Myths And Legends Of Our Own Land

by

Charles M. Skinner

Myths And Legends Of Our Own Land
by Charles M. Skinner

Copyright © 2023

All Rights reserved.

No part of this publication may be reproduced, stored in a retrieval system, or transmitted in any form or by any means, electronic, mechanical, photocopying or Otherwise, without the written permission of the publisher.
The author/editor asserts the moral right to be identified as the author/editor of this work.

ISBN: 978-93-59328-30-0

Published by

DOUBLE 9 BOOKS

2/13-B, Ansari Road
Daryaganj, New Delhi – 110002
info@double9books.com
www.double9books.com
Tel. 011-40042856

This book is under public domain

ABOUT THE AUTHOR

Charles Montgomery Skinner (March 15, 1852 - January 7, 1907) was an American author. Skinner was born in the town of Victor, New York. His literary and journalistic career included serving as editor of the Brooklyn Eagle. In 1903, the Atlantic Monthly published his analysis on the paper's legendary Walt Whitman. He published collections of myths, tales, and folklore from the US and around the globe. He intended to preserve traditions threatened by the industrial age by combining folkloric customs with New England transcendentalism. Skinner's writings covered a wide range of topics. He was a playwright who wrote the play Villon, the Vagabond. Skinner was also fascinated with the changing seasons, particularly as they occurred within industrializing cities. He wrote a gardening and urban beautifying handbook to help improve the urban environment. In Workers and the Trusts and American Communes, he also commented on the tumultuous economy of turn-of-the-century America. Natural history books such as with Feet to the Earth and Do-Nothing Days were among his other contributions to American literature.

CONTENTS

PREFACE 15

THE HUDSON AND ITS HILLS
   RIP VAN WINKLE 17
   CATSKILL GNOMES 20
   THE CATSKILL WITCH 21
   THE REVENGE OF SHANDAKEN 22
   CONDEMNED TO THE NOOSE 23
   BIG INDIAN 25
   THE BAKER'S DOZEN 26
   THE DEVIL'S DANCE-CHAMBER 28
   THE CULPRIT FAY 30
   POKEPSIE 32
   DUNDERBERG 33
   ANTHONY'S NOSE 34
   MOODUA CREEK 35
   A TRAPPER'S GHASTLY VENGEANCE 36
   THE VANDERDECKEN OF TAPPAN ZEE 39
   THE GALLOPING HESSIAN 40
   STORM SHIP OF THE HUDSON 42
   WHY SPUYTEN DUYVIL IS SO NAMED 43
   THE RAMAPO SALAMANDER 45
   CHIEF CROTON 48
   THE RETREAT FROM MAHOPAC 49
   NIAGARA 51

THE DEFORMED OF ZOAR	53
HORSEHEADS	54
KAYUTA AND WANETA	55
THE DROP STAR	57
THE PROPHET OF PALMYRA	59
A VILLAIN'S CREMATION	60
THE MONSTER MOSQUITOE	61
THE GREEN PICTURE	62
THE NUNS OF CARTHAGE	63
THE SKULL IN THE WALL	64
THE HAUNTED MILL	65
OLD INDIAN FACE	67
THE DIVISION OF THE SARANACS	68
AN EVENT IN INDIAN PARK	70
THE INDIAN PLUME	71
BIRTH OF THE WATER-LILY	72
ROGERS'S SLIDE	73
THE FALLS AT COHOES	75
FRANCIS WOOLCOTT'S NIGHT-RIDERS	76
POLLY'S LOVER	77
CROSBY, THE PATRIOT SPY	79
THE LOST GRAVE OF PAINE	82
THE RISING OF GOUVERNEUR MORRIS	83

THE ISLE OF MANHATTOES AND NEARBY

DOLPH HEYLIGER	85
THE KNELL AT THE WEDDING	88
ROISTERING DIRCK VAN DARA	90
THE PARTY FROM GIBBET ISLAND	92
MISS BRITTON'S POKER	94

THE DEVIL'S STEPPING-STONES 95

THE SPRINGS OF BLOOD AND WATER 96

THE CRUMBLING SILVER 97

THE CORTELYOU ELOPEMENT 98

VAN WEMPEL'S GOOSE 99

THE WEARY WATCHER 101

THE RIVAL FIDDLERS 102

WYANDANK 104

MARK OF THE SPIRIT HAND 106

THE FIRST LIBERAL CHURCH 107

ON AND NEAR THE DELAWARE

THE PHANTOM DRAGOON 108

DELAWARE WATER GAP 110

THE PHANTOM DRUMMER 111

THE MISSING SOLDIER OF VALLEY FORGE 113

THE LAST SHOT AT GERMANTOWN 114

A BLOW IN THE DARK 116

THE TORY'S CONVERSION 118

LORD PERCY'S DREAM 120

SAVED BY THE BIBLE 122

PARRICIDE OF THE WISSAHICKON 124

THE BLACKSMITH AT BRANDYWINE 126

FATHER AND SON 127

THE ENVY OF MANITOU 129

THE LAST REVEL IN PRINTZ HALL 130

THE TWO RINGS 133

FLAME SCALPS OF THE CHARTIERS 135

THE CONSECRATION OF WASHINGTON 136

TALES OF PURITAN LAND

EVANGALINE 139
THE SNORING OF SWUNKSUS 141
THE LEWISTON HERMIT 142
THE DEAD SHIP OF HARPSWELL 143
THE SCHOOLMASTER HAD NOT REACHED ORRINGTON 144
JACK WELCH'S DEATH LIGHT 145
THE LADY URSULA 147
FATHER MOODY'S BLACK VEIL 148
THE HOME OF THUNDER 150
THE PARTRIDGE WITCH 151
THE MARRIAGE OF MOUNT KATAHDIN 153
THE MOOSE OF MOUNT KINEO 154
THE OWL TREE 155
A CHESTNUT LOG 157
THE WATCHER ON WHITE ISLAND 158
CHOCORUA 159
PASSACONAWAY'S RIDE TO HEAVEN 160
THE BALL GAME BY THE SACO 162
THE WHITE MOUNTAINS 163
THE VISION ON MOUNT ADAMS 166
THE GREAT CARBUNCLE 167
SKINNER'S CAVE 168
YET THEY CALL IT LOVER'S LEAP 169
SALEM AND OTHER WITCHCRAFT 170
THE GLOUCESTER LEAGUERS 177
SATAN AND HIS BURIAL-PLACE 179
PETER RUGG, THE MISSING MAN 181
THE LOSS OF WEETAMOO 183

THE FATAL FORGET-ME-NOT	184
THE OLD MILL AT SOMERVILLE	185
EDWARD RANDOLPH'S PORTRAIT	187
LADY ELEANORE'S MANTLE	189
HOWE'S MASQUERADE	191
OLD ESTHER DUDLEY	193
THE LOSS OF JACOB HURD	195
THE HOBOMAK	196
BERKSHIRE TORIES	198
THE REVENGE OF JOSIAH BREEZE	200
THE MAY-POLE OF MERRYMOUNT	203
THE DEVIL AND TOM WALKER	205
THE GRAY CHAMPION	208
THE FOREST SMITHY	210
WAHCONAH FALLS	212
KNOCKING AT THE TOMB	214
THE WHITE DEER OF ONOTA	215
WIZARD'S GLEN	217
BALANCED ROCK	218
SHONKEEK-MOONKEEK	219
THE SALEM ALCHEMIST	221
ELIZA WHARTON	223
SALE OF THE SOUTHWICKS	224
THE COURTSHIP OF MYLES STANDISH	225
MOTHER CREWE	226
AUNT RACHEL'S CURSE	228
NIX'S MATE	230
THE WILD MAN OF CAPE COD	231
NEWBURY'S OLD ELM	232

SAMUEL SEWALL'S PROPHECY	233
THE SHRIEKING WOMAN	234
AGNES SURRIAGE	235
SKIPPER IRESON'S RIDE	237
HEARTBREAK HILL	238
HARRY MAIN: THE TREASURE AND THE CATS	239
THE WESSAGUSCUS HANGING	240
THE UNKNOWN CHAMPION	242
GOODY COLE	244
GENERAL MOULTON AND THE DEVIL	246
THE SKELETON IN ARMOR	248
MARTHA'S VINEYARD AND NANTUCKET	249
LOVE AND TREASON	250
THE HEADLESS SKELETON OF SWAMPTOWN	251
THE CROW AND CAT OF HOPKINSHILL	252
THE OLD STONE MILL	253
ORIGIN OF A NAME	254
MICAH ROOD APPLES	255
A DINNER AND ITS CONSEQUENCES	256
THE NEW HAVEN STORM SHIP	257
THE WINDAM FROGS	258
THE LAMB OF SACRIFICE	259
MOODUS NOISES	260
HADDAM ENCHANTMENTS	262
BLOCK ISLAND AND THE PALATINE	264
THE BUCCANEER	266
ROBERT LOCKWOOD'S FATE	268
LOVE AND RUM	270

LIGHTS AND SHADOWS OF THE SOUTH

THE SWIM AT INDIAN HEAD 271

THE MOANING SISTERS 273

A RIDE FOR A BRIDE 274

SPOOKS OF THE HIAWASSEE 277

LAKE OF THE DISMAL SWAMP 278

THE BARGE OF DEFEAT 279

NATURAL BRIDGE 280

THE SILENCE BROKEN 281

SIREN OF THE FRENCH BROAD 283

THE HUNTER OF CALAWASSEE 284

REVENGE OF THE ACCABEE 285

TOCCOA FALLS 287

TWO LIVES FOR ONE 289

A GHOSTLY AVENGER 291

THE WRAITH RINGER OF ATLANTA 293

THE SWALLOWING EARTHQUAKE 294

LAST STAND OF THE BILOXI 295

THE SACRED FIRE OF NACHEZ 297

PASS CHRISTIAN 298

THE UNDER LAND 300

THE CENRAL STATES AND THE GREAT LAKES

AN AVERTED PERIL 301

THE OBSTINACY OF SAINT CLAIR 303

THE HUNDREDTH SKULL 305

THE CRIME OF BLACK SWAMP 307

THE HOUSE ACCURSED 309

MICHEL DE COUCY'S TROUBLES 311

WALLEN'S RIDGE 313

THE SKY WALKER OF HURON 315

THE COFFIN OF SNAKES 317

MACKINACK 319

LAKE SUPERIOR WATER GODS 321

THE WITCH OF PICTURED ROCKS 322

THE ORIGIN OF WHITE-FISH 324

THE SPIRIT OF CLOUDY 325

THE SUN FIRE AT SAULT SAINTE MARIE 326

THE SNAKE GOD OF BELLE ISLE 328

WERE-WOLVES OF DETROIT 330

THE ESCAPE OF FRANCOIS NAVARRE 332

THE OLD LODGER 334

THE NAIN ROUGE 336

TWO REVENGES 338

HIAWATHA 339

THE INDIAN MESSIAH 342

THE VISION OF RESCUE 344

DEVIL'S LAKE 345

THE KEUSCA ELOPEMENT 346

PIPESTONE 347

THE VIRGINS' FEAST 348

FALLS OF ST. ANTHONY 350

FLYING SHADOW AND TRACK MAKER 351

SAVED BY A LIGHTNING-STROKE 353

THE KILLING OF CLOUDY SKY 355

PROVIDENCE HOLE 357

THE SCARE CURE 358

TWELFTH NIGHT AT CAHOKIA 359

THE SPELL OF CREVE CIUR LAKE	361
HOW THE CRIME WAS REVEALED	362
BANSHEE OF THE BAD LANDS	363
STANDING ROCK	365
THE SALT WITCH	366

ALONG THE ROCKY RANGE

OVER THE DIVIDE	367
THE PHANTOM TRAIN OF MARSHALL PASS	368
THE RIVER OF LOST SOULS	370
RIDERS OF THE DESERT	371
THE DIVISION OF TWO TRIBES	373
BESIEGED BY STARVATION	375
A YELLOWSTONE TRAGEDY	377
THE BROAD HOUSE	379
THE DEATH WALTZ	380
THE FLOOD AT SANTA FE	382
GODDESS OF SALT	383
THE COMING OF THE NAVAJOS	384
THE ARK ON SUPERSTITION MOUNTAINS	386
THE PALE FACED LIGHTNING	388
THE WEIRD SENTINEL AT SQUAW PEAK	390
SACRIFICE OF THE TOLTECS	391
TA-VWOTS CONQUERS THE SUN	393
THE COMANCHE RIDER	396
HORNED TOAD AND GIANTS	398
THE SPIDER TOWER	400
THE LOST TRAIL	401
A BATTLE IN THE AIR	403

ON THE PACIFIC COAST
- THE VOYAGER OF WHULGE 404
- TAMANOUS OF TACOMA 405
- THE DEVIL AND THE DALLES.. 407
- CASCADES OF THE COLUMBIA 409
- THE DEATH OF UMATILLA.. 410
- HUNGER VALLEY 412
- THE WRATH OF MANITOU 413
- THE SPOOK OF MISERY HILL.. 414
- THE QUEEN OF DEATH VALLEY 416
- BRIDAL VEIL FALL... 417
- THE GOVERNOR'S RIGHT EYE 418
- THE PRISONER IN AMERICAN SHAFT... 420

AS TO BURIED RICHES
- KIDD'S TREASURE.. 421
- OTHER BURIED WEALTH 426

STORIED WATERS, CLIFFS AND MOUNTAINS
- MONSTERS AND SEA-SERPENTS... 436
- STONE-THROWING DEVILS 441
- STORIED SPRINGS.. 444
- LOVERS' LEAPS.. 449
- GOD ON THE MOUNTAINS... 455

PREFACE

It is unthinkingly said and often, that America is not old enough to have developed a legendary era, for such an era grows backward as a nation grows forward. No little of the charm of European travel is ascribed to the glamour that history and fable have flung around old churches, castles, and the favored haunts of tourists, and the Rhine and Hudson are frequently compared, to the prejudice of the latter, not because its scenery lacks in loveliness or grandeur, but that its beauty has not been humanized by love of chivalry or faerie, as that of the older stream has been. Yet the record of our country's progress is of deep import, and as time goes on the figures seen against the morning twilight of our history will rise to more commanding stature, and the mists of legend will invest them with a softness or glory that shall make reverence for them spontaneous and deep. Washington hurling the stone across the Potomac may live as the Siegfried of some Western saga, and Franklin invoking the lightnings may be the Loki of our mythology. The bibliography of American legends is slight, and these tales have been gathered from sources the most diverse: records, histories, newspapers, magazines, oral narrative—in every case reconstructed. The pursuit of them has been so long that a claim may be set forth for some measure of completeness.

But, whatever the episodes of our four historic centuries may furnish to the poet, painter, dramatist, or legend-building idealist of the future, it is certain that we are not devoid of myth and folk-lore. Some characters, prosaic enough, perhaps, in daily life, have impinged so lightly on society before and after perpetrating their one or two great deeds, that they have already become shadowy and their achievements have acquired a color of the supernatural. It is where myth and history combine that legend is most interesting and appeals to our fancy or our sympathy most strongly; and it is not too early for us to begin the collation of those quaint happenings and those spoken reports that gain in picturesqueness with each transmission. An attempt has been made in this instance to assemble only legends, for, doubtful as some historians profess to find them, certain occurrences, like the story of Captain Smith and Pocahontas, and the ride of General Putnam down Breakneck Stairs, are taught as history; while as to folk-lore, that of the Indian tribes and of the Southern negro is too copious to be recounted in this work. It will be noted that traditions do not thrive in brick and brownstone, and that the stories once rife in the colonial cities have almost as effectually disappeared as the architectural landmarks of last century. The field entered by the writer is not untrodden. Hawthorne and Irving have made paths across it, and it is hoped that others may deem its farther exploration worthy of their efforts.

THE HUDSON AND ITS HILLS

RIP VAN WINKLE

The story of Rip Van Winkle, told by Irving, dramatized by Boucicault, acted by Jefferson, pictured by Darley, set to music by Bristow, is the best known of American legends. Rip was a real personage, and the Van Winkles are a considerable family at this day. An idle, good-natured, happy-go-lucky fellow, he lived, presumably, in the village of Catskill, and began his long sleep in 1769. His wife was a shrew, and to escape her abuse Rip often took his dog and gun and roamed away to the Catskills, nine miles westward, where he lounged or hunted, as the humor seized him. It was on a September evening, during a jaunt on South Mountain, that he met a stubby, silent man, of goodly girth, his round head topped with a steeple hat, the skirts of his belted coat and flaps of his petticoat trousers meeting at the tops of heavy boots, and the face—ugh!—green and ghastly, with unmoving eyes that glimmered in the twilight like phosphorus. The dwarf carried a keg, and on receiving an intimation, in a sign, that he would like Rip to relieve him of it, that cheerful vagabond shouldered it and marched on up the mountain.

At nightfall they emerged on a little plateau where a score of men in the garb of long ago, with faces like that of Rip's guide, and equally still and speechless, were playing bowls with great solemnity, the balls sometimes rolling over the plateau's edge and rumbling down the rocks with a boom like thunder. A cloaked and snowy-bearded figure, watching aloof, turned like the others, and gazed uncomfortably at the visitor who now came blundering in among them. Rip was at first for making off, but the sinister glare in the circle of eyes took the run out of his legs, and he was not displeased when they signed to him to tap the keg and join in a draught of the ripest schnapps that ever he had tasted,—and he knew the flavor of every brand in Catskill. While these strange men grew no more genial with passing of the flagons, Rip was pervaded by a satisfying glow; then, overcome by sleepiness and resting his head on a stone, he stretched his tired legs out and fell to dreaming.

Morning. Sunlight and leaf shadow were dappled over the earth when he awoke, and rising stiffly from his bed, with compunctions in his bones, he reached for his gun. The already venerable implement was so far gone with rot and rust that it fell to pieces in his hand, and looking down at the fragments of it, he saw that his clothes were dropping from his body in rags and mould, while a white beard flowed over his breast. Puzzled and alarmed, shaking his head ruefully as he recalled the carouse of the silent, he hobbled down the mountain as fast as he might for the grip of the rheumatism on his knees and elbows, and entered his native village. What! Was this Catskill? Was this the place that he left yesterday? Had all these houses sprung up overnight, and these streets been pushed across the meadows in a day? The people, too: where were his friends? The children who had romped with him, the rotund topers whom he had left cooling their hot noses in pewter pots at the tavern door, the dogs that used to bark a welcome, recognizing in him a kindred spirit of vagrancy: where were they?

And his wife, whose athletic arm and agile tongue had half disposed him to linger in the mountains how happened it that she was not awaiting him at the gate? But gate there was none in the familiar place: an unfenced yard of weeds and ruined foundation wall were there. Rip's home was gone. The idlers jeered at his bent, lean form, his snarl of beard and hair, his disreputable dress, his look of grieved astonishment. He stopped, instinctively, at the tavern, for he knew that place in spite of its new sign: an officer in blue regimentals and a cocked hat replacing the crimson George III. of his recollection, and labelled "General Washington." There was a quick gathering of ne'er-do-weels, of tavern-haunters and gaping 'prentices, about him, and though their faces were strange and their manners rude, he made bold to ask if they knew such and such of his friends.

"Nick Vedder? He's dead and gone these eighteen years." "Brom Dutcher? He joined the army and was killed at Stony Point." "Van Brummel? He, too, went to the war, and is in Congress now."

"And Rip Van Winkle?"

"Yes, he's here. That's him yonder."

And to Rip's utter confusion he saw before him a counterpart of himself, as young, lazy, ragged, and easy-natured as he remembered himself to be, yesterday—or, was it yesterday?

"That's young Rip," continued his informer. "His father was Rip Van Winkle, too, but he went to the mountains twenty years ago and never came back. He probably fell over a cliff, or was carried off by Indians, or eaten by bears."

Twenty years ago! Truly, it was so. Rip had slept for twenty years without awaking. He had left a peaceful colonial village; he returned to a bustling republican town. How he eventually found, among the oldest inhabitants, some who admitted that they knew him; how he found a comfortable home with his married daughter and the son who took after him so kindly; how he recovered from the effect of the tidings that his wife had died of apoplexy, in a quarrel; how he resumed his seat at the tavern tap and smoked long pipes and told long yarns for the rest of his days, were matters of record up to the beginning of this century.

And a strange story Rip had to tell, for he had served as cup-bearer to the dead crew of the Half Moon. He had quaffed a cup of Hollands with no other than Henry Hudson himself. Some say that Hudson's spirit has made its home amid these hills, that it may look into the lovely valley that he discovered; but others hold that every twenty years he and his men assemble for a revel in the mountains that so charmed them when first seen swelling against the western heavens, and the liquor they drink on this night has the bane of throwing any mortal who lips it into a slumber whence nothing can arouse him until the day dawns when the crew shall meet again. As you climb the east front of the mountains by the old carriage road, you pass, half-way up the height, the stone that Rip Van Winkle slept on, and may see that it is slightly hollowed by his form. The ghostly revellers are due in the Catskills in 1909, and let all tourists who are among the mountains in September of that year beware of accepting liquor from strangers.

CATSKILL GNOMES

Behind the New Grand Hotel, in the Catskills, is an amphitheatre of mountain that is held to be the place of which the Mohicans spoke when they told of people there who worked in metals, and had bushy beards and eyes like pigs. From the smoke of their forges, in autumn, came the haze of Indian summer; and when the moon was full, it was their custom to assemble on the edge of a precipice above the hollow and dance and caper until the night was nigh worn away. They brewed a liquor that had the effect of shortening the bodies and swelling the heads of all who drank it, and when Hudson and his crew visited the mountains, the pygmies held a carouse in his honor and invited him to drink their liquor. The crew went away, shrunken and distorted by the magic distillation, and thus it was that Rip Van Winkle found them on the eve of his famous sleep.

THE CATSKILL WITCH

When the Dutch gave the name of Katzbergs to the mountains west of the Hudson, by reason of the wild-cats and panthers that ranged there, they obliterated the beautiful Indian Ontiora, "mountains of the sky." In one tradition of the red men these hills were bones of a monster that fed on human beings until the Great Spirit turned it into stone as it was floundering toward the ocean to bathe. The two lakes near the summit were its eyes. These peaks were the home of an Indian witch, who adjusted the weather for the Hudson Valley with the certainty of a signal service bureau. It was she who let out the day and night in blessed alternation, holding back the one when the other was at large, for fear of conflict. Old moons she cut into stars as soon as she had hung new ones in the sky, and she was often seen perched on Round Top and North Mountain, spinning clouds and flinging them to the winds. Woe betide the valley residents if they showed irreverence, for then the clouds were black and heavy, and through them she poured floods of rain and launched the lightnings, causing disastrous freshets in the streams and blasting the wigwams of the mockers. In a frolic humor she would take the form of a bear or deer and lead the Indian hunters anything but a merry dance, exposing them to tire and peril, and vanishing or assuming some terrible shape when they had overtaken her. Sometimes she would lead them to the cloves and would leap into the air with a mocking "Ho, ho!" just as they stopped with a shudder at the brink of an abyss. Garden Rock was a spot where she was often found, and at its foot a lake once spread. This was held in such awe that an Indian would never wittingly pursue his quarry there; but once a hunter lost his way and emerged from the forest at the edge of the pond. Seeing a number of gourds in crotches of the trees he took one, but fearing the spirit he turned to leave so quickly that he stumbled and it fell. As it broke, a spring welled from it in such volume that the unhappy man was gulfed in its waters, swept to the edge of Kaaterskill clove and dashed on the rocks two hundred and sixty feet below. Nor did the water ever cease to run, and in these times the stream born of the witch's revenge is known as Catskill Creek.

THE REVENGE OF SHANDAKEN

On the rock platform where the Catskill Mountain House now stands, commanding one of the fairest views in the world, old chief Shandaken set his wigwam,—for it is a mistake to suppose that barbarians are indifferent to beauty,—and there his daughter, Lotowana, was sought in marriage by his braves. She, however, kept faith to an early vow exchanged with a young chief of the Mohawks. A suitor who was particularly troublesome was Norsereddin, proud, morose, dark-featured, a stranger to the red man, a descendant, so he claimed, from Egyptian kings, and who lived by himself on Kaaterskill Creek, appearing among white settlements but rarely.

On one of his visits to Catskill, a tavern-lounging Dutchman wagered him a thousand golden crowns that he could not win Lotowana, and, stung by avarice as well as inflamed by passion, Norsereddin laid new siege to her heart. Still the girl refused to listen, and Shandaken counselled him to be content with the smiles of others, thereby so angering the Egyptian that he assailed the chief and was driven from the camp with blows; but on the day of Lotowana's wedding with the Mohawk he returned, and in a honeyed speech asked leave to give a jewel to the bride to show that he had stifled jealousy and ill will. The girl took the handsome box he gave her and drew the cover, when a spring flew forward, driving into her hand the poisoned tooth of a snake that had been affixed to it. The venom was strong, and in a few minutes Lotowana lay dead at her husband's feet.

Though the Egyptian had disappeared into the forest directly on the acceptance of his treacherous gift, twenty braves set off in pursuit, and overtaking him on the Kalkberg, they dragged him back to the rock where father and husband were bewailing the maid's untimely fate. A pile of fagots was heaped within a few feet of the precipice edge, and tying their captive on them, they applied the torch, dancing about with cries of exultation as the shrieks of the wretch echoed from the cliffs. The dead girl was buried by the mourning tribe, while the ashes of Norsereddin were left to be blown abroad. On the day of his revenge Shandaken left his ancient dwelling-place, and his camp-fires never glimmered afterward on the front of Ontiora.

CONDEMNED TO THE NOOSE

Ralph Sutherland, who, early in the last century, occupied a stone house a mile from Leeds, in the Catskills, was a man of morose and violent disposition, whose servant, a Scotch girl, was virtually a slave, inasmuch as she was bound to work for him without pay until she had refunded to him her passage-money to this country. Becoming weary of bondage and of the tempers of her master, the girl ran away. The man set off in a raging chase, and she had not gone far before Sutherland overtook her, tied her by the wrists to his horse's tail, and began the homeward journey. Afterward, he swore that the girl stumbled against the horse's legs, so frightening the animal that it rushed off madly, pitching him out of the saddle and dashing the servant to death on rocks and trees; yet, knowing how ugly-tempered he could be, his neighbors were better inclined to believe that he had driven the horse into a gallop, intending to drag the girl for a short distance, as a punishment, and to rein up before he had done serious mischief. On this supposition he was arrested, tried, and sentenced to die on the scaffold.

The tricks of circumstantial evidence, together with pleas advanced by influential relatives of the prisoner, induced the court to delay sentence until the culprit should be ninety-nine years old, but it was ordered that, while released on his own recognizance, in the interim, he should keep a hangman's noose about his neck and show himself before the judges in Catskill once every year, to prove that he wore his badge of infamy and kept his crime in mind. This sentence he obeyed, and there were people living recently who claimed to remember him as he went about with a silken cord knotted at his throat. He was always alone, he seldom spoke, his rough, imperious manner had departed. Only when children asked him what the rope was for were his lips seen to quiver, and then he would hurry away. After dark his house was avoided, for gossips said that a shrieking woman passed it nightly, tied at the tail of a giant horse with fiery eyes and smoking nostrils; that a skeleton in a winding sheet had been found there; that a curious thing, somewhat like a woman, had been known to sit on his garden wall, with lights shining from her finger-tips, uttering unearthly laughter; and that domestic animals reproached the man by groaning and howling beneath his windows.

These beliefs he knew, yet he neither grieved, nor scorned, nor answered when he was told of them. Years sped on. Every year deepened his reserve and loneliness, and some began to whisper that he would take his own way out of the world, though others answered that men who were born to be hanged would never be drowned; but a new republic was created; new laws were made; new judges sat to minister them; so, on Ralph Sutherland's ninety-ninth birthday anniversary, there were none who would accuse him or execute sentence. He lived yet another year, dying in 1801. But was it from habit, or was it in self-punishment and remorse, that he never took off the cord? for, when he drew his last breath, though it was in his own house, his throat was still encircled by the hangman's rope.

BIG INDIAN

Intermarriages between white people and red ones in this country were not uncommon in the days when our ancestors led as rude a life as the natives, and several places in the Catskills commemorate this fact. Mount Utsayantha, for example, is named for an Indian woman whose life, with that of her baby and her white husband, was lost there. For the white men early found friends among these mountains. As far back as 1663 they spared Catherine Dubois and her three children, after some rash spirits had abducted them and carried them to a place on the upper Walkill, to do them to death; for the captives raised a Huguenot hymn and the hearts of their captors were softened.

In Esopus Valley lived Winnisook, whose height was seven feet, and who was known among the white settlers as "the big Indian." He loved a white girl of the neighborhood, one Gertrude Molyneux, and had asked for her hand; but while she was willing, the objections of her family were too strong to be overcome, and she was teased into marriage with Joseph Bundy, of her own race, instead. She liked the Indian all the better after that, however, because Bundy proved to be a bad fellow, and believing that she could be happier among barbarians than among a people that approved such marriages, she eloped with Winnisook. For a long time all trace of the runaway couple was lost, but one day the man having gone down to the plain to steal cattle, it was alleged, was discovered by some farmers who knew him, and who gave hot chase, coming up with him at the place now called Big Indian.

Foremost in the chase was Bundy. As he came near to the enemy of his peace he exclaimed, "I think the best way to civilize that yellow serpent is to let daylight into his heart," and, drawing his rifle to his shoulder, he fired. Mortally wounded, yet instinctively seeking refuge, the giant staggered into the hollow of a pine-tree, where the farmers lost sight of him. There, however, he was found by Gertrude, bolt upright, yet dead. The unwedded widow brought her dusky children to the place and spent the remainder of her days near his grave. Until a few years ago the tree was still pointed out, but a railroad company has now covered it with an embankment.

THE BAKER'S DOZEN

Baas [Boss] Volckert Jan Pietersen Van Amsterdam kept a bake-shop in Albany, and lives in history as the man who invented New Year cakes and made gingerbread babies in the likeness of his own fat offspring. Good churchman though he was, the bane of his life was a fear of being bewitched, and perhaps it was to keep out evil spirits, who might make one last effort to gain the mastery over him, ere he turned the customary leaf with the incoming year, that he had primed himself with an extra glass of spirits on the last night of 1654. His sales had been brisk, and as he sat in his little shop, meditating comfortably on the gains he would make when his harmless rivals—the knikkerbakkers (bakers of marbles)—sent for their usual supply of olie-koeks and mince-pies on the morrow, he was startled by a sharp rap, and an ugly old woman entered. "Give me a dozen New Year's cookies!" she cried, in a shrill voice.

"Vell, den, you needn' sbeak so loud. I aind teaf, den."

"A dozen!" she screamed. "Give me a dozen. Here are only twelve."

"Vell, den, dwalf is a dozen."

"One more! I want a dozen."

"Vell, den, if you vant anodder, go to de duyvil and ged it."

Did the hag take him at his word? She left the shop, and from that time it seemed as if poor Volckert was bewitched, indeed, for his cakes were stolen; his bread was so light that it went up the chimney, when it was not so heavy that it fell through the oven; invisible hands plucked bricks from that same oven and pelted him until he was blue; his wife became deaf, his children went unkempt, and his trade went elsewhere. Thrice the old woman reappeared, and each time was sent anew to the devil; but at last, in despair, the baker called on Saint Nicolaus to come and advise him. His call was answered with startling quickness, for, almost while he was making it, the venerable patron of Dutch feasts stood before him. The good soul advised the trembling man to be more generous in his dealings with his fellows, and after a lecture on charity he vanished, when, lo! the old woman was there in his place.

She repeated her demand for one more cake, and Volckert Jan Pietersen, etc., gave it, whereupon she exclaimed, "The spell is broken, and from this time a dozen is thirteen!" Taking from the counter a gingerbread effigy of Saint Nicolaus, she made the astonished Dutchman lay his hand upon it and swear to give more liberal measure in the future. So, until thirteen new States arose from the ruins of the colonies,—when the shrewd Yankees restored the original measure,—thirteen made a baker's dozen.

THE DEVIL'S DANCE-CHAMBER

Most storied of our New World rivers is the Hudson. Historic scenes have been enacted on its shores, and Indian, Dutchman, Briton, and American have invested it with romance. It had its source, in the red man's fancy, in a spring of eternal youth; giants and spirits dwelt in its woods and hills, and before the river-Shatemuc, king of streams, the red men called it—had broken through the highlands, those mountains were a pent for spirits who had rebelled against the Manitou. After the waters had forced a passage to the sea these evil ones sought shelter in the glens and valleys that open to right and left along its course, but in time of tempest, when they hear Manitou riding down the ravine on wings of storm, dashing thunderbolts against the cliffs, it is the fear that he will recapture them and force them into lightless caverns to expiate their revolt, that sends them huddling among the rocks and makes the hills resound with roars and howls.

At the Devil's Dance-Chamber, a slight plateau on the west bank, between Newburg and Crom Elbow, the red men performed semi-religious rites as a preface to their hunting and fishing trips or ventures on the war-path. They built a fire, painted themselves, and in that frenzy into which savages are so readily lashed, and that is so like to the action of mobs in trousers, they tumbled, leaped, danced, yelled, sang, grimaced, and gesticulated until the Manitou disclosed himself, either as a harmless animal or a beast of prey. If he came in the former shape the augury was favorable, but if he showed himself as a bear or panther, it was a warning of evil that they seldom dared to disregard.

The crew of Hudson's ship, the Half Moon, having chanced on one of these orgies, were so impressed by the fantastic spectacle that they gave the name Duyvels Dans-Kamer to the spot. Years afterwards, when Stuyvesant ascended the river, his doughty retainers were horrified, on landing below the Dans-Kamer, to discover hundreds of painted figures frisking there in the fire-light. A few surmised that they were but a new generation of savages holding a powwow, but most of the sailors fancied that the assemblage was demoniac, and that the figures were spirits of bad Indians repeating a scalp-dance and revelling in the mysterious fire-water that they had brought down from the river source in jars and skins. The spot was at least once profaned with blood, for a young Dutchman and his wife, of Albany, were captured here by an angry Indian, and although the young man succeeded in stabbing his captor to death, he was burned alive on the rock by the friends of the Indian whose wrath he had provoked. The wife, after being kept in captivity for a time, was ransomed.

THE CULPRIT FAY

The wood-tick's drum convokes the elves at the noon of night on Cro' Nest top, and, clambering out of their flower-cup beds and hammocks of cobweb, they fly to the meeting, not to freak about the grass or banquet at the mushroom table, but to hear sentence passed on the fay who, forgetting his vestal vow, has loved an earthly maid. From his throne under a canopy of tulip petals, borne on pillars of shell, the king commands silence, and with severe eye but softened voice he tells the culprit that while he has scorned the royal decree he has saved himself from the extreme penalty, of imprisonment in walnut shells and cobweb dungeons, by loving a maid who is gentle and pure. So it shall be enough if he will go down to the Hudson and seize a drop from the bow of mist that a sturgeon leaves when he makes his leap; and after, to kindle his darkened flame-wood lamp at a meteor spark. The fairy bows, and without a word slowly descends the rocky steep, for his wing is soiled and has lost its power; but once at the river, he tugs amain at a mussel shell till he has it afloat; then, leaping in, he paddles out with a strong grass blade till he comes to the spot where the sturgeon swims, though the watersprites plague him and toss his boat, and the fish and the leeches bunt and drag; but, suddenly, the sturgeon shoots from the water, and ere the arch of mist that he tracks through the air has vanished, the sprite has caught a drop of the spray in a tiny blossom, and in this he washes clean his wings.

The water-goblins torment him no longer. They push his boat to the shore, where, alighting, he kisses his hand, then, even as a bubble, he flies back to the mountain top, dons his acorn helmet, his corselet of bee-hide, his shield of lady-bug shell, and grasping his lance, tipped with wasp sting, he bestrides his fire-fly steed and off he goes like a flash. The world spreads out and then grows small, but he flies straight on. The ice-ghosts leer from the topmost clouds, and the mists surge round, but he shakes his lance and pipes his call, and at last he comes to the Milky Way, where the sky-sylphs lead him to their queen, who lies couched in a palace ceiled with stars, its dome held up by northern lights and the curtains made of the morning's flush. Her mantle is twilight purple, tied with threads of gold from the eastern dawn, and her face is as fair as the silver moon.

She begs the fay to stay with her and taste forever the joys of heaven, but the knightly elf keeps down the beating of his heart, for he remembers a face on earth that is fairer than hers, and he begs to go. With a sigh she fits him a car of cloud, with the fire-fly steed chained on behind, and he hurries away to the northern sky whence the meteor comes, with roar and whirl, and as it passes it bursts to flame. He lights his lamp at a glowing spark, then wheels away to the fairy-land. His king and his brothers hail him stoutly, with song and shout, and feast and dance, and the revel is kept till the eastern sky has a ruddy streak. Then the cock crows shrill and the fays are gone.

POKEPSIE

The name of this town has forty-two spellings in old records, and with singular pertinacity in ill-doing, the inhabitants have fastened on it the longest and clumsiest of all. It comes from the Mohegan words Apo-keep-sink, meaning a safe, pleasant harbor. Harbor it might be for canoes, but for nothing bigger, for it was only the little cove that was so called between Call Rock and Adder Cliff,—the former indicating where settlers awaiting passage hailed the masters of vessels from its top, and the latter taking its name from the snakes that abounded there.

Hither came a band of Delawares with Pequot captives, among them a young chief to whom had been offered not only life but leadership if he would renounce his tribe, receive the mark of the turtle on his breast, and become a Delaware. On his refusal, he was bound to a tree, and was about to undergo the torture, when a girl among the listeners sprang to his side. She, too, was a Pequot, but the turtle totem was on her bosom, and when she begged his life, because they had been betrothed, the captors paused to talk of it. She had chosen well the time to interfere, for a band of Hurons was approaching, and even as the talk went on their yell was heard in the wood. Instant measures for defence were taken, and in the fight that followed both chief and maiden were forgotten; but though she cut the cords that bound him, they were separated in the confusion, he disappearing, she falling captive to the Hurons, who, sated with blood, retired from the field. In the fantastic disguise of a wizard the young Pequot entered their camp soon after, and on being asked to try his enchantments for the cure of a young woman, he entered her tent, showing no surprise at finding her to be the maiden of his choice, who was suffering from nothing worse than nerves, due to the excitement of the battle. Left alone with his patient, he disclosed his identity, and planned a way of escape that proved effective on that very night, for, though pursued by the angry Hurons, the couple reached "safe harbor," thence making a way to their own country in the east, where they were married.

DUNDERBERG

Dunderberg, "Thunder Mountain," at the southern gate of the Hudson Highlands, is a wooded eminence, chiefly populated by a crew of imps of stout circumference, whose leader, the Heer, is a bulbous goblin clad in the dress worn by Dutch colonists two centuries ago, and carrying a speaking-trumpet, through which he bawls his orders for the blowing of winds and the touching off of lightnings. These orders are given in Low Dutch, and are put into execution by the imps aforesaid, who troop into the air and tumble about in the mist, sometimes smiting the flag or topsail of a ship to ribbons, or laying the vessel over before the wind until she is in peril of going on beam ends. At one time a sloop passing the Dunderberg had nearly foundered, when the crew discovered the sugar-loaf hat of the Heer at the mast-head. None dared to climb for it, and it was not until she had driven past Pollopel's Island—the limit of the Heer's jurisdiction—that she righted. As she did so the little hat spun into the air like a top, creating a vortex that drew up the storm-clouds, and the sloop kept her way prosperously for the rest of the voyage. The captain had nailed a horse-shoe to the mast. The "Hat Rogue" of the Devil's Bridge in Switzerland must be a relative of this gamesome sprite, for his mischief is usually of a harmless sort; but, to be on the safe side, the Dutchmen who plied along the river lowered their peaks in homage to the keeper of the mountain, and for years this was a common practice. Mariners who paid this courtesy to the Heer of the Donder Berg were never molested by his imps, though skipper Ouselsticker, of Fishkill,—for all he had a parson on board,—was once beset by a heavy squall, and the goblin came out of the mist and sat astraddle of his bowsprit, seeming to guide his schooner straight toward the rocks. The dominie chanted the song of Saint Nicolaus, and the goblin, unable to endure either its spiritual potency or the worthy parson's singing, shot upward like a ball and rode off on the gale, carrying with him the nightcap of the parson's wife, which he hung on the weathercock of Esopus steeple, forty miles away.

ANTHONY'S NOSE

The Hudson Highlands are suggestively named Bear Mountain, Sugar Loaf, Cro' Nest, Storm King, called by the Dutch Boterberg, or Butter Hill, from its likeness to a pat of butter; Beacon Hill, where the fires blazed to tell the country that the Revolutionary war was over; Dunderberg, Mount Taurus, so called because a wild bull that had terrorized the Highlands was chased out of his haunts on this height, and was killed by falling from a cliff on an eminence to the northward, known, in consequence, as Breakneck Hill. These, with Anthony's Nose, are the principal points of interest in the lovely and impressive panorama that unfolds before the view as the boats fly onward.

Concerning the last-named elevation, the aquiline promontory that abuts on the Hudson opposite Dunderberg, it takes title from no resemblance to the human feature, but is so named because Anthony Van Corlaer, the trumpeter, who afterwards left a reason for calling the upper boundary of Manhattan Island Spuyten Duyvil Creek, killed the first sturgeon ever eaten at the foot of this mountain. It happened in this wise: By assiduous devotion to keg and flagon Anthony had begotten a nose that was the wonder and admiration of all who knew it, for its size was prodigious; in color it rivalled the carbuncle, and it shone like polished copper. As Anthony was lounging over the quarter of Peter Stuyvesant's galley one summer morning this nose caught a ray from the sun and reflected it hissing into the water, where it killed a sturgeon that was rising beside the vessel. The fish was pulled aboard, eaten, and declared good, though the singed place savored of brimstone, and in commemoration of the event Stuyvesant dubbed the mountain that rose above his vessel Anthony's Nose.

MOODUA CREEK

Moodua is an evolution, through Murdy's and Moodna, from Murderer's Creek, its present inexpressive name having been given to it by N. P. Willis. One Murdock lived on its shore with his wife, two sons, and a daughter; and often in the evening Naoman, a warrior of a neighboring tribe, came to the cabin, caressed the children, and shared the woodman's hospitality. One day the little girl found in the forest an arrow wrapped in snake-skin and tipped with crow's feather; then the boy found a hatchet hanging by a hair from a bough above the door; then a glare of evil eyes was caught for an instant in a thicket. Naoman, when he came, was reserved and stern, finding voice only to warn the family to fly that night; so, when all was still, the threatened family made its way softly, but quickly, to the Hudson shore, and embarked for Fisher's Kill, across the river.

The wind lagged and their boat drew heavily, and when, from the shade of Pollopel's Island, a canoe swept out, propelled by twelve men, the hearts of the people in the boat sank in despair. The wife was about to leap over, but Murdock drew her back; then, loading and firing as fast as possible, he laid six of his pursuers low; but the canoe was savagely urged forward, and in another minute every member of the family was a helpless captive. When the skiff had been dragged back, the prisoners were marched through the wood to an open spot where the principal members of the tribe sat in council.

The sachem arose, twisted his hands in the woman's golden hair, bared his knife, and cried, "Tell us what Indian warned you and betrayed his tribe, or you shall see husband and children bleed before your eyes." The woman answered never a word, but after a little Naoman arose and said, "'Twas I;" then drew his blanket about him and knelt for execution. An axe cleft his skull. Drunk with the sight of blood, the Indians rushed upon the captives and slew them, one by one. The prisoners neither shrank nor cried for mercy, but met their end with hymns upon their lips, and, seeing that they could so meet death, one member of the band let fall his arm and straight became a Christian. The cabin was burned, the bodies flung into the stream, and the stain of blood was seen for many a year in Murderer's Creek.

A TRAPPER'S GHASTLY VENGEANCE

About a mile back from the Hudson, at Coxsackie, stood the cabin of Nick Wolsey, who, in the last century, was known to the river settlements as a hunter and trapper of correct aim, shrewdness, endurance, and taciturn habit. For many years he lived in this cabin alone, except for the company of his dog; but while visiting a camp of Indians in the wilderness he was struck with the engaging manner of one of the girls of the tribe; he repeated the visit; he found cause to go to the camp frequently; he made presents to the father of the maid, and at length won her consent to be his wife. The simple marriage ceremony of the tribe was performed, and Wolsey led Minamee to his home; but the wedding was interrupted in an almost tragic manner, for a surly fellow who had loved the girl, yet who never had found courage to declare himself, was wrought to such a jealous fury at the discovery of Wolsey's good fortune that he sprang at him with a knife, and would have despatched him on the spot had not the white man's faithful hound leaped at his throat and borne him to the ground.

Wolsey disarmed the fellow and kicked and cuffed him to the edge of the wood, while the whole company shouted with laughter at this ignominious punishment, and approved it. A year or more passed. Wolsey and his Indian wife were happy in their free and simple life; happy, too, in their little babe. Wolsey was seldom absent from his cabin for any considerable length of time, and usually returned to it before the night set in. One evening he noticed that the grass and twigs were bent near his house by some passing foot that, with the keen eye of the woodman, he saw was not his wife's.

"Some hunter," he said, "saw the house when he passed here, and as, belike, he never saw one before, he stopped to look in." For the trail led to his window, and diverged thence to the forest again. A few days later, as he was returning, he came on the footprints that were freshly made, and a shadow crossed his face. On nearing the door he stumbled on the body of his dog, lying rigid on the ground. "How did this happen, Minamee?" he cried, as he flung open the door. The wife answered, in a low voice, "O Hush! you'll wake the child."

Nick Wolsey entered the cabin and stood as one turned to marble. Minamee, his wife, sat on the gold hearth, her face and hands cut and blackened, her dress torn, her eyes glassy, a meaningless smile on her lips. In her arms she pressed the body of her infant, its dress soaked with blood, and the head of the little creature lay on the floor beside her. She crooned softly over the cold clay as if hushing it to sleep, and when Wolsey at length found words, she only whispered, "Hush! you will wake him." The night went heavily on; day dawned, and the crooning became lower and lower; still, through all that day the bereft woman rocked to and fro upon the floor, and the agonized husband hung about her, trying in vain to give comfort, to bind her wounds, to get some explanation of the mystery that confronted him. The second night set in, and it was evident that it would be the last for Minamee. Her strength failed until she allowed herself to be placed on a couch of skins, while the body of her child was gently lifted from her arms. Then, for a few brief minutes, her reason was restored, and she found words to tell her husband how the Indian whose murderous attack he had thwarted at the wedding had come to the cabin, shot the dog that had rushed out to defend the place, beat the woman back from the door, tore the baby from its bed, slashed its head off with a knife, and, flinging the little body into her lap, departed with the words, "This is my revenge. I am satisfied." Before the sun was in the east again Minamee was with her baby.

Wolsey sat for hours in the ruin of his happiness, his breathing alone proving that he was alive, and when at last he arose and went out of the house, there were neither tears nor outcry; he saddled his horse and rode off to the westward. At nightfall he came to the Indian village where he had won his wife, and relating to the assembled tribe what had happened, he demanded that the murderer be given up to him. His demand was readily granted, whereupon the white man advanced on the cowering wretch, who had confidently expected the protection of his people, and with the quick fling and jerk of a raw-hide rope bound his arms to his side. Then casting a noose about his neck and tying the end of it to his saddle-bow, he set off for the Hudson. All that night he rode, the Indian walking and running at the horse's heels, and next day he reached his cabin. Tying his prisoner to a tree, the trapper cut a quantity of young willows, from which he fashioned a large cradle-like receptacle; in this he placed the culprit, face upward, and tied so stoutly that he could not move a finger; then going into his house, he emerged with the body of Minamee, and laid it, face downward, on the wretch, who could not repress a groan of horror as the awful burden sank on his breast. Wolsey bound together the living and the dead, and with a swing of his powerful arms he flung them on his horse's back, securing them there with so many turns of rope that nothing could displace them. Now he began to lash his horse until the poor beast trembled with anger and pain, when, flinging off the halter, he gave it a final lash, and the animal plunged, foaming and snorting, into the wilderness. When it had vanished and the hoof-beats were no longer heard, Nick Wolsey took his rifle on his arm and left his home forever. And tradition says that the horse never stopped in its mad career, but that on still nights it can be heard sweeping through the woods along the Hudson and along the Mohawk like a whirlwind, and that as the sound goes by a smothered voice breaks out in cursing, in appeal, then in harsh and dreadful laughter.

THE VANDERDECKEN OF TAPPAN ZEE

It is Saturday night; the swell of the Hudson lazily heaves against the shores of Tappan Zee, the cliff above Tarrytown where the white lady cries on winter nights is pale in starlight, and crickets chirp in the boskage. It is so still that the lap of oars can be heard coming across the water at least a mile away. Some small boat, evidently, but of heavy build, for it takes a vigorous hand to propel it, and now there is a grinding of oars on thole-pins. Strange that it is not yet seen, for the sound is near. Look! Is that a shadow crossing that wrinkle of starlight in the water? The oars have stopped, and there is no wind to make that sound of a sigh.

Ho, Rambout Van Dam! Is it you? Are you still expiating your oath to pull from Kakiat to Spuyten Duyvil before the dawn of Sabbath, if it takes you a month of Sundays? Better for you had you passed the night with your roistering friends at Kakiat, or started homeward earlier, for Sabbath-breaking is no sin now, and you, poor ghost, will find little sympathy for your plight. Grant that your month of Sundays, or your cycle of months of Sundays, be soon up, for it is sad to be reminded that we may be punished for offences many years forgotten. When the sun is high to-morrow a score of barges will vex the sea of Tappan, each crowded with men and maids from New Amsterdam, jigging to profane music and refreshing themselves with such liquors as you, Rambout, never even smelled—be thankful for that much. If your shade sits blinking at them from the wooded buttresses of the Palisades, you must repine, indeed, at the hardness of your fate.

THE GALLOPING HESSIAN

In the flower-gemmed cemetery of Tarrytown, where gentle Irving sleeps, a Hessian soldier was interred after sustaining misfortune in the loss of his head in one of the Revolutionary battles. For a long time after he was buried it was the habit of this gentleman to crawl from his grave at unseemly hours and gallop about the country, sending shivers through the frames of many worthy people, who shrank under their blankets when they heard the rush of hoofs along the unlighted roads.

In later times there lived in Tarrytown—so named because of the tarrying habits of Dutch gossips on market days, though some hard-minded people insist that Tarwe-town means Wheat-towna gaunt schoolmaster, one Ichabod Crane, who cherished sweet sentiments for Katrina Van Tassell, the buxom daughter of a farmer, also a famous maker of pies and doughnuts. Ichabod had been calling late one evening, and, his way home being long, Katrina's father lent him a horse to make the journey; but even with this advantage the youth set out with misgivings, for he had to pass the graveyard.

As it was near the hour when the Hessian was to ride, he whistled feebly to keep his courage up, but when he came to the dreaded spot the whistle died in a gasp, for he heard the tread of a horse. On looking around, his hair bristled and his heart came up like a plug in his throat to hinder his breathing, for he saw a headless horseman coming over the ridge behind him, blackly defined against the starry sky. Setting spurs to his nag with a hope of being first to reach Sleepy Hollow bridge, which the spectre never passed, the unhappy man made the best possible time in that direction, for his follower was surely overtaking him. Another minute and the bridge would be reached; but, to Ichabod's horror, the Hessian dashed alongside and, rising in his stirrups, flung his head full at the fugitive's back. With a squeal of fright the schoolmaster rolled into a mass of weeds by the wayside, and for some minutes he remained there, knowing and remembering nothing.

Next morning farmer Van Tassell's horse was found grazing in a field near Sleepy Hollow, and a man who lived some miles southward reported that he had seen Mr. Crane striding as rapidly along the road to New York as his lean legs could take him, and wearing a pale and serious face as he kept his march. There were yellow stains on the back of his coat, and the man who restored the horse found a smashed pumpkin in the broken bushes beside the road. Ichabod never returned to Tarrytown, and when Brom Bones, a stout young ploughman and taphaunter, married Katrina, people made bold to say that he knew more about the galloping Hessian than any one else, though they believed that he never had reason to be jealous of Ichabod Crane.

STORM SHIP OF THE HUDSON

It was noised about New Amsterdam, two hundred years ago, that a round and bulky ship flying Dutch colors from her lofty quarter was careering up the harbor in the teeth of a north wind, through the swift waters of an ebbing tide, and making for the Hudson. A signal from the Battery to heave to and account for herself being disregarded, a cannon was trained upon her, and a ball went whistling through her cloudy and imponderable mass, for timbers she had none. Some of the sailor-folk talked of mirages that rose into the air of northern coasts and seas, but the wise ones put their fingers beside their noses and called to memory the Flying Dutchman, that wanderer of the seas whose captain, having sworn that he would round Cape Horn in spite of heaven and hell, has been beating to and fro along the bleak Fuegian coast and elsewhere for centuries, being allowed to land but once in seven years, when he can break the curse if he finds a girl who will love him. Perhaps Captain Vanderdecken found this maiden of his hopes in some Dutch settlement on the Hudson, or perhaps he expiated his rashness by prayer and penitence; howbeit, he never came down again, unless he slipped away to sea in snow or fog so dense that watchers and boatmen saw nothing of his passing. A few old settlers declared the vessel to be the Half Moon, and there were some who testified to seeing that identical ship with Hudson and his spectre crew on board making for the Catskills to hold carouse.

This fleeting vision has been confounded with the storm ship that lurks about the foot of the Palisades and Point-no-Point, cruising through Tappan Zee at night when a gale is coming up. The Hudson is four miles wide at Tappan, and squalls have space enough to gather force; hence, when old skippers saw the misty form of a ship steal out from the shadows of the western hills, then fly like a gull from shore to shore, catching the moonlight on her topsails, but showing no lanterns, they made to windward and dropped anchor, unless their craft were stanch and their pilot's brains unvexed with liquor. On summer nights, when falls that curious silence which is ominous of tempest, the storm ship is not only seen spinning across the mirror surface of the river, but the voices of the crew are heard as they chant at the braces and halyards in words devoid of meaning to the listeners.

WHY SPUYTEN DUYVIL IS SO NAMED

The tide-water creek that forms the upper boundary of Manhattan Island is known to dwellers in tenements round about as "Spittin' Divvle." The proper name of it is Spuyten Duyvil, and this, in turn, is the compression of a celebrated boast by Anthony Van Corlaer. This redoubtable gentleman, famous for fat, long wind, and long whiskers, was trumpeter for the garrison at New Amsterdam, which his countrymen had just bought for twenty-four dollars, and he sounded the brass so sturdily that in the fight between the Dutch and Indians at the Dey Street peach orchard his blasts struck more terror into the red men's hearts than did the matchlocks of his comrades. William the Testy vowed that Anthony and his trumpet were garrison enough for all Manhattan Island, for he argued that no regiment of Yankees would approach near enough to be struck with lasting deafness, as must have happened if they came when Anthony was awake.

Peter Stuyvesant-Peter the Headstrong—showed his appreciation of Anthony's worth by making him his esquire, and when he got news of an English expedition on its way to seize his unoffending colony, he at once ordered Anthony to rouse the villages along the Hudson with a trumpet call to war. The esquire took a hurried leave of six or eight ladies, each of whom delighted to believe that his affections were lavished on her alone, and bravely started northward, his trumpet hanging on one side, a stone bottle, much heavier, depending from the other. It was a stormy evening when he arrived at the upper end of the island, and there was no ferryman in sight, so, after fuming up and down the shore, he swallowed a mighty draught of Dutch courage,—for he was as accomplished a performer on the horn as on the trumpet,—and swore with ornate and voluminous oaths that he would swim the stream "in spite of the devil" [En spuyt den Duyvil].

He plunged in, and had gone half-way across when the Evil One, not to be spited, appeared as a huge moss-bunker, vomiting boiling water and lashing a fiery tail. This dreadful fish seized Anthony by the leg; but the trumpeter was game, for, raising his instrument to his lips, he exhaled his last breath through it in a defiant blast that rang through the woods for miles and made the devil himself let go for a moment. Then he was dragged below, his nose shining through the water more and more faintly, until, at last, all sight of him was lost. The failure of his mission resulted in the downfall of the Dutch in America, for, soon after, the English won a bloodless victory, and St. George's cross flaunted from the ramparts where Anthony had so often saluted the setting sun. But it was years, even then, before he was hushed, for in stormy weather it was claimed that the shrill of his trumpet could be heard near the creek that he had named, sounding above the deeper roar of the blast.

THE RAMAPO SALAMANDER

A curious tale of the Rosicrucians runs to the effect that more than two centuries ago a band of German colonists entered the Ramapo valley and put up houses of stone, like those they had left in the Hartz Mountains, and when the Indians saw how they made knives and other wonderful things out of metal, which they extracted from the rocks by fire, they believed them to be manitous and went away, not wishing to resist their possession of the land. There was treasure here, for High Tor, or Torn Mountain, had been the home of Amasis, youngest of the magi who had followed the star of Bethlehem. He had found his way, through Asia and Alaska, to this country, had taken to wife a native woman, by whom he had a child, and here on the summit he had built a temple. Having refused the sun worship, when the Indians demanded that he should take their faith, he was set upon, and would have been killed had not an earthquake torn the ground at his feet, opening a new channel for the Hudson and precipitating into it every one but the magus and his daughter. To him had been revealed in magic vision the secrets of wealth in the rocks.

The leader in the German colony, one Hugo, was a man of noble origin, who had a wife and two children: a boy, named after himself; a girl,—Mary. Though it had been the custom in the other country to let out the forge fires once in seven years, Hugo opposed that practice in the forge he had built as needless. But his men murmured and talked of the salamander that once in seven years attains its growth in unquenched flame and goes forth doing mischief. On the day when that period was ended the master entered his works and saw the men gazing into the furnace at a pale form that seemed made from flame, that was nodding and turning in the fire, occasionally darting its tongue at them or allowing its tail to fall out and lie along the stone floor. As he came to the door he, too, was transfixed, and the fire seemed burning his vitals, until he felt water sprinkled on his face, and saw that his wife, whom he had left at home too ill to move, stood behind him and was casting holy water into the furnace, speaking an incantation as she did so. At that moment a storm arose, and a rain fell that put out the fire; but as the last glow faded the lady fell dead.

When her children were to be consecrated, seven years later, those who stood outside of the church during the ceremony saw a vivid flash, and the nurse turned from the boy in her fright. She took her hands from her eyes. The child was gone. Twice seven years had passed and the daughter remained unspotted by the world, for, on the night when her father had led her to the top of High Torn Mountain and shown her what Amasis had seen,—the earth spirits in their caves heaping jewels and offering to give them if Hugo would speak the word that binds the free to the earth forces and bars his future for a thousand years,—it was her prayer that brought him to his senses and made the scene below grow dim, though the baleful light of the salamander clinging to the rocks at the bottom of the cave sent a glow into the sky.

Many nights after that the glow was seen on the height and Hugo was missing from his home, but for lack of a pure soul to stand as interpreter he failed to read the words that burned in the triangle on the salamander's back, and returned in rage and jealousy. A knightly man had of late appeared in the settlement, and between him and Mary a tender feeling had arisen, that, however, was unexpressed until, after saving her from the attack of a panther, he had allowed her to fall into his arms. She would willingly then have declared her love for him, but he placed her gently and regretfully from him and said, "When you slept I came to you and put a crown of gems on your head: that was because I was in the power of the earth spirit. Then I had power only over the element of fire, that either consumes or hardens to stone; but now water and life are mine. Behold! Wear these, for thou art worthy." And touching the tears that had fallen from her eyes, they turned into lilies in his hands, and he put them on her brow.

"Shall we meet again?" asked the girl.

"I do not know," said he. "I tread the darkness of the universe alone, and I peril my redemption by yielding to this love of earth. Thou art redeemed already, but I must make my way back to God through obedience tested in trial. Know that I am one of those that left heaven for love of man. We were of that subtle element which is flame, burning and glowing with love,—and when thy mother came to me with the power of purity to cast me out of the furnace, I lost my shape of fire and took that of a human being,—a child. I have been with thee often, and was rushing to annihilation, because I could not withstand the ordeal of the senses. Had I yielded, or found thee other than thou art, I should have become again an earth spirit. I have been led away by wish for power, such as I have in my grasp, and forgot the mission to the suffering. I became a wanderer over the earth until I reached this land, the land that you call new. Here was to be my last trial and here I am to pass the gate of fire."

As he spoke voices arose from the settlement.

"They are coming," said he. The stout form of Hugo was in advance. With a fierce oath he sprang on the young man. "He has ruined my household," he cried. "Fling him into the furnace!" The young man stood waiting, but his brow was serene. He was seized, and in a few moments had disappeared through the mouth of the burning pit. But Mary, looking up, saw a shape in robes of silvery light, and it drifted upward until it vanished in the darkness. The look of horror on her face died away, and a peace came to it that endured until the end.

CHIEF CROTON

Between the island of Manhattoes and the Catskills the Hudson shores were plagued with spooks, and even as late as the nineteenth century Hans Anderson, a man who tilled a farm back of Peekskill, was worried into his grave by the leaden-face likeness of a British spy whom he had hanged on General Putnam's orders. "Old Put" doubtless enjoyed immunity from this vexatious creature, because he was born with few nerves. A region especially afflicted was the confluence of the Croton and the Hudson, for the Kitchawan burying-ground was here, and the red people being disturbed by the tramping of white men over their graves, "the walking sachems of Teller's Point" were nightly to be met on their errands of protest.

These Indians had built a palisade on Croton Point, and here they made their last stand against their enemies from the north. Throughout the fight old chief Croton stood on the wall with arrows showering around him, and directed the resistance with the utmost calm. Not until every one of his men was dead and the fort was going up in flame about him did he confess defeat. Then standing amid the charring timbers, he used his last breath in calling down the curse of the Great Spirit against the foe. As the victorious enemy rushed into the enclosure to secure the scalps of the dead he fell lifeless into the fire, and their jubilant yell was lost upon his ears. Yet, he could not rest nor bear to leave his ancient home, even after death, and often his form, in musing attitude, was seen moving through the woods. When a manor was built on the ruins of his fort, he appeared to the master of it, to urge him into the Continental army, and having seen this behest obeyed and laid a solemn injointure to keep the freedom of the land forever, he vanished, and never appeared again.

THE RETREAT FROM MAHOPAC

After the English had secured the city of New Amsterdam and had begun to extend their settlements along the Hudson, the Indians congregated in large numbers about Lake Mahopac, and rejected all overtures for the purchase of that region. In their resolution they were sustained by their young chief Omoyao, who refused to abandon on on any terms the country where his fathers had solong hunted, fished, and built their lodges. A half-breed, one Joliper, a member of this tribe, was secretly in the pay of the English, but the allurements and insinuations that he put forth on their behalf were as futile as the breathing of wind in the leaves. At last the white men grew angry. Have the land they would, by evil course if good ways were refused, and commissioning Joliper to act for them in a decisive manner, they guaranteed to supply him with forces if his negotiations fell through. This man never thought it needful to negotiate. He knew the temper of his tribe and he was too jealous of his chief to go to him for favors, because he loved Maya, the chosen one of Omoyao.

At the door of Maya's tent he entreated her to go with him to the white settlements, and on her refusal he broke into angry threats, declaring, in the self-forgetfulness of passion, that he would kill her lover and lead the English against the tribe. Unknown to both Omoyao had overheard this interview, and he immediately sent runners to tell all warriors of his people to meet him at once on the island in the lake. Though the runners were cautioned to keep their errand secret, it is probable that Joliper suspected that the alarm had gone forth, and he resolved to strike at once; so he summoned his renegades, stole into camp next evening and made toward Maya's wigwam, intending to take her to a place of safety. Seeing the chief at the door, he shot an arrow at him, but the shaft went wide and slew the girl's father. Realizing, upon this assault, that he was outwitted and that his people were outnumbered, the chief called to Maya to meet him at the island, and plunged into the brush, after seeing that she had taken flight in an opposite direction. The vengeful Joliper was close behind him with his renegades, and the chief was captured; then, that he might not communicate with his people or delay the operations against them, it was resolved to put him to death.

He was tied to a tree, the surrounding wood was set on fire, and he was abandoned to his fate, his enemies leaving him to destruction in their haste to reach the place of the council and slay or capture all who were there. Hardly were they out of hearing ere the plash of a paddle sounded through the roar of flame and Maya sprang upon the bank, cut her lover's bonds, and with him made toward the island, which they reached by a protected way before the assailants had arrived. They told the story of Joliper's cruelty and treason, and when his boats were seen coming in to shore they had eyes and hands only for Joliper. He was the first to land. Hardly had he touched the strand before he was surrounded by a frenzied crowd and had fallen bleeding from a hundred gashes.

The Indians were overpowered after a brief and bloody resistance. They took safety in flight. Omoyao and Maya, climbing upon the rock above their "council chamber," found that while most of their people had escaped their own retreat was cut off, and that it would be impossible to reach any of the canoes. They preferred death to torture and captivity, so, hand in hand, they leaped together down the cliff, and the English claimed the land next day.

NIAGARA

The cataract of Niagara (properly pronounced Nee-ah-gah-rah), or Oniahgarah, is as fatal as it is fascinating, beautiful, sublime, and the casualties occurring there justify the tradition that "the Thundering Water asks two victims every year." It was reputed, before white men looked for the first time on these falls—and what thumping yarns they told about them!—that two lives were lost here annually, and this average has been kept up by men and women who fall into the flood through accident, recklessness or despair, while bloody battles have been fought on the shores, and vessels have been hurled over the brink, to be dashed to splinters on the rocks.

The sound of the cataract was declared to be the voice of a mighty spirit that dwelt in the waters, and in former centuries the Indians offered to it a yearly sacrifice. This sacrifice was a maiden of the tribe, who was sent over in a white canoe, decorated with fruit and flowers, and the girls contended for this honor, for the brides of Manitou were objects of a special grace in the happy hunting-grounds. The last recorded sacrifice was in 1679, when Lelawala, the daughter of chief Eagle Eye, was chosen, in spite of the urgings and protests of the chevalier La Salle, who had been trying to restrain the people from their idolatries by an exposition of the Christian dogma. To his protests he received the unexpected answer, "Your words witness against you. Christ, you say, set us an example. We will follow it. Why should one death be great, while our sacrifice is horrible?" So the tribe gathered at the bank to watch the sailing of the white canoe. The chief watched the embarkation with the stoicism usual to the Indian when he is observed by others, but when the little bark swung out into the current his affection mastered him, and he leaped into his own canoe and tried to overtake his daughter. In a moment both were beyond the power of rescue. After their death they were changed into spirits of pure strength and goodness, and live in a crystal heaven so far beneath the fall that its roaring is a music to them: she, the maid of the mist; he, the ruler of the cataract. Another version of the legend makes a lover and his mistress the chief actors. Some years later a patriarch of the tribe and all his sons went over the fall when the white men had seized their lands, preferring death to flight or war.

In about the year 200 the Stone Giants waded across the river below the falls on their northward march. These beings were descended from an ancient family, and being separated from their stock in the year 150 by the breaking of a vine bridge across the Mississippi, they left that region. Indian Pass, in the Adirondacks, bore the names of Otneyarheh, Stony Giants; Ganosgwah, Giants Clothed in Stone; and Dayohjegago, Place Where the Storm Clouds Fight the Great Serpent. Giants and serpents were held to be harmful inventions of the Evil Spirit, and the Lightning god, catching up clouds as he stood on the crags, broke them open, tore their lightnings out and hurled them against the monsters. These cannibals had almost exterminated the Iroquois, for they were of immense size and had made themselves almost invincible by rolling daily in the sand until their flesh was like stone. The Holder of the Heavens, viewing their evil actions from on high, came down disguised as one of their number—he used often to meditate on Manitou Rock, at the Whirlpool—and leading them to a valley near Onondaga, on pretence of guiding them to a fairer country, he stood on a hill above them and hurled rocks upon their heads until all, save one, who fled into the north, were dead. Yet, in the fulness of time, new children of the Stone Giants (mail-clad Europeans?) entered the region again and were destroyed by the Great Spirit,—oddly enough where the famous fraud known as the Cardiff giant was alleged to have been found. The Onondagas believed this statue to be one of their ancient foes.

THE DEFORMED OF ZOAR

The valley of Zoar, in western New York, is so surrounded by hills that its discoverers—a religious people, who gave it a name from Scripture said, "This is Zoar; it is impregnable. From her we will never go." And truly, for lack of roads, they found it so hard to get out, having got in, that they did not leave it. Among the early settlers here were people of a family named Wright, whose house became a sort of inn for the infrequent traveller, inasmuch as they were not troubled with piety, and had no scruples against the selling of drink and the playing of cards at late hours. A peddler passed through the valley on his way to Buffalo and stopped at the Wright house for a lodging, but before he went to bed he incautiously showed a number of golden trinkets from his pack and drew a considerable quantity of money out of his pocket when he paid the fee for his lodging. Hardly had he fallen asleep before his greedy hosts were in the room, searching for his money. Their lack of caution caused him to awake, and as he found them rifling his pockets and his pack he sprang up and showed fight.

A blow sent him to the bottom of the stairs, where his attempt to escape was intercepted, and the family closed around him and bound his arms and legs. They showed him the money they had taken and asked where he had concealed the rest. He vowed that it was all he had. They insisted that he had more, and seizing a knife from the table the elder Wright slashed off one of his toes "to make him confess." No result came from this, and six toes were cut off,—three from each foot; then, in disgust, the unhappy peddler was knocked on the head and flung through a trap-door into a shallow cellar. Presently he arose and tried to draw himself out, but with hatchet and knife they chopped away his fingers and he fell back. Even the women shared in this work, and leaned forward to gaze into the cellar to see if he might yet be dead. While listening, they heard the man invoke the curse of heaven on them: he asked that they should wear the mark of crime even to the fourth generation, by coming into the world deformed and mutilated as he was then. And it was so. The next child born in that house had round, hoof-like feet, with only two toes, and hands that tapered from the wrist into a single long finger. And in time there were twenty people so deformed in the valley: The "crab-clawed Zoarites" they were called.

HORSEHEADS

The feeling recently created by an attempt to fasten the stupid names of Fairport or of North Elmira on the village in central New York that, off and on for fifty years, had been called Horseheads, caused an inquiry as to how that singular name chanced to be adopted for a settlement. In 1779, when General Sullivan was retiring toward the base of his supplies after a destructive campaign against the Indians in Genesee County, he stopped near this place and rested his troops. The country was then rude, unbroken, and still beset with enemies, however, and when the march was resumed it was thought best to gain time over a part of the way by descending the Chemung River on rafts.

As there were no appliances for building large floats, and the depth of the water was not known, the general ordered a destruction of all impedimenta that could be got rid of, and commanded that the poor and superfluous horses should be killed. His order was obeyed. As soon as the troops had gone, the wolves, that were then abundant, came forth and devoured the carcasses of the steeds, so that the clean-picked bones were strewn widely over the camp-ground. When the Indians ventured back into this region, some of them piled the skulls of the horses into heaps, and these curious monuments were found by white settlers who came into the valley some years later, and who named their village Horseheads, in commemoration of these relics. The Indians were especially loth to leave this region, for their tradition was that it had been the land of the Senecas from immemorial time, the tribe being descended from a couple that had a home on a hill near Horseheads.

KAYUTA AND WANETA

The Indians loved our lakes. They had eyes for their beauty, and to them they were abodes of gracious spirits. They used to say of Oneida Lake, that when the Great Spirit formed the world "his smile rested on its waters and Frenchman's Island rose to greet it; he laughed and Lotus Island came up to listen." So they built lodges on their shores and skimmed their waters in canoes. Much of their history relates to them, and this is a tale of the Senecas that was revived a few years ago by the discovery of a deer-skin near Lakes Waneta and Keuka, New York, on which some facts of the history were rudely drawn, for all Indians are artists.

Waneta, daughter of a chief, had plighted her troth to Kayuta, a hunter of a neighboring tribe with which her people were at war. Their tryst was held at twilight on the farther shore of the lake from her village, and it was her gayety and happiness, after these meetings had taken place, that roused the suspicion and jealousy of Weutha, who had marked her for his bride against the time when he should have won her father's consent by some act of bravery. Shadowing the girl as she stole into the forest one evening, he saw her enter her canoe and row to a densely wooded spot; he heard a call like the note of a quail, then an answer; then Kayuta emerged on the shore, lifted the maiden from her little bark, and the twain sat down beside the water to listen to the lap of its waves and watch the stars come out.

Hurrying back to camp, the spy reported that an enemy was near them, and although Waneta had regained her wigwam by another route before the company of warriors had reached the lake, Kayuta was seen, pursued, and only escaped with difficulty. Next evening, not knowing what had happened after her homeward departure on the previous night—for the braves deemed it best to keep the knowledge of their military operations from the women—the girl crept away to the lake again and rowed to the accustomed place, but while waiting for the quail call a twig dropped on the water beside her. With a quick instinct that civilization has spoiled she realized this to be a warning, and remaining perfectly still, she allowed her boat to drift toward shore, presently discovering that her lover was standing waist-deep in the water. In a whisper he told her that they were watched, and bade her row to a dead pine that towered at the foot of the lake, where he would soon meet her. At that instant an arrow grazed his side and flew quivering into the canoe.

Pushing the boat on its course and telling her to hasten, Kayuta sprang ashore, sounded the warwhoop, and as Weutha rose into sight he clove his skull with a tomahawk. Two other braves now leaped forward, but, after a struggle, Kayuta left them dead or senseless, too. He would have stayed to tear their scalps off had he not heard his name uttered in a shriek of agony from the end of the lake, and, tired and bleeding though he was, he bounded along its margin like a deer, for the voice that he heard was Waneta's. He reached the blasted pine, gave one look, and sank to the earth. Presently other Indians came, who had heard the noise of fighting, and burst upon him with yells and brandished weapons, but something in his look restrained them from a close advance. His eyes were fixed on a string of beads that lay on the bottom of the lake, just off shore, and when the meaning of it came to them, the savages thought no more of killing, but moaned their grief; for Waneta, in stepping from her canoe to wade ashore, had been caught and swallowed by a quagmire. All night and all next day Kayuta sat there like a man of stone. Then, just as the hour fell when he was used to meet his love, his heart broke, and he joined her in the spiritland.

THE DROP STAR

A little maid of three years was missing from her home on the Genesee. She had gone to gather water-lilies and did not return. Her mother, almost crazed with grief, searched for days, weeks, months, before she could resign herself to the thought that her little one—Kayutah, the Drop Star, the Indians called her—had indeed been drowned. Years went by. The woman's home was secure against pillage, for it was no longer the one house of a white family in that region, and the Indians had retired farther and farther into the wilderness. One day a hunter came to the woman and said, "I have seen old Skenandoh,—the last of his tribe, thank God! who bade me say this to you: that the ice is broken, and he knows of a hill of snow where a red berry grows that shall be yours if you will claim it." When the meaning of this message came upon her the woman fainted, but on recovering speech she despatched her nephew to the hut of the aged chief and passed that night in prayer.

The young man set off at sunset, and by hard riding, over dim trails, with only stars for light, he came in the gray of dawn to an upright timber, colored red and hung with scalps, that had been cut from white men's heads at the massacre of Wyoming. The place they still call Painted Post. Without drawing rein he sped along the hills that hem Lake Seneca, then, striking deeper into the wilds, he reached a smaller lake, and almost fell from his saddle before a rude tent near the shore. A new grave had been dug close by, and he shuddered to think that perhaps he had come too late, but a wrinkled Indian stepped forth at that moment and waited his word.

"I come," cried the youth,—"to see the berry that springs from snow."

"You come in time," answered Skenandoh. "No, 'tis not in that grave. It is my own child that is buried there. She was as a sister to the one you seek, and she bade me restore the Drop Star to her mother,—the squaw that we know as the New Moon's Light."

Stepping into the wigwam, he emerged again, clasping the wrist of a girl of eighteen, whose robe he tore asunder at the throat, showing the white breast, and on it a red birth-mark; then, leading her to the young man, he said,—"And now I must go to the setting sun." He slung a pouch about him, loaded, not with arms and food, but stones, stepped into his canoe, and paddled out upon the water, singing as he went a melancholy chant—his deathsong. On gaining the middle of the lake he swung his tomahawk and clove the bottom of the frail boat, so that it filled in a moment and the chief sank from sight. The young man took his cousin to her overjoyed mother, helped to win her back to the ways of civilized life, and eventually married her. She took her Christian name again, but left to the lake on whose banks she had lived so long her Indian name of Drop Star—Kayutah.

THE PROPHET OF PALMYRA

It was at Palmyra, New York, that the principles of Mormonism were first enunciated by Joseph Smith, who claimed to have found the golden plates of the Book of Mormon in a hill-side in neighboring Manchester,—the "Hill of Cumorah,"—to which he was led by angels. The plates were written in characters similar to the masonic cabala, and he translated them by divine aid, giving to the world the result of his discovery. The Hebrew prophet Mormon was the alleged author of the record, and his son Moroni buried it. The basis of Mormonism was, however, an unpublished novel, called "The Manuscript Found," that was read to Sidney Rigdon (afterwards a Mormon elder) by its author, a clergyman, and that formulated a creed for a hypothetical church. Smith had a slight local celebrity, for he and his father were operators with the divining-rod, and when he appropriated this creed a harmless and beneficent one, for polygamy was a later "inspiration" of Brigham Young—and began to preach it, in 1844, it gained many converts. His arrogation of the presidency of the "Church of Latter Day Saints" and other rash performances won for him the enmity of the Gentiles, who imprisoned and killed him at Carthage, Missouri, leaving Brigham Young to lead the people across the deserts to Salt Lake, where they prospered through thrift and industry.

It was claimed that in the van of this army, on the march to Utah, was often seen a venerable man with silver beard, who never spoke, but who would point the way whenever the pilgrims were faint or discouraged. When they reached the spot where the temple was afterwards built, he struck his staff into the earth and vanished.

At Hydesville, near Palmyra, spiritualism, as it is commonly called, came into being on March 31, 1849, when certain of the departed announced themselves by thumping on doors and tables in the house of the Fox family, the survivors of which confessed the fraud nearly forty years after. It is of interest to note that the ground whence these new religions sprang was peopled by the Onondagas, the sacerdotal class of the Algonquin tribe, who have preserved the ancient religious rites of that great family until this day.

A VILLAIN'S CREMATION

Bramley's Mountain, near the present village of Bloomfield, New York, on the edge of the Catskill group, was the home of a young couple that had married with rejoicing and had taken up the duties and pleasures of housekeeping with enthusiasm. To be sure, in those days housekeeping was not a thing to be much afraid of, and the servant question had not come up for discussion. The housewives did the work themselves, and the husband had no valets. The domicile of this particular pair was merely a tent of skins stretched around a frame of poles, and their furniture consisted principally of furs strewn over the earth floor; but they loved each other truly. The girl was thankful to be taken from her home to live, because, up to the time of her marriage, she had been persecuted by a morose and ill-looking fellow of her tribe, who laid siege to her affection with such vehemence that the more he pleaded the greater was her dislike; and now she hoped that she had seen the last of him. But that was not to be. He lurked about the wigwam of the pair, torturing himself with the sight of their felicity, and awaiting his chance to prove his hate. This chance came when the husband had gone to Lake Delaware to fish, for he rowed after and gave battle in the middle of the pond. Taken by surprise, and being insufficiently armed, the husband was killed and his body flung into the water. Then, casting an affectionate leer at the wife who had watched this act of treachery and malice with speechless horror from the mountain-side, he drove his canoe ashore and set off in pursuit of her. She retreated so slowly as to allow him to keep her in sight, and when she entered a cave he pressed forward eagerly, believing that now her escape was impossible; but she had purposely trapped him there, for she had already explored a tortuous passage that led to the upper air, and by this she had left the cavern in safety while he was groping and calling in the dark. Returning to the entrance, she loosened, by a jar, a ledge that overhung it, so that the door was almost blocked; then, gathering light wood from the dry trees around her, she made a fire and hurled the burning sticks into the prison where the wretch was howling, until he was dead in smoke and flame. When his yells and curses had been silenced she told a friend what she had done, then going back to the lake, she sang her death-song and cast herself into the water, hoping thus to rejoin her husband.

THE MONSTER MOSQUITOE

They have some pretty big mosquitoes in New Jersey and on Long Island, but, if report of their ancestry is true, they have degenerated in size and voracity; for the grandfather of all mosquitoes used to live in the neighborhood of Fort Onondaga, New York, and sallying out whenever he was hungry, would eat an Indian or two and pick his teeth with their ribs. The red men had no arms that could prevail against it, but at last the Holder of the Heavens, hearing their cry for aid, came down and attacked the insect. Finding that it had met its match, the mosquito flew away so rapidly that its assailant could hardly keep it in sight. It flew around the great lake, then turned eastward again. It sought help vainly of the witches that brooded in the sink-holes, or Green Lakes (near Janesville, New York), and had reached the salt lake of Onondaga when its pursuer came up and killed it, the creature piling the sand into hills in its dying struggles.

As its blood poured upon the earth it became small mosquitoes, that gathered about the Holder of the Heavens and stung him so sorely that he half repented the service that he had done to men. The Tuscaroras say that this was one of two monsters that stood on opposite banks of the Seneca River and slew all men that passed. Hiawatha killed the other one. On their reservation is a stone, marked by the form of the Sky Holder, that shows where he rested during the chase, while his tracks were until lately seen south of Syracuse, alternating with footprints of the mosquito, which were shaped like those of a bird, and twenty inches long. At Brighton, New York, where these marks appeared, they were reverentially renewed by the Indians for many years.

THE GREEN PICTURE

In a cellar in Green Street, Schenectady, there appeared, some years ago, the silhouette of a human form, painted on the floor in mould. It was swept and scrubbed away, but presently it was there again, and month by month, after each removal, it returned: a mass of fluffy mould, always in the shape of a recumbent man. When it was found that the house stood on the site of the old Dutch burial ground, the gossips fitted this and that together and concluded that the mould was planted by a spirit whose mortal part was put to rest a century and more ago, on the spot covered by the house, and that the spirit took this way of apprising people that they were trespassing on its grave. Others held that foul play had been done, and that a corpse, hastily and shallowly buried, was yielding itself back to the damp cellar in vegetable form, before its resolution into simpler elements. But a darker meaning was that it was the outline of a vampire that vainly strove to leave its grave, and could not because a virtuous spell had been worked about the place.

A vampire is a dead man who walks about seeking for those whose blood he can suck, for only by supplying new life to its cold limbs can he keep the privilege of moving about the earth. He fights his way from his coffin, and those who meet his gray and stiffened shape, with fishy eyes and blackened mouth, lurking by open windows, biding his time to steal in and drink up a human life, fly from him in terror and disgust. In northern Rhode Island those who die of consumption are believed to be victims of vampires who work by charm, draining the blood by slow draughts as they lie in their graves. To lay this monster he must be taken up and burned; at least, his heart must be; and he must be disinterred in the daytime when he is asleep and unaware. If he died with blood in his heart he has this power of nightly resurrection. As late as 1892 the ceremony of heart-burning was performed at Exeter, Rhode Island, to save the family of a dead woman that was threatened with the same disease that removed her, namely, consumption. But the Schenectady vampire has yielded up all his substance, and the green picture is no more.

THE NUNS OF CARTHAGE

At Carthage, New York, where the Black River bends gracefully about a point, there was a stanch old house, built in the colonial fashion and designed for the occupancy of some family of hospitality and wealth, but the family died out or moved away, and for some years it remained deserted. During the war of 1812 the village gossips were excited by the appearance of carpenters, painters and upholsterers, and it was evident that the place was to be restored to its manorial dignities; but their curiosity was deepened instead of satisfied when, after the house had been put in order and high walls built around it, the occupants presented themselves as four young women in the garb of nuns. Were they daughters of the family? Were they English sympathizers in disguise, seeking asylum in the days of trouble? Had they registered a vow of celibacy until their lovers should return from the war? Were they on a secret and diplomatic errand? None ever knew, at least in Carthage. The nuns lived in great privacy, but in a luxury before unequalled in that part of the country. They kept a gardener, they received from New York wines and delicacies that others could not afford, and when they took the air, still veiled, it was behind a splendid pair of bays.

One afternoon, just after the close of the war, a couple of young American officers went to the convent, and, contrary to all precedent, were admitted. They remained within all that day, and no one saw them leave, but a sound of wheels passed through the street that evening. Next day there were no signs of life about the place, nor the day following, nor the next. The savage dog was quiet and the garden walks had gone unswept. Some neighbors climbed over the wall and reported that the place had been deserted. Why and by whom no one ever knew, but a cloud remained upon its title until a recent day, for it was thought that at some time the nuns might return.

THE SKULL IN THE WALL

A skull is built into the wall above the door of the court-house at Goshen, New York. It was taken from a coffin unearthed in 1842, when the foundation of the building was laid. People said there was no doubt about it, only Claudius Smith could have worn that skull, and he deserved to be publicly pilloried in that manner. Before the Revolutionary war Smith was a farmer in Monroe, New York, and being prosperous enough to feel the king's taxes no burden, to say nothing of his jealousy of the advantage that an independent government would be to the hopes of his poorer neighbors, he declared for the king. After the declaration of independence had been published, his sympathies were illustrated in an unpleasantly practical manner by gathering a troop of other Tories about him, and, emboldened by the absence of most of the men of his vicinage in the colonial army, he began to harass the country as grievously in foray as the red-coats were doing in open field.

He pillaged houses and barns, then burned them; he insulted women, he drove away cattle and horses, he killed several persons who had undertaken to defend their property. His "campaigns" were managed with such secrecy that nobody knew when or whence to look for him. His murder of Major Nathaniel Strong, of Blooming Grove, roused indignation to such a point that a united effort was made to catch him, a money reward for success acting as a stimulus to the vigilance of the hunters, and at last he was captured on Long Island. He was sent back to Goshen, tried, convicted, and on January 22, 1779, was hanged, with five of his band. The bodies of the culprits were buried in the jail-yard, on the spot where the court-house stands, and old residents identified Smith's skeleton, when it was accidentally exhumed, by its uncommon size. A farmer from an adjacent town made off with a thigh bone, and a mason clapped mortar into the empty skull and cemented it into the wall, where it long remained.

THE HAUNTED MILL

Among the settlers in the Adirondacks, forty or fifty years ago, was Henry Clymer, from Brooklyn, who went up to Little Black Creek and tried to make a farm out of the gnarly, stumpy land; but being a green hand at that sort of thing, he soon gave it up and put up the place near Northwood, that is locally referred to as the haunted mill. When the first slab was cut, a big party was on hand to cheer and eat pie in honor of the Clymers, for Mr. Clymer, who was a dark, hearty, handsome fellow, and his bright young wife had been liberal in their hospitality. The couple had made some talk, they were so loving before folks—too loving to last; and, besides, it was evident that Mrs. Clymer was used to a better station in life than her husband. It was while the crowd was laughing and chattering at the picnic-table of new boards from the mill that Mrs. Clymer stole away to her modest little house, and a neighbor who had followed her was an accidental witness to a singular episode. Mrs. Clymer was kneeling beside her bed, crying over the picture of a child, when Clymer entered unexpectedly and attempted to take the picture from her.

She faced him defiantly. "You kept that because it looked like him, I reckon," he said. "You might run back to him. You know what he'd call you and where you'd stand with your aristocracy."

The woman pointed to the door, and the man left without another word, and so did the listener. Next morning the body of Mrs. Clymer was found hanging to a beam in the mill. At the inquest the husband owned that he had "had a few words" with her on the previous day, and thought that she must have suddenly become insane. The jury took this view. News of the suicide was printed in some of the city papers, and soon after that the gossips had another sensation, for a fair-haired man, also from Brooklyn, arrived at the place and asked where the woman was buried. When he found the grave he sat beside it for some time, his head resting on his hand; then he inquired for Clymer, but Clymer, deadly pale, had gone into the woods as soon as he heard that a stranger had arrived. The new-comer went to Trenton, where he ordered a gravestone bearing the single word "Estella" to be placed where the woman's body had been interred. Clymer quickly sold out and disappeared. The mill never prospered, and has long been in a ruinous condition. People of the neighborhood think that the ghost of Mrs. Clymer—was that her name?—still troubles it, and they pass the place with quickened steps.

OLD INDIAN FACE

On Lower Ausable Pond is a large, ruddy rock showing a huge profile, with another, resembling a pappoose, below it. When the Tahawi ruled this region their sachem lived here at "the Dark Cup," as they called this lake, a man renowned for virtue and remarkable, in his age, for gentleness. When his children had died and his manly grandson, who was the old man's hope, had followed them to the land of the cloud mountains, Adota's heart withered within him, and standing beneath this rock, he addressed his people, recounting what he had done for them, how he had swept their enemies from the Lakes of the Clustered Stars (the Lower Saranac) and Silver Sky (Upper Saranac) to the Lake of Wandah, gaining a land where they might hunt and fish in peace. The little one, the Star, had been ravished away to crown the brow of the thunder god, who, even now, was advancing across the peaks, bending the woods and lighting the valleys with his jagged torches.

Life was nothing to him longer; he resigned it.

As he spoke these words he fell back, and the breath passed out of him. Then came the thunder god, and with an appalling burst of fire sent the people cowering. The roar that followed seemed to shake the earth, but the medicine-man of the tribe stood still, listening to the speech of the god in the clouds. "Tribe of the Tahawi," he translated, "Adota treads the star-path to the happy hunting-grounds, and the sun is shining on his heart. He will never walk among you again, but the god loves both him and you, and he will set his face on the mountains. Look!" And, raising their eyes, they beheld the likeness of Adota and of his beloved child, the Star, graven by lightning-stroke on the cliff. There they buried the body of Adota and held their solemn festivals until the white men drove them out of the country.

THE DIVISION OF THE SARANACS

In the middle of the last century a large body of Saranac Indians occupied the forests of the Upper Saranac through which ran the Indian carrying-place, called by them the Eagle Nest Trail. Whenever they raided the Tahawi on the slopes of Mount Tahawus (Sky-splitter), there was a pleasing rivalry between two young athletes, called the Wolf and the Eagle, as to which would carry off the more scalps, and the tribe was divided in admiration of them. There was one who did not share this liking: an old sachem, one of the wizards who had escaped when the Great Spirit locked these workers of evil in the hollow trees that stood beside the trail. In their struggles to escape the less fortunate ones thrust their arms through the closing bark, and they are seen there, as withered trunks and branches, to this day. Oquarah had not been softened by this exhibition of danger nor the qualification of mercy that allowed him still to exist. Rather he was more bitter when he saw, as he fancied, that the tribe thought more of the daring and powerful warriors than it did of the bent and malignant-minded counsellor.

It was in the moon of green leaves that the two young men set off to hunt the moose, and on the next day the Wolf returned alone. He explained that in the hunt they had been separated; he had called for hours for his friend, and had searched so long that he concluded he must have returned ahead of him. But he was not at the camp. Up rose the sachem with visage dark. "I hear a forked tongue," he cried. "The Wolf was jealous of the Eagle and his teeth have cut into his heart."

"The Wolf cannot lie," answered the young man.

"Where is the Eagle?" angrily shouted the sachem, clutching his hatchet.

"The Wolf has said," replied the other.

The old sachem advanced upon him, but as he raised his axe to strike, the wife of the Wolf threw herself before her husband, and the steel sank into her brain. The sachem fell an instant later with the Wolf's knife in his heart, and instantly the camp was in turmoil. Before the day had passed it had been broken up, and the people were divided into factions, for it was no longer possible to hold it together in peace. The Wolf, with half of the people, went down the Sounding River to new hunting-grounds, and the earth that separated the families was reddened whenever one side met the other.

    Years had passed when, one morning, the upper tribe saw a canoe advancing across the Lake of the Silver Sky. An old man stepped from it: he was the Eagle. After the Wolf had left him he had fallen into a cleft in a rock, and had lain helpless until found by hunters who were on their way to Canada. He had joined the British against the French, had married a northern squaw, but had returned to die among the people of his early love. Deep was his sorrow that his friend should have been accused of doing him an injury, and that the once happy tribe should have been divided by that allegation. The warriors and sachems of both branches were summoned to a council, and in his presence they swore a peace, so that in the fulness of time he was able to die content. That peace was always kept.

AN EVENT IN INDIAN PARK

It was during the years when the Saranacs were divided that Howling Wind, one of the young men of Indian Carry, saw and fell in love with a girl of the family on Tupper Lake. He quickly found a way to tell his liking, and the couple met often in the woods and on the shore. He made bold to row her around the quieter bays, and one moonlight evening he took her to Devil's Rock, or Devil's Pulpit, where he told her the story of the place. This was to the effect that the fiend had paddled, on timbers, by means of his tail, to that rock, and had assembled fish and game about him in large numbers by telling them that he was going to preach to them, instead of which moral procedure he pounced upon and ate all that were within his grasp.

As so often happened in Indian history, the return of these lovers was seen by a disappointed rival, who had hurried back to camp and secured the aid of half a dozen men to arrest the favored one as soon as he should land. The capture was made after a struggle, and Howling Wind was dragged to the chief's tent for sentence. That sentence was death, and with a refinement of cruelty that was rare even among the Indians, the girl was ordered to execute it. She begged and wept to no avail. An axe was put into her hands, and she was ordered to despatch the prisoner. She took the weapon; her face grew stern and the tears dried on her cheeks; her lover, bound to a tree, gazed at her in amazement; his rival watched, almost in glee. Slowly the girl crossed the open space to her lover. She raised the tomahawk and at a blow severed the thongs that held him, then, like a flash, she leaped upon his rival, who had sprung forward to interfere, and clove his skull with a single stroke. The lovers fled as only those can fly who run for life. Happily for them, they met a party from the Carry coming to rescue Howling Wind from the danger to which his courtship had exposed him, and it was even said that this party entered the village and by presenting knives and arrows at the breast of the chief obtained his now superfluous consent to the union of the fugitives. The pair reached the Carry in safety and lived a long and happy life together.

THE INDIAN PLUME

Brightest flower that grows beside the brooks is the scarlet blossom of the Indian plume: the blood of Lenawee. Hundreds of years ago she lived happily among her brother and sister Saranacs beside Stony Creek, the Stream of the Snake, and was soon to marry the comely youth who, for the speed of his foot, was called the Arrow. But one summer the Quick Death came on the people, and as the viewless devil stalked through the village young and old fell before him. The Arrow was the first to die. In vain the Prophet smoked the Great Calumet: its smoke ascending took no shape that he could read. In vain was the white dog killed to take aloft the people's sins. But at last the Great Spirit himself came down to the mountain called the Storm Darer, splendid in lightning, awful in his thunder voice and robe of cloud. "My wrath is against you for your sins," he cried, "and naught but human blood will appease it."

In the morning the Prophet told his message, and all sat silent for a time. Then Lenawee entered the circle. "Lenawee is a blighted flower," she sobbed. "Let her blood flow for her people." And catching a knife from the Prophet's belt, she ran with it to the stream on which she and the Arrow had so often floated in their canoe. In another moment her blood had bedewed the earth. "Lay me with the Arrow," she murmured, and, smiling in their sad faces, breathed her last. The demon of the quick death shrank from the spot, and the Great Spirit smiled once more on the tribe that could produce such heroism. Lenawee's body was placed beside her lover's, and next morning, where her blood had spilt, the ground was pure, and on it grew in slender spires a new flower,—the Indian plume: the transformed blood of sacrifice. The people loved that flower in all years after. They decked their hair and dresses with it and made a feast in its honor. When parents taught their children the beauty of unselfishness they used as its emblem a stalk of Indian plume.

BIRTH OF THE WATER-LILY

Back from his war against the Tahawi comes the Sun, chief of the Lower Saranacs,—back to the Lake of the Clustered Stars, afterward called, by dullards, Tupper's Lake. Tall and invincible he comes among his people, boasting of his victories, Indian fashion, and stirring the scalps that hang at his breast. "The Eagle screams," he cries. "He greets the chief, the Blazing Sun. Wayotah has made the Tahawi tremble. They fly from him. Hooh, hooh! He is the chief." Standing apart with wistful glance stands Oseetah, the Bird. She loves the strong young chief, but she knows that another has his promise, and she dares not hope; yet the chief loves her, and when the feasting is over he follows her footprints to the shore, where he sees her canoe turning the point of an island. He silently pursues and comes upon her as she sits waving and moaning. He tries to embrace her, but she draws apart. He asks her to sing to him; she bids him begone.

He takes a more imperious tone and orders her to listen to her chief. She moves away. He darts toward her. Turning on him a face of sorrow, she runs to the edge of a steep rock and waves him back. He hastens after. Then she springs and disappears in the deep water. The Sun plunges after her and swims with mad strength here and there. He calls. There is no answer. Slowly he returns to the village and tells the people what has happened. The Bird's parents are stricken and the Sun moans in his sleep. At noon a hunter comes in with strange tidings: flowers are growing on the water! The people go to their canoes and row to the Island of Elms. There, in a cove, the still water is enamelled with flowers, some as white as snow, filling the air with perfume, others strong and yellow, like the lake at sunset.

"Explain to us," they cry, turning to the old Medicine of his tribe, "for this was not so yesterday."

"It is our daughter," he answered. "These flowers are the form she takes. The white is her purity, the yellow her love. You shall see that her heart will close when the sun sets, and will reopen at his coming." And the young chief went apart and bowed his head.

ROGERS'S SLIDE

The shores of Lakes George and Champlain were ravaged by war. Up and down those lovely waters swept the barges of French and English, and the green hills rang to the shrill of bugles, the boom of cannon, and the yell of savages. Fiction and history have been weft across the woods and the memory of deeds still echoes among the heights. It was at Glen's Falls, in the cave on the rock in the middle of the river, that the brave Uncas held the watch with Hawkeye. Bloody Defile and Bloody Pond, between there and Lake George, take their names from the "Bloody morning scout" sent out by Sir William Johnson on a September day in 1755 to check Dieskau until Fort William Henry could be completed. In the action that ensued, Colonel Williams, founder of Williams College, and Captain Grant, of the Connecticut line, great-grandfather of the President who bore that name, were killed. The victims, dead and wounded alike, having been flung into Bloody Pond, it was thick and red for days, and tradition said that in after years it resumed its hue of crimson at sunset and held it until dawn. The captured, who were delivered to the Indians, had little to hope, for their white allies could not stay their savagery. Blind Rock was so called because the Indians brought a white man there, and tearing his eyes out, flung them into embers at the foot of the stone. Captives were habitually tortured, blazing splinters of pine being thrust into their flesh, their nails torn out, and their bodies slashed with knives before they went to the stake. An English prisoner was allowed to run the gauntlet here. They had already begun to strike at him as he sped between the lines, when he seized a pappoose, flung it on a fire, and, in the instant of confusion that followed, snatched an axe, cut the bonds of a comrade who had been doomed to die, and both escaped.

But the best-known history of this region is that of Rogers's Rock, or Rogers's Slide, a lofty precipice at the lower end of Lake George. Major Rogers did not toboggan down this rock in leather trousers, but his escape was no less remarkable than if he had. On March 13, 1758, while reconnoitring near Ticonderoga with two hundred rangers, he was surprised by a force of French and Indians. But seventeen of his men escaped death or capture, and he was pursued nearly to the brink of this cliff. During a brief delay among the red men, arising from the loss of his trail, he had time to throw his pack down the slide, reverse his snow-shoes, and go back over his own track to the head of a ravine before they emerged from the woods, and, seeing that his shoe-marks led to the rock, while none pointed back, they concluded that he had flung himself off and committed suicide to avoid capture. Great was their disappointment when they saw the major on the frozen surface of the lake beneath going at a lively rate toward Fort William Henry. He had gained the ice by way of the cleft in the rocks, but the savages, believing that he had leaped over the precipice, attributed his preservation to the Great Spirit and forbore to fire on him. Unconsciously, he had chosen the best possible place to disappear from, for the Indians held it in superstitious regard, believing that spirits haunted the wood and hurled bad souls down the cliff, drowning them in the lake, instead of allowing them to go to the happy hunting grounds. The major reached his quarters in safety, and lived to take up arms against the land of his birth when the colonies revolted, seventeen years later.

THE FALLS AT COHOES

When Occuna, a young Seneca, fell in love with a girl whose cabin was near the present town of Cohoes, he behaved very much as Americans of a later date have done. He picked wild flowers for her; he played on the bone pipe and sang sentimental songs in the twilight; he roamed the hills with her, gathering the loose quartz crystals that the Indians believed to be the tears of stricken deer, save on Diamond Rock, in Lansingburgh, where they are the tears of Moneta, a bereaved mother and wife; and in fine weather they went boating on the Mohawk above the rapids. They liked to drift idly on the current, because it gave them time to gaze into each other's eyes, and to build air castles that they would live in in the future. They were suddenly called to a realization of danger one evening, for the stream had been subtly drawing them on and on until it had them in its power. The stroke of the paddle failed and the air castles fell in dismal ruin. Sitting erect they began their death-song in this wise:

Occuna: "Daughter of a mighty warrior, the Manitou calls me hence. I hear the roaring of his voice; I see the lightning of his glance along the river; he walks in clouds and spray upon the waters."

The Maiden: "Thou art thyself a warrior, O Occuna. Hath not thine axe been often bathed in blood? Hath the deer ever escaped thine arrow or the beaver avoided thy chase? Thou wilt not fear to go into the presence of Manitou."

Occuna: "Manitou, indeed, respects the strong. When I chose thee from the women of our tribe I promised that we should live and die together. The Thunderer calls us now. Welcome, O ghost of Oriska, chief of the invincible Senecas! A warrior and the daughter of a warrior come to join you in the feast of the blessed!"

The boat leaped over the falls, and Occuna, striking on the rocks below, was killed at once; but, as by a miracle, the girl fell clear of them and was whirled on the seething current to shoal water, where she made her escape. For his strength and his virtues the dead man was canonized. His tribe raised him above the regions of the moon, whence he looked down on the scenes of his youth with pleasure, and in times of war gave pleasant dreams and promises to his friends, while he confused the enemy with evil omens. Whenever his tribe passed the falls they halted and with brief ceremonials commemorated the death of Occuna.

FRANCIS WOOLCOTT'S NIGHT-RIDERS

In Copake, New York, among the Berkshire Hills, less than a century ago, lived Francis Woolcott, a dark, tall man, with protruding teeth, whose sinister laugh used to give his neighbors a creep along their spines. He had no obvious trade or calling, but the farmers feared him so that he had no trouble in making levies: pork, flour, meal, cider, he could have what he chose for the asking, for had he not halted horses at the plow so that neither blows nor commands could move them for two hours? Had he not set farmer Raught's pigs to walking on their hind legs and trying to talk? When he shouted "Hup! hup! hup!" to farmer Williams's children, had they not leaped to the moulding of the parlor wainscot,—a yard above the floor and only an inch wide,—and walked around it, afterward skipping like birds from chair-back to chair-back, while the furniture stood as if nailed to the floor? And was he not the chief of thirteen night-riders, whose faces no man had seen, nor wanted to see, and whom he sent about the country on errands of mischief every night when the moon was growing old? As to moons, had he not found a mystic message from our satellite on Mount Riga, graven on a meteor?

Horses' tails were tied, hogs foamed at the mouth and walked like men, cows gave blood for milk. These night-riders met Woolcott in a grove of ash and chestnut trees, each furnished with a stolen bundle of oat straw, and these bundles Woolcott changed to black horses when the night had grown dark enough not to let the way of the change be seen. These horses could not cross streams of water, and on the stroke of midnight they fell to pieces and were oaten sheaves once more, but during their time of action they rushed through woods, bearing their riders safely, and tore like hurricanes across the fields, leaping bushes, fences, even trees, without effort. Never could traces be found of them the next day. At last the devil came to claim his own. Woolcott, who was ninety years old, lay sick and helpless in his cabin. Clergymen refused to see him, but two or three of his neighbors stifled their fears and went to the wizard's house to soothe his dying moments. With the night came storm, and with its outbreak the old man's face took on such a strange and horrible look that the watchers fell back in alarm. There was a burst of purple flame at the window, a frightful peal, a smell of sulphur, and Woolcott was dead. When the watchers went out the roads were dry, and none in the village had heard wind, rain, or thunder. It was the coming of the fiend.

POLLY'S LOVER

In about the middle of this century a withered woman of ninety was buried from a now deserted house in White Plains, New York, Polly Carter the name of her, but "Crazy Polly" was what the neighbors called her, for she was eccentric and not fond of company. Among the belongings of her house was a tall clock, such as relic hunters prize, that ticked solemnly in a landing on the stairs.

For a time, during the Revolution, the house stood within the British lines, and as her father was a colonel in Washington's army she was left almost alone in it. The British officers respected her sex, but they had an unpleasant way of running in unannounced and demanding entertainment, in the king's name, which she felt forced to grant. One rainy afternoon the door was flung open, then locked on the inside, and she found herself in the arms of a stalwart, handsome lieutenant, who wore the blue. It was her cousin and fiance. Their glad talk had not been going long when there came a rousing summons at the door. Three English officers were awaiting admittance.

Perhaps they had seen Lawrence Carter go into the house, and if caught he would be killed as a spy. He must be hidden, but in some place where they would not think of looking. The clock! That was the place. With a laugh and a kiss the young man submitted to be shut in this narrow quarter, and throwing his coat and hat behind some furniture the girl admitted the officers, who were wet and surly and demanded dinner. They tramped about the best room in their muddy boots, talking loudly, and in order to break the effect of the chill weather they passed the brandy bottle freely. Polly served them with a dinner as quickly as possible, for she wanted to get them out of the house, but they were in no mood to go, and the bottle passed so often that before the dinner was over they were noisy and tipsy and were using language that drove Polly from the room.

At last, to her relief, she heard them preparing to leave the house, but as they were about to go the senior officer, looking up at the landing, now dim in the paling light, said to one of the others, "See what time it is." The officer addressed, who happened to be the drunkest of the party, staggered up the stair and exclaimed, "The d—-d thing's stopped." Then, as if he thought it a good joke, he added, "It'll never go again." Drawing his sabre he gave the clock a careless cut and ran the blade through the panel of the door; after this the three passed out. When their voices had died in distant brawling, Polly ran to release her lover. Something thick and dark was creeping from beneath the clock-case. With trembling fingers she pulled open the door, and Lawrence, her lover, fell heavily forward into her arms, dead. The officer was right: the clock never went again.

CROSBY, THE PATRIOT SPY

It was at the Jay house, in Westchester, New York, that Enoch Crosby met Washington and offered his services to the patriot army. Crosby was a cobbler, and not a very thriving one, but after the outbreak of hostilities he took a peddler's outfit on his back and, as a non-combatant, of Tory sympathies, he obtained admission through the British lines. After his first visit to head quarters it is certain that he always carried Sir Henry Clinton's passport in the middle of his pack, and so sure were his neighbors that he was in the service of the British that they captured him and took him to General Washington, but while his case was up for debate he managed to slip his handcuffs, which were not secure, and made off. Clinton, on the other hand, was puzzled by the unaccountable foresight of the Americans, for every blow that he prepared to strike was met, and he lost time and chance and temper. As if the suspicion of both armies and the hatred of his neighbors were not enough to contend against, Crosby now became an object of interest to the Skinners and Cowboys, who were convinced that he was making money, somehow, and resolved to have it.

The Skinners were camp-followers of the American troops and the Cowboys a band of Tories and renegade British. Both factions were employed, ostensibly, in foraging for their respective armies, but, in reality, for themselves, and the farmers and citizens occupying the neutral belt north of Manhattan Island had reason to curse them both impartially. While these fellows were daring thieves, they occasionally got the worst of it, even in the encounters with the farmers, as on the Neperan, near Tarrytown, where the Cowboys chased a woman to death, but were afterward cut to pieces by the enraged neighbors. Hers is but one of the many ghosts that haunt the neutral ground, and the croaking of the birds of ill luck that nest at Raven rock is blended with the cries of her dim figure. Still, graceless as these fellows were, they affected a loyalty to their respective sides, and were usually willing to fight each other when they met, especially for the plunder that was to be got by fighting.

In October, 1780, Claudius Smith, "king of the Cowboys," and three scalawag sons came to the conclusion that it was time for Crosby's money to revert to the crown, and they set off toward his little house one evening, sure of finding him in, for his father was seriously ill. The Smiths arrived there to find that the Skinners had preceded them on the same errand, and they recognized through the windows, in the leader of the band, a noted brigand on whose head a price was laid. He was searching every crack and cranny of the room, while Crosby, stripped to shirt and trousers, stood before the empty fireplace and begged for that night to be left alone with his dying father.

"To hell with the old man!" roared the Skinner. "Give up your gold, or we'll put you to the torture," and he significantly whirled the end of a rope that he carried about his waist. At that moment the faint voice of the old man was heard calling from another room.

"Take all that I have and let me go!" cried Crosby, and turning up a brick in the fire-place he disclosed a handful of gold, his life savings. The leader still tried to oppose his exit, but Crosby flung him to the floor and rushed away to his father, while the brigand, deeming it well to delay rising, dug his fingers into the hollow and began to extract the sovereigns. At that instant four muskets were discharged from without: there was a crash of glass, a yell of pain, and four of the Skinners rolled bleeding on the floor; two others ran into the darkness and escaped; their leader, trying to follow, was met at the threshold by the Smiths, who clutched the gold out of his hand and pinioned his elbows in a twinkling.

"I thought ye'd like to know who's got ye," said old Smith, peering into the face of the astonished and crestfallen robber, "for I've told ye many a time to keep out of my way, and now ye've got to swing for getting into it."

Within five minutes of the time that he had got his clutch on Crosby's money the bandit was choking to death at the end of his own rope, hung from the limb of an apple-tree, and, having secured the gold, the Cowboys went their way into the darkness. Crosby soon made his appearance in the ranks of the Continentals, and, though they looked askant at him for a time, they soon discovered the truth and hailed him as a hero, for the information he had carried to Washington from Clinton's camp had often saved them from disaster. He had survived attack in his own house through the falling out of rogues, and he survived the work and hazard of war through luck and a sturdy frame. Congress afterwards gave him a sum of money larger than had been taken from him, for his chief had commended him in these lines: "Circumstances of political importance, which involved the lives and fortunes of many, have hitherto kept secret what this paper now reveals. Enoch Crosby has for years been a faithful and unrequited servant of his country. Though man does not, God may reward him for his conduct. GEORGE WASHINGTON."

Associated with Crosby in his work of getting information from the enemy was a man named Gainos, who kept an inn on the neutral ground, that was often raided. Being assailed by Cowboys once, Gainos, with his tenant and stable-boys, fired at the bandits together, just as the latter had forced his front door, then stepping quickly forward he slashed off the head of the leader with a cutlass. The retreating crew dumped the body into a well on the premises, and there it sits on the crumbling curb o' nights looking disconsolately for its head.

It may also be mentioned that the Skinners had a chance to revenge themselves on the Cowboys for their defeat at the Crosby house. They fell upon the latter at the tent-shaped cave in Yonkers,—it is called Washington's Cave, because the general napped there on bivouac,—and not only routed them, but secured so much of their treasure that they were able to be honest for several years after.

THE LOST GRAVE OF PAINE

Failure to mark the resting-places of great men and to indicate the scenes of their deeds has led to misunderstanding and confusion among those who discover a regard for history and tradition in this practical age. Robert Fulton, who made steam navigation possible, lies in an unmarked tomb in the yard of Trinity Church—the richest church in America. The stone erected to show where Andre was hanged was destroyed by a cheap patriot, who thought it represented a compliment to the spy. The spot where Alexander Hamilton was shot in the duel by Aaron Burr is known to few and will soon be forgotten. It was not until a century of obloquy had been heaped on the memory of Thomas Paine that his once enemies were brought to know him as a statesman of integrity, a philanthropist, and philosopher. His deistic religion, proclaimed in "The Age of Reason," is unfortunately no whit more independent than is preached in dozens of pulpits to-day. He died ripe in honors, despite his want of creed, and his mortal part was buried in New Rochelle, New York, under a large walnut-tree in a hay-field. Some years later his friends removed the body to a new grave in higher ground, and placed over it a monument that the opponents of his principles quickly hacked to pieces. Around the original grave there still remains a part of the old inclosure, and it was proposed to erect a suitable memorial—the Hudson and its Hills the spot, but the owner of the tract would neither give nor sell an inch of his land for the purpose of doing honor to the man. Some doubt has already been expressed as to whether the grave is beneath the monument or in the inclosure; and it is also asserted that Paine's ghost appears at intervals, hovering in the air between the two burial-places, or flitting back and forth from one to the other, lamenting the forgetfulness of men and wailing, "Where is my grave? I have lost my grave!"

THE RISING OF GOUVERNEUR MORRIS

Gouverneur Morris, American minister to the court of Louis XVI, was considerably enriched, at the close of the reign of terror, by plate, jewels, furniture, paintings, coaches, and so on, left in his charge by members of the French nobility, that they might not be confiscated in the sack of the city by the *sans culottes*; for so many of the aristocracy were killed and so many went into exile or disguised their names, that it was impossible to find heirs or owners for these effects. Some of the people who found France a good country to be out of came to America, where adventurers had found prosperity and refugees found peace so many times before. Marshal Ney and Bernadotte are alleged to have served in the American army during the Revolution, and at Hogansburg, New York, the Reverend Eleazer Williams, an Episcopal missionary, who lies buried in the church-yard there, was declared to be the missing son of Louis XVI. The question, "Have we a Bourbon among us?" was frequently canvassed; but he avoided publicity and went quietly on with his pastoral work.

All property left in Mr. Morris's hands that had not been claimed was removed to his mansion at Port Morris, when he returned from his ministry, and he gained in the esteem and envy of his neighbors when the extent of these riches was seen. Once, at the wine, he touched glasses with his wife, and said that if she bore a male child that son should be heir to his wealth. Two relatives who sat at the table exchanged looks at this and cast a glance of no gentle regard on his lady. A year went by. The son was born, but Gouverneur Morris was dead.

It is the first night of the year 1817, the servants are asleep, and the widow sits late before the fire, her baby in her arms, listening betimes to the wind in the chimney, the beat of hail on the shutters, the brawling of the Bronx and the clash of moving ice upon it; yet thinking of her husband and the sinister look his promise had brought to the faces of his cousins, when a tramp of horses is heard without, and anon a summons at the door. The panels are beaten by loaded riding-whips, and a man's voice cries, "Anne Morris, fetch us our cousin's will, or we'll break into the house and take it." The woman clutches the infant to her breast, but makes no answer. Again the clatter of the whips; but now a mist is gathering in the room, and a strange enchantment comes over her, for are not the lions breathing on the coat of arms above the door, and are not the portraits stirring in their frames?

They are, indeed. There is a rustle of robes and clink of steel and one old warrior leaps down, his armor sounding as he alights, and striking thrice his sword and shield together he calls on Gouverneur Morris to come forth. Somebody moves in the room where Morris died; there is a measured footfall in the corridor, with the clank of a scabbard keeping time; the door is opened, and on the blast that enters the widow hears a cry, then a double gallop, passing swiftly into distance. As she gazes, her husband appears, apparelled as in life, and with a smile he takes a candelabrum from the mantel and, beckoning her to follow, moves from room to room. Then, for the first time, the widow knows to what wealth her baby has been born, for the ghost discloses secret drawers in escritoires where money, title deeds, and gems are hidden, turns pictures and wainscots on unsuspected hinges, revealing shelves heaped with fabrics, plate, and lace; then, returning to the fireside, he stoops as if to kiss his wife and boy, but a bell strikes the first hour of morning and he vanishes into his portrait on the wall.

THE ISLE OF MANHATTOES AND NEARBY

DOLPH HEYLIGER

New York was New Amsterdam when Dolph Heyliger got himself born there,—a graceless scamp, though a brave, good-natured one, and being left penniless on his father's death he was fain to take service with a doctor, while his mother kept a shop. This doctor had bought a farm on the island of Manhattoes—away out of town, where Twenty-third Street now runs, most likely—and, because of rumors that its tenants had noised about it, he seemed likely to enjoy the responsibilities of landholding and none of its profits. It suited Dolph's adventurous disposition that he should be deputed to investigate the reason for these rumors, and for three nights he kept his abode in the desolate old manor, emerging after daybreak in a lax and pallid condition, but keeping his own counsel, to the aggravation of the populace, whose ears were burning for his news.

Not until long after did he tell of the solemn tread that woke him in the small hours, of his door softly opening, though he had bolted and locked it, of a portly Fleming, with curly gray hair, reservoir boots, slouched hat, trunk and doublet, who entered and sat in the arm-chair, watching him until the cock crew. Nor did he tell how on the third night he summoned courage, hugging a Bible and a catechism to his breast for confidence, to ask the meaning of the visit, and how the Fleming arose, and drawing Dolph after him with his eyes, led him downstairs, went through the front door without unbolting it, leaving that task for the trembling yet eager youth, and how, after he had proceeded to a disused well at the bottom of the garden, he vanished from sight.

Dolph brooded long upon these things and dreamed of them in bed. He alleged that it was in obedience to his dreams that he boarded a schooner bound up the Hudson, without the formality of adieu to his employer, and after being spilled ashore in a gale at the foot of Storm King, he fell into the company of Anthony Vander Hevden, a famous landholder and hunter, who achieved a fancy for Dolph as a lad who could shoot, fish, row, and swim, and took him home with him to Albany. The Heer had commodious quarters, good liquor, and a pretty daughter, and Dolph felt himself in paradise until led to the room he was to occupy, for one of the first things that he set eyes on in that apartment was a portrait of the very person who had kept him awake for the worse part of three nights at the bowerie in Manhattoes. He demanded to know whose picture it was, and learned that it was that of Killian Vander Spiegel, burgomaster and curmudgeon, who buried his money when the English seized New Amsterdam and fretted himself to death lest it should be discovered. He remembered that his mother had spoken of this Spiegel and that her father was the miser's rightful heir, and it now appeared that he was one of Heyden's forbears too. In his dream that night the Fleming stepped out of the portrait, led him, as he had done before, to the well, where he smiled and vanished. Dolph reflected, next morning, that these things had been ordered to bring together the two branches of the family and disclose the whereabouts of the treasure that it should inherit. So full was he of this idea that he went back to New Amsterdam by the first schooner, to the surprise of the Heer and the regret of his daughter.

After the truant had been received with execrations by the doctor and with delight by his mother, who believed that spooks had run off with him, and with astonishment, as a hero of romance, by the public, he made for the haunted premises at the first opportunity and began to angle at the disused well. Presently he found his hook entangled in something at the bottom, and on lifting slowly he discovered that he had secured a fine silver porringer, with lid held down by twisted wire. It was the work of a moment to wrench off the lid, when he found the vessel to be filled with golden pieces. His fishing that day was attended with such luck as never fell to an angler before, for there were other pieces of plate down there, all engraved with the Spiegel arms and all containing treasure.

By encouraging the most dreadful stories about the spot, in order to keep the people wide away from it, he accomplished the removal of his prizes bit by bit from their place of concealment to his home. His unaccounted absence in Albany and his dealings with the dead had prepared his neighbors for any change in himself or his condition, and now that he always had a bottle of schnapps for the men and a pot of tea for the women, and was good to his mother, they said that they had always known that when he changed it would be for the better,—at which his old detractors lifted their eyebrows significantly—and when asked to dinner by him they always accepted.

Moreover, they made merry when the day came round for his wedding with the little maid of Albany. They likewise elected him a member of the corporation, to which he bequeathed some of the Spiegel plate and often helped the other city fathers to empty the big punch-bowl. Indeed, it was at one of these corporation feasts that he died of apoplexy. He was buried with honors in the yard of the Dutch church in Garden Street.

THE KNELL AT THE WEDDING

A young New Yorker had laid such siege to the heart of a certain belle—this was back in the Knickerbocker days when people married for love—that everybody said the banns were as good as published; but everybody did not know, for one fine morning my lady went to church with another gentleman—not her father, though old enough to be—and when the two came out they were man and wife. The elderly man was rich. After the first paroxysm of rage and disappointment had passed, the lover withdrew from the world and devoted himself to study; nor when he learned that she had become a widow, with comfortable belongings derived from the estate of the late lamented, did he renew acquaintance with her, and he smiled bitterly when he heard of her second marriage to a young adventurer who led her a wretched life, but atoned for his sins, in a measure, by dying soon enough afterward to leave a part of her fortune unspent.

In the lapse of time the doubly widowed returned to New York, where she met again the lover of her youth. Mr. Ellenwood had acquired the reserve of a scholar, and had often puzzled his friends with his eccentricities; but after a few meetings with the object of his young affection he came out of his glooms, and with respectful formality laid again at her feet the heart she had trampled on forty years before. Though both of them were well on in life, the news of their engagement made little of a sensation. The widow was still fair; the wooer was quiet, refined, and courtly, and the union of their fortunes would assure a competence for the years that might be left to them. The church of St. Paul, on Broadway, was appointed for the wedding, and it was a whim of the groom that his bride should meet him there. At the appointed hour a company of the curious had assembled in the edifice; a rattle of wheels was heard, and a bevy of bridesmaids and friends in hoop, patch, velvet, silk, powder, swords, and buckles walked down the aisle; but just as the bride had come within the door, out of the sunlight that streamed so brilliantly on the mounded turf and tombstones in the churchyard, the bell in the steeple gave a single boom.

The bride walked to the altar, and as she took her place before it another clang resounded from the belfry. The bridegroom was not there. Again and again the brazen throat and iron tongue sent out a doleful knell, and faces grew pale and anxious, for the meaning of it could not be guessed. With eyes fixed on the marble tomb of her first husband, the woman tremblingly awaited the solution of the mystery, until the door was darkened by something that made her catch her breath—a funeral. The organ began a solemn dirge as a black-cloaked cortege came through the aisle, and it was with amazement that the bride discovered it to be formed of her oldest friends,—bent, withered; paired, man and woman, as in mockery—while behind, with white face, gleaming eyes, disordered hair, and halting step, came the bridegroom, in his shroud.

"Come," he said,—"let us be married. The coffins are ready. Then, home to the tomb."

"Cruel!" murmured the woman.

"Now, Heaven judge which of us has been cruel. Forty years ago you took away my faith, destroyed my hopes, and gave to others your youth and beauty. Our lives have nearly run their course, so I am come to wed you as with funeral rites." Then, in a softer manner, he took her hand, and said, "All is forgiven. If we cannot live together we will at least be wedded in death. Time is almost at its end. We will marry for eternity. Come." And tenderly embracing her, he led her forward. Hard as was the ordeal, confusing, frightening, humiliating, the bride came through it a better woman.

"It is true," she said, "I have been vain and worldly, but now, in my age, the truest love I ever knew has come back to me. It is a holy love. I will cherish it forever." Their eyes met, and they saw each other through tears. Solemnly the clergyman read the marriage service, and when it was concluded the low threnody that had come from the organ in key with the measured clang of the bell, merged into a nobler motive, until at last the funeral measures were lost in a burst of exultant harmony. Sobs of pent feeling and sighs of relief were heard as the bridal party moved away, and when the newmade wife and husband reached the portal the bell was silent and the sun was shining.

ROISTERING DIRCK VAN DARA

In the days when most of New York stood below Grand Street, a roistering fellow used to make the rounds of the taverns nightly, accompanied by a friend named Rooney. This brave drinker was Dirck Van Dara, one of the last of those swag-bellied topers that made merry with such solemnity before the English seized their unoffending town. It chanced that Dirck and his chum were out later than usual one night, and by eleven o'clock, when all good people were abed, a drizzle set in that drove the watch to sleep in doorways and left Broadway tenantless. As the two choice spirits reeled out of a hostelry near Wall Street and saw the lights go out in the tap-room windows they started up town to their homes in Leonard Street, but hardly had they come abreast of old St. Paul's when a strange thing stayed them: crying was heard in the churchyard and a phosphorescent light shone among the tombs. Rooney was sober in a moment, but not so Dirck Van Dara, who shouted, "Here is sport, friend Rooney. Let's climb the wall. If the dead are for a dance, we will take partners and show them how pigeons' wings are cut nowadays."

"No," exclaimed the other; "those must perish who go among the dead when they come out of their graves. I've heard that if you get into their clutches, you must stay in purgatory for a hundred years, and no priest can pray you out."

"Bah! old wives' tales! Come on!" And pulling his friend with him, they were over the fence. "Hello! what have we here?" As he spoke a haggard thing arose from behind a tombstone, a witchlike creature, with rags falling about her wasted form and hair that almost hid her face. The twain were set a-sneezing by the fumes of sulphur, and Rooney swore afterwards that there were little things at the end of the yard with grinning faces and lights on the ends of their tails. Old Hollands are heady. Dirck began to chaff the beldam on her dilapidation, but she stopped his talk by dipping something from a caldron behind her and flinging it over both of her visitors. Whatever it was, it burned outrageously, and with a yell of pain they leaped the wall more briskly than they had jumped it the other way, and were soon in full flight. They had not gone far when the clock struck twelve.

"Arrah! there's a crowd of them coming after," panted Rooney. "Ave Mary! I've heard that if you die with witch broth being thrown over you,

you're done for in the next world, as well as this. Let us get to Father Donagan's. Wow!"

As he made this exclamation the fugitives found their way opposed by a woman, who looked at them with immodest eyes and said, "Dirck Van Dara, your sire, in wig and bob, turned us Cyprians out of New York, after ducking us in the Collect. But we forgive him, and to prove it we ask you to our festival."

At the stroke of midnight the street before the church had swarmed with a motley throng, that now came onward, waving torches that sparkled like stars. They formed a ring about Dirck and began to dance, and he, nothing loth, seized the nymph who had addressed him and joined in the revel. Not a soul was out or awake except themselves, and no words were said as the dance went wilder to strains of weird and unseen instruments. Now and then one would apply a torch to the person of Dirck, meanly assailing him in the rear, and the smart of the burn made him feet it the livelier. At last they turned toward the Battery as by common consent, and went careering along the street in frolic fashion. Rooney, whose senses had thus far been pent in a stupor, fled with a yell of terror, and as he looked back he saw the unholy troop disappearing in the mist like a moving galaxy. Never from that night was Dirck Van Data seen or heard of more, and the publicans felt that they had less reason for living.

THE PARTY FROM GIBBET ISLAND

Ellis Island, in New York harbor, once bore the name of Gibbet Island, because pirates and mutineers were hanged there in chains. During the times when it was devoted to this fell purpose there stood in Communipaw the Wild Goose tavern, where Dutch burghers resorted, to smoke, drink Hollands, and grow fat, wise, and sleepy in each others' company. The plague of this inn was Yan Yost Vanderscamp, a nephew of the landlord, who frequently alarmed the patrons of the house by putting powder into their pipes and attaching briers beneath their horses' tails, and who naturally turned pirate when he became older, taking with him to sea his boon companion, an ill-disposed, ill-favored blackamoor named Pluto, who had been employed about the tavern. When the landlord died, Vanderscamp possessed himself of this property, fitted it up with plunder, and at intervals he had his gang ashore,—such a crew of singing, swearing, drinking, gaming devils as Communipaw had never seen the like of; yet the residents could not summon activity enough to stop the goings-on that made the Wild Goose a disgrace to their village. The British authorities, however, caught three of the swashbucklers and strung them up on Gibbet Island, and things that went on badly in Communipaw after that went on with quiet and secrecy.

The pirate and his henchmen were returning to the tavern one night, after a visit to a rakish-looking vessel in the offing, when a squall broke in such force as to give their skiff a leeway to the place of executions. As they rounded that lonely reef a creaking noise overhead caused Vanderscamp to look up, and he could not repress a shudder as he saw the bodies of his three messmates, their rags fluttering and their chains grinding in the wind.

"Don't you want to see your friends?" sneered Pluto. "You, who are never afraid of living men, what do you fear from the dead?"

"Nothing," answered the pirate. Then, lugging forth his bottle, he took a long pull at it, and holding it toward the dead felons, he shouted, "Here's fair weather to you, my lads in the wind, and if you should be walking the rounds to-night, come in to supper."

A clatter of bones and a creak of chains sounded like a laugh. It was midnight when the boat pulled in at Communipaw, and as the storm continued Vanderscamp, drenched to the skin, made quick time to the Wild

Goose. As he entered, a sound of revelry overhead smote his ear, and, being no less astonished than in need of cordials, he hastened up-stairs and flung open the door. A table stood there, furnished with jugs and pipes and cans, and by light of candles that burned as blue as brimstone could be seen the three gallows-birds from Gibbet Island, with halters on their necks, clinking their tankards together and trolling forth a drinking-song.

Starting back with affright as the corpses hailed him with lifted arms and turned their fishy eyes on him, Vanderscamp slipped at the door and fell headlong to the bottom of the stairs. Next morning he was found there by the neighbors, dead to a certainty, and was put away in the Dutch churchyard at Bergen on the Sunday following. As the house was rifled and deserted by its occupants, it was hinted that the negro had betrayed his master to his fellow-buccaneers, and that he, Pluto, was no other than the devil in disguise. But he was not, for his skiff was seen floating bottom up in the bay soon after, and his drowned body lodged among the rocks at the foot of the pirates' gallows.

For a long time afterwards the island was regarded as a place that required purging with bell, book, and candle, for shadows were reported there and faint lights that shot into the air, and to this day, with the great immigrant station on it and crowds going and coming all the time, the Battery boatmen prefer not to row around it at night, for they are likely to see the shades of the soldier and his mistress who were drowned off the place one windy night, when the girl was aiding the fellow to escape confinement in the guard-house, to say nothing of Vanderscamp and his felons.

MISS BRITTON'S POKER

The maids of Staten Island wrought havoc among the royal troops who were quartered among them during the Revolution. Near quarantine, in an old house,—the Austen mansion,—a soldier of King George hanged himself because a Yankee maid who lived there would not have him for a husband, nor any gentleman whose coat was of his color; and, until ghosts went out of fashion, his spirit, in somewhat heavy boots, with jingling spurs, often disturbed the nightly quiet of the place.

The conduct of a damsel in the old town of Richmond was even more stern. She was the granddaughter, and a pretty one, of a farmer named Britton; but though Britton by descent and name, she was no friend of Britons, albeit she might have had half the officers in the neighboring camp at her feet, if she had wished them there. Once, while mulling a cup of cider for her grandfather, she was interrupted by a self-invited myrmidon, who undertook, in a fashion rude and unexpected, to show the love in which he held her. Before he could kiss her, the girl drew the hot poker from the mug of drink and jabbed at the vitals of her amorous foe, burning a hole through his scarlet uniform and printing on his burly person a lasting memento of the adventure. With a howl of pain the fellow rushed away, and the privacy of the Britton family was never again invaded, at least whilst cider was being mulled.

THE DEVIL'S STEPPING-STONES

When the devil set a claim to the fair lands at the north of Long Island Sound, his claim was disputed by the Indians, who prepared to fight for their homes should he attempt to serve his writ of ejectment. Parley resulted in nothing, so the bad one tried force, but he was routed in open fight and found it desirable to get away from the scene of action as soon as possible. He retreated across the Sound near the head of East River. The tide was out, so he stepped from island to island, without trouble, and those reefs and islands are to this day the Devil's Stepping-Stones. On reaching Throgg's Neck he sat down in a despairing attitude and brooded on his defeat, until, roused to a frenzy at the thought of it, he resolved to renew the war on terms advantageous entirely to himself. In that day Connecticut was free from rocks, but Long Island was covered with them; so he gathered all he could lay his hands on and tossed them at the Indians that he could see across the Sound near Cold Spring until the supply had given out. The red men who last inhabited Connecticut used to show white men where the missiles landed and where the devil struck his heel into the ground as he sprang from the shore in his haste to reach Long Island. At Cold Spring other footprints and one of his toes are shown. Establishing himself at Coram, he troubled the people of the country for many years, so that between the devil on the west and the Montauks on the east they were plagued indeed; for though their guard at Watch Hill, Rhode Island, and other places often apprised them of the coming of the Montauks, they never knew which way to look for the devil.

THE SPRINGS OF BLOOD AND WATER

A great drought had fallen on Long Island, and the red men prayed for water. It is true that they could get it at Lake Ronkonkoma, but some of them were many miles from there, and, beside, they feared the spirits at that place: the girl who plied its waters in a phosphor-shining birch, seeking her recreant lover; and the powerful guardians that the Great Spirit had put in charge to keep the fish from being caught, for these fish were the souls of men, awaiting deliverance into another form. The people gathered about their villages in bands and besought the Great Spirit to give them drink. His voice was heard at last, bidding their chief to shoot an arrow into the air and to watch where it fell, for there would water gush out. The chief obeyed the deity, and as the arrow touched the earth a spring of sweet water spouted into the air. Running forward with glad cries the red men drank eagerly of the liquor, laved their faces in it, and were made strong again; and in memory of that event they called the place the Hill of God, or Manitou Hill, and Manet or Manetta Hill it is to this day. Hereabouts the Indians settled and lived in peace, thriving under the smile of their deity, making wampum for the inland tribes and waxing rich with gains from it. They made the canal from bay to sea at Canoe Place, that they might reach open water without dragging their boats across the sand-bars, and in other ways they proved themselves ingenious and strong.

When the English landed on the island they saw that the Indians were not a people to be trifled with, and in order to properly impress them with their superiority, they told them that John Bull desired a treaty with them. The officers got them to sit in line in front of a cannon, the nature of which instrument was unknown to them, and during the talk the gun was fired, mowing down so many of the red people that the survivors took to flight, leaving the English masters at the north shore, for this heartless and needless massacre took place at Whale's Neck. So angry was the Great Spirit at this act of cruelty and treachery that he caused blood to ooze from the soil, as he had made water leap for his thirsting children, and never again would grass grow on the spot where the murder had been done.

THE CRUMBLING SILVER

There is a clay bank on Little Neck, Long Island, where metallic nodules are now and then exposed by rain. Rustics declare them to be silver, and account for their crumbling on the theory that the metal is under a curse. A century ago the Montauks mined it, digging over enough soil to unearth these pellets now and again, and exchanging them at the nearest settlements for tobacco and rum. The seeming abundance of these lumps of silver aroused the cupidity of one Gardiner, a dweller in the central wilderness of the island, but none of the Indians would reveal the source of their treasure. One day Gardiner succeeded in getting an old chief so tipsy that, without realizing what he was doing, he led the white man to the clay bed and showed him the metallic spots glittering in the sun. With a cry of delight Gardiner sprang forward and tore at the earth with his fingers, while the Indian stood by laughing at his eagerness.

Presently a shade crossed the white man's face, for he thought that this vast treasure would have to be shared by others. It was too much to endure. He wanted all. He would be the richest man on earth. Stealing behind the Indian as he stood swaying and chuckling, he wrenched the hatchet from his belt and clove his skull at a blow. Then, dragging the body to a thicket and hiding it under stones and leaves, he hurried to his house for cart and pick and shovel, and returning with speed he dug out a half ton of the silver before sunset. The cart was loaded, and he set homeward, trembling with excitement and conjuring bright visions for his future, when a wailing sound from a thicket made him halt and turn pale. Noiselessly a figure glided from the bush. It was the Indian he had killed. The form approached the treasure, flung up its arm, uttered a few guttural words; then a rising wind seemed to lift it from the ground and it drifted toward the Sound, fading like a cloud as it receded.

Full of misgiving, Gardiner drove to his home, and, by light of a lantern, transferred his treasure to his cellar. Was it the dulness of the candle that made the metal look so black? After a night of feverish tossing on his bed he arose and went to the cellar to gloat upon his wealth. The light of dawn fell on a heap of gray dust, a few brassy looking particles showing here and there. The curse of the ghost had been of power and the silver was silver no more. Mineralogists say that the nodules are iron pyrites. Perhaps so; but old residents know that they used to be silver.

THE CORTELYOU ELOPEMENT

In the Bath district of Brooklyn stands Cortelyou manor, built one hundred and fifty years ago, and a place of defence during the Revolution when the British made sallies from their camp in Flatbush and worried the neighborhood. It was in one of these forays on pigs and chickens that a gallant officer of red-coats met a pretty lass in the fields of Cortelyou. He stilled her alarm by aiding her to gather wild-flowers, and it came about that the girl often went into the fields and came back with prodigious bouquets of daisies. The elder Cortelyou had no inkling of this adventure until one of his sons saw her tryst with the red-coat at a distance. Be sure the whole family joined him in remonstrance. As the girl declared that she would not forego the meetings with her lover, the father swore that she should never leave his roof again, and he tried to be as good, or bad, as his word. The damsel took her imprisonment as any girl of spirit would, but was unable to effect her escape until one evening, as she sat at her window, watching the moon go down and paint the harbor with a path of light. A tap at the pane, as of a pebble thrown against it, roused her from her revery. It was her lover on the lawn.

At her eager signal he ran forward with a light ladder, planted it against the window-sill, and in less than a minute the twain were running toward the beach; but the creak of the ladder had been heard, and grasping their muskets two of the men hurried out. In the track of the moon the pursuers descried a moving form, and, without waiting to challenge, they levelled the guns and fired. A woman's cry followed the report; then a dip of oars was heard that fast grew fainter until it faded from hearing. On returning to the house they found the girl's room empty, and next morning her slipper was brought in from the mud at the landing. Nobody inside of the American lines ever learned what that shot had done, but if it failed to take a life it robbed Cortelyou of his mind. He spent the rest of his days in a single room, chained to a staple in the floor, tramping around and around, muttering and gesturing, and sometimes startling the passer-by as he showed his white face and ragged beard at the window.

VAN WEMPEL'S GOOSE

Allow us to introduce Nicholas Van Wempel, of Flatbush: fat, phlegmatic, rich, and henpecked. He would like to be drunk because he is henpecked, but the wife holds the purse-strings and only doles out money to him when she wants groceries or he needs clothes. It was New Year's eve, the eve of 1739, when Vrouw Van Wempel gave to her lord ten English shillings and bade him hasten to Dr. Beck's for the fat goose that had been bespoken. "And mind you do not stop at the tavern," she screamed after him in her shrillest tone. But poor Nicholas! As he went waddling down the road, snapping through an ice-crust at every step, a roguish wind—or perhaps it was one of the bugaboos that were known to haunt the shores of Gravesend Bay—snatched off his hat and rolled it into the very doorway of the tavern that he had been warned, under terrible penalties, to avoid.

As he bent to pick it up the door fell ajar, and a pungency of schnapps and tobacco went into his nostrils. His resolution, if he had one, vanished. He ordered one glass of schnapps; friends came in and treated him to another; he was bound to do as much for them; shilling by shilling the goose money passed into the till of the landlord. Nicholas was heard to make a muttered assertion that it was his own money anyhow, and that while he lived he would be the head of his own house; then the mutterings grew faint and merged into snores. When he awoke it was at the low sound of voices in the next room, and drowsily turning his head he saw there two strangers,—sailors, he thought, from their leather jackets, black beards, and the rings in their ears. What was that they said? Gold? On the marshes? At the old Flatlands tide-mill? The talkers had gone before his slow and foggy brain could grasp it all, but when the idea had fairly eaten its way into his intellect, he arose with the nearest approach to alacrity that he had exhibited in years, and left the place. He crunched back to his home, and seeing nobody astir went softly into his shed, where he secured a shovel and lantern, and thence continued with all consistent speed to the tumbledown tide-mill on the marsh,—a trying journey for his fat legs on a sharp night, but hope and schnapps impelled him.

He reached the mill, and, hastening to the cellar, began to probe in the soft, unfrozen earth. Presently his spade struck something, and he dug and dug until he had uncovered the top of a canvas bag,—the sort that sailors call a "round stern-chest." It took all his strength to lug it out, and as he did so a seam burst, letting a shower of gold pieces over the ground. He loosed the band of his breeches, and was filling the legs thereof with coin, when a tread of feet sounded overhead and four men came down the stair. Two of them he recognized as the fellows of the tavern. They saw the bag, the lantern, then Nicholas. Laden though he was with gold until he could hardly budge, these pirates, for such they were, got him up-stairs, forced him to drink hot Hollands to the success of their flag, then shot him through the window into the creek. As he was about to make this unceremonious exit he clutched something to save himself, and it proved to be a plucked goose that the pirates had stolen from a neighboring farm and were going to sup on when they had scraped their gold together. He felt the water and mud close over him; he struggled desperately; he was conscious of breathing more freely and of staggering off at a vigorous gait; then the power of all the schnapps seemed to get into his head, and he remembered no more until he heard his wife shrilling in his ears, when he sat up and found himself in a snow-bank close to his house, with a featherless goose tight in his grasp.

Vrouw Van Wempel cared less about the state of her spouse when she saw that he had secured the bird, and whenever he told his tale of the pirates she turned a deaf ear to him, for if he had found the gold why did he not manage to bring home a few pieces of it? He, in answer, asked how, as he had none of his own money, she could have come by the goose? He often told his tale to sympathetic ears, and would point to the old mill to prove that it was true.

THE WEARY WATCHER

Before the opening of the great bridge sent commerce rattling up Washington Street in Brooklyn that thoroughfare was a shaded and beautiful avenue, and among the houses that attested its respectability was one, between Tillary and Concord Streets, that was long declared to be haunted. A man and his wife dwelt there who seemed to be fondly attached to each other, and whose love should have been the stronger because of their three children none grew to years. A mutual sorrow is as close a tie as a common affection. One day, while on a visit to a friend, the wife saw her husband drive by in a carriage with a showy woman beside him. She went home at once, and when the supposed recreant returned she met him with bitter reproaches. He answered never a word, but took his hat and left the house, never to be seen again in the places that had known him.

The wife watched and waited, daily looking for his return, but days lengthened into weeks, months, years, and still he came not. Sometimes she lamented that she had spoken hastily and harshly, thinking that, had she known all, she might have found him blameless. There was no family to look after, no wholesome occupation that she sought, so the days went by in listening and watching, until, at last, her body and mind gave way, and the familiar sight of her face, watching from a second floor window, was seen no longer. Her last day came. She had risen from her bed; life and mind seemed for a moment to be restored to her; and standing where she had stood so often, her form supported by a half-closed shutter and a grasp on the sash, she looked into the street once more, sighed hopelessly, and so died. It was her shade that long watched at the windows; it was her waxen face, heavy with fatigue and pain, that was dimly seen looking over the balusters in the evening.

THE RIVAL FIDDLERS

Before Brooklyn had spread itself beyond Greenwood Cemetery a stone could be seen in Martense's Lane, south of that burial-ground, that bore a hoof mark. A negro named Joost, in the service of the Van Der Something-or-others, was plodding home on Saturday night, his fiddle under his arm. He had been playing for a wedding in Flatbush and had been drinking schnapps until he saw stars on the ground and fences in the sky; in fact, the universe seemed so out of order that he seated himself rather heavily on this rock to think about it. The behavior of the stars in swimming and rolling struck him as especially curious, and he conceived the notion that they wanted to dance. Putting his fiddle to his chin, he began a wild jig, and though he made it up as he went along, he was conscious of doing finely, when the boom of a bell sent a shiver down his spine. It was twelve o'clock, and here he was playing a dance tune on Sunday. However, the sin of playing for one second on the Sabbath was as great as that of playing all day; so, as long as he was in for it, he resolved to carry the tune to the end, and he fiddled away with a reckless vehemence. Presently he became aware that the music was both wilder and sweeter than before, and that there was more of it. Not until then did he observe that a tall, thin stranger stood beside him; and that he was fiddling too,—composing a second to Joost's air, as if he could read his thought before he put it into execution on the strings. Joost paused, and the stranger did likewise.

"Where de debble did you come frum?" asked the first. The other smiled.

"And how did you come to know dat music?" Joost pursued.

"Oh, I've known that tune for years," was the reply. "It's called 'The Devil's joy at Sabbath Breaking.'"

"You're a liar!" cried the negro. The stranger bowed and burst into a roar of laughter. "A liar!" repeated Joost,—"for I made up dat music dis very minute."

"Yet you notice that I could follow when you played."

"Humph! Yes, you can follow."

"And I can lead, too. Do you know the tune 'Go to the Devil and Shake Yourself?'"

"Yes; but I play second to nobody."

"Very well, I'll beat you at any air you try."

"Done!" said Joost. And then began a contest that lasted until daybreak. The stranger was an expert, but Joost seemed to be inspired, and just as the sun appeared he sounded, in broad and solemn harmonies, the hymn of Von Catts:

"Now behold, at dawn of day, Pious Dutchmen sing and pray."

At that the stranger exclaimed, "Well, that beats the devil!" and striking his foot angrily on the rock, disappeared in a flash of fire like a burst bomb. Joost was hurled twenty feet by the explosion, and lay on the ground insensible until a herdsman found him some hours later. As he suffered no harm from the contest and became a better fiddler than ever, it is supposed that the recording angel did not inscribe his feat of Sabbath breaking against him in large letters. There were a few who doubted his story, but they had nothing more to say when he showed them the hoof-mark on the rock. Moreover, there are fewer fiddlers among the negroes than there used to be, because they say that the violin is the devil's instrument.

WYANDANK

From Brooklyn Heights, or Ihpetonga, "highplace of trees," where the Canarsie Indians made wampum or sewant, and where they contemplated the Great Spirit in the setting of the sun across the meeting waters, to Montauk Point, Long Island has been swept by the wars of red men, and many are the tokens of their occupancy. A number of their graves were to be seen until within fifty years, as clearly marked as when the warriors were laid there in the hope of resurrection among the happy hunting grounds that lay to the west and south. The casting of stones on the death-spots or graves of some revered or beloved Indians was long continued, and was undoubtedly for the purpose of raising monuments to them, though at Monument Mountain, Massachusetts, Sacrifice Rock, between Plymouth and Sandwich, Massachusetts, and some other places the cairns merely mark a trail. Even the temporary resting-place of Sachem Poggatacut, near Sag Harbor, was kept clear of weeds and leaves by Indians who passed it in the two centuries that lapsed between the death of the chief and the laying of the road across it in 1846. This spot is not far from Whooping Boy's Hollow, so named because of a boy who was killed by Indians, and because the rubbing of two trees there in a storm gave forth a noise like crying. An older legend has it that this noise is the angry voice of the magician who tried to slay Wyandank, the "Washington of the Montauks," who is buried on the east end of the island. Often he led his men into battle, sounding the warwhoop, copied from the scream of the eagle, so loudly that those who heard it said that the Montauks were crying for prey.

It was while killing an eagle on Block Island, that he might use the plumes for his hair, that this chief disclosed himself to the hostiles and brought on a fight in which every participant except himself was slain. He was secretly followed back to Long Island by a magician who had hopes of enlisting the evil ones of that region against him,—the giants that left their tracks in "Blood-stone Rock" and "Printed Rock," near Napeague, and such renegades as he who, having betrayed his people, was swallowed by the earth, his last agony being marked by a stamp of the foot that left its print on a slab near the Indian burial-ground at Kongonok. Failing in these alliances the wizard hid among the hollows of the moors, and there worked spells of such malice that the chief's hand lost steadiness in the hunt and his voice was seldom heard in council. When the haunt of this evil one was made known, a number of young men undertook to trap him. They went to the hills by night, and moved stealthily through the shrubbery until they were almost upon him; but his familiars had warned him of their approach, though they had wakened him only to betray him for a cloud swept in from the sea, fell about the wretch, burst into flame, and rolled back toward the ocean, bearing him in the centre of its burning folds. Because of the cry he uttered the place long bore the name of Whooping Hollow, and it used to be said that the magician visited the scene of his ill-doing every winter, when his shrieks could be heard ringing over the hills.

MARK OF THE SPIRIT HAND

Andover, New Jersey, was quaint and quiet in the days before the Revolution—it is not a roaring metropolis, even yet—and as it offered few social advantages there was more gathering in taprooms and more drinking of flip than there should have been. Among those who were not averse to a cheering cup were three boon companions, Bailey, Hill, and Evans, farmers of the neighborhood. They loved the tavern better than the church, and in truth the church folk did not love them well, for they were suspected of entertaining heresies of the most forbidden character. It was while they were discussing matters of belief over their glasses that one of them proposed, in a spirit of bravado, that whichever of the trio might be first to die should come back from the grave and reveal himself to the others—if he could—thus settling the question as to whether there was a future.

Not long after this agreement—for consent was unanimous—Hill departed this life. His friends lamented his absence, especially at the tavern, but they anticipated no attempt on his part to express the distinguished consideration that he had felt for his old chums. Some weeks passed, yet there was no sign, and the two survivors of the party, as they jogged homeward to the house where both lived, had begun to think and speak less frequently of the absent one. But one night the household was alarmed by a terrible cry. Bailey got a light and hurried to the bedside of his friend, whom he found deathly white and holding his chest as if in pain. "He has been here!" gasped Evans. "He stood here just now."

"Who?" asked Bailey, a creep passing down his spine.

"Hill! He stood there, where you are now, and touched me with a hand that was so cold—cold—" and Evans shivered violently. On turning back the collar of his shirt the impression of a hand appeared on the flesh near the shoulder: a hand in white, with one finger missing. Hill had lost a finger. There was less of taverns after that night, for Evans carried the token of that ghostly visit on his person until he, too, had gone to solve the great secret.

THE FIRST LIBERAL CHURCH

In 1770 the brig Hand-in-Hand went ashore at Good Luck, New Jersey. Among the passengers on board the vessel, that it would perhaps be wrong to call ill fated, was John Murray, founder of Universalism in America. He had left England in despair, for his wife and children were dead, and so broken was he in his power of thought and purpose that he felt as if he should never preach again.

In fact, his rescue from the wreck was passive, on his part, and he suffered himself to be carried ashore, recking little whether he reached it or no. After he had been for half an hour or so on the soil of the new country, to which he had made his entrance in so unexpected a manner, he began to feel hungry, and set off afoot along the desolate beach. He came to a cabin where an old man stood in a doorway with a basket of fish beside him. "Will you sell me a fish?" asked Murray.

"No. The fish is all yours. I expected you."

"You do not know me."

"You are the man who is to tell us of God."

"I will never preach of Him again."

"I built that log church yonder. Don't say that you will not preach in it. Whenever a clergyman, Presbyterian, Methody, or Baptist, came here, I asked him to preach in my kitchen. I tried to get him to stay; but no—he always had work elsewhere. Last night I saw the brig driven on the bar, and a voice said to me, 'In that ship is the man who will teach of God. Not the old God of terrors, but one of love and mercy. He has come through great sorrow to do this work.' I have made ready for you. Do not go away."

The minister felt a strange lifting in his heart. He fell on his knees before the little house and offered up a prayer. Long he staid in that place, preaching gentle doctrines and ministering to the men and women of that lonely village, and when the fisherman apostle, Thomas Potter, died he left the church to Murray, who, in turn, bequeathed it, "free, for the use of all Christian people."

ON AND NEAR THE DELAWARE

THE PHANTOM DRAGOON

The height that rises a mile or so to the south of Newark, Delaware, is called Iron Hill, because it is rich in hematite ore, but about the time of General Howe's advance to the Brandywine it might well have won its name because of the panoply of war—the sullen guns, the flashing swords, and glistening bayonets—that appeared among the British tents pitched on it. After the red-coats had established camp here the American outposts were advanced and one of the pickets was stationed at Welsh Tract Church. On his first tour of duty the sentry was thrown into great alarm by the appearance of a figure robed from head to foot in white, that rode a horse at a charging gait within ten feet of his face. When guard was relieved the soldier begged that he might never be assigned to that post again. His nerves were strong in the presence of an enemy in the flesh—but an enemy out of the grave! Ugh! He would desert rather than encounter that shape again. His request was granted. The sentry who succeeded him was startled, in the small hours, by a rush of hoofs and the flash of a pallid form. He fired at it, and thought that he heard the sound of a mocking laugh come back.

Every night the phantom horseman made his rounds, and several times the sentinels shot at him without effect, the white horse and white rider showing no annoyance at these assaults. When it came the turn of a sceptical and unimaginative old corporal to take the night detail, he took the liberty of assuming the responsibilities of this post himself. He looked well to the priming of his musket, and at midnight withdrew out of the moonshine and waited, with his gun resting on a fence. It was not long before the beat of hoofs was heard approaching, and in spite of himself the corporal felt a thrill along his spine as a mounted figure that might have represented Death on the pale horse came into view; but he jammed his hat down, set his teeth, and sighted his flint-lock with deliberation. The rider was near, when bang went the corporal's musket, and a white form was lying in the road, a horse speeding into the distance. Scrambling over the fence, the corporal, reassured, ran to the form and turned it over: a British scout, quite dead. The daring fellow, relying on the superstitious fears of the rustics in his front, had made a nightly ride as a ghost, in order to keep the American outposts from advancing, and also to guess, from elevated points, at the strength and disposition of their troops. He wore a cuirass of steel, but that did not protect his brain from the corporal's bullet.

DELAWARE WATER GAP

The Indian name of this beautiful region, Minisink, "the water is gone," agrees with the belief of geologists that a lake once existed behind the Blue Ridge, and that it burst its way through the hills at this point. Similar results were produced by a cataclysm on the Connecticut at Mount Holyoke, on the Lehigh at Mauch Chunk, and Runaway Pond, New Hampshire, got its name by a like performance. The aborigines, whatever may be said against them, enjoyed natural beauty, and their habitations were often made in this delightful region, their councils being attended by chief Tamanend, or Tammany, a Delaware, whose wisdom and virtues were such as to raise him to the place of patron saint of America. The notorious Tammany Society of New York is named for him. When this chief became old and feeble his tribe abandoned him in a hut at New Britain, Pennsylvania, and there he tried to kill himself by stabbing, but failing in that, he flung burning leaves over himself, and so perished. He was buried where he died. It was a princess of his tribe that gave the name of Lover's Leap to a cliff on Mount Tammany, by leaping from it to her death, because her love for a young European was not reciprocated.

There is a silver-mine somewhere on the opposite mountain of Minsi, the knowledge of its location having perished with the death of a recluse, who coined the metal he took from it into valuable though illegal dollars, going townward every winter to squander his earnings. During the Revolution "Oran the Hawk," a Tory and renegade, was vexatious to the people of Delaware Valley, and a detachment of colonial troops was sent in pursuit of him. They overtook him at the Gap and chased him up the slopes of Tammany, though he checked their progress by rolling stones among them. One rock struck a trooper, crushed him, and bore him down to the base of a cliff, his blood smearing it in his descent. But though he seemed to have eluded his pursuers, Oran was shot in several places during his flight, and when at last he cast himself into a thicket, to rest and get breath, it was never to rise again. His bones, cracked by bullets and gnawed by beasts, were found there when the leaves fell.

THE PHANTOM DRUMMER

Colonel Howell, of the king's troops, was a gay fellow, framed to make women false; but when he met the rosy, sweet-natured daughter of farmer Jarrett, near Valley Forge, he attempted no dalliance, for he fell too seriously in love. He might not venture into the old man's presence, for Jarrett had a son with Washington, and he hated a red-coat as he did the devil; but the young officer met the girl in secret, and they plighted troth beneath the garden trees, hidden in gray mist. As Howell bent to take his first kiss that night, a rising wind went past, bringing from afar the roll of a drum, and as they talked the drum kept drawing nearer, until it seemed at hand. The officer peered across the wall, then hurried to his mistress' side, as pale as death. The fields outside were empty of life.

Louder came the rattling drum; it seemed to enter the gate, pass but a yard away, go through the wall, and die in the distance. When it ceased, Howell started as if a spell had been lifted, laxed his grip on the maiden's hand, then drew her to his breast convulsively. Ruth's terror was more vague but no less genuine than his own, and some moments passed before she could summon voice to ask him what this visitation meant. He answered, "Something is about to change my fortunes for good or ill; probably for ill. Important events in my family for the past three generations have been heralded by that drum, and those events were disasters oftener than benefits." Few more words passed, and with another kiss the soldier scaled the wall and galloped away, the triple beat of his charger's hoofs sounding back into the maiden's ears like drum-taps. In a skirmish next day Colonel Howell was shot. He was carried to farmer Jarrett's house and left there, in spite of the old man's protest, for he was willing to give no shelter to his country's enemies. When Ruth saw her lover in this strait she was like to have fallen, but when she learned that it would take but a few days of quiet and care to restore him to health, she was ready to forgive her fellow-countrymen for inflicting an injury that might result in happiness for both of them.

It took a great deal of teasing to overcome the scruples of the farmer, but he gruffly consented to receive the young man until his hurt should heal. Ruth attended him faithfully, and the cheerful, manly nature of the officer so won the farmer's heart that he soon forgot the color of Howell's coat. Nor was he surprised when Howell told him that he loved his daughter and asked for her hand; indeed, it had been easy to guess their affection, and the old man declared that but for his allegiance to a tyrant he would gladly own him as a son-in-law. It was a long struggle between love and duty that ensued in Howell's breast, and love was victor. If he might marry Ruth he would leave the army. The old man gave prompt consent, and a secret marriage was arranged. Howell had been ordered to rejoin his regiment; he could not honorably resign on the eve of an impending battle, and, even had he done so, a long delay must have preceded his release. He would marry the girl, go to the country, live there quietly until the British evacuated Philadelphia, when he would return and cast his lot with the Jarrett household.

Howell donned citizen's dress, and the wedding took place in the spacious best room of the mansion, but as he slipped the ring on the finger of his bride the roll of a drum was heard advancing up the steps into the room, then on and away until all was still again. The young colonel was pale; Ruth clung to him in terror; clergymen and guests looked at each other in amazement. Now there were voices at the porch, the door was flung open, armed men entered, and the bridegroom was a prisoner. He was borne to his quarters, and afterward tried for desertion, for a servant in the Jarrett household, hating all English and wishing them to suffer, even at each other's hands, had betrayed the plan of his master's guest. The court-martial found him guilty and condemned him to be shot. When the execution took place, Ruth, praying and sobbing in her chamber, knew that her husband was no more. The distant sound of musketry reverberated like the roll of a drum.

THE MISSING SOLDIER OF VALLEY FORGE

During the dreadful winter of the American encampment at Valley Forge six or eight soldiers went out to forage for provisions. Knowing that little was to be hoped for near the camp of their starving comrades, they set off in the direction of French Creek. At this stream the party separated, and a little later two of the men were attacked by Tory farmers. Flying along the creek for some distance they came to a small cave in a bluff, and one of them, a young Southerner named Carrington, scrambled into it. His companion was not far behind, and was hurrying toward the cave, when he was arrested by a rumble and a crash: a block of granite, tons in weight, that had hung poised overhead, slid from its place and completely blocked the entrance. The stifled cry of despair from the living occupant of the tomb struck to his heart. He hid in a neighboring wood until the Tories had dispersed, then, returning to the cave, he strove with might and main to stir the boulder from its place, but without avail.

When he reached camp, as he did next day, he told of this disaster, but the time for rescue was believed to be past, or the work was thought to be too exhausting and dangerous for a body of men who had much ado to keep life in their own weak frames. It was a double tragedy, for the young man's sweetheart never recovered from the shock that the news occasioned, and on her tomb, near Richmond, Virginia, these words are chiselled: "Died, of a broken heart, on the 1st of March, 1780, Virginia Randolph, aged 21 years, 9 days. Faithful unto death." In the summer of 1889 some workmen, blasting rock near the falls on French Creek, uncovered the long-concealed cavern and found there a skeleton with a few rags of a Continental uniform. In a bottle beside it was an account, signed by Arthur L. Carrington, of the accident that had befallen him, and a letter declaring undying love for his sweetheart.

He had starved to death. The bones were neatly coffined, and were sent to Richmond to be buried beside those of the faithful Miss Randolph.

THE LAST SHOT AT GERMANTOWN

Many are the tales of prophecy that have been preserved to us from war times. In the beginning of King Philip's war in Connecticut, in 1675, it was reported that the firing of the first gun was heard all over the State, while the drumbeats calling settlers to defence were audible eight miles away. Braddock's defeat and the salvation of Washington were foretold by a Miami chief at a council held in Fort Ponchartrain, on Detroit River, the ambush and the slaughter having been revealed to him in a dream. The victims of that battle, too, had been apprised, for one or two nights before the disaster a young lieutenant in Braddock's command saw his fellow-officers pass through his tent, bloody and torn, and when the first gun sounded he knew that it spoke the doom of nearly all his comrades. At Killingly, Connecticut, in the autumn before the outbreak of the Revolution, a distant roar of artillery was heard for a whole day and night in the direction of Boston, mingled with a rattle of musketry, and so strong was the belief that war had begun and the British were advancing, that the minute men mustered to await orders. It was afterward argued that these noises came from an explosion of meteors, a shower of these missiles being then in progress, invisible, of course, in the day-time. Just after the signing of the Declaration of Independence the royal arms on the spire of the Episcopal church at Hampton, Virginia, were struck off by lightning. Shortly before the surrender of Cornwallis a display of northern lights was seen in New England, the rays taking the form of cannon, facing southward. In Connecticut sixty-four of these guns were counted.

At the battle of Germantown the Americans were enraged by the killing of one of their men who had gone out with a flag of truce. He was shot from the windows of Judge Chew's house, which was crowded with British soldiers, and as he fell to the lawn, dyeing the peaceful emblem with his blood, at least one of the Continentals swore that his death should be well avenged. The British reinforcements, sixteen thousand strong, came hurrying through the street, their officers but half-dressed, so urgent had been the summons for their aid. Except for their steady tramp the place was silent; doors were locked and shutters bolted, and if people were within doors no sign of them was visible. General Agnew alone of all the troop seemed depressed and anxious. Turning to an aide as they passed the Mennonist graveyard, he said, "This field is the last I shall fight on."

An eerie face peered over the cemetery wall, a scarred, unshaven face framed in long hair and surmounting a body clothed in skins, with the question, "Is that the brave General Gray who beat the rebels at Paoli?" One of the soldiers, with a careless toss of the hand, seemed to indicate General Agnew. A moment later there was a report, a puff of smoke from the cemetery wall, and a bullet whizzed by the head of the general, who smiled wanly, to encourage his men. Summary execution would have been done upon the stranger had not a body of American cavalry dashed against the red-coats at that moment, and a fierce contest was begun. When the day was over, General Agnew, who had been separated from his command in the confusion of battle, came past the graves again. Tired and depressed, he drew rein for a moment to breathe the sweet air, so lately fouled with dust and smoke, and to watch the gorgeous light of sunset. Again, like a malignant genius of the place, the savage-looking stranger arose from behind the wall. A sharp report broke the quiet of evening and awoke clattering echoes from the distant houses. A horse plunged and General Agnew rolled from his saddle, dead: the last victim in the strife at Germantown.

A BLOW IN THE DARK

The Tory Manheim sits brooding in his farmhouse near Valley Forge, and his daughter, with a hectic flush on her cheek, looks out into the twilight at the falling snow. She is worn and ill; she has brought on a fever by exposure incurred that very day in a secret journey to the American camp, made to warn her lover of another attempt on the life of Washington, who must pass her father's house on his return from a distant settlement. The Tory knows nothing of this; but he starts whenever the men in the next room rattle the dice or break into a ribald song, and a frown of apprehension crosses his face as the foragers crunch by, half-barefoot, through the snow. The hours go on, and the noise in the next room increases; but it hushes suddenly when a knock at the door is heard. The Tory opens it, and trembles as a tall, grave man, with the figure of an athlete, steps into the fire-light and calmly removes his gloves. "I have been riding far," said he. "Can you give me some food and the chance to sleep for an hour, until the storm clears up?"

Manheim says that he can, and shuffling into the next room, he whispers, "Washington!" The girl is sent out to get refreshments. It is in vain that she seeks to sign or speak to the man who sits there so calmly before the fire, for her father is never out of sight or hearing. After Washington has finished his modest repast he asks to be left to himself for a while, but the girl is told to conduct him to the room on the left of the landing on the next floor.

Her father holds the candle at the foot of the stairs until he sees his guest enter; then he bids his daughter go to her own bed, which is in the chamber on the right of the landing. There is busy whispering in the room below after that, and the dice box is shaken to see to whose lot it shall fall to steal up those stairs and stab Washington in his sleep. An hour passes and all in the house appear to be at rest, but the stairs creak slightly as Manheim creeps upon his prey. He blows his candle out and softly enters the chamber on the left. The men, who listen in the dark at the foot of the stair, hear a moan, and the Tory hurries back with a shout of gladness, for the rebel chief is no more and Howe's reward will enrich them for life.

Glasses are filled, and in the midst of the rejoicing a step is heard on the stair. Washington stands before them. In calm, deep tones he thanks the farmer for his shelter, and asks that his horse be brought to the door and his reckoning be made out. The Tory stares as one bereft. Then he rushes aloft, flings open the door of the room on the left, and gazes at the face that rests on the pillow,—a pillow that is dabbled with red. The face is that of his daughter. The name of father is one that he will never hear again in this world. The candle falls from his hand; he sinks to the floor; be his sin forgiven! Outside is heard the tramp of a horse. It is that of Washington, who rides away, ignorant of the peril he has passed and the sacrifice that averted it.

THE TORY'S CONVERSION

In his firelit parlor, in his little house at Valley Forge, old Michael Kuch sits talking with his daughter. But though it is Christmas eve the talk has little cheer in it. The hours drag on until the clock strikes twelve, and the old man is about to offer his evening prayer for the safety of his son, who is one of Washington's troopers, when hurried steps are heard in the snow, there is a fumbling at the latch, then the door flies open and admits a haggard, panting man who hastily closes it again, falls into a seat, and shakes from head to foot. The girl goes to him. "John!" she says. But he only averts his face. "What is wrong with thee, John Blake?" asks the farmer. But he has to ask again and again ere he gets an answer. Then, in a broken voice, the trembling man confesses that he has tried to shoot Washington, but the bullet struck and killed his only attendant, a dragoon. He has come for shelter, for men are on his track already. "Thou know'st I am neutral in this war, John Blake," answered the farmer,—"although I have a boy down yonder in the camp. It was a cowardly thing to do, and I hate you Tories that you do not fight like men; yet, since you ask me for a hiding-place, you shall have it, though, mind you, 'tis more on the girl's account than yours. The men are coming. Out—this way—to the spring-house. So!"

Before old Michael has time to return to his chair the door is again thrust open, this time by men in blue and buff. They demand the assassin, whose footsteps they have tracked there through the snow. Michael does not answer. They are about to use violence when, through the open door, comes Washington, who checks them with a word. The general bears a drooping form with a blood splash on its breast, and deposits it on the hearth as gently as a mother puts a babe into its cradle. As the firelight falls on the still face the farmer's eyes grow round and big; then he shrieks and drops upon his knees, for it is his son who is lying there. Beside him is a pistol; it was dropped by the Tory when he entered. Grasping it eagerly the farmer leaps to his feet. His years have fallen from him. With a tiger-like bound he gains the door, rushes to the spring-house where John Blake is crouching, his eyes sunk and shining, gnawing his fingers in a craze of dismay. But though hate is swift, love is swifter, and the girl is there as soon as he. She strikes his arm aside, and the bullet he has fired lodges in the wood. He draws out his knife, and the murderer, to whom has now come the calmness of despair, kneels and offers his breast to the blade. Before he can strike, the soldiers hasten up, and seizing Blake, they drag him to the house—the little room—where all had been so peaceful but a few minutes before.

The culprit is brought face to face with Washington, who asks him what harm he has ever suffered from his fellow countrymen that he should turn against them thus. Blake hangs his head and owns his willingness to die. His eyes rest on the form extended on the floor, and he shudders; but his features undergo an almost joyous change, for the figure lifts itself, and in a faint voice calls, "Father!" The young man lives. With a cry of delight both father and sister raise him in their arms. "You are not yet prepared to die," says Washington to the captive. "I will put you under guard until you are wanted. Take him into custody, my dear young lady, and try to make an American of him. See, it is one o'clock, and this is Christmas morning. May all be happy here. Come." And beckoning to his men he rides away, though Blake and his affianced would have gone on their knees before him. Revulsion of feeling, love, thankfulness and a latent patriotism wrought a quick change in Blake. When young Kuch recovered Blake joined his regiment, and no soldier served the flag more honorably.

LORD PERCY'S DREAM

Leaving the dissipations of the English court, Lord Percy came to America to share the fortunes of his brethren in the contest then raging on our soil. His father had charged him with the delivery of a certain package to an Indian woman, should he meet her in his rambles through the western wilds, and, without inquiring into the nature of the gift or its occasion, he accepted the trust. At the battle of the Brandywine—strangely foretold by Quaker prophecy forty years before—he was detailed by Cornwallis to drive the colonial troops out of a graveyard where they had intrenched themselves, and though he set upon this errand with the enthusiasm of youth, his cheek paled as he drew near the spot where the enemy was waiting.

It was not that he had actual physical fear of the onset: he had dreamed a dream a few nights before, the purport of which he had hinted to his comrades, and as he rode into the clearing at the top of Osborn's Hill he drew rein and exclaimed, "My dream! Yonder is the graveyard. I am fated to die there." Giving a few of his effects to his brother officers, and charging one of them to take a message of love to his betrothed in England, he set his lips and rode forward.

His cavalry bound toward the scene of action and are within thirty paces of the cemetery wall, when from behind it rises a battalion of men in the green uniform of the Santee Rangers and pours a withering fire into the ranks. The shock is too great to withstand, and the red-coats stagger away with broken ranks, leaving many dead and wounded on the ground. Lord Percy is the coolest of all. He urges the broken columns forward, and almost alone holds the place until the infantry, a hundred yards behind, come up. Thereupon ensues one of those hand-to-hand encounters that are so rare in recent war, and that are the sorest test of valor and discipline. Now rides forward Captain Waldemar, chief of the rangers and a half-breed Indian, who, seeing Percy, recognizes him as an officer and engages him in combat. There is for a minute a clash of steel on steel; then the nobleman falls heavily to the earth—dead. His dream has come true. That night the captain Waldemar seeks out the body of this officer, attracted by something in the memory of his look, and from his bosom takes the packet that was committed to his care.

By lantern-light he reads, carelessly at first, then rapidly and eagerly, and at the close he looks long and earnestly at the dead man, and seems to brush away a tear. Strange thing to do over the body of an enemy! Why had fate decreed that they should be enemies? For Waldemar is the half-brother of Percy. His mother was the Indian girl that the earl, now passing his last days in England, had deceived with a pretended marriage, and the letters promise patronage to her son. The half-breed digs a grave that night with his own hands and lays the form of his brother in it.

SAVED BY THE BIBLE

It was on the day after the battle of Germantown that Warner, who wore the blue, met his hated neighbor, the Tory Dabney, near that bloody field.

By a common impulse the men fell upon each other with their knives, and Warner soon had his enemy in a position to give him the death-stroke, but Dabney began to bellow for quarter. "My brother cried for quarter at Paoli," answered the other, "and you struck him to the heart."

"I have a wife and child. Spare me for their sakes."

"My brother had a wife and two children. Perhaps you would like to beg your life of them."

Though made in mockery, this proposition was caught at so earnestly that Warner at length consented to take his adversary, firmly bound, to the house where the bereaved family was living. The widow was reading the Bible to her children, but her grief was too fresh to gather comfort from it. When Dabney was flung into the room he grovelled at her feet and begged piteously for mercy. Her face did not soften, but there was a kind of contempt in the settled sadness of her tone as she said, "It shall be as God directs. I will close this Bible, open it at chance, and when this boy shall put his finger at random on a line, by that you must live or die."

The book was opened, and the child put his finger on a line: "That man shall die."

Warner drew his knife and motioned his prisoner to the door. He was going to lead him into the wood to offer him as a sacrifice to his brother's spirit.

"No, no!" shrieked the wretch. "Give me one more chance; one more! Let the girl open the book."

The woman coldly consents, and when the book is opened for the second time she reads, "Love your enemies." There are no other words. The knife is used, but it is to cut the prisoner's bonds, and he walks away with head hung down, never more to take arms against his countrymen. And glad are they all at this, when the husband is brought home—not dead, though left among the corpses at Paoli, but alive and certain of recovery, with such nursing as his wife will give him. After tears of joy have been shed she tells him the story of the Bible judgment, and all the members of the family fall on their knees in thanksgiving that the blood of Dabney is not upon their heads.

PARRICIDE OF THE WISSAHICKON

Farmer Derwent and his four stout sons set off on an autumn night for the meeting of patriots at a house on the Wissahickon,—a meeting that bodes no good to the British encamped in Philadelphia, let the red-coats laugh as they will at the rag-tag and bob-tail that are joining the army of Mr. Washington in the wilds of the Skippack. The farmer sighs as he thinks that his younger son alone should be missing from the company, and wonders for the thousandth time what has become of the boy. They sit by a rock that juts into the road to trim their lantern, and while they talk together they are startled by an exclamation. It is from Ellen, the adopted daughter of Derwent and the betrothed of his missing son. On the night that the boy stole away from his father's house he asked her to meet him in this place in a year's time, and the year is up to-night.

But it is not to meet him that she is hastening now: she has heard that the British have learned of the patriot gathering and will try to make prisoners of the company. Even as she tells of this there is a sound to the southward: the column is on the march. The farmer's eye blazes with rage and hate. "Boys," he says, "yonder come those who intend to kill us. Let them taste of their own warfare. Stand here in the shadow and fire as they pass this rock."

The troopers ride on, chuckling over their sure success, when there is a report of rifles and four of the red-coats are in the dust. The survivors, though taken by surprise, prove their courage by halting to answer the volley, and one of them springs from his saddle, seizes Derwent, and plunges a knife into his throat. The rebel falls. His blood pools around him. The British are successful, for two of the young men are bound and two of them have fallen, and there is a cheer of victory, but the trooper with the knife in his hand does not raise his voice. He bends above the farmer as still as one dead, until his captain claps him on the shoulder. As he rises, the prisoners start in wonder, for the face they see in the lantern-light is that of their brother, yet strange in its haggardness and its smear of blood on the cheek. The girl runs from her hiding-place with a cry, but stands in horror when her foot touches the gory pool in the road. The trooper opens his coat and offers her a locket. It contains her picture, and he has worn it above his heart for a year, but she lets it fall and sinks down, moaning. The soldier tears off his red coat, tramples it in the dust, then vaulting to his saddle he plunges into the river, fords it, and crashes through the underbrush on the other side. In a few minutes he has reached the summit of a rock that rises nearly a hundred feet above the stream. The horse halts at the edge, but on a fierce stab of the spur into his flank he takes the leap. With a despairing yell the traitor and parricide goes into eternity.

THE BLACKSMITH AT BRANDYWINE

Terrible in the field at Brandywine was the figure of a man armed only with a hammer, who plunged into the ranks of the enemy, heedless of his own life, yet seeming to escape their shots and sabre cuts by magic, and with Thor strokes beat them to the earth. But yesterday war had been to him a distant rumor, a thing as far from his cottage at Dilworth as if it had been in Europe, but he had revolted at a plot that he had overheard to capture Washington and had warned the general. In revenge the Tories had burned his cottage, and his wife and baby had perished in the flames. All day he had sat beside the smoking ruins, unable to weep, unable to think, unable almost to suffer, except dumbly, for as yet he could not understand it. But when the drums were heard they roused the tiger in him, and gaunt with sleeplessness and hunger he joined his countrymen and ranged like Ajax on the field. Every cry for quarter was in vain: to every such appeal he had but one reply, his wife's name—Mary.

Near the end of the fight he lay beside the road, his leg broken, his flesh torn, his life ebbing from a dozen wounds. A wagoner, hasting to join the American retreat, paused to give him drink. "I've only five minutes more of life in me," said the smith. "Can you lift me into that tree and put a rifle in my hands?" The powerful teamster raised him to the crotch of an oak, and gave him the rifle and ammunition that a dying soldier had dropped there. A band of red-coats came running down the road, chasing some farmers. The blacksmith took careful aim; there was a report, and the leader of the band fell dead. A pause; again a report rang out, and a trooper sprawled upon the ground. The marksman had been seen, and a lieutenant was urging his men to hurry on and cut him down. There was a third report, and the lieutenant reeled forward into the road, bleeding and cursing. "That's for Mary," gasped the blacksmith. The rifle dropped from his hands, and he, too, sank lifeless against the boughs.

FATHER AND SON

It was three soldiers, escaping from the rout of Braddock's forces, who caught the alleged betrayer of their general and put him to the death. They threw his purse of ill-gotten louis d'or into the river, and sent him swinging from the edge of a ravine, with a vine about his neck and a placard on his breast. And so they left him.

Twenty years pass, and the war-fires burn more fiercely in the vales of Pennsylvania, but, too old to fight, the schoolmaster sits at his door near Chad's Ford and smokes and broods upon the past. He thinks of the time when he marched with Washington, when with two wounded comrades he returned along the lonely trail; then comes the vision of a blackening face, and he rises and wipes his brow. "It was right," he mutters. "He sent a thousand of his brothers to their deaths."

Gilbert Gates comes that evening to see the old man's daughter: a smooth, polite young fellow, but Mayland cannot like him, and after some short talk he leaves him, pleading years and rheumatism, and goes to bed. But not to sleep; for toward ten o'clock his daughter goes to him and urges him to fly, for men are gathering near the house—Tories, she is sure,—and they mean no good. Laughing at her fears, but willing to relieve her anxiety, the old man slips into his clothes, goes into the cellar, and thence starts for the barn, while the girl remains for a few minutes to hide the silver.

He does not go far before Gates is at his elbow with the whispered words, "Into the stack-quick. They are after you." Mayland hesitates with distrust, but the appearance of men with torches leaves no time for talk. With Gilbert's help he crawls deep into the straw and is covered up. Presently a rough voice asks which way he has gone. Gilbert replies that he has gone to the wood, but there is no need for getting into a passion, and that on no account would it be advisable to fire the stack. "Won't we though?" cries one of the party. "We'll burn the rebel out of house and home," and thrusting his torch into the straw it is ablaze in an instant. The crowd hurries away toward the wood, and does not hear the stifled groan that comes out of the middle of the fire. Gates takes a paper from his pocket, and, after reading it for the last time, flings it upon the flame. It bears the inscription, "Isaac Gates, Traitor and Spy, hung by three soldiers of his majesty's army. Isaac Mayland."

From his moody contemplation he rouses with a start, for Mayland's daughter is there. Her eyes are bent on a distorted thing that lies among the embers, and in the dying light of the flames it seems to move. She studies it close, then with a cry of pain and terror she falls upon the hot earth, and her senses go out, not to be regained in woful years. With head low bowed, Gilbert Gates trudges away. In the fight at Brandywine next day, Black Samson, a giant negro, armed with a scythe, sweeps his way through the red ranks like a sable figure of Time. Mayland had taught him; his daughter had given him food. It is to avenge them that he is fighting. In the height of the conflict he enters the American ranks leading a prisoner—Gilbert Gates. The young man is pale, stern, and silent. His deed is known, he is a spy as well as a traitor, but he asks no mercy. It is rumored that next day he alone, of the prisoners, was led to a wood and lashed by arms and legs to a couple of hickory trees that had been bent by a prodigious effort and tied together by their tops. The lashing was cut by a rifle-ball, the trees regained their straight position with a snap like whips, and that was the way Gilbert Gates came to his end.

THE ENVY OF MANITOU

Behind the mountains that gloom about the romantic village of Mauch Chunk, Pennsylvania, was once a lake of clear, bright water, its winding loops and bays extending back for several miles. On one of its prettiest bits of shore stood a village of the Leni Lenape, and largest of its wigwams, most richly pictured without, most luxurious in its couching of furs within, was that of the young chief, Onoko. This Indian was a man of great size, strength, and daring. Single-handed he had slain the bear on Mauch Chunk [Bear Mountain], and it was no wonder that Wenonah, the fairest of her tribe, was flattered when he sued for her hand, and promptly consented to be his wife. It was Onoko's fortune in war, the chase, and love that roused the envy of Mitche Manitou.

One day, as the couple were floating in their shallop of bark on the calm lake, idly enjoying the sunshine and saying pretty things to each other, the Manitou arose among the mountains. Terrible was his aspect, for the scowl of hatred was on his face, thunder crashed about his head, and fire snapped from his eyes. Covering his right hand with his invincible magic mitten, he dealt a blow on the hills that made the earth shake, and rived them to a depth of a thousand feet. Through the chasm thus created the lake poured a foaming deluge, and borne with it was the canoe of Onoko and Wenonah. One glance at the wrathful face in the clouds above them and they knew that escape was hopeless, so, clasping each other in a close embrace, they were whirled away to death. Manitou strode away moodily among the hills, and ever since that time the Lehigh has rolled through the chasm that he made. The memory of Onoko is preserved in the name of a glen and cascade a short distance above Mauch Chunk.

It is not well to be too happy in this world. It rouses the envy of the gods.

THE LAST REVEL IN PRINTZ HALL

"Young man, I'll give thee five dollars a week to be care-taker in Printz Hall," said Quaker Quidd to fiddler Matthews, on an autumn evening.

Young Matthews had just been taunting the old gentleman with being afraid to sleep on his own domain, and as the eyes of all the tavern loungers were on him he could hardly decline so flattering a proposition, so, after some hemming and hawing, he said he would take the Quaker at his word. He played but two or three more tunes that evening, did Peter Matthews, and played them rather sadly; then, as Quidd had finished his mulled cider and departed, he took his homeward way in thoughtful mood. Printz Hall stood in a lonely, weed-grown garden near Chester, Pennsylvania, and thither repaired Peter, as next day's twilight shut down, with a mattress, blanket, comestibles, his beloved fiddle, and a flask of whiskey. Ensconcing himself in the room that was least depressing in appearance he stuffed rags into the vacant panes, lighted a candle, started a blaze in the fireplace, and ate his supper.

"Not so bad a place, after all," mumbled Peter, as he warmed himself at the fire and the flask; then, taking out his violin, he began to play. The echo of his music emphasized the emptiness of the house, the damp got into the strings so that they sounded tubby, and there were unintentional quavers in the melody whenever the trees swung against the windows and splashed them with rain, or when a distant shutter fell a-creaking. Finally, he stirred the fire, bolted the door, snuffed his candle, took a courageous pull at the liquor, flung off his coat and shoes, rolled his blanket around him, stretched himself on the mattress, and fell asleep. He was awakened by—well, he could not say what, exactly, only he became suddenly as wide awake as ever he had been in his life, and listened for some sound that he knew was going to come out of the roar of the wind and the slamming, grating, and whistling about the house. Yes, there it was: a tread and a clank on the stair. The door, so tightly bolted, flew open, and there entered a dark figure with steeple-crowned hat, cloak, jack-boots, sword, and corselet. The terrified fiddler wanted to howl, but his voice was gone. "I am Peter Printz, governor-general of his Swedish Majesty's American colonies, and builder of this house," said the figure. "'Tis the night of the autumnal equinox, when my friends meet here for revel. Take thy fiddle and come. Play, but speak not."

And whether he wished or no, Peter was drawn to follow the figure, which he could make out by the phosphor gleam of it. Down-stairs they went, doors swinging open before them, and along corridors that clanged to the stroke of the spectre's boot heels. Now they came to the ancient reception-room, and as they entered it Peter was dazzled. The floor was smooth with wax, logs snapped in the fireplace, though the flame was somewhat blue, the old hangings and portraits looked fresh, and in the light of wax candles a hundred people, in the brave array of old times, walked, courtesied, and seemed to laugh and talk together. As the fiddler appeared, every eye was turned on him in a disquieting way, and when he addressed himself to his bottle, from every throat came a hollow laugh. Finding his way to a chair he sank into it and put his instrument in position. At the first note the couples took hands, and as he struck into a jig they began to circle swiftly, leaping wondrous high.

Faster went the music, for the whiskey was at work in Peter's noddle, and wilder grew the dance. It was as if the storm had come in through the windows and was blowing these people hither and yon, around and around. The fiddler vaguely wondered at himself, for he had never played so well, though he had never heard the tune before. Now loomed Governor Printz in the middle of the room, and extending his hand he ordered the dance to cease. "Thou bast played well, fiddler," he said, "and shalt be paid." Then, at his signal, came two negro men tugging at a strong box that Printz unlocked. It was filled with gold pieces. "Hold thy fiddle bag," commanded the governor, and Peter did so, watching, open mouthed, the transfer of a double handful of treasure from box to sack. Another such handful followed, and another. At the fourth Peter could no longer contain himself. He forgot the injunction not to speak, and shouted gleefully, "Lord Harry! Here's luck!"

There was a shriek of demon laughter, the scene was lost in darkness, and Peter fell insensible. In the morning a tavern-haunting friend, anxious to know if Peter had met with any adventure, entered the house and went cautiously from room to room, calling on the watcher to show himself. There was no response. At last he stumbled on the whiskey bottle, empty, and knew that Peter must be near. Sure enough, there he lay in the great room, with dust and mould thick on everything, and his fiddle smashed into a thousand pieces. Peter on being awakened looked ruefully about him, then sprang up and eagerly demanded his money. "What money?" asked his friend. The fiddler clutched at his green bag, opened it, shook it; there was nothing. Nor was there any delay in Peter's exit from that mansion, and when, twenty-four hours after, the house went up in flames, he averred that the ghosts had set it afire, and that he knew where they brought their coals from.

THE TWO RINGS

Gabrielle de St. Pierre, daughter of the commandant of Fort Le Boeuf, now—Waterford, Pennsylvania, that the French had setup on the Ohio River, was Parisian by birth and training, but American by choice, for she had enjoyed on this lonesome frontier a freedom equal to that of the big-handed, red-faced half-breeds, and she was as wild as an Indian in her sports. Returning from a hunt, one day, she saw three men advancing along the trail, and, as it was easy to see that they were not Frenchmen, her guide slipped an arrow to the cord and discharged it; but Gabrielle was as quick as he, for she struck the missile as it was leaving the bow and it quivered harmlessly into a beech. The younger of the men who were advancing—he was Harry Fairfax, of Virginia—said to his chief, "Another escape for you, George. Heaven sent one of its angels to avert that stroke."

Washington, for it was he, answered lightly, and, as no other hostile demonstrations were made, the new-comers pressed on to the fort, where St. Pierre received them cordially, though he knew that their errand was to claim his land on behalf of the English and urge the French to retire to the southwest. The days that were spent in futile negotiation passed all too swiftly for Fairfax, for he had fallen in love with Gabrielle. She would not consent to a betrothal until time had tried his affection, but as a token of friendship she gave him a stone circlet of Indian manufacture, and received in exchange a ring that had been worn by the mother of Fairfax.

After the diplomats had returned the English resolved to enforce their demand with arms, and Fairfax was one of the first to be despatched to the front.

Early in the campaign his company engaged the enemy near the Ohio River, and in the heat of battle he had time to note and wonder at the strange conduct of one of the French officers, a mere stripling, who seemed more concerned to check the fire of his men than to secure any advantage in the fight. Presently the French gave way, and with a cheer the English ran forward to claim the field, the ruder spirits among them at once beginning to plunder the wounded. A cry for quarter drew Fairfax with a bound to the place whence it came, and, dashing aside a pilfering soldier, he bent above a slight form that lay extended on the earth: the young officer whose strange conduct had so surprised him. In another moment he recognized his mother's ring on one of the slender hands. It was Gabrielle. Her father had perished in the fight, but she had saved her lover.

In due time she went with her affianced to his home in Williamsburg, Virginia, and became mistress of the Fairfax mansion. But she never liked the English, as a people, and when, in later years, two sturdy sons of hers asked leave to join the Continental army, she readily consented.

FLAME SCALPS OF THE CHARTIERS

Before Pittsburg had become worthy to be called a settlement, a white man rowed his boat to the mouth of Chartiers creek, near that present city. He was seeking a place in which to make his home, and a little way up-stream, where were timber, water, and a southern slope, he marked a "tomahawk claim," and set about clearing the land. Next year his wife, two children, and his brother came to occupy the cabin he had built, and for a long time all went happily, but on returning from a long hunt the brothers found the little house in ashes and the charred remains of its occupants in the ruins. Though nearly crazed by this catastrophe they knew that their own lives were in hourly peril, and they wished to live until they could punish the savages for this crime. After burying the bodies, they started east across the hills, leaving a letter on birch bark in a cleft stick at the mouth of Chartiers creek, in which the tragedy was recounted.

This letter was afterward found by trappers. The men themselves were never heard from, and it is believed that they, too, fell at the hands of the Indians. Old settlers used to affirm that on summer nights the cries of the murdered innocents could be heard in the little valley where the cabin stood, and when storms were coming up these cries were often blended with the yells of savages. More impressive are the death lights—the will-o'-the-wisps—that wander over the scene of the tragedy, and up and down the neighboring slopes. These apparitions are said to be the spirits of husband and wife seeking each other, or going together in search of their children; but some declare that in their upward streaming rays it can readily be seen that they are the scalps of the slain. Two of them have a golden hue, and these are the scalps of the children. From beneath them drops of red seem to distil on the grass and are found to have bedewed the flowers on the following morning.

THE CONSECRATION OF WASHINGTON

In 1773 some of the Pietist monks were still living in their rude monastery whose ruins are visible on the banks of the Wissahickon. Chief among these mystics was an old man who might have enjoyed the wealth and distinction warranted by a title had he chosen to remain in Germany, but he had forsworn vanities, and had come to the new world to pray, to rear his children, and to live a simple life. Some said he was an alchemist, and many believed him to be a prophet. The infrequent wanderer beside the romantic river had seen lights burning in the window of his cell and had heard the solemn sound of song and prayer. On a winter night, when snow lay untrodden about the building and a sharp air stirred in the trees with a sound like harps, the old man sat in a large room of the place, with his son and daughter, waiting. For a prophecy had run that on that night, at the third hour of morning, the Deliverer would present himself. In a dream was heard a voice, saying, "I will send a deliverer to the new world who shall save my people from bondage, as my Son saved them from spiritual death." The night wore on in prayer and meditation, and the hours tolled heavily across the frozen wilderness, but, at the stroke of three, steps were heard in the snow and the door swung open. The man who entered was of great stature, with a calm, strong face, a powerful frame, and a manner of dignity and grace.

"Friends, I have lost my way," said he. "Can you direct me?"

The old man started up in a kind of rapture. "You have not lost your way," he cried, "but found it. You are called to a great mission. Kneel at this altar and receive it."

The stranger looked at the man in surprise and a doubt passed over his face. "Nay, I am not mad," urged the recluse, with a slight smile. "Listen: to-night, disturbed for the future of your country, and unable to sleep, you mounted horse and rode into the night air to think on the question that cannot be kept out of your mind, Is it lawful for the subject to draw sword against his king? The horse wandered, you knew and cared not whither, until he brought you here."

"How do you know this?" asked the stranger, in amazement.

"Be not surprised, but kneel while I anoint thee deliverer of this land."

Moved and impressed, the man bowed his knee before one of his fellows for the first time in his life. The monk touched his finger with oil, and laying it on the brow of the stranger said, "Do you promise, when the hour shall strike, to take the sword in defence of your country? Do you promise, when you shall see your soldiers suffer for bread and fire, and when the people you have led to victory shall bow before you, to remember that you are but the minister of God in the work of a nation's freedom?"

With a new light burning in his eyes, the stranger bent his head.

"Then, in His name, I consecrate thee deliverer of this oppressed people. When the time comes, go forth to victory, for, as you are faithful, be sure that God will grant it. Wear no crown, but the blessings and honor of a free people, save this." As he finished, his daughter, a girl of seventeen, came forward and put a wreath of laurel on the brow of the kneeling man. "Rise," continued the prophet, "and take my hand, which I have never before offered to any man, and accept my promise to be faithful to you and to this country, even if it cost my life."

As he arose, the son of the priest stepped to him and girt a sword upon his hip, and the old man held up his hands in solemn benediction. The stranger laid his hand on the book that stood open on the altar and kissed the hilt of his sword. "I will keep the faith," said he. At dawn he went his way again, and no one knew his name, but when the fires of battle lighted the western world America looked to him for its deliverance from tyranny. Years later it was this spot that he revisited, alone, to pray, and here Sir William Howe offered to him, in the name of his king, the title of regent of America. He took the parchment and ground it into a rag in the earth at his feet. For this was Washington. MARION

Blooming and maidenly, though she dressed in leather and used a rifle like a man, was Marion, grand-daughter of old Abraham, who counted his years as ninety, and who for many of those years had lived with his books in the tidy cabin where the Youghiogheny and Monongahela come together. This place stood near the trail along which Braddock marched to his defeat, and it was one of the stragglers from this command, a bony half-breed with red hair, called Red Wolf, that knocked at the door and asked for water. Seeing no one but Marion he ventured in, and would have tried not only to make free with the contents of the little house but would have kissed the girl as well, only that she seized her rifle and held him at bay. Still, the fellow would have braved a shot, had not a young officer in a silver-laced uniform glanced through the open door in passing and discovered the situation. He doffed his chapeau to Marion, then said sternly to the rogue, "Retire. Your men are waiting for you." Red Wolf slunk away, and Washington, for it was he, begged that he might rest for a little time under the roof.

This request was gladly complied with, both by the girl and by her grandfather, who presently appeared, and the fever that threatened the young soldier was averted by a day of careful nursing. Marion's innate refinement, her gentleness, her vivacity, could not fail to interest Washington, and the vision of her face was with him for many a day. He promised to return, then he rode forward and caught up with the troops. He survived the battle in which seven hundred of his comrades were shot or tomahawked and scalped. One Indian fired at him eleven times, and five of the bullets scratched him; after that the savage forbore, believing that the officer was under Manitou's protection. When the retreating column approached the place where Marion lived he hastened on in advance to see her. The cabin was in ashes. He called, but there was no answer. When he turned away, with sad and thoughtful mien, a brown tress was wrapped around his finger, and in his cabinet he kept it until his death, folded in a paper marked "Marion, July 11, 1755."

TALES OF PURITAN LAND

EVANGALINE

The seizure by England of the country that soon afterward was rechristened Nova Scotia was one of the cruellest events in history. The land was occupied by a good and happy people who had much faith and few laws, plenty to eat and drink, no tax collectors nor magistrates, in brief, a people who were entitled to call themselves Acadians, for they made their land an Arcady. Upon them swooped the British ships, took them unarmed and unoffending, crowded them aboard their transports,—often separating husband and wife, parents and children,—scattered them far and wide, beyond hope of return, and set up the cross of St. George on the ruins of prosperity and peace. On the shore of the Basin of Minas can still be traced the foundations of many homes that were perforce deserted at that time, and among them are the ruins of Grand Pre.

Here lived Evangeline Bellefontaine and Gabriel Lajeunesse, who were betrothed with the usual rejoicings just before the coming of the English. They had expected, when their people were arrested, to be sent away together; but most of the men were kept under guard, and Gabriel was at sea, bound neither he nor she knew whither, when Evangeline found herself in her father's house alone, for grief and excitement had been more than her aged parent could bear, and he was buried at the shore just before the women of the place were crowded on board of a transport. As the ship set off her sorrowing passengers looked behind them to see their homes going up in flame and smoke, and Acadia knew them no more. The English had planned well to keep these people from coming together for conspiracy or revenge: they scattered them over all America, from Newfoundland to the southern savannas.

Evangeline was not taken far away, only to New England; but without Gabriel all lands were drear, and she set off in the search for him, working here and there, sometimes looking timidly at the headstones on new graves, then travelling on. Once she heard that he was a *coureur des bois* on the prairies, again that he was a voyageur in the Louisiana lowlands; but those of his people who kept near her inclined to jest at her faith and urged her to marry Leblanc, the notary's son, who truly loved her. To these she only replied, "I cannot."

Down the Ohio and Mississippi she went—on a raft—with a little band of those who were seeking the French settlements, where the language, religion, and simplicity of life recalled Acadia. They found it on the banks of the Teche, and they reached the house of the herdsman Gabriel on the day that he had departed for the north to seek Evangeline. She and the good priest who had been her stay in a year of sorrow turned back in pursuit, and for weary months, over prairie and through forest, skirting mountain and morass, going freely among savages, they followed vain clues, and at last arrived in Philadelphia. Broken in spirit then, but not less sweet of nature for the suffering that she had known, she who had been named for the angels became a minister of mercy, and in the black robe of a nun went about with comforts to the sick and poor. A pestilence was sweeping through the city, and those who had no friends nor attendants were taken to the almshouse, whither, as her way was, Evangeline went on a soft Sabbath morning to calm the fevered and brighten the hearts of the dying.

Some of the patients of the day before had gone and new were in their places. Suddenly she turned white and sank on her knees at a bedside, with a cry of "Gabriel, my beloved!" breathed into the ears of a prematurely aged man who lay gasping in death before her. He came out of his stupor, slowly, and tried to speak her name. She drew his head to her bosom, kissed him, and for one moment they were happy. Then the light went out of his eyes and the warmth from his heart. She pressed his eyelids down and bowed her head, for her way was plainer now, and she thanked God that it was so.

THE SNORING OF SWUNKSUS

The original proprietor of Deer Isle, off the coast of Maine—at least, the one who was in possession one hundred and thirty years ago—had the liquid name of Swunksus. His name was not the only liquid thing in the neighborhood, however, for, wherever Swunksus was, fire-water was not far. Shortly before the Revolution a renegade from Boston, one Conary, moved up to the island and helped himself to as much of it as he chose, but the longer he lived there the more he wanted. Swunksus was willing enough to divide his domain with the white intruder, but Conary was not satisfied with half. He did not need it all; he just wanted it. Moreover, he grew quarrelsome and was continually nagging poor Swunksus, until at last he forced the Indian to accept a challenge, not to immediate combat, but to fight to the death should they meet thereafter.

The red man retired to his half of the island and hid among the bushes near his home to await the white man, but in this little fastness he discovered a jug of whiskey that either fate or Conary had placed there. Before an hour was over he was "as full and mellow as a harvest moon," and it was then that his enemy appeared. There was no trouble in finding Swunksus, for he was snoring like a fog horn, and walking boldly up to him, Conary blew his head off with a load of slugs. Then he took possession of the place and lived happily ever after. Swunksus takes his deposition easily, for, although he has more than once paraded along the beaches, his ghost spends most of the time in slumber, and terrific snores have been heard proceeding from the woods in daylight.

THE LEWISTON HERMIT

On an island above the falls of the Androscoggin, at Lewiston, Maine, lived a white recluse at the beginning of the eighteenth century. The natives, having had good reason to mistrust all palefaces, could think no good of the man who lived thus among but not with them. Often they gathered at the bank and looked across at his solitary candle twinkling among the leaves, and wondered what manner of evil he could be planning against them. Wherever there are many conspirators one will be a gabbler or a traitor; so, when the natives had resolved on his murder, he, somehow, learned of their intent and set himself to thwart it. So great was their fear of this lonely man, and of the malignant powers he might conjure to his aid, that nearly fifty Indians joined the expedition, to give each other courage.

Their plan was to go a little distance up the river and come down with the current, thus avoiding the dip of paddles that he might hear in a direct crossing. When it was quite dark they set off, and keeping headway on their canoes aimed them toward the light that glimmered above the water. But the cunning hermit had no fire in his cabin that night. It was burning on a point below his shelter, and from his hiding-place among the rocks he saw their fleet, as dim and silent as shadows, go by him on the way to the misguiding beacon.

Presently a cry arose. The savages had passed the point of safe sailing; their boats had become unmanageable. Forgetting their errand, their only hope now was to save themselves, but in vain they tried to reach the shore: the current was whirling them to their doom. Cries and death-songs mingled with the deepening roar of the waters, the light barks reached the cataract and leaped into the air. Then the night was still again, save for the booming of the flood. Not one of the Indians who had set out on this errand of death survived the hermit's stratagem.

THE DEAD SHIP OF HARPSWELL

At times the fisher-folk of Maine are startled to see the form of a ship, with gaunt timbers showing through the planks, like lean limbs through rents in a pauper's garb, float shoreward in the sunset. She is a ship of ancient build, with tall masts and sails of majestic spread, all torn; but what is her name, her port, her flag, what harbor she is trying to make, no man can tell, for on her deck no sailor has ever been seen to run up colors or heard to answer a hail. Be it in calm or storm, in-come or ebb of tide, the ship holds her way until she almost touches shore.

There is no creak of spars or whine of cordage, no spray at the bow, no ripple at the stern—no voice, and no figure to utter one. As she nears the rocks she pauses, then, as if impelled by a contrary current, floats rudder foremost off to sea, and vanishes in twilight. Harpswell is her favorite cruising-ground, and her appearance there sets many heads to shaking, for while it is not inevitable that ill luck follows her visits, it has been seen that burial-boats have sometimes had occasion to cross the harbor soon after them, and that they were obliged by wind or tide or current to follow her course on leaving the wharf.

THE SCHOOLMASTER HAD NOT REACHED ORRINGTON

The quiet town of Orrington, in Maine, was founded by Jesse Atwood, of Wellfleet, Cape Cod, in 1778, and has become known, since then, as a place where skilful farmers and brave sailors could always be found. It also kept Maine supplied for years with oldest inhabitants. It is said that the name was an accident of illiteracy, and that it is the only place in the world that owes its title to bad spelling. The settlers who followed Atwood there were numerous enough to form a township after ten years, and the name they decided on for their commonwealth was Orangetown, so called for a village in Maryland where some of the people had associations, but the clerk of the town meeting was not a college graduate and his spelling of Orange was Orring, and of town, ton. His draft of the resolutions went before the legislature, and the people directly afterward found themselves living in Orrington.

JACK WELCH'S DEATH LIGHT

Pond Cove, Maine, is haunted by a light that on a certain evening, every summer, rises a mile out at sea, drifts to a spot on shore, then whirls with a buzz and a glare to an old house, where it vanishes. Its first appearance was simultaneous with the departure of Jack Welch, a fisherman. He was seen one evening at work on his boat, but in the morning he was gone, nor has he since shown himself in the flesh.

On the tenth anniversary of this event three fishermen were hurrying up the bay, hoping to reach home before dark, for they dreaded that uncanny light, but a fog came in and it was late before they reached the wharf. As they were tying their boat a channel seemed to open through the mist, and along that path from the deep came a ball of pallid flame with the rush of a meteor. There was one of the men who cowered at the bottom of the boat with ashen face and shaking limbs, and did not watch the light, even though it shot above his head, played through the rigging, and after a wide sweep went shoreward and settled on his house. Next day one of his comrades called for him, but Tom Wright was gone, gone, his wife said, before the day broke. Like Jack Welch's disappearance, this departure was unexplained, and in time he was given up for dead.

Twenty years had passed, when Wright's presumptive widow was startled by the receipt of a letter in a weak, trembling hand, signed with her husband's name. It was written on his death-bed, in a distant place, and held a confession. Before their marriage, Jack Welch had been a suitor for her hand, and had been the favored of the two. To remove his rival and prosper in his place, Wright stole upon the other at his work, killed him, took his body to sea, and threw it overboard. Since that time the dead man had pursued him, and he was glad that the end of his days was come. But, though Tom Wright is no more, his victim's light comes yearly from the sea, above the spot where his body sank, floats to the scene of the murder on the shore, then flits to the house where the assassin lived and for years simulated the content that comes of wedded life. MOGG MEGONE

Hapless daughter of a renegade is Ruth Bonython. Her father is as unfair to his friends as to his enemies, but to neither of them so merciless as to Ruth. Although he knows that she loves Master Scammon—in spite of his desertion and would rather die than wed another, he has promised her to Mogg Megone, the chief who rules the Indians at the Saco mouth. He, blundering savage, fancies that he sees to the bottom of her grief, and one day, while urging his suit, he opens his blanket and shows the scalp of Scammon, to prove that he has avenged her. She looks in horror, but when he flings the bloody trophy at her feet she baptizes it with a forgiving tear. What villainy may this lead to? Ah, none for him, for Bonython now steps in and plies him with flattery and drink, gaining from the chief, at last, his signature—the bow totem—to a transfer of the land for which he is willing to sell his daughter. Ruth, maddened at her father's meanness and the Indian's brutality, rushes on the imbruted savage, grasps from his belt the knife that has slain her lover, cleaves his heart in twain, and flies into the wood, leaving Bonython stupid with amazement.

Father Rasles, in his chapel at Norridgewock, is affecting his Indian converts against the Puritans, who settled to the southward of him fifty years before. To him comes a woman with torn garments and frightened face. Her dead mother stood before her last night, she says, and looked at her reprovingly, for she had killed Mogg Megone. The priest starts back in wrath, for Mogg was a hopeful agent of the faith, and bids her go, for she can ask no pardon. Brooding within his chapel, then, he is startled by the sound of shot and hum of arrows. Harmon and Moulton are advancing with their men and crying, "Down with the beast of Rome! Death to the Babylonish dog!" Ruth, knowing not what this new misfortune may mean, runs from the church and disappears.

Some days later, old Baron Castine, going to Norridgewock to bury and revenge the dead, finds a woman seated on the earth and gazing over a field strewn with ashes and with human bones. He touches her. She is cold. There has been no life for days. It is Ruth.

THE LADY URSULA

In 1690 a stately house stood in Kittery, Maine, a strongly guarded place with moat and drawbridge (which was raised at night) and a moated grange adjacent where were cattle, sheep, and horses. Here, in lonely dignity, lived Lady Ursula, daughter of the lord of Grondale Abbey, across the water, whose distant grandeurs were in some sort reflected in this manor of the wilderness. Silver, mahogany, paintings, tapestries, waxed floors, and carven chests of linen represented wealth; prayers were said by a chaplain every morning and evening in the chapel, and, though the main hall would accommodate five hundred people, the lady usually sat at meat there with her thirty servants, her part of the table being raised two feet above theirs.

It was her happiness to believe that Captain Fowler, now absent in conflict with the French, would return and wed her according to his promise, but one day came a tattered messenger with bitter news of the captain's death. She made no talk of her grief, and, while her face was pale and step no longer light, she continued in the work that custom exacted from women of that time: help for the sick, alms for the poor, teaching for the ignorant, religion for the savage. Great was her joy, then, when a ship came from England bringing a letter from Captain Fowler himself, refuting the rumor of defeat and telling of his coming. Now the hall took on new life, reflecting the pleasure of its mistress; color came back to her cheek and sparkle to her eye, and she could only control her impatience by more active work and more aggressive charities. The day was near at hand for the arrival of her lover, when Ursula and her servants were set upon by Indians, while away from the protection of the manor, and slain. They were buried where they fell, and Captain Fowler found none to whom his love or sorrow could be told.

FATHER MOODY'S BLACK VEIL

In 1770 the Reverend Joseph Moody died at York, Maine, where he had long held the pastorate of a church, and where in his later years his face was never seen by friend or relative. At home, when any one was by, on the street, and in the pulpit his visage was concealed by a double fold of crape that was knotted above his forehead and fell to his chin, the lower edge of it being shaken by his breath. When first he presented himself to his congregation with features masked in black, great was the wonder and long the talk about it. Was he demented? His sermons were too logical for that. Had he been crossed in love? He could smile, though the smile was sad. Had he been scarred by accident or illness? If so, no physician knew of it.

After a time it was given out that his eyes were weakened by reading and writing at night, and the wonder ceased, though the veiled parson was less in demand for weddings, christenings, and social gatherings, and more besought for funerals than he had been. If asked to take off his crape he only replied, "We all wear veils of one kind or another, and the heaviest and darkest are those that hang about our hearts. This is but a material veil. Let it stay until the hour strikes when all faces shall be seen and all souls reveal their secrets."

Little by little the clergyman felt himself enforced to withdraw from the public gaze. There were rough people who were impertinent and timid people who turned out of their road to avoid him, so that he found his outdoor walks and meditations almost confined to the night, unless he chose the grave-yard for its seclusion or strolled on the beach and listened to the wallowing and grunting of the Black Boars—the rocks off shore that had laughed on the night when the York witch went up the chimney in a gale. But his life was long and kind and useful, and when at last the veiled head lay on the pillow it was never to rise from consciously, a fellow-clergyman came to soothe his dying moments and commend his soul to mercy.

To him, one evening, Father Moody said, "Brother, my hour is come and the veil of eternal darkness is falling over my eyes. Men have asked me why I wear this piece of crape about my face, as if it were not for them a reminder and a symbol, and I have borne the reason so long within me that only now have I resolved to tell it. Do you recall the finding of young Clark beside the river, years ago? He had been shot through the head. The man who killed him did so by accident, for he was a bosom friend; yet he could never bring himself to confess the fact, for he dreaded the blame of his townsmen, the anguish of the dead man's parents, the hate of his betrothed. It was believed that the killing was a murder, and that some roving Indian had done it. After years of conscience-darkened life, in which the face of his dead friend often arose accusingly before him, the unhappy wretch vowed that he would never again look his fellows openly in the face: he would pay a penalty and conceal his shame. Then it was that I put a veil between myself and the world."

Joseph Moody passed away and, as he wished, the veil still hid his face in the coffin, but the clergyman who had raised it for a moment to compose his features, found there a serenity and a beauty that were majestic.

THE HOME OF THUNDER

Some Indians believe that the Thunder Bird is the agent of storm; that the flashes of his eyes cause lightning and the flapping of his cloud-vast wings make thunder. Not so the Passamaquoddies, for they hold that Katahdin's spirit children are Thunders, and in this way an Indian found them: He had been seeking game along the Penobscot and for weeks had not met one of his fellow creatures. On a winter day he came on the print of a pair of snow-shoes; next morning the tracks appeared in another part of the forest, and so for many days he found them.

After a time it occurred to him to see where these tracks went to, and he followed them until they merged with others in a travelled road, ending at a precipice on the side of Katahdin (Great Mountain).

While lost in wonder that so many tracks should lead nowhere, he was roused by a footfall, and a maiden stepped from the precipice to the ledge beside him. Though he said nothing, being in awe of her stateliness and beauty, she replied in kind words to every unspoken thought and bade him go with her. He approached the rock with fear, but at a touch from the woman it became as mist, and they entered it together.

Presently they were in a great cave in the heart of Katahdin, where sat the spirit of the mountain, who welcomed them and asked the girl if her brothers had come. "I hear them coming," she replied. A blinding flash, a roar of thunder, and there stepped into the cave two men of giant size and gravely beautiful faces, hardened at the cheeks and brows to stone. "These," said the girl to the hunter, "are my brothers, the Thunder and the Lightning. My father sends them forth whenever there is wrong to redress, that those who love us may not be smitten. When you hear Thunder, know that they are shooting at our enemies."

At the end of that day the hunter returned to his home, and behold, he had been gone seven years. Another legend says that the stone-faced sons of the mountain adopted him, and that for seven years he was a roaming Thunder, but at the end of that time while a storm was raging he was allowed to fall, unharmed, into his own village.

THE PARTRIDGE WITCH

Two brothers, having hunted at the head of the Penobscot until their snow-shoes and moccasins gave out, looked at each other ruefully and cried, "Would that there was a woman to help us!" The younger brother went to the lodge that evening earlier than the elder, in order to prepare the supper, and great was his surprise on entering the wigwam to find the floor swept, a fire built, a pot boiling, and their clothing mended. Returning to the wood he watched the place from a covert until he saw a graceful girl enter the lodge and take up the tasks of housekeeping.

When he entered she was confused, but he treated her with respect, and allowed her to have her own way so far as possible, so that they became warm friends, sporting together like children when the work of the day was over. But one evening she said, "Your brother is coming. I fear him. Farewell." And she slipped into the wood. When the young man told his elder brother what had happened there—the elder having been detained for a few days in the pursuit of a deer—he declared that he would wish the woman to come back, and presently, without any summons, she returned, bringing a toboggan-load of garments and arms. The luck of the hunters improved, and they remained happily together until spring, when it was time to return with their furs.

They set off down the Penobscot in their canoe and rowed merrily along, but as they neared the home village the girl became uneasy, and presently "threw out her soul"—became clairvoyant—and said, "Let me land here. I find that your father would not like me, so do not speak to him about me." But the elder brother told of her when they reached home, whereon the father exclaimed, "I had feared this. That woman is a sister of the goblins. She wishes to destroy men."

At this the elder brother was afraid, lest she should cast a spell on him, and rowing up the river for a distance he came upon her as she was bathing and shot at her. The arrow seemed to strike, for there was a flutter of feathers and the woman flew away as a partridge. But the younger did not forget the good she had done and sought her in the wood, where for many days they played together as of old.

"I do not blame your father: it is an affair of old, this hate he bears me," she said. "He will choose a wife for you soon, but do not marry her, else all will come to an end for you." The man could not wed the witch, and he might not disobey his father, in spite of this adjuration; so when the old man said to him, "I have a wife for you, my son," he answered, "It is well."

They brought the bride to the village, and for four days the wedding-dance was held, with a feast that lasted four days more. Then said the young man, "Now comes the end," and lying down on a bear-skin he sighed a few times and his spirit ascended to the Ghosts' road—the milky way. The father shook his head, for he knew that this was the witch's work, and, liking the place no longer, he went away and the tribe was scattered.

THE MARRIAGE OF MOUNT KATAHDIN

An Indian girl gathering berries on the side of Mount Katahdin looked up at its peak, rosy in the afternoon light, and sighed, "I wish that I had a husband. If Katahdin were a man he might marry me." Her companions laughed at this quaint conceit, and, filled with confusion at being overheard, she climbed higher up the slope and was lost to sight. For three years her tribe lost sight of her; then she came back with a child in her arms a beautiful boy with brows of stone. The boy had wonderful power: he had only to point at a moose or a duck or a bear, and it fell dead, so that the tribe never wanted food. For he was the son of the Indian girl and the spirit of the mountain, who had commanded her not to reveal the boy's paternity. Through years she held silence on this point, holding in contempt, like other Indians, the prying inquiries of gossips and the teasing of young people, and knowing that Katahdin had designed the child for the founder of a mighty race, with the sinews of the very mountains in its frame, that should fill and rule the earth. Yet, one day, in anger at some slight, the mother spoke: "Fools! Wasps who sting the fingers that pick you from the water! Why do you torment me about what you might all see? Look at the boy's face—his brows: in them do you not see Katahdin? Now you have brought the curse upon yourselves, for you shall hunt your own venison from this time forth." Leading the child by the hand she turned toward the mountain and went out from their sight. And since then the Indians who could not hold their tongues, and who might otherwise have been great, have dwindled to a little people.

THE MOOSE OF MOUNT KINEO

Eastern traditions concerning Hiawatha differ in many respects from those of the West. In the East he is known as Glooskap, god of the Passamaquoddies, and his marks are left in many places in the maritime provinces and Maine. It was he who gave names to things, created men, filled them with life, and moved their wonder with storms. He lived on the rocky height of Blomidon, at the entrance to Minas Basin, Nova Scotia, and the agates to be found along its foot are jewels that he made for his grandmother's necklace, when he restored her youth. He threw up a ridge between Fort Cumberland and Parrsboro, Nova Scotia, that he might cross, dry shod, the lake made by the beavers when they dammed the strait at Blomidon, but he afterward killed the beavers, and breaking down their dam he let the lake flow into the sea, and went southward on a hunting tour. At Mount Desert he killed a moose, whose bones he flung to the ground at Bar Harbor, where they are still to be seen, turned to stone, while across the bay he threw the entrails, and they, too, are visible as rocks, dented with his arrow-points. Mount Kineo was anciently a cow moose of colossal size that he slew and turned into a height of land, and the Indians trace the outline of the creature in the uplift to this day. Little Kineo was a calf moose that he slew at the same time, and Kettle Mountain is his camp-caldron that he flung to the ground in the ardor of the chase.

THE OWL TREE

One day in October, 1827, Rev. Charles Sharply rode into Alfred, Maine, and held service in the meeting-house. After the sermon he announced that he was going to Waterborough to preach, and that on his circuit he had collected two hundred and seventy dollars to help build a church in that village. Would not his hearers add to that sum? They would and did, and that evening the parson rode away with over three hundred dollars in his saddlebags. He never appeared in Waterborough. Some of the country people gave tongue to their fear that the possession of the money had made him forget his sacred calling and that he had fled the State.

On the morning after his disappearance, however, Deacon Dickerman appeared in Alfred riding on a horse that was declared to be the minister's, until the tavern hostler affirmed that the minister's horse had a white star on forehead and breast, whereas this horse was all black. The deacon said that he found the horse grazing in his yard at daybreak, and that he would give it to whoever could prove it to be his property. Nobody appeared to demand it, and people soon forgot that it was not his. He extended his business at about that time and prospered; he became a rich man for a little place; though, as his wealth increased, he became morose and averse to company.

One day a rumor went around that a belated traveller had seen a misty thing under "the owl tree" at a turn of a road where owls were hooting, and that it took on a strange likeness to the missing clergyman. Dickerman paled when he heard this story, but he shook his head and muttered of the folly of listening to boy nonsense. Ten years had gone by-during that time the boys had avoided the owl tree after dark—when a clergyman of the neighborhood was hastily summoned to see Mr. Dickerman, who was said to be suffering from overwork. He found the deacon in his house alone, pacing the floor, his dress disordered, his cheek hectic.

"I have not long to live," said he, "nor would I live longer if I could. I am haunted day and night, and there is no peace, no rest for me on earth. They say that Sharply's spirit has appeared at the owl tree. Well, his body lies there. They accused me of taking his horse. It is true. A little black dye on his head and breast was all that was needed to deceive them. Pray for me, for I fear my soul is lost. I killed Sharply." The clergyman recoiled. "I killed him," the wretched man went on, "for the money that he had. The devil prospered me with it. In my will I leave two thousand dollars to his widow and five thousand dollars to the church he was collecting for. Will there be mercy for me there? I dare not think it. Go and pray for me." The clergyman hastened away, but was hardly outside the door when the report of a pistol brought him back. Dickerman lay dead on the floor. Sharply's body was exhumed from the shade of the owl tree, and the spot was never haunted after.

A CHESTNUT LOG

There is no doubt that farmer Lovel had read ancient history or he would not have been so ready in the emergency that befell him one time in the last century. He had settled among the New Hampshire hills near the site that is now occupied by the village of Washington and had a real good time there with bears and Indians. It was when he was splitting rails on Lovel Mountain—they named it for him afterward—that he found himself surrounded by six Indians, who told him that he was their prisoner. He agreed that they had the advantage over him and said that he would go quietly along if they would allow him to finish the big chestnut log that he was at work on. As he was a powerful fellow and was armed with an axe worth any two of their tomahawks, and as he would be pretty sure to have the life of at least one of them if they tried to drive him faster than he wanted to go, they consented. He said that he would be ready all the sooner if they would help him to pull the big log apart, and they agreed to help him. Driving a wedge into the long split he asked them to take hold, and when they had done this he knocked out the wedge with a single blow and the twelve hands were caught tight in the closing wood. Struggle as the savages might, they could not get free, and after calmly enjoying the situation for a few minutes he walked slowly from one to the other and split open the heads of all six. Then he went to work again splitting up more chestnuts.

THE WATCHER ON WHITE ISLAND

The isles of Shoals, a little archipelago of wind and wave-swept rocks that may be seen on clear days from the New Hampshire coast, have been the scene of some mishaps and some crimes. On Boone Island, where the Nottingham galley went down one hundred and fifty years ago, the survivors turned cannibals to escape starvation, while Haley's Island is peopled by shipwrecked Spanish ghosts that hail vessels and beg for passage back to their country. The pirate Teach, or Blackbeard, used to put in at these islands to hide his treasure, and one of his lieutenants spent some time on White Island with a beautiful girl whom he had abducted from her home in Scotland and who, in spite of his rough life, had learned to love him. It was while walking with her on this rock, forgetful of his trade and the crimes he had been stained with, that one of his men ran up to report a sail that was standing toward the islands. The pirate ship was quickly prepared for action, but before embarking, mindful of possible flight or captivity, the lieutenant made his mistress swear that she would guard the buried treasure if it should be till doomsday.

The ship he was hurrying to meet came smoothly on until the pirate craft was well in range, when ports flew open along the stranger's sides, guns were run out, and a heavy broadside splintered through the planks of the robber galley. It was a man-of-war, not a merchantman, that had run Blackbeard down. The war-ship closed and grappled with the corsair, but while the sailors were standing at the chains ready to leap aboard and complete the subjugation of the outlaws a mass of flame burst from the pirate ship, both vessels were hurled in fragments through the air, and a roar went for miles along the sea. Blackbeard's lieutenant had fired the magazine rather than submit to capture, and had blown the two ships into a common ruin. A few of both crews floated to the islands on planks, sore from burns and bruises, but none survived the cold and hunger of the winter. The pirate's mistress was among the first to die; still, true to her promise, she keeps her watch, and at night is dimly seen on a rocky point gazing toward the east, her tall figure enveloped in a cloak, her golden hair unbound upon her shoulders, her pale face still as marble.

CHOCORUA

This beautiful alp in the White Mountains commemorates in its name a prophet of the Pequawket tribe who, prior to undertaking a journey, had confided his son to a friendly settler, Cornelius Campbell, of Tamworth. The boy found some poison in the house that had been prepared for foxes, and, thinking it to be some delicacy, he drank of it and died. When Chocorua returned he could not be persuaded that his son had fallen victim to his own ignorance, but ascribed his death to the white man's treachery, and one day, when Campbell entered his cabin from the fields, he found there the corpses of his wife and children scalped and mangled.

He was not a man to lament at such a time: hate was stronger than sorrow. A fresh trail led from his door. Seizing his rifle he set forth in pursuit of the murderer. A mark in the dust, a bent grass blade, a torn leaf-these were guides enough, and following on through bush and swamp and wood they led him to this mountain, and up the slope he scrambled breathlessly. At the summit, statue-like, Chocorua stood. He saw the avenger coming, and knew himself unarmed, but he made no attempt to escape his doom. Drawing himself erect and stretching forth his hands he invoked anathema on his enemies in these words: "A curse upon you, white men! May the Great Spirit curse you when he speaks in the clouds, and his words are fire! Chocorua had a son and you killed him while the sky looked bright. Lightning blast your crops! Winds and fire destroy your dwellings! The Evil One breathe death upon your cattle! Your graves lie in the war-path of the Indian! Panthers howl and wolves fatten over your bones! Chocorua goes to the Great Spirit. His curse stays with the white man."

The report of Campbell's rifle echoed from the ledges and Chocorua leaped into the air, plunging to the rocks below. His mangled remains were afterward found and buried near the Tamworth path. The curse had its effect, for pestilence and storm devastated the surrounding country and the smaller settlements were abandoned. Campbell became a morose hermit, and was found dead in his bed two years afterward.

PASSACONAWAY'S RIDE TO HEAVEN

The personality of Passaconaway, the powerful chief and prophet, is involved in doubt, but there can be no misprision of his wisdom. By some historians he has been made one with St. Aspenquid, the earliest of native missionaries among the Indians, who, after his conversion by French Jesuits, travelled from Maine to the Pacific, preaching to sixty-six tribes, healing the sick and working miracles, returning to die at the age of ninety-four. He was buried on the top of Agamenticus, Maine, where his manes were pacified with offerings of three thousand slain animals, and where his tombstone stood for a century after, bearing the legend, "Present, useful; absent, wanted; living, desired; dying, lamented."

By others Passaconaway is regarded as a different person. The Child of the Bear—to English his name—was the chief of the Merrimacs and a convert of the apostle Eliot. Natives and colonists alike admired him for his eloquence, his bravery, and his virtue. Before his conversion he was a reputed wizard who sought by magic arts to repel the invasion of his woods and mountains by the white men, invoking the spirits of nature against them from the topmost peak of the Agiochooks, and his native followers declared that in pursuance of this intent he made water burn, rocks move, trees dance, and transformed himself into a mass of flame.

Such was his power over the forces of the earth that he could burn a tree in winter and from its ashes bring green leaves; he made dead wood blossom and a farmer's flail to bud, while a snake's skin he could cause to run. At the age of one hundred and twenty he retired from his tribe and lived in a lonely wigwam among the Pennacooks. One winter night the howling of wolves was heard, and a pack came dashing through the village harnessed by threes to a sledge of hickory saplings that bore a tall throne spread with furs. The wolves paused at Passaconaway's door. The old chief came forth, climbed upon the sledge, and was borne away with a triumphal apostrophe that sounded above the yelping and snarling of his train. Across Winnepesaukee's frozen surface they sped like the wind, and the belated hunter shrank aside as he saw the giant towering against the northern lights and heard his death-song echo from the cliffs. Through pathless woods, across ravines, the wolves sped on, with never slackened speed, into the mazes of the Agiochooks to that highest peak we now call Washington. Up its steep wilderness of snow the ride went furiously; the summit was neared, the sledge burst into flame, still there was no pause; the height was gained, the wolves went howling into darkness, but the car, wrapped in sheaves of fire, shot like a meteor toward the sky and was lost amid the stars of the winter night. So passed the Indian king to heaven.

THE BALL GAME BY THE SACO

Water-Goblins from the streams about Katahdin had left their birthplace and journeyed away to the Agiochooks, making their presence known to the Indians of that region by thefts and loss of life. When the manitou, Glooskap, learned that these goblins were eating human flesh and committing other outrages, he took on their own form, turning half his body into stone, and went in search of them. The wigwam had been pitched near the Home of the Water Fairies,—a name absurdly changed by the people of North Conway to Diana's Bath,—and on entering he was invited to take meat. The tail of a whale was cooked and offered to him, but after he had taken it upon his knees one of the goblins exclaimed, "That is too good for a beggar like you," and snatched it away. Glooskap had merely to wish the return of the dainty when it flew back into his platter. Then he took the whale's jaw, and snapped it like a reed; he filled his pipe and burned the tobacco to ashes in one inhalation; when his hosts closed the wigwam and smoked vigorously, intending to foul the air and stupefy him, he enjoyed it, while they grew sick; so they whispered to each other, "This is a mighty magician, and we must try his powers in another way."

A game of ball was proposed, and, adjourning to a sandy level at the bend of the Saco, they began to play, but Glooskap found that the ball was a hideous skull that rolled and snapped at him and would have torn his flesh had it not been immortal and immovable from his bones. He crushed it at a blow, and breaking off the bough of a tree he turned it by a word into a skull ten times larger than the other that flew after the wicked people as a wildcat leaps upon a rabbit. Then the god stamped on the sands and all the springs were opened in the mountains, so that the Saco came rising through the valley with a roar that made the nations tremble. The goblins were caught in the flood and swept into the sea, where Glooskap changed them into fish.

THE WHITE MOUNTAINS

From times of old these noble hills have been the scenes of supernatural visitations and mysterious occurrences. The tallest peak of the Agiochooks — as they were, in Indian naming — was the seat of God himself, and the encroachment there of the white man was little liked. Near Fabyan's was once a mound, since levelled by pick and spade, that was known as the Giant's Grave. Ethan Allen Crawford, a skilful hunter, daring explorer, and man of herculean frame, lived, died, and is buried here, and near the ancient hillock he built one of the first public houses in the mountains. It was burned. Another, and yet another hostelry was builded on the site, but they likewise were destroyed by fire. Then the enterprise was abandoned, for it was remembered that an Indian once mounted this grave, waved a torch from its top, and cried in a loud voice, "No pale-face shall take root on this spot. This has the Great Spirit whispered in my ear."

Governor Wentworth, while on a lonely tour through his province, found this cabin of Crawford's and passed a night there, tendering many compliments to the austere graces of the lady of the house and drinking himself into the favor of the husband, who proclaimed him the prince of good fellows. On leaving, the guest exacted of Crawford a visit to Wolfeborough, where he was to inquire for "Old Wentworth." This visit was undertaken soon after, and the sturdy frontiersman was dismayed at finding himself in the house of the royal governor; but his reception was hearty enough to put him at his ease, and when he returned to the mountains he carried in his pocket a deed of a thousand acres of forest about his little farm. The family that he founded became wealthy and increased, by many an acre, the measure of that royal grant.

Not far below this spot, in the wildest part of the Notch, shut in by walls of rock thousands of feet high, is the old Willey House, and this, too, was the scene of a tragedy, for in 1826 a storm loosened the soil on Mount Willey and an enormous landslide occurred. The people in the house rushed forth on hearing the approach of the slide and met death almost at their door. Had they remained within they would have been unharmed, for the avalanche was divided by a wedge of rock behind the house, and the little inn was saved. Seven people are known to have been killed, and it was rumored that there was another victim in a young man whose name was unknown and who was walking through the mountains to enjoy their beauty. The messenger who bore the tidings of the destruction of the family was barred from reaching North Conway by the flood in the Saco, so he stood at the brink of the foaming river and rang a peal on a trumpet. This blast echoing around the hills in the middle of the night roused several men from their beds to know its meaning. The dog belonging to the inn is said to have given first notice to people below the Notch that something was wrong, but his moaning and barking were misunderstood, and after running back and forth, as if to summon help, he disappeared. At the hour of the accident James Willey, of Conway, had a dream in which he saw his dead brother standing by him. He related the story of the catastrophe to the sleeping man and said that when "the world's last knell" sounded they were going for safety to the foot of the steep mountain, for the Saco had risen twenty-four feet in seven hours and threatened to ingulf them in front.

Another spot of interest in the Notch is Nancy's Brook. It was at the point where this stream comes foaming from Mount Nancy into the great ravine that the girl whose name is given to it was found frozen to death in a shroud of snow in the fall of 1788. She had set out alone from Jefferson in search of a young farmer who was to have married her, and walked thirty miles through trackless snow between sunset and dawn. Then her strength gave out and she sank beside the road never to rise again. Her recreant lover went mad with remorse when he learned the manner of her death and did not long survive her, and men who have traversed the savage passes of the Notch on chill nights in October have fancied that they heard, above the clash of the stream and whispering of the woods, long, shuddering groans mingled with despairing cries and gibbering laughter.

The birth of Peabody River came about from a cataclysm of less violent nature than some of the avalanches that have so scarred the mountains. In White's "History of New England," Mr. Peabody, for whom the stream is named, is reported as having taken shelter in an Indian cabin on the heights where the river has its source. During the night a loud roaring waked the occupants of the hut and they sprang forth, barely in time to save their lives; for, hardly had they gained the open ground before a cavern burst open in the hill and a flood of water gushed out, sweeping away the shelter and cutting a broad swath through the forest.

Although the Pilot Mountains are supposed to have taken their name from the fact that they served as landmarks to hunters who were seeking the Connecticut River from the Lancaster district, an old story is still told of one Willard, who was lost amid the defiles of this range, and nearly perished with hunger. While lying exhausted on the mountainside his dog would leave him every now and then and return after a couple of hours. Though

Willard was half dead, he determined to use his last strength in following the animal, and as a result was led by a short cut to his own camp, where provisions were plenty, and where the intelligent creature had been going for food. The dog was christened Pilot, in honor of this service, and the whole range is thought by many to be named in his honor.

Waternomee Falls, on Hurricane Creek, at Warren, are bordered with rich moss where fairies used to dance and sing in the moonlight. These sprites were the reputed children of Indians that had been stolen from their wigwams and given to eat of fairy bread, that dwarfed and changed them in a moment. Barring their kidnapping practices the elves were an innocent and joyous people, and they sought more distant hiding-places in the wilderness when the stern churchmen and cruel rangers penetrated their sylvan precincts.

An old barrack story has it that Lieutenant Chamberlain, who fought under Lovewell, was pursued along the base of Melvin Peak by Indians and was almost in their grasp when he reached Ossipee Falls. It seemed as if there were no alternative between death by the tomahawk and death by a fall to the rocks below, for the chasm here is eighteen feet wide; but without stopping to reckon chances he put his strength into a running jump, and to the amazement of those in pursuit and perhaps to his own surprise he cleared the gap and escaped into the woods. The foremost of the Indians attempted the leap, but plunged to his death in the ravine.

The Eagle Range was said to be the abode, two hundred years ago, of a man of strange and venerable appearance, whom the Indians regarded with superstitious awe and never tried to molest. He slept in a cave on the south slope and ranged the forest in search of game, muttering and gesturing to himself. He is thought to be identified with Thomas Crager, whose wife had been hanged in Salem as a witch, and whose only child had been stolen by Indians. After a long, vain search for the little one he gave way to a bitter moroseness, and avoided the habitations of civilized man and savages alike. It is a satisfaction to know that before he died he found his daughter, though she was the squaw of an Indian hunter and was living with his tribe on the shore of the St. Lawrence.

THE VISION ON MOUNT ADAMS

There are many traditions connected with Mount Adams that have faded out of memory. Old people remember that in their childhood there was talk of the discovery of a magic stone; of an Indian's skeleton that appeared in a speaking storm; of a fortune-teller that set off on a midnight quest, far up among the crags and eyries. In October, 1765, a detachment of nine of Rogers's Rangers began the return from a Canadian foray, bearing with them plate, candlesticks, and a silver statue that they had rifled from the Church of St. Francis. An Indian who had undertaken to guide the party through the Notch proved faithless, and led them among labyrinthine gorges to the head of Israel's River, where he disappeared, after poisoning one of the troopers with a rattlesnake's fang. Losing all reckoning, the Rangers tramped hither and thither among the snowy hills and sank down, one by one, to die in the wilderness, a sole survivor reaching a settlement after many days, with his knapsack filled with human flesh.

In 1816 the candlesticks were recovered near Lake Memphremagog, but the statue has never been laid hold upon. The spirits of the famished men were wont, for many winters, to cry in the woods, and once a hunter, camped on the side of Mount Adams, was awakened at midnight by the notes of an organ. The mists were rolling off, and he found that he had gone to sleep near a mighty church of stone that shone in soft light. The doors were flung back, showing a tribe of Indians kneeling within. Candles sparkled on the altar, shooting their rays through clouds of incense, and the rocks shook with thunder-gusts of music. Suddenly church, lights, worshippers vanished, and from the mists came forth a line of uncouth forms, marching in silence. As they started to descend the mountain a silver image, floating in the air, spread a pair of gleaming pinions and took flight, disappearing in the chaos of battlemented rocks above.

THE GREAT CARBUNCLE

High on the eastern face of Mount Monroe shone the Great Carbuncle, its flash scintillating for miles by day, its dusky crimson glowing among the ledges at night. The red men said that it hung in the air, and that the soul of an Indian—killed, that he might guard the spot—made approach perilous to men of all complexions and purposes. As late as Ethan Crawford's time one search band took a "good man" to lay the watcher, when they strove to scale the height, but they returned "sorely bruised, treasureless, and not even saw that wonderful sight." The value of the stone tempted many, but those who sought it had to toil through a dense forest, and on arriving at the mountain found its glories eclipsed by intervening abutments, nor could they get near it. Rocks covered with crystals, at first thought to be diamonds, were readily despoiled of their treasure, but the Great Carbuncle burned on, two thousand feet above them, at the head of the awful chasm of Oakes Gulf, and baffled seekers likened it to the glare of an evil eye.

There was one who had grown old in searching for this gem, often scrambling over the range in wind and snow and cloud, and at last he reached a precipitous spot he had never attained before. Great was his joy, for the Carbuncle was within his reach, blazing into his eyes in the noon sunlight as if it held, crystallized in its depths, the brightness of all the wine that had ever gladdened the tired hearts of men. There were rivals in the search, and on reaching the plateau they looked up and saw him kneeling on a narrow ledge with arms extended as in rapture. They called to him. He answered not. He was dead—dead of joy and triumph. While they looked a portion of the crag above him fell away and rolled from rock to rock, marking its course with flashes of bloody fire, until it reached the Lake of the Clouds, and the waters of that tarn drowned its glory. Yet those waters are not always black, and sometimes the hooked crest of Mount Monroe is outlined against the night sky in a ruddy glow.

SKINNER'S CAVE

The abhorrence to paying taxes and duties—or any other levy from which an immediate and personal good is not promised—is too deeply rooted in human nature to be affected by statutes, and whenever it is possible to buy commodities that have escaped the observation of the revenue officers many are tempted to do so for the mere pleasure of defying the law. In the early part of this century the northern farmers and their wives were, in a way, providing themselves with laces, silver-ware, brandy, and other protected and dreadful articles, on which it was evident that somebody had forgotten to pay duty. The customs authorities on the American side of the border were long puzzled by the irruption of these forbidden things, but suspicion ultimately fell on a fellow of gigantic size, named Skinner.

It was believed that this outlaw carried on the crime of free trade after sunset, hiding his merchandise by day on the islands of Lake Memphremagog. This delightful sheet of water lies half in Canada and half in Vermont—agreeably to the purpose of such as he. Province Island is still believed to contain buried treasure, but the rock that contains Skinner's Cave was the smuggler's usual haunt, and when pursued he rowed to this spot and effected a disappearance, because he entered the cave on the northwest side, where it was masked by shrubbery. One night the officers landed on this island after he had gone into hiding, and after diligent search discovered his boat drawn up in a covert. They pushed it into the lake, where the winds sent it adrift, and, his communication with the shore thus cut off, the outlaw perished miserably of hunger. His skeleton was found in the cavern some years later.

YET THEY CALL IT LOVER'S LEAP

In the lower part of the township of Cavendish, Vermont, the Black River seeks a lower level through a gorge in the foot-hills of the Green Mountains. The scenery here is romantic and impressive, for the river makes its way along the ravine in a series of falls and rapids that are overhung by trees and ledges, while the geologist finds something worth looking at in the caves and pot-holes that indicate an older level of the river. At a turn in the ravine rises the sheer precipice of Lover's Leap. It is a vertical descent of about eighty feet, the water swirling at its foot in a black and angry maelstrom. It is a spot whence lovers might easily step into eternity, were they so disposed, and the name fits delightfully into the wild and somber scene; but ask any good villager thereabout to relate the legend of the place and he will tell you this:

About forty years ago a couple of young farmers went to the Leap—which then had no name—to pry out some blocks of the schistose rock for a foundation wall. They found a good exposure of the rock beneath the turf and began to quarry it. In the earnestness of the work one of the men forgot that he was standing on the verge of a precipice, and through a slip of his crowbar he lost his balance and went reeling into the gulf. His horrified companion crept to the edge, expecting to see his mangled corpse tossing in the whirlpool, but, to his amazement, the unfortunate was crawling up the face of a huge table of stone that had fallen from the opposite wall and lay canted against it.

"Hello!" shouted the man overhead. "Are you hurt much?"

The victim of the accident slowly got upon his feet, felt cautiously of his legs and ribs, and began to search through his pockets, his face betraying an anxiety that grew deeper and deeper as the search went on. In due time the answer came back, deliberate, sad, and nasal, but distinct above the roar of the torrent: "Waal, I ain't hurt much, but I'll be durned if I haven't lost my jack-knife!"

And he was pulled out of the gorge without it.

SALEM AND OTHER WITCHCRAFT

The extraordinary delusion recorded as Salem witchcraft was but a reflection of a kindred insanity in the Old World that was not extirpated until its victims had been counted by thousands. That human beings should be accused of leaguing themselves with Satan to plague their fellows and overthrow the powers of righteousness is remarkable, but that they should admit their guilt is incomprehensible, albeit the history of every popular delusion shows that weak minds are so affected as to lose control of themselves and that a whimsey can be as epidemic as small-pox.

Such was the case in 1692 when the witchcraft madness, which might have been stayed by a seasonable spanking, broke out in Danvers, Massachusetts, the first victim being a wild Irishwoman, named Glover, and speedily involved the neighboring community of Salem. The mischiefs done by witches were usually trifling, and it never occurred to their prosecutors that there was an inconsistency between their pretended powers and their feeble deeds, or that it was strange that those who might live in regal luxury should be so wretchedly poor. Aches and pains, blight of crops, disease of cattle, were charged to them; children complained of being pricked with thorns and pins (the pins are still preserved in Salem), and if hysterical girls spoke the name of any feeble old woman, while in flighty talk, they virtually sentenced her to die. The word of a child of eleven years sufficed to hang, burn, or drown a witch.

Giles Corey, a blameless man of eighty, was condemned to the mediaeval *peine forte et dure*, his body being crushed beneath a load of rocks and timbers. He refused to plead in court, and when the beams were laid upon him he only cried, "More weight!" The shade of the unhappy victim haunted the scene of his execution for years, and always came to warn the people of calamities. A child of five and a dog were also hanged after formal condemnation. Gallows Hill, near Salem, witnessed many sad tragedies, and the old elm that stood on Boston Common until 1876 was said to have served as a gallows for witches and Quakers. The accuser of one day was the prisoner of the next, and not even the clergy were safe.

A few escapes were made, like that of a blue-eyed maid of Wenham, whose lover aided her to break the wooden jail and carried her safely beyond the Merrimac, finding a home for her among the Quakers; and that of Miss

Wheeler, of Salem, who had fallen under suspicion, and whose brothers hurried her into a boat, rowed around Cape Ann, and safely bestowed her in "the witch house" at Pigeon Cove. Many, however, fled to other towns rather than run the risk of accusation, which commonly meant death.

When the wife of Philip English was arrested he, too, asked to share her fate, and both were, through friendly intercession, removed to Boston, where they were allowed to have their liberty by day on condition that they would go to jail every night. Just before they were to be taken back to Salem for trial they went to church and heard the Rev. Joshua Moody preach from the text, "If they persecute you in one city, flee unto another." The good clergyman not only preached goodness, but practised it, and that night the door of their prison was opened. Furnished with an introduction from Governor Phipps to Governor Fletcher, of New York, they made their way to that settlement, and remained there in safe and courteous keeping until the people of Salem had regained their senses, when they returned. Mrs. English died, soon after, from the effects of cruelty and anxiety, and although Mr. Moody was generally commended for his substitution of sense and justice for law, there were bigots who persecuted him so constantly that he removed to Plymouth.

According to the belief of the time a witch or wizard compacted with Satan for the gift of supernatural power, and in return was to give up his soul to the evil one after his life was over. The deed was signed in blood of the witch and horrible ceremonies confirmed the compact. Satan then gave his ally a familiar in the form of a dog, ape, cat, or other animal, usually small and black, and sometimes an undisguised imp. To suckle these "familiars" with the blood of a witch was forbidden in English law, which ranked it as a felony; but they were thus nourished in secret, and by their aid the witch might raise storms, blight crops, abort births, lame cattle, topple over houses, and cause pains, convulsions, and illness. If she desired to hurt a person she made a clay or waxen image in his likeness, and the harms and indignities wreaked on the puppet would be suffered by the one bewitched, a knife or needle thrust in the waxen body being felt acutely by the living one, no matter how far distant he might be. By placing this image in running water, hot sunshine, or near a fire, the living flesh would waste as this melted or dissolved, and the person thus wrought upon would die. This belief is still current among negroes affected by the voodoo superstitions of the South. The witch, too, had the power of riding winds, usually with a broomstick for a conveyance, after she had smeared the broom or herself with magic ointment, and the flocking of the unhallowed to their sabbaths in snaky bogs or on lonely mountain tops has been described minutely by those who claim to have seen the sight. Sometimes they cackled and gibbered through the night before the houses of the clergy, and it was only at Christmas that their power failed them. The meetings were devoted to wild and obscene orgies, and the intercourse of fiends and witches begot a progeny of toads and snakes.

Naturally the Indians were accused, for they recognized the existence of both good and evil spirits, their medicine-men cured by incantations in the belief that devils were thus driven out of their patients, and in the early history of the country the red man was credited by white settlers with powers hardly inferior to those of the oriental and European magicians of the middle ages. Cotton Mather detected a relation between Satan and the Indians, and he declares that certain of the Algonquins were trained from boyhood as powahs, powwows, or wizards, acquiring powers of second sight and communion with gods and spirits through abstinence from food and sleep and the observance of rites. Their severe discipline made them victims of nervous excitement and the responsibilities of conjuration had on their minds an effect similar to that produced by gases from the rift in Delphos on the Apollonian oracles, their manifestations of insanity or frenzy passing for deific or infernal possession. When John Gibb, a Scotchman, who had gone mad through religious excitement, was shipped to this country by his tired fellow-countrymen, the Indians hailed him as a more powerful wizard than any of their number, and he died in 1720, admired and feared by them because of the familiarity with spirits out of Hobbomocko (hell) that his ravings and antics were supposed to indicate. Two Indian servants of the Reverend Mr. Purvis, of Salem, having tried by a spell to discover a witch, were executed as witches themselves. The savages, who took Salem witchcraft at its worth, were astonished at its deadly effect, and the English may have lost some influence over the natives in consequence of this madness. "The Great Spirit sends no witches to the French," they said. Barrow Hill, near Amesbury, was said to be the meeting-place for Indian powwows and witches, and at late hours of the night the light of fires gleamed from its top, while shadowy forms glanced athwart it. Old men say that the lights are still there in winter, though modern doubters declare that they were the aurora borealis.

But the belief in witches did not die even when the Salem people came to their senses. In the Merrimac valley the devil found converts for many years after: Goody Mose, of Rocks village, who tumbled down-stairs when a big beetle was killed at an evening party, some miles away, after it had been bumping into the faces of the company; Goody Whitcher, of Ameshury, whose loom kept banging day and night after she was dead; Goody Sloper, of West Newbury, who went home lame directly that a man had struck his axe into the beam of a house that she had bewitched, but who recovered her strength and established an improved reputation when, in 1794, she swam out to a capsized boat and rescued two of the people who were in peril; Goodman Nichols, of Rocks village, who "spelled" a neighbor's son, compelling him to run up one end of the house, along the ridge, and down the other end, "troubling the family extremely by his strange proceedings;" Susie Martin, also of Rocks, who was hanged in spite of her devotions in jail, though the rope danced so that it could not be tied, but a crow overhead called for a withe and the law was executed with that; and Goody Morse, of Market and High Streets, Newburyport, whose baskets and pots danced through her house continually and who was seen "flying about the sun as if she had been cut in twain, or as if the devil did hide the lower part of her." The hill below Easton, Pennsylvania, called Hexenkopf (Witch's head), was described by German settlers as a place of nightly gathering for weird women, who whirled about its top in "linked dances" and sang in deep tones mingled with awful laughter. After one of these women, in Williams township, had been punished for enchanting a twenty-dollar horse, their sabbaths were held more quietly. Mom Rinkle, whose "rock" is pointed out beside the Wissahickon, in Philadelphia, "drank dew from acorn-cups and had the evil eye." Juan Perea, of San Mateo, New Mexico, would fly with his chums to meetings in the mountains in the shape of a fire-ball. During these sallies he left his own eyes at home and wore those of some brute animal. It was because his dog ate his eyes when he had carelessly put them on a table that he had always afterward to wear those of a cat. Within the present century an old woman who lived in a hut on the Palisades of the Hudson was held to be responsible for local storms and accidents. As late as 1889 two Zuni Indians were hanged on the wall of an old Spanish church near their pueblo in Arizona on a charge of having blown away the rainclouds in a time of drouth. It was held that there was something uncanny in the event that gave the name of Gallows Hill to an eminence near Falls Village, Connecticut, for a strange black man was found hanging, dead, to a tree near its top one morning.

Moll Pitcher, a successful sorcerer and fortune-teller of old Lynn, has figured in obsolete poems, plays, and romances. She lived in a cottage at the foot of High Rock, where she was consulted, not merely by people of respectability, but by those who had knavish schemes to prosecute and who wanted to learn in advance the outcome of their designs. Many a ship was deserted at the hour of sailing because she boded evil of the voyage. She was of medium height, big-headed, tangle-haired, long-nosed, and had a searching black eye. The sticks that she carried were cut from a hazel that hung athwart a brook where an unwedded mother had drowned her child. A girl who went to her for news of her lover lost her reason when the witch, moved by a malignant impulse, described his death in a fiercely dramatic manner. One day the missing ship came bowling into port, and the shock of joy that the girl experienced when the sailor clasped her in his arms restored her erring senses. When Moll Pitcher died she was attended by the little daughter of the woman she had so afflicted.

John, or Edward, Dimond, grandfather of Moll Pitcher, was a benevolent wizard. When vessels were trying to enter the port of Marblehead in a heavy gale or at night, their crews were startled to hear a trumpet voice pealing from the skies, plainly audible above the howling and hissing of any tempest, telling them how to lay their course so as to reach smooth water. This was the voice of Dimond, speaking from his station, miles away in the village cemetery. He always repaired to this place in troublous weather and shouted orders to the ships that were made visible to him by mystic power as he strode to and fro among the graves. When thieves came to him for advice he charmed them and made them take back their plunder or caused them to tramp helplessly about the streets bearing heavy burdens.

"Old Mammy Redd, of Marblehead, Sweet milk could turn to mould in churn."

Being a witch, and a notorious one, she could likewise curdle the milk as it came from the cow, and afterward transform it into blue wool. She had the evil eye, and, if she willed, her glance or touch could blight like palsy. It only needed that she should wish a bloody cleaver to be found in a cradle to cause the little occupant to die, while the whole town ascribed to her the annoyances of daily housework and business. Her unpleasant celebrity led to her death at the hands of her fellow-citizens who had been "worried" by no end of queer happenings: ships had appeared just before they were wrecked and had vanished while people looked at them; men were seen walking on the water after they had been comfortably buried; the wind was heard to name the sailors doomed never to return; footsteps and voices were heard in the streets before the great were to die; one man was chased by a corpse in its coffin; another was pursued by the devil in a carriage drawn by four white horses; a young woman who had just received a present of some fine fish from her lover was amazed to see him melt into the air, and was heart-broken when she learned next morning that he had died at sea. So far away as Amesbury the devil's power was shown by the appearance of a man who walked the roads carrying his head under his arm, and by the freak of a windmill that the miller always used to shut up at sundown but that started by itself at midnight. Evidently it was high time to be rid of Mammy Redd.

Margaret Wesson, "old Meg," lived in Gloucester until she came to her death by a shot fired at the siege of Louisburg, five hundred miles away, in 1745. Two soldiers of Gloucester, while before the walls of the French town, were annoyed by a crow, that flew over and around them, cawing harshly and disregarding stones and shot, until it occurred to them that the bird could be no other than old Meg in another form, and, as silver bullets are an esteemed antidote for the evils of witchcraft, they cut two silver buttons from their uniforms and fired them at the crow. At the first shot its leg was broken; at the second, it fell dead. On returning to Gloucester they learned that old Meg had fallen and broken her leg at the moment when the crow was fired on, and that she died quickly after. An examination of her body was made, and the identical buttons were extracted from her flesh that had been shot into the crow at Louisburg.

As a citizen of New Haven was riding home—this was at the time of the goings on at Salem—he saw shapes of women near his horse's head, whispering earnestly together and keeping time with the trot of his animal without effort of their own. "In the name of God, tell me who you are," cried the traveller, and at the name of God they vanished. Next day the man's orchard was shaken by viewless hands and the fruit thrown down. Hogs ran about the neighborhood on their hind legs; children cried that somebody was sticking pins into them; one man would roll across the floor as if pushed, and he had to be watched lest he should go into the fire; when housewives made their bread they found it as full of hair as food in a city boarding-house; when they made soft soap it ran from the kettle and over the floor like lava; stones fell down chimneys and smashed crockery. One of the farmers cut off an ear from a pig that was walking on its hind legs, and an eccentric old body of the neighborhood appeared presently with one of her ears in a muffle, thus satisfying that community that she had caused the troubles. When a woman was making potash it began to leap about, and a rifle was fired into the pot, causing a sudden calm. In the morning the witch was found dead on her floor. Yet killing only made her worse, for she moved to a deserted house near her own, and there kept a mad revel every night; fiddles were heard, lights flashed, stones were thrown, and yells gave people at a distance a series of cold shivers; but the populace tried the effect of tearing down the house, and quiet was brought to the town.

In the early days of this century a skinny old woman known as Aunt Woodward lived by herself in a log cabin at Minot Corner, Maine, enjoying the awe of the people in that secluded burg. They moved around but little at night, on her account, and one poor girl was in mortal fear lest by mysterious arts she should be changed, between two days, into a white horse. One citizen kept her away from his house by nailing a horseshoe to his door, while another took the force out of her spells by keeping a branch of "round wood" at his threshold. At night she haunted a big, square house where the ghost of a murdered infant was often heard to cry, and by day she laid charms on her neighbors' provisions and utensils, and turned their cream to buttermilk. "Uncle" Blaisdell hurried into the settlement to tell the farmers that Aunt Woodward had climbed into his sled in the middle of the road, and that his four yoke of oxen could not stir it an inch, but that after she had leaped down one yoke of cattle drew the load of wood without an effort. Yet she died in her bed.

THE GLOUCESTER LEAGUERS

Strange things had been reported in Gloucester. On the eve of King Philip's War the march of men was heard in its streets and an Indian bow and scalp were seen on the face of the moon, while the boom of cannon and roll of drums were heard at Malden and the windows of Plymouth rattled to the passage of unseen horsemen. But the strangest thing was the arrival on Cape Ann of a force of French and Indians that never could be caught, killed, or crippled, though two regiments were hurried into Gloucester and battled with them for a fortnight. Thus, the rumor went around that these were not an enemy of flesh and blood, but devils who hoped to work a moral perversion of the colony. From 1692, when they appeared, until Salem witchcraft was at an end, Cape Ann was under military and spiritual guard against "the spectre leaguers."

Another version of the episode, based on sworn evidence, has it that Ebenezer Babson, returning late on a summer night, saw two men run from his door and vanish in a field. His family denied that visitors had called, so he gave chase, for he believed the men to have a mischievous intention. As he left the threshold they sprang from behind a log, one saying to the other, "The master of the house is now come, else we might have taken the house," and again they disappeared in a swamp. Babson woke the guard, and on entering the quarters of the garrison the sound of many feet was heard without, but when the doors were flung open only the two men were visible and they were retreating. Next evening the yeoman was chased by these elusive gentry, who were believed to be scouts of the enemy, for they wore white breeches and waistcoats and carried bright guns.

For several nights they appeared, and on the 4th of July half a dozen of them were seen so plainly that the soldiers made a sally, Babson bringing three of "ye unaccountable troublers" to the ground with a single shot, and getting a response in kind, for a bullet hissed by his ear and buried itself in a tree. When the company approached the place where lay the victims of that remarkable shot, behold, they arose and scampered away as blithely as if naught had happened to them. One of the trio was cornered and shot anew, but when they would pick him up he melted into air. There was fierce jabbering in an unknown tongue, through all the swamp, and by the time the garrison had returned the fellows were skulking in the shrubbery again.

Richard Dolliver afterward came on eleven of them engaged in incantations and scattered them with a gunshot, but they would not down. They lurked about the cape until terror fell on all the people, remaining for "the best part of a month together," so it was deemed that "Satan had set ambushments against the good people of Gloucester, with demons in the shape of armed Indians and Frenchmen."

Stones were thrown, barns were beaten with clubs, the marching of unseen hosts was heard after dark, the mockers grew so bold that they ventured close to the redoubtable Babson, gazed scornfully down the barrel of his gun, and laid a charm on the weapon, so that, no matter how often he snapped it at them, it flashed in the pan. Neighboring garrisons were summoned, but all battling with goblins was fruitless. One night a dark and hostile throng emerged from the wood and moved toward the blockhouse, where twenty musketeers were keeping guard. "If you be ghosts or devils I will foil you," cried the captain, and tearing a silver button from his doublet he rammed it into his gun and fired on the advancing host. Even as the smoke of his musket was blown on the wind, so did the beleaguering army vanish, the silver bullet proving that they were not of human kind. The night was wearing on when a cry went out that the devils were coming again. Arms were laid aside this time, and the watchers sank to their knees in prayer. Directly that the name of God was uttered the marching ceased and heaven rang with the howls of the angry fiends. Never again were leaguers seen in Gloucester.

SATAN AND HIS BURIAL-PLACE

Satan appears to have troubled the early settlers in America almost as grievously as he did the German students. He came in many shapes to many people, and sometimes he met his match. Did he not try to stop old Peter Stuyvesant from rowing through Hell Gate one moonlight night, and did not that tough old soldier put something at his shoulder that Satan thought must be his wooden leg? But it wasn't a leg: it was a gun, loaded with a silver bullet that had been charged home with prayer. Peter fired and the missile whistled off to Ward's Island, where three boys found it afterward and swapped it for double handfuls of doughnuts and bulls' eyes. Incidentally it passed between the devil's ribs and the fiend exploded with a yell and a smell, the latter of sulphur, to Peter's blended satisfaction and alarm. And did not the same spirit of evil plague the old women of Massachusetts Bay and craze the French and Spaniards in the South? At Hog Rock, west of Milford, Connecticut, he broke up a pleasant diversion:

"Once four young men upon ye rock

Sate down at chuffle board to play

When ye Deuill appearde in shape of a hogg

And frightend ym so they scampered away

And left Old Nick to finish ye play."

One of the first buildings to be put up in Ipswich, Massachusetts, was a church built on a ledge above the river, and in that church Satan tried to conceal himself for purposes of mischief. For this act he was hurled from the steeple-top by some unseen instrument of righteousness with such force that his hoofmark was stamped into a solid stone near by. This did not deter him from mounting to the ridge-pole and assuming a defiant air, with folded arms, when Whitefield began to preach, but when that clergyman's tremendous voice was loosed below him he bounced into the air in terror and disappeared.

The Shakers report that in the waning of the eighteenth century they chased the evil one through the coverts of Mount Sinai, Massachusetts, and just before dawn of a summer morning they caught and killed and buried him. Shakers are spiritualists, and they believe their numbers to have been augmented by distinguished dead, among whom they already number Washington, Lafayette, Napoleon, Tamerlane, and Pocahontas. The two first named of these posthumous communists are still seen by members of the faith who pass Satan's grave at night, for they sit astride of white horses and watch the burial spot, lest the enemy of man arise and begin anew his career of trouble. Some members of the brotherhood say that this legend typifies a burial of evil tendencies in the hearts of those who hunted the fiend, but it has passed down among others as a circumstance. The Shakers have many mystic records, transmitted verbally to the present disciples of "Mother Ann," but seldom told to scoffers "in the world," as those are called who live without their pure and peaceful communes. Among these records is that of the appearance of John the Baptist in the meeting-house at Mount Lebanon, New York, one Sunday, clothed in light and leading the sacred dance of the worshippers, by which they signify the shaking out of all carnal things from the heart.

PETER RUGG, THE MISSING MAN

The idea of long wandering as a penalty, symbolized in "The Wandering Jew," "The Flying Dutchman," and the character of Kundry, in "Parsifal," has application in the legend of Peter Rugg. This strange man, who lived in Middle Street, Boston, with his wife and daughter, was esteemed, as a person of probity and good manners except in his swearing fits, for he was subject to outbursts of passion, when he would kick his way through doors instead of opening them, bite tenpenny nails in two, and curse his wig off In the autumn of 1770 he visited Concord, with his little girl, and on the way home was overtaken by a violent storm. He took shelter with a friend at Menotomy, who urged him to stay all night, for the rain was falling heavier every moment; but Rugg would not be stayed, and seeing that there was no hope of a dry journey back to town he roared a fearful oath and cried, "Let the storm increase. I will see home to-night in spite of it, or may I never see home!" With that he tossed the child into the open chaise, leaped in after her, lashed his horse, and was off.

Several nights afterward, while Rugg's neighbors were out with lanterns trying to discover the cause of a heavy jarring that had begun to disturb them in bad weather, the excitable gentleman, who had not been seen since his Concord visit, came whirling along the pavement in his carriage, his daughter beside him, his black horse plunging on in spite of his efforts to stop him. The lanterns that for a moment twinkled in Peter's face showed him as a wet and weary man, with eyes turned up longingly at the windows where his wife awaited him; then he was gone, and the ground trembled as with an earthquake, while the rain fell more heavily.

Mrs. Rugg died within a twelvemonth, and Peter never reached home, but from all parts of New England came stories of a man and child driving rapidly along the highways, never stopping except to inquire the way to Boston. Half of the time the man would be headed in a direction opposite to the one he seemed to want to follow, and when set right would cry that he was being deceived, and was sometimes heard to mutter, "No home to-night." In Hartford, Providence, Newburyport, and among the New Hampshire hills the anxious face of the man became known, and he was referred to as "the stormbreeder," for so surely as he passed there would be rain, wind, lightning, thunder, and darkness within the hour.

Some years ago a man in a Connecticut town stopped this hurrying traveller, who said, in reply to a question, "I have lost the road to Boston. My name is Peter Rugg." Then Rugg's disappearance half a century before was cited by those who had long memories, and people began to look askant at Peter and gave him generous road room when they met him. The toll-taker on Charlestown bridge declared that he had been annoyed and alarmed by a prodigious tramping of hoofs and rattling of wheels that seemed to pass toward Boston before his very face, yet he could see nothing. He took courage one night to plant himself in the middle of the bridge with a three-legged stool, and when the sound approached he dimly saw a large black horse driven by a weary looking man with a child beside him. The stool was flung at the horse's head, but passed through the animal as through smoke and skipped across the floor of the bridge. Thus much the toll-collector said, but when asked if Rugg had appeared again he made no reply.

THE LOSS OF WEETAMOO

Winnepurkit, sagamore of the coast settlements between Nahant and Cape Ann, had married Weetamoo, daughter of Passaconaway, king of the Pennacooks, and had taken her to his home. Their honeymoon was happy, but old ties are strong, and after a little time the bride felt a longing to see her people again. When she made known this wish the husband not only consented to her visit, but gave her a guard of his most trusty hunters who saw her safe in her father's lodge (near the site of Concord, New Hampshire), and returned directly. Presently came a messenger from Passaconaway, informing his son-in-law that Weetamoo had finished her visit and wished again to be with her husband, to whom he looked for an escort to guide her through the wilderness. Winnepurkit felt that his dignity as a chief was slighted by this last request, and he replied that as he had supplied her with a guard for the outward journey it was her father's place to send her back, "for it stood not with Winnepurkit's reputation either to make himself or his men so servile as to fetch her again."

Passaconaway returned a sharp answer that irritated Winnepurkit still more, and he was told by the young sagamore that he might send his daughter or keep her, for she would never be sent for. In this unhappy strife for precedent, which has been repeated on later occasions by princes and society persons, the young wife seemed to be fated as an unwilling sacrifice; but summoning spirit to leave her father's wigwam she launched a canoe on the Merrimack, hoping to make her way along that watery highway to her husband's domain. It was winter, and the stream was full of floating ice; at the best of times it was not easy to keep a frail vessel of bark in the current away from the rapids, and a wandering hunter reported that a canoe had come down the river guided by a woman, that it had swung against the Amoskeag rocks, where Manchester stands now, and a few moments later was in a quieter reach of water, broken and empty. No more was seen of Weetamoo.

THE FATAL FORGET-ME-NOT

Three miles out from the Nahant shore, Massachusetts, rises Egg Rock, a dome of granite topped by a light-house. In the last century the forget-me-nots that grew in a little marsh at its summit were much esteemed, for it was reported that if a girl should receive one of these little flowers from her lover the two would be faithful to each other through all their married life. It was before a temporary separation that a certain young couple strolled together on the Nahant cliffs. The man was to sail for Italy next day, to urge parental consent to their union. As he looked dreamily into the sea the legend of the forget-me-not came into his mind, and in a playful tone he offered to gather a bunch as a memento. Unthinkingly the girl consented. He ran down the cliff to his boat, pushed out, and headed toward the rock, but a fisherman shouted that a gale was rising and the tide was coming in; indeed, the horizon was whitening and the rote was growing plain.

Alice had heard the cry of warning and would have called him back, but she was forsaken by the power of speech, and watched, with pale face and straining eyes, the boat beating smartly across the surges. It was seen to reach Egg Rock, and after a lapse came dancing toward the shore again; but the tide, was now swirling in rapidly, the waves were running high, and the wind freshened as the sun sank. At times the boat was out of sight in the hollowed water, and as it neared Nahant it became unmanageable. Apparently it had filled with water and the tiller-rope had broken. Nothing could be done by the spectators who had gathered on the rocks, except to shout directions that were futile, even if they could be heard. At last the boat was lifted by a breaker and hurled against a mass of granite at the very feet of the man's mistress. When the body was recovered next day, a bunch of forget-me-not was clasped in the rigid hand.

THE OLD MILL AT SOMERVILLE

The "old powder-house," as the round stone tower is called that stands on a gravel ridge in Somerville, Massachusetts, is so named because at the outbreak of the Revolutionary War it was used temporarily as a magazine; but long before that it was a wind-mill. Here in the old days two lovers held their tryst: a sturdy and honest young farmer of the neighborhood and the daughter of a man whose wealth puffed him with purse-pride. It was the plebeian state of the farmer that made him look at him with an unfavorable countenance, and when it was whispered to him that the young people were meeting each other almost every evening at the mill, he resolved to surprise them there and humiliate, if he did not punish them. From the shadow of the door they saw his approach, and, yielding to the girl's imploring, the lover secreted himself while she climbed to the loft. The flutter of her dress caught the old man's eye and he hastened, panting, into the mill. For some moments he groped about, for his eyes had not grown used to the darkness of the place, and hearing his muttered oaths, the girl crept backward from the stair.

She was beginning to hope that she had not been seen, when her foot caught in a loose board and she stumbled, but in her fall she threw out her hand to save herself and found a rope within her grasp. Directly that her weight had been applied to it there was a whir and a clank. The cord had set the great fans in motion. At the same moment a fall was heard, then a cry, passing from anger into anguish. She rushed down the stair, the lover appeared from his hiding-place at the same moment, and together they dragged the old man to his feet. At the moment when the wind had started the sails he had been standing on one of the mill-stones and the sudden jerk had thrown him down. His arm caught between the grinding surfaces and had been crushed to pulp. He was carried home and tenderly nursed, but he did not live long; yet before he died he was made to see the folly of his course, and he consented to the marriage that it had cost him so dear to try to prevent. Before she could summon heart to fix the wedding-day the girl passed many months of grief and repentance, and for the rest of her life she avoided the old mill. There was good reason for doing so, people said, for on windy nights the spirit of the old man used to haunt the place, using such profanity that it became visible in the form of blue lights, dancing and exploding about the building.

EDWARD RANDOLPH'S PORTRAIT

Nothing is left of Province House, the old home of the royal governors, in Boston, but the gilded Indian that served as its weathercock and aimed his arrow at the winds from the cupola. The house itself was swept away long ago in the so-called march of improvement. In one of its rooms hung a picture so dark that when Lieutenant-Governor Hutchinson went to live there hardly anybody could say what it represented. There were hints that it was a portrait of the devil, painted at a witch-meeting near Salem, and that on the eve of disasters in the province a dreadful face had glared from the canvas. Shirley had seen it on the night of the fall of Ticonderoga, and servants had gone shuddering from the room, certain that they had caught the glance of a malignant eye.

It was known to the governors, however, that the portrait, if not that of the arch fiend, was that of one who in the popular mind was none the less a devil: Edward Randolph, the traitor, who had repealed the first provincial charter and deprived the colonists of their liberties. Under the curse of the people he grew pale and pinched and ugly, his face at last becoming so hateful that men were unwilling to look at it. Then it was that he sat for his portrait. Threescore or odd years afterward, Hutchinson sat in the hall wondering vaguely if coming events would consign him to the obloquy that had fallen on his predecessor, for at his bidding a fleet had come into the harbor with three regiments of red coats on board, despatched from Halifax to overawe the city. The coming of the selectmen to protest against quartering these troops on the people and the substitution of martial for civic law, interrupted his reverie, and a warm debate arose. At last the governor seized his pen impatiently, and cried, "The king is my master and England is my home. Upheld by them, I defy the rabble."

He was about to sign the order for bringing in the troops when a curtain that had hung before the picture was drawn aside. Hutchinson stared at the canvas in amazement, then muttered, "It is Randolph's spirit! It wears the look of hell." The picture was seen to be that of a man in antique garb, with a despairing, hunted, yet evil expression in the face, and seemed to stare at Hutchinson.

"It is a warning," said one of the company.

Hutchinson recovered himself with an effort and turned away. "It is a trick," he cried; and bending over the paper he fixed his name, as if in desperate haste. Then he trembled, turned white, and wiped a sweat from his brow. The selectmen departed in silence but in anger, and those who saw Hutchinson on the streets next day affirmed that the portrait had stepped out of its canvas and stood at his side through the night. Afterward, as he lay on his death-bed, he cried that the blood of the Boston massacre was filling his throat, and as his soul passed from him his face, in its agony and rage, was the face of Edward Randolph.

LADY ELEANORE'S MANTLE

Lady Eleanore Rochcliffe, being orphaned, was admitted to the family of her distant relative, Governor Shute, of Massachusetts Bay, and came to America to take her home with him. She arrived at the gates of Province House, in Boston, in the governor's splendid coach, with outriders and guards, and as the governor went to receive her, a pale young man, with tangled hair, sprang from the crowd and fell in the dust at her feet, offering himself as a footstool for her to tread upon. Her proud face lighted with a smile of scorn, and she put out her hand to stay the governor, who was in the act of striking the fellow with his cane.

"Do not strike him," she said. "When men seek to be trampled, it is a favor they deserve."

For a moment she bore her weight on the prostrate form, "emblem of aristocracy trampling on human sympathies and the kindred of nature," and as she stood there the bell on South Church began to toll for a funeral that was passing at the moment. The crowd started; some looked annoyed; Lady Eleanore remained calm and walked in stately fashion up the passage on the arm of His Excellency. "Who was that insolent fellow?" was asked of Dr. Clarke, the governor's physician.

"Gervase Helwyse," replied the doctor; "a youth of no fortune, but of good mind until he met this lady in London, when he fell in love with her, and her pride and scorn have crazed him."

A few nights after a ball was given in honor of the governor's ward, and Province House was filled with the elect of the city. Commanding in figure, beautiful in face, richly dressed and jewelled, the Lady Eleanore was the admired of the whole assembly, and the women were especially curious to see her mantle, for a rumor went out that it had been made by a dying girl, and had the magic power of giving new beauty to the wearer every time it was put on. While the guests were taking refreshment, a young man stole into the room with a silver goblet, and this he offered on his knee to Lady Eleanore. As she looked down she recognized the face of Helwyse.

"Drink of this sacramental wine," he said, eagerly, "and pass it among the guests."

"Perhaps it is poisoned," whispered a man, and in another moment the liquor was overturned, and Helwyse was roughly dragged away.

"Pray, gentlemen, do not hurt my poor admirer," said the lady, in a tone of languor and condescension that was unusual to her. Breaking from his captives, Helwyse ran back and begged her to cast her mantle into the fire. She replied by throwing a fold of it above her head and smiling as she said, "Farewell. Remember me as you see me now."

Helwyse shook his head sadly and submitted to be led away. The weariness in Eleanore's manner increased; a flush was burning on her cheek; her laugh had grown infrequent. Dr. Clarke whispered something in the governor's ear that made that gentleman start and look alarmed. It was announced that an unforeseen circumstance made it necessary to close the festival at once, and the company went home. A few days after the city was thrown into a panic by an outbreak of small-pox, a disease that in those times could not be prevented nor often cured, and that gathered its victims by thousands. Graves were dug in rows, and every night the earth was piled hastily on fresh corpses. Before all infected houses hung a red flag of warning, and Province House was the first to show it, for the plague had come to town in Lady Eleanore's mantle. The people cursed her pride and pointed to the flags as her triumphal banners. The pestilence was at its height when Gervase Helwyse appeared in Province House. There were none to stay him now, and he climbed the stairs, peering from room to room, until he entered a darkened chamber, where something stirred feebly under a silken coverlet and a faint voice begged for water. Helwyse tore apart the curtains and exclaimed, "Fie! What does such a thing as you in Lady Eleanore's apartment?"

The figure on the bed tried to hide its hideous face. "Do not look on me," it cried. "I am cursed for my pride that I wrapped about me as a mantle. You are avenged. I am Eleanore Rochcliffe."

The lunatic stared for a moment, then the house echoed with his laughter. The deadly mantle lay on a chair. He snatched it up, and waving also the red flag of the pestilence ran into the street. In a short time an effigy wrapped in the mantle was borne to Province House and set on fire by a mob. From that hour the pest abated and soon disappeared, though graves and scars made a bitter memory of it for many a year. Unhappiest of all was the disfigured creature who wandered amid the shadows of Province House, never showing her face, unloved, avoided, lonely.

HOWE'S MASQUERADE

During the siege of Boston Sir William Howe undertook to show his contempt for the raw fellows who were disrespectfully tossing cannon-balls at him from the batteries in Cambridge and South Boston, by giving a masquerade. It was a brilliant affair, the belles and blades of the loyalist set being present, some in the garb of their ancestors, for the past is ever more picturesque than the present, and a few roisterers caricaturing the American generals in ragged clothes, false noses, and absurd wigs. At the height of the merriment a sound of a dirge echoing through the streets caused the dance to stop. The funeral music paused before the doors of Province House, where the dance was going on, and they were flung open. Muffled drums marked time for a company that began to file down the great stair from the floor above the ball-room: dark men in steeple-hats and pointed beards, with Bibles, swords, and scrolls, who looked sternly at the guests and descended to the street.

Colonel Joliffe, a Whig, whose age and infirmity had prevented him from joining Washington, and whose courtesy and intelligence had made him respected by his foes, acted as chorus: "These I take to be the Puritan governors of Massachusetts: Endicott, Winthrop, Vane, Dudley, Haynes, Bellingham, Leverett, Bradstreet." Then came a rude soldier, mailed, begirt with arms: the tyrant Andros; a brown-faced man with a sailor's gait: Sir William Phipps; a courtier wigged and jewelled: Earl Bellomont; the crafty, well-mannered Dudley; the twinkling, red-nosed Shute; the ponderous Burnet; the gouty Belcher; Shirley, Pownall, Bernard, Hutchinson; then a soldier, whose cocked hat he held before his face. "'Tis the shape of Gage!" cried an officer, turning pale. The lights were dull and an uncomfortable silence had fallen on the company. Last, came a tall man muffled in a military cloak, and as he paused on the landing the guests looked from him to their host in amazement, for it was the figure of Howe himself. The governor's patience was at an end, for this was a part of the masquerade that had not been looked for. He fiercely cried to Joliffe, "There is a plot in this. Your head has stood too long on a traitor's shoulders."

"Make haste to cut it off, then," was the reply, "for the power of Sir William Howe and of the king, his master, is at an end. These shadows are mourners at his funeral. Look! The last of the governors."

Howe rushed with drawn sword on the figure of himself, when it turned and looked at him. The blade clanged to the floor and Howe fell back with a gasp of horror, for the face was his own. Hand nor voice was raised to stay the double-goer as it mournfully passed on. At the threshold it stamped its foot and shook its fists in air; then the door closed. Mingled with the strains of the funeral march, as it died along the empty streets, came the tolling of the bell on South Church steeple, striking the hour of midnight. The festivities were at an end and, oppressed by a nameless fear, the spectators of this strange pageant made ready for departure; but before they left the booming of cannon at the southward announced that Washington had advanced. The glories of Province House were over. When the last of the royal governors left it he paused on the threshold, beat his foot on the stone, and flung up his hands in an attitude of grief and rage.

OLD ESTHER DUDLEY

Boston had surrendered. Washington was advancing from the heights where he had trained his guns on the British works, and Sir William Howe lingered at the door of Province House,—last of the royal governors who would stand there,—and cursed and waved his hands and beat his heel on the step, as if he were crushing rebellion by that act. The sound brought an old woman to his side. "Esther Dudley!" he exclaimed. "Why are you not gone?"

"I shall never leave. As housekeeper for the governors and pensioner of the king, this has been my home; the only home I know. Go back, but send more troops. I will keep the house till you return."

"Grant that I may return," he cried. "Since you will stay, take this bag of guineas and keep this key until a governor shall demand it."

Then, with fierce and moody brow, the governor went forth, and the faded eyes of Esther Dudley saw him nevermore. When the soldiers of the republic cast about for quarters in Boston town, they spared the official mansion to this old woman. Her bridling toryism and assumption of old state amused them and did no harm; indeed, her loyalty was half admired; beside, nobody took the pride in the place that she did, or would keep it in better order. That she sometimes had a half-dozen of unrepentant codgers in to dinner, and that they were suspected of drinking healths to George III. in crusted port, was a fact to blink. Rumor had it that not all her guests were flesh and blood, but that she had an antique mirror across which ancient occupants of the house would pass in shadowy procession at her command, and that she was wont to have the Shirleys, Olivers, Hutchinsons, and Dudleys out of their graves to hold receptions there; so a touch of dread may have mingled in the feeling that kept the populace aloof.

Living thus by herself, refusing to hear of rebel victories, construing the bonfires, drumming, hurrahs, and bell-ringing to signify fresh triumphs for England, she drifted farther and farther out of her time and existed in the shadows of the past. She lighted the windows for the king's birthday, and often from the cupola watched for a British fleet, heeding not the people below, who, as they saw her withered face, repeated the prophecy, with a laugh "When the golden Indian on Province House shall shoot his arrow and the cock on South Church spire shall crow, look for a royal governor again." So, when it was bandied about the streets that the governor was coming, she took it in no wise strange, but dressed herself in silk and hoops, with store of ancient jewels, and made ready to receive him. In truth, there was a function, for already a man of stately mien, and richly dressed, was advancing through the court, with a staff of men in wigs and laced coats behind him, and a company of troops at a little distance. Esther Dudley flung the door wide and dropping on her knees held forth the key with the cry, "Thank heaven for this hour! God save the king!"

The governor put off his hat and helped the woman to her feet. "A strange prayer," said he; "yet we will echo it to this effect: For the good of the realm that still owns him to be its ruler, God save King George."

Esther Dudley stared wildly. That face she remembered now,—the proscribed rebel, John Hancock; governor, not by royal grant, but by the people's will.

"Have I welcomed a traitor? Then let me die."

"Alas! Mistress Dudley, the world has changed for you in these later years. America has no king." He offered her his arm, and she clung to it for a moment, then, sinking down, the great key, that she so long had treasured, clanked to the floor.

"I have been faithful unto death," she gasped. "God save the king!"

The people uncovered, for she was dead.

"At her tomb," said Hancock, "we will bid farewell forever to the past. A new day has come for us. In its broad light we will press onward."

THE LOSS OF JACOB HURD

Jacob Hurd, stern witch-harrier of Ipswich, can abide nothing out of the ordinary course of things, whether it be flight on a broomstick or the wrong adding of figures; so his son gives him trouble, for he is an imaginative boy, who walks alone, talking to the birds, making rhymes, picking flowers, and dreaming. That he will never be a farmer, mechanic, or tradesman is as good as certain, and one day when the child runs in with a story of a golden horse, with tail and mane of silver, on which he has ridden over land and sea, climbing mountains and swimming rivers, he turns pale with fright lest the boy be bewitched; then, as the awfulness of the invention becomes manifest, he cries, "Thou knowest thou art lying," and strikes the little fellow.

The boy staggers into his mother's arms, and that night falls into a fever, in which he raves of his horse and the places he will see, while Jacob sits by his side, too sore in heart for words, and he never leaves the cot for food or sleep till the fever is burned out. Just before he closes his eyes the child looks about him and says that he hears the horse pawing in the road, and, either for dust or cloud or sun gleam, it seems for an instant as if the horse were there. The boy gives a cry of joy, then sinks upon his pillow, lifeless.

Some time after this Jacob sets off one morning, while the stars are out, to see three witches hanged, but at evening his horse comes flying up the road, splashed with blood and foam, and the neighbors know from that of Jacob's death, for he is lying by the wayside with an Indian arrow in his heart and an axemark on his head. The wife runs to the door, and, though she shakes with fear at its approach, she sees that in the sunset glow the horse's sides have a shine like gold, and its mane and tail are silver white. Now the animal is before the house, but the woman does not faint or cry at the blood splash on the saddle, for—is it the dust-cloud that takes that shape?—she sees on its back a boy with a shining face, who throws a kiss at her,—her Paul. He, little poet, lives in spirit, and has found happiness.

THE HOBOMAK

Such was the Indian name of the site of Westboro, Massachusetts, and the neighboring pond was Hochomocko. The camp of the red men near the shore was full of bustle one day, for their belle, Iano, was to marry the young chief, Sassacus. The feast was spread and all were ready to partake of it, when it was found that the bride was missing. One girl had seen her steal into the wood with a roguish smile on her lip, and knew that she intended to play hide-and-seek with Sassacus before she should be proclaimed a wife, but the day wore on and she did not come. Among those who were late in reaching camp was Wequoash, who brought a panther in that he had slain on Boston Hill, and he bragged about his skill, as usual. There had been a time when he was a rival of the chief for the hand of Iano, and he showed surprise and concern at her continued absence. The search went on for two days, and, at the end of that time, the girl's body was taken from the lake.

At the funeral none groaned so piteously as Wequoash. Yet Sassacus felt his loss so keenly that he fell into a sickness next day, and none was found so constant in his ministrations as Wequoash; but all to no avail, for within a week Sassacus, too, was dead. As the strongest and bravest remaining in the tribe, Wequoash became heir to his honors by election.

A year later he sat moodily by the lakeside, when a flame burst up from the water, and a canoe floated toward him that a mysterious agency impelled him to enter. The boat sped toward the flame, that, at his approach, assumed Iano's form. He heard the water gurgle as he passed over the spot where the shape had glimmered, but there was no other sound or check. Next year this thing occurred again, and then the spirit spoke: "Only once more."

Yet a third time his fate took him to the spot, and as the hour came on he called his people to him: "This," said he, "is my death-day. I have done evil, and the time comes none too soon. Sassacus was your chief. I envied him his happiness, and gave him poison when I nursed him. Worse than that, I saw Iano in her canoe on her wedding-day. She had refused my hand. I entered my canoe and chased her over the water, in pretended sport, but in the middle of the lake I upset her birch and she was drowned. See! she comes!"

For, as he spoke, the light danced up again, and the boat came, self-impelled, to the strand. Wequoash entered it, and with head bent down was hurried away. Those on the shore saw the flame condense to a woman's shape, and a voice issued from it: "It is my hour!" A blinding bolt of lightning fell, and at the appalling roar of thunder all hid their faces. When they looked up, boat and flame had vanished. Whenever, afterward, an Indian rowed across the place where the murderer had sunk, he dropped a stone, and the monument that grew in that way can be seen on the pond floor to this day.

BERKSHIRE TORIES

The tories of Berkshire, Massachusetts, were men who had been endeared to the king by holding office under warrant from that sacred personage. They have been gently dealt with by historians, but that is "overstrained magnanimity which concentrates its charities and praises for defeated champions of the wrong, and reserves its censures for triumphant defenders of the right." While the following incidents have been so well avouched that they deserve to stand as history, their picturesqueness justifies renewed acquaintance.

Among the loyalists was Gideon Smith, of Stockbridge, who had helped British prisoners to escape, and had otherwise made himself so obnoxious that he was forced for a time to withdraw and pass a season of penitence and meditation in a cavern near Lenox, that is called the Tories' Glen. Here he lay for weeks, none but his wife knowing where he was, but at his request she walked out every day with her children, leading them past his cave, where he fed on their faces with hungry eyes. They prattled on, never dreaming that their father was but a few feet from them. Smith survived the war and lived to be on good terms with his old foes.

In Lenox lived a Tory, one of those respectable buffers to whom wealth and family had given immunity in the early years of the war, but who sorely tried the temper of his neighbors by damning everything American from Washington downward. At last they could endure his abuse no longer; his example had affected other Anglomaniacs, and a committee waited on him to tell him that he could either swear allegiance to the colonies or be hanged. He said he would be hanged if he would swear, or words to that effect, and hanged he was, on a ready-made gallows in the street. He was let down shortly, "brought around" with rum, and the oath was offered again. He refused it. This had not been looked for. It had been taken for granted that he would abjure his fealty to the king at the first tightening of the cord. A conference was held, and it was declared that retreat would be undignified and unsafe, so the Tory was swung up again, this time with a yank that seemed to "mean business." He hung for some time, and when lowered gave no sign of life. There was some show of alarm at this, for nobody wanted to kill the old fellow, and every effort was made to restore consciousness. At last the lungs heaved, the purple faded from his cheek, his eyes opened, and he gasped, "I'll swear." With a shout of joy the company hurried him to the tavern, seated him before the fire, and put a glass of punch in his hand. He drank the punch to Washington's health, and after a time was heard to remark to himself, "It's a hard way to make Whigs, but it'll do it."

Nathan Jackson, of Tyringham, was another Yankee who had seen fit to take arms against his countrymen, and when captured he was charged with treason and remanded for trial. The jail, in Great Barrington, was so little used in those days of sturdy virtue that it had become a mere shed, fit to hold nobody, and Jackson, after being locked into it, might have walked out whenever he felt disposed; but escape, he thought, would have been a confession of the wrongness of Tory principles, or of a fear to stand trial. He found life so monotonous, however, that he asked the sheriff to let him go out to work during the day, promising to sleep in his cell, and such was his reputation for honesty that his request was granted without a demur, the prisoner returning every night to be locked up. When the time approached for the court to meet in Springfield heavy harvesting had begun, and, as there was no other case from Berkshire County to present, the sheriff grumbled at the bother of taking his prisoner across fifty miles of rough country, but Jackson said that he would make it all right by going alone. The sheriff was glad to be released from this duty, so off went the Tory to give himself up and be tried for his life. On the way he was overtaken by Mr. Edwards, of the Executive Council, then about to meet in Boston, and without telling his own name or office, he learned the extraordinary errand of this lonely pedestrian. Jackson was tried, admitted the charges against him, and was sentenced to death. While he awaited execution of the law upon him, the council in Boston received petitions for clemency, and Mr. Edwards asked if there was none in favor of Nathan Jackson. There was none. Mr. Edwards related the circumstance of his meeting with the condemned man, and a murmur of surprise and admiration went around the room. A despatch was sent to Springfield. When it reached there the prison door was flung open and Jackson walked forth free.

THE REVENGE OF JOSIAH BREEZE

Two thousand Cape Cod fishermen had gone to join the colonial army, and in their absence the British ships had run in shore to land crews on mischievous errands. No man, woman, or child on the Cape but hated the troops and sailors of King George, and would do anything to work them harm. When the Somerset was wrecked off Truro, in 1778, the crew were helped ashore, 'tis true, but they were straightway marched to prison, and it was thought that no other frigate would venture near the shifting dunes where she had laid her skeleton, as many a good ship had done before and has done since. It was November, and ugly weather was shutting in, when a three-decker, that had been tacking off shore and that flew the red flag, was seen to yaw wildly while reefing sail and drift toward land with a broken tiller. No warning signal was raised on the bluffs; not a hand was stirred to rescue. Those who saw the accident watched with sullen satisfaction the on-coming of the vessel, nor did they cease to look for disaster when the ship anchored and stowed sail.

Ezekiel and Josiah Breeze, father and son, stood at the door of their cottage and watched her peril until three lights twinkling faintly through the gray of driving snow were all that showed where the enemy lay, straining at her cables and tossing on a wrathful sea. They stood long in silence, but at last the boy exclaimed, "I'm going to the ship."

"If you stir from here, you're no son of mine," said Ezekiel.

"But she's in danger, dad."

"As she oughter be. By mornin' she'll be strewed along the shore and not a spar to mark where she's a-swingin' now."

"And the men?"

"It's a jedgment, boy."

The lad remembered how the sailors of the Ajax had come ashore to burn the homes of peaceful fishermen and farmers; how women had been insulted; how his friends and mates had been cut down at Long Island with British lead and steel; how, when he ran to warn away a red-faced fellow that was robbing his garden, the man had struck him on the shoulder with a cutlass. He had sworn then to be revenged. But to let a host go down to death and never lift a helping hand—was that a fair revenge? "I've got to go, dad," he burst forth. "Tomorrow morning there'll be five hundred faces turned up on the beach, covered with ice and staring at the sky, and five hundred mothers in England will wonder when they're goin' to see those faces again. If ever they looked at me the sight of 'em would never go out of my eyes. I'd be harnted by 'em, awake and asleep. And to-morrow is Thanksgiving. I've got to go, dad, and I will." So speaking, he rushed away and was swallowed in the gloom.

The man stared after him; then, with a revulsion of feeling, he cried, "You're right, 'Siah. I'll go with you." But had he called in tones of thunder he would not have been heard in the roar of the wind and crash of the surf. As he reached the shore he saw faintly on the phosphorescent foam a something that climbed a hill of water; it was lost over its crest and reappeared on the wave beyond; it showed for a moment on the third wave, then it vanished in the night. "Josiah!" It was a long, querulous cry. No answer. In half an hour a thing rode by the watcher on the sands and fell with a crash beside him—a boat bottom up: his son's.

Next day broke clear, with new snow on the ground. In his house at Provincetown, Captain Breeze was astir betimes, for his son Ezekiel, his grandson Josiah, and all other relatives who were not at the front with Washington were coming for the family reunion. Plump turkeys were ready for the roasting, great loaves of bread and cake stood beside the oven, redoubtable pies of pumpkin and apple filled the air with maddening odors. The people gathered and chattered around his cheery fire of the damage that the storm had done, when Ezekiel stumbled in, his brown face haggard, his lips working, and a tremor in his hands. He said, "Josiah!" in a thick voice, then leaned his arms against the chimney and pressed his face upon them. Among fishermen whose lives are in daily peril the understanding of misfortune is quick, and the old man put his hand on the shoulder of his son and bent his head. The day of joy was become a day of gloom. As the news went out, the house began to fill with sympathizing friends, and there was talking in low voices through the rooms, when a cry of surprise was heard outside. A ship, cased in tons of ice, was forging up the harbor, her decks swarming with blue jackets, some of whom were beating off the frozen masses from lower spars and rigging. She followed the channel so steadily, it was plain to be seen that a wise hand was at her helm; her anchor ran out and she swung on the tide. "The Ajax, as I'm a sinner!" exclaimed a sailor on shore. A boat put off from her, and people angrily collected at the wharf, with talk of getting out their guns, when a boyish figure arose in the stern, and was greeted with a shout of surprise and welcome.

The boat touched the beach, Josiah Breeze leaped out of it, and in another minute his father had him in a bear's embrace, making no attempt to stop the tears that welled out of his eyes. An officer had followed Josiah on shore, and going to the group he said, "That boy is one to be proud of. He put out in a sea that few men could face, to save an enemy's ship and pilot it into the harbor. I could do no less than bring him back." There was praise and laughter and clasping of hands, and when the Thanksgiving dinner was placed, smoking, on the board, the commander of H. M. S. Ajax was among the jolliest of the guests at Captain Breeze's table.

THE MAY-POLE OF MERRYMOUNT

The people of Merrymount—unsanctified in the eyes of their Puritan neighbors, for were they not Episcopals, who had pancakes at Shrovetide and wassail at Christmas?—were dancing about their May-pole one summer evening, for they tried to make it May throughout the year. Some were masked like animals, and all were tricked with flowers and ribbons. Within their circle, sharing in song and jest, were the lord and lady of the revels, and an English clergyman waiting to join the pair in wedlock. Life, they sang, should be all jollity: away with care and duty; leave wisdom to the weak and old, and sanctity for fools. Watching the sport from a neighboring wood stood a band of frowning Puritans, and as the sun set they stalked forth and broke through the circle. All was dismay. The bells, the laughter, the song were silent, and some who had tasted Puritan wrath before shrewdly smelled the stocks. A Puritan of iron face—it was Endicott, who had cut the cross from the flag of England—warning aside the "priest of Baal," proceeded to hack the pole down with his sword. A few swinging blows, and down it sank, with its ribbons and flowers.

"So shall fall the pride of vain people; so shall come to grief the preachers of false religion," quoth he. "Truss those fellows to the trees and give them half a dozen of blows apiece as token that we brook no ungodly conduct and hostility to our liberties. And you, king and queen of the May, have you no better things to think about than fiddling and dancing? How if I punish you both?"

"Had I the power I'd punish you for saying it," answered the swain; "but, as I have not, I am compelled to ask that the girl go unharmed."

"Will you have it so, or will you share your lover's punishment?" asked Endicott.

"I will take all upon myself," said the woman.

The face of the governor softened. "Let the young fellow's hair be cut, in pumpkin-shell fashion," he commanded; "then bring them to me but gently."

He was obeyed, and as the couple came before him, hand in hand, he took a chain of roses from the fallen pole and cast it about their necks. And so they were married. Love had softened rigor and all were better for the assertion of a common humanity. But the May-pole of Merrymount was never set up again. There were no more games and plays and dances, nor singing of worldly music. The town went to ruin, the merrymakers were scattered, and the gray sobriety of religion and toil fell on Pilgrim land again.

THE DEVIL AND TOM WALKER

When Charles River was lined with groves and marshes there lived in a cabin, near Brighton, Massachusetts, an ill-fed rascal named Tom Walker. There was but one in the commonwealth who was more penurious, and that was his wife. They squabbled over the spending of a penny and each grudged food to the other. One day as Tom walked through the pine wood near his place, by habit watching the ground—for even there a farthing might be discovered—he prodded his stick into a skull, cloven deep by an Indian tomahawk. He kicked it, to shake the dirt off, when a gruff voice spake: "What are you doing in my grounds?" A swarthy fellow, with the face of a charcoal burner, sat on a stump, and Tom wondered that he had not seen him as he approached.

He replied, "Your grounds! They belong to Deacon Peabody."

"Deacon Peabody be damned!" cried the black fellow; "as I think he will be, anyhow, if he does not look after his own sins a little sharper and a little less curiously after his neighbors'. Look, if you want to see how he is faring," and, pointing to a tree, he called Tom to notice that the deacon's name was written on the bark and that it was rotten at the core. To his surprise, Tom found that nearly every tree had the name of some prominent man cut upon it.

"Who are you?" he asked.

"I go by different names in different places," replied the dark one. "In some countries I am the black miner; in some the wild huntsman; here I am the black woodman. I am the patron of slave dealers and master of Salem witches."

"I think you are the devil," blurted Tom.

"At your service," replied his majesty.

Now, Tom, having lived long with Mrs. Walker, had no fear of the devil, and he stopped to have a talk with him. The devil remarked, in a careless tone, that Captain Kidd had buried his treasure in that wood, under his majesty's charge, and that whoever wished could find and keep it by making the usual concession. This Tom declined. He told his wife about it, however, and she was angry with him for not having closed the bargain at once, declaring that if he had not courage enough to add this treasure to their possessions she would not hesitate to do it. Tom showed no disposition to check her. If she got the money he would try to get a share of it, and if the devil took away his helpmate—well, there were things that he had made his mind to endure, when he had to. True enough, the woman started for the wood before sundown, with her spoons in her apron. When Tom discovered that the spoons were gone he, too, set off, for he wanted those back, anyway; but he did not overtake his wife. An apron was found in a tree containing a dried liver and a withered heart, and near that place the earth had been trampled and strewn with handfuls of coarse hair that reminded Tom of the man that he had met in the woods. "Egad!" he muttered, "Old Nick must have had a tough time with her." Half in gratitude and half in curiosity, Tom waited to speak to the dark man, and was next day rewarded by seeing that personage come through the wood with an axe, whistling carelessly. Tom at once approached him on the subject of the buried treasure—not the vanished wife, for her he no longer regarded as a treasure.

After some haggling the devil proposed that Tom should start a loan office in Boston and use Kidd's money in exacting usury. This suited Tom, who promised to screw four per cent. a month out of the unfortunates who might ask his aid, and he was seen to start for town with a bag which his neighbors thought to hold his crop of starveling turnips, but which was really a king's ransom in gold and jewels—the earnings of Captain Kidd in long years of honest piracy. It was in Governor Belcher's time, and cash was scarce. Merchants and professional men as well as the thriftless went to Tom for money, and, as he always had it, his business grew until he seemed to have a mortgage on half the men in Boston who were rich enough to be in debt. He even went so far as to move into a new house, to ride in his own carriage, and to eat enough to keep body and soul together, for he did not want to give up his soul to the one who would claim it just yet.

The most singular proof of his thrift—showing that he wanted to save soul and money both—was shown in his joining the church and becoming a prayerful Christian. He kept a Bible in his pocket and another on his desk, resolved to be prepared if a certain gentleman should call. He buried his old horse feet uppermost, for he was taught that on resurrection day the world would be turned upside down, and he was resolved, if his enemy appeared, to give him a run for it. While employed one afternoon in the congenial task of foreclosing a mortgage his creditor begged for another day to raise the money. Tom was irritable on account of the hot weather and talked to him as a good man of the church ought not to do.

"You have made so much money out of me," wailed the victim of Tom's philanthropies.

"Now, the devil take me if I have made a farthing!" exclaimed Tom.

At that instant there were three knocks at the door, and, stepping out to see who was there, the money lender found himself in presence of his fate. His little Bible was in a coat on a nail, and the bigger one was on his desk. He was without defence. The evil one caught him up like a child, had him on the back of his snorting steed in no time, and giving the beast a cut he flew like the wind in the teeth of a rising storm toward the marshes of Brighton. As he reached there a lightning flash descended into the wood and set it on fire. At the same moment Tom's house was discovered to be in flames. When his effects were examined nothing was found in his strong boxes but cinders and shavings.

THE GRAY CHAMPION

It befell Sir Edmund Andros to make himself the most hated of the governors sent to represent the king in New England. A spirit of independence, born of a free soil, was already moving in the people's hearts, and the harsh edicts of this officer, as well as the oppressive measures of his master, brought him into continual conflict with the people. He it was who went to Hartford to demand the surrender of the liberties of that colony. The lights were blown out and the patent of those liberties was hurried away from under his nose and hidden from his reach in a hollow of the Charter Oak.

In Boston, too, he could call no American his friend, and it was there that he met one of the first checks to his arrogance. It was an April evening in 1689, and there was an unusual stir in the streets. People were talking in low tones, and one caught such phrases as, "If the Prince of Orange is successful, this Andros will lose his head." "Our pastors are to be burned alive in King Street." "The pope has ordered Andros to celebrate the eve of St. Bartholomew in Boston: we are to be killed." "Our old Governor Bradstreet is in town, and Andros fears him." While talk was running in this excited strain the sound of a drum was heard coming through Cornhill. Now was seen a file of soldiers with guns on shoulder, matches twinkling in the falling twilight, and behind them, on horseback, Andros and his councillors, including the priest of King's Chapel, all wearing crucifixes at their throats, all flushed with wine, all looking down with indifference at the people in their dark cloaks and broadbrimmed hats, who looked back at them with suspicion and hate. The soldiers trod the streets like men unused to giving way, and the crowd fell back, pressed against the buildings. Groans and hisses were heard, and a voice sent up this cry, "Lord of Hosts, provide a champion for thy people!"

Ere the echo of that call had ceased there came from the other end of the street, stepping as in time to the drum, an aged man, in cloak and steeple hat, with heavy sword at his thigh. His port was that of a king, and his dignity was heightened by a snowy beard that fell to his waist. Taking the middle of the way he marched on until he was but a few paces from the advancing column. None knew him and he seemed to recognize none among the crowd. As he drew himself to his height, it seemed in the dusk as if he were of no mortal mould. His eye blazed, he thrust his staff before him, and in a voice of invincible command cried, "Halt!"

Half because it was habit to obey the word, half because they were cowed by the majestic presence, the guard stood still and the drum was silenced. Andros spurred forward, but even he made a pause when he saw the staff levelled at his breast. "Forward!" he blustered. "Trample the dotard into the street. How dare you stop the king's governor?"

"I have stayed the march of a king himself," was the answer. "The king you serve no longer sits on the throne of England. To-morrow you will be a prisoner. Back, lest you reach the scaffold!"

A moment of hesitation on Andros's part encouraged the people to press closer, and many of them took no pains to hide the swords and pistols that were girt upon them. The groans and hisses sounded louder. "Down with Andros! Death to tyrants! A curse on King James!" came from among the throng, and some of them stooped as if to tear up the pavings. Doubtful, yet overawed, the governor wheeled about and gloomily marched back through the streets where he had ridden so arrogantly. In truth, his next night was spent in prison, for James had fled from England, and William held the throne. All eyes being on the retreating company, the champion of the people was not seen to depart, but when they turned to praise and thank him he had vanished, and there were those who said that he had melted into twilight.

The incident had passed into legend, and fourscore years had followed it, when the soldiers of another king of England marched down State Street, and fired on the people of Boston who were gathered below the old State House. Again it was said that the form of a tall, white-bearded man in antique garb was seen in that street, warning back the troops and encouraging the people to resist them. On the little field of Lexington in early dawn, and at the breastwork on Bunker Hill, where farmers worked by lantern-light, this dark form was seen—the spirit of New England. And it is told that whenever any foreign foe or domestic oppressor shall dare the temper of the people, in the van of the resisting army shall be found this champion.

THE FOREST SMITHY

Early in this century a man named Ainsley appeared at Holyoke, Massachusetts, and set up a forge in a wood at the edge of the village, with a two-room cottage to live in. A Yankee peddler once put up at his place for shelter from a storm, and as the rain increased with every hour he begged to remain in the house over night, promising to pay for his accommodation in the morning. The blacksmith, who seemed a mild, considerate man, said that he was willing, but that, as the rooms were small, it would be well to refer the matter to his wife. As the peddler entered the house the wife—a weary-looking woman with white hair—seated herself at once in a thickly-cushioned arm-chair, and, as if loath to leave it, told the peddler that if he would put up with simple fare and a narrow berth he was welcome. After a candle had been lighted the three sat together for some time, talking of crops and trade, when there came a rush of hoofs without and a hard-looking man, who had dismounted at the door, entered without knocking. The blacksmith turned pale and the wife's face expressed sore anxiety.

"What brings you here?" asked the smith.

"I must pass the night here," answered the man.

"But, stranger, I can't accommodate you. We have but one spare room, and that has been taken by the man who is sitting there."

"Then give me a bit to eat."

"Get the stranger something," said the woman to her husband, without rising.

"Are you lame, that you don't get it yourself?"

The woman paused; then said, "Husband, you are tired. Sit here and I will wait on the stranger."

The blacksmith took the seat, when the stranger again blustered, "It would be courtesy to offer me that chair, tired as I am. Perhaps you don't know that I am an officer of the law?"

When supper was ready they took their places, the woman drawing up the arm-chair for her own use, but, as the custom was, they all knelt to say grace, and while their faces were buried in their hands the candle was blown out. The stranger jumped up and began walking around the room.

When a light could be found he had gone and the cushion had disappeared from the chair. "Oh! After all these years!" wailed the woman, and falling on her knees she sobbed like a child, while her husband in vain tried to comfort her. The peddler, who had already gone to bed, but who had seen a part of this puzzling drama through the open door, knew not what to do, but, feeling some concern for the safety of his own possessions, he drew his pack into bed with him, and, being tired, fell asleep with the sobs of the woman sounding in his ears.

When he awoke it was broad day and the earth was fresh and bright from its bath. After dressing he passed into the other room, finding the table still set, the chair before it without its cushion, the fire out, and nobody in or about the house. The smithy was deserted, and to his call there was no response but the chattering of jays in the trees; so, shouldering his pack, he resumed his journey. He opened his pack at a farm-house to repair a clock, when he discovered that his watches were gone, and immediately lodged complaint with the sheriff, but nothing was ever seen again of Ainsley, his wife, or the rough stranger. Who was the thief? What was in the cushion? And what brought the stranger to the house?

WAHCONAH FALLS

The pleasant valley of Dalton, in the Berkshire Hills, had been under the rule of Miacomo for forty years when a Mohawk dignitary of fifty scalps and fifty winters came a-wooing his daughter Wahconah. On a June day in 1637, as the girl sat beside the cascade that bears her name, twining flowers in her hair and watching leaves float down the stream, she became conscious of a pair of eyes bent on her from a neighboring coppice, and arose in some alarm. Finding himself discovered, the owner of the eyes, a handsome young fellow, stepped forward with a quieting air of friendliness, and exclaimed, "Hail, Bright Star!"

"Hail, brother," answered Wahconah.

"I am Nessacus," said the man, "one of King Philip's soldiers. Nessacus is tired with his flight from the Long Knives (the English), and his people faint. Will Bright Star's people shut their lodges against him and his friends?"

The maiden answered, "My father is absent, in council with the Mohawks, but his wigwams are always open. Follow."

Nessacus gave a signal, and forth from the wood came a sad-eyed, battle-worn troop that mustered about him. Under the girl's lead they went down to the valley and were hospitably housed. Five days later Miacomo returned, with him the elderly Mohawk lover, and a priest, Tashmu, of repute a cringing schemer, with whom hunters and soldiers could have nothing in common, and whom they would gladly have put out of the way had they not been deterred by superstitious fears. The strangers were welcomed, though Tashmu looked at them gloomily, and there were games in their honor, Nessacus usually proving the winner, to Wahconah's joy, for she and the young warrior had fallen in love at first sight, and it was not long before he asked her father for her hand. Miacomo favored the suit, but the priest advised him, for politic reasons, to give the girl to the old Mohawk, and thereby cement a tribal friendship that in those days of English aggression might be needful. The Mohawk had three wives already, but he was determined to add Wahconah to his collection, and he did his best, with threats and flattery, to enforce his suit. Nessacus offered to decide the matter in a duel with his rival, and the challenge was accepted, but the wily Tashmu discovered in voices of wind and thunder, flight of birds and shape of clouds, such omens that the scared Indians unanimously forbade a resort to arms. "Let the Great Spirit speak," cried Tashmu, and all yielded their consent.

Invoking a ban on any who should follow, Tashmu proclaimed that he would pass that night in Wizard's Glen, where, by invocations, he would learn the divine will. At sunset he stalked forth, but he had not gone far ere the Mohawk joined him, and the twain proceeded to Wahconah Falls. There was no time for magical hocus-pocus that night, for both of them toiled sorely in deepening a portion of the stream bed, so that the current ran more swiftly and freely on that side, and in the morning Tashmu announced in what way the Great Spirit would show his choice. Assembling the tribe on the river-bank, below a rock that midway split the current, a canoe, with symbols painted on it, was set afloat near the falls. If it passed the dividing rock on the side where Nessacus waited, he should have Wahconah. If it swerved to the opposite shore, where the Mohawk and his counsellor stood, the Great Spirit had chosen the old chief for her husband. Of course, the Mohawk stood on the deeper side. On came the little boat, keeping the centre of the stream. It struck the rock, and all looked eagerly, though Tashmu and the Mohawk could hardly suppress an exultant smile. A little wave struck the canoe: it pivoted against the rock and drifted to the feet of Nessacus. A look of blank amazement came over the faces of the defeated wooer and his friend, while a shout of gladness went up, that the Great Spirit had decided so well. The young couple were wed with rejoicings; the Mohawk trudged homeward, and, to the general satisfaction, Tashmu disappeared with him. Later, when Tashmu was identified as the one who had guided Major Talcott's soldiers to the valley, the priest was caught and slain by Miacomo's men.

KNOCKING AT THE TOMB

Knock, knock, knock! The bell has just gone twelve, and there is the clang again upon the iron door of the tomb. The few people of Lanesboro who are paying the penance of misdeeds or late suppers, by lying awake at that dread hour, gather their blankets around their shoulders and mutter a word of prayer for deliverance against unwholesome visitors of the night. Why is the old Berkshire town so troubled? Who is it that lies buried in that tomb, with its ornament of Masonic symbols? Why was the heavy iron knocker placed on the door? The question is asked, but no one will answer it, nor will any say who the woman is that so often visits the cemetery at the stroke of midnight and sounds the call into the chamber of the dead. Starlight, moonlight, or storm—it makes no difference to the woman. There she goes, in her black cloak, seen dim in the night, except where there are snow and moon together, and there she waits, her hand on the knocker, for the bell to strike to set up her clangor. Some say that she is crazy, and it is her freak to do this thing. Is she calling on the corpses to rise and have a dance among the graves? or has she been asked to call the occupant of that house at a given hour? Perhaps, weary of life, she is asking for admittance to the rest and silence of the tomb. She has long been beneath the sod, this troubler of dreams. Who knows her secret?

THE WHITE DEER OF ONOTA

Beside quiet Onota, in the Berkshire Hills, dwelt a band of Indians, and while they lived here a white deer often came to drink. So rare was the appearance of an animal like this that its visits were held as good omens, and no hunter of the tribe ever tried to slay it. A prophet of the race had said, "So long as the white doe drinks at Onota, famine shall not blight the Indian's harvest, nor pestilence come nigh his lodge, nor foeman lay waste his country." And this prophecy held true. That summer when the deer came with a fawn as white and graceful as herself, it was a year of great abundance. On the outbreak of the French and Indian War a young officer named Montalbert was despatched to the Berkshire country to persuade the Housatonic Indians to declare hostility to the English, and it was as a guest in the village of Onota that he heard of the white deer. Sundry adventurers had made valuable friendships by returning to the French capital with riches and curiosities from the New World. Even Indians had been abducted as gifts for royalty, and this young ambassador resolved that when he returned to his own country the skin of the white deer should be one of the trophies that would win him a smile from Louis.

He offered a price for it—a price that would have bought all their possessions and miles of the country roundabout, but their deer was sacred, and their refusal to sacrifice it was couched in such indignant terms that he wisely said no more about it in the general hearing. There was in the village a drunken fellow, named Wondo, who had come to that pass when he would almost have sold his soul for liquor, and him the officer led away and plied with rum until he promised to bring the white doe to him. The pretty beast was so familiar with men that she suffered Wondo to catch her and lead her to Montalbert. Making sure that none was near, the officer plunged his sword into her side and the innocent creature fell. The snowy skin, now splashed with red, was quickly stripped off, concealed among the effects in Montalbert's outfit, and he set out for Canada; but he had not been many days on his road before Wondo, in an access of misery and repentance, confessed to his share of the crime that had been done and was slain on the moment.

With the death of the deer came an end to good fortune. Wars, blights, emigration followed, and in a few years not a wigwam was left standing beside Onota.

There is a pendant to this legend, incident to the survival of the deer's white fawn. An English hunter, visiting the lake with dog and gun, was surprised to see on its southern bank a white doe. The animal bent to drink and at the same moment the hunter put his gun to his shoulder. Suddenly a howl was heard, so loud, so long, that the woods echoed it, and the deer, taking alarm, fled like the wind. The howl came from the dog, and, as that animal usually showed sagacity in the presence of game, the hunter was seized with a fear that its form was occupied, for the time, by a hag who lived alone in the "north woods," and who was reputed to have appeared in many shapes—for this was not so long after witch times that their influence was forgotten.

Drawing his ramrod, the man gave his dog such a beating that the poor creature had something worth howling for, because it might be the witch that he was thrashing. Then running to the shanty of the suspected woman he flung open her door and demanded to see her back, for, if she had really changed her shape, every blow that he had given to the dog would have been scored on her skin. When he had made his meaning clear, the crone laid hold on the implement that served her for horse at night, and with the wooden end of it rained blows on him so rapidly that, if the dog had had half the meanness in his nature that some people have, the spectacle would have warmed his heart, for it was a prompt and severe revenge for his sufferings. And to the last the hunter could not decide whether the beating that he received was prompted by indignation or vengeance.

WIZARD'S GLEN

Four miles from Pittsfield, Massachusetts, among the Berkshire Hills, is a wild valley, noted for its echoes, that for a century and more has been called Wizard's Glen. Here the Indian priests performed their incantations, and on the red-stained Devil's Altar, it was said, they offered human sacrifice to Hobomocko and his demons of the wood. In Berkshire's early days a hunter, John Chamberlain, of Dalton, who had killed a deer and was carrying it home on his shoulders, was overtaken on the hills by a storm and took shelter from it in a cavernous recess in Wizard's Glen. In spite of his fatigue he was unable to sleep, and while lying on the earth with open eyes he was amazed to see the wood bend apart before him, disclosing a long aisle that was mysteriously lighted and that contained hundreds of capering forms. As his eyes grew accustomed to the faint light he made out tails and cloven feet on the dancing figures; and one tall form with wings, around whose head a wreath of lightning glittered, and who received the deference of the rest, he surmised to be the devil himself. It was such a night and such a place as Satan and his imps commonly chose for high festivals.

As he lay watching them through the sheeted rain a tall and painted Indian leaped on Devil's Altar, fresh scalps dangling round his body in festoons, and his eyes blazing with fierce command. In a brief incantation he summoned the shadow hordes around him. They came, with torches that burned blue, and went around and around the rock singing a harsh chant, until, at a sign, an Indian girl was dragged in and flung on the block of sacrifice. The figures rushed toward her with extended arms and weapons, and the terrified girl gave one cry that rang in the hunter's ears all his life after. The wizard raised his axe: the devils and vampires gathered to drink the blood and clutch the escaping soul, when in a lightning flash the girl's despairing glance fell on the face of Chamberlain. That look touched his manhood, and drawing forth his Bible he held it toward the rabble while he cried aloud the name of God. There was a crash of thunder. The light faded, the demons vanished, the storm swept past, and peace settled on the hills.

BALANCED ROCK

Balanced Rock, or Rolling Rock, near Pittsfield, Massachusetts, is a mass of limestone that was deposited where it stands by the great continental glacier during the ice age, and it weighs four hundred and eighty tons (estimated) in spite of its centuries of weathering. Here one of the Atotarhos, kings of the Six Nations, had his camp. He was a fierce man, who ate and drank from bowls made of the skulls of enemies, and who, when he received messages and petitions, wreathed himself from head to foot with poison snakes. The son of this ferocious being inherited none of his war-like tendencies; indeed, the lad was almost feminine in appearance, and on succeeding to power he applied himself to the cultivation of peaceful arts. Later historians have uttered a suspicion that he was a natural son of Count Frontenac, but that does not suit with this legend.

The young Atotarho stood near Balanced Rock watching a number of big boys play duff. In this game one stone is placed upon another and the players, standing as far from it as they fancy they can throw, attempt to knock it out of place with other stones. The silence of Atotarho and his slender, girlish look called forth rude remarks from the boys, who did not know him, and who dared him to test his skill. The young chief came forward, and as he did so the jeers and laughter changed to cries of astonishment and fear, for at each step he grew in size until he towered above them, a giant. Then they knew him, and fell down in dread, but he took no revenge. Catching up great bowlders he tossed them around as easily as if they had been beechnuts, and at last, lifting the balanced rock, he placed it lightly where it stands to-day, gave them a caution against ill manners and hasty judgments, and resumed his slender form. For many years after, the old men of the tribe repeated this story and its lesson from the top of Atotarho's duff.

SHONKEEK-MOONKEEK

This is the Mohegan name of the pretty lake in the Berkshires now called Pontoosuc. Shonkeek was a boy, Moonkeek a girl, and they were cousins who grew up as children commonly do, whether in house or wigwam: they roamed the woods and hills together, filled their baskets with flowers and berries, and fell in love. But the marriage of cousins was forbidden in the Mohegan polity, and when they reached an age in which they found companionship most delightful their rambles were interdicted and they were even told to avoid each other. This had the usual effect, and they met on islands in the lake at frequent intervals, to the torment of one Nockawando, who wished to wed the girl himself, and who reported her conduct to her parents.

The lovers agreed, after this, to fly to an Eastern tribe into which they would ask to be adopted, but they were pledged, if aught interfered with their escape, to meet beneath the lake. Nockawando interfered. On the next night, as the unsuspecting Shonkeek was paddling over to the island where the maid awaited him, the jealous rival, rowing softly in his wake, sent an arrow into his back, and Shonkeek, without a cry, pitched headlong into the water. Yet, to the eyes of Nockawando, he appeared to keep his seat and urge his canoe forward. The girl saw the boat approach: it sped, now, like an eagle's flight. One look, as it passed the rock; one glance at the murderer, crouching in his birchen vessel, and with her lover's name on her lips she leaped into her own canoe and pushed out from shore. Nockawando heard her raise the death-song and rowed forward as rapidly as he could, but near the middle of the lake his arm fell palsied.

The song had ended and the night had become strangely, horribly still. Not a chirp of cricket, not a lap of wave, not a rustle of leaf. Motionless the girl awaited, for his boat was still moving by the impetus of his last stroke of the paddle. The evening star was shining low on the horizon, and as her figure loomed in the darkness the star shone through at the point where her eye had looked forth. It was no human creature that sat there. Then came the dead man's boat. The two shadows rowed noiselessly together, and as they disappeared in the mist that was now settling on the landscape, an unearthly laugh rang over the lake; then all was still. When Nockawando reached the camp that night he was a raving maniac. The Indians never found the bodies of the pair, but they believed that while water remains in Pontoosuc its surface will be vexed by these journeys of the dead.

THE SALEM ALCHEMIST

In 1720 there lived in a turreted house at North and Essex Streets, in Salem, a silent, dark-visaged man,—a reputed chemist. He gathered simples in the fields, and parcels and bottles came and went between him and learned doctors in Boston; but report went around that it was not drugs alone that he worked with, nor medicines for passing ailments that he distilled. The watchman, drowsily pacing the streets in the small hours, saw his shadow move athwart the furnace glare in his tower, and other shadows seemed at the moment to flit about it—shadows that could be thrown by no tangible form, yet that had a grotesque likeness to the human kind. A clink of hammers and a hiss of steam were sometimes heard, and his neighbors devoutly hoped that if he secured the secret of the philosopher's stone or the universal solvent, it would be honestly come by.

But it was neither gold nor the perilous strong water that he wanted. It was life: the elixir that would dispel the chill and decrepitude of age, that would bring back the youthful sparkle to the eye and set the pulses bounding. He explored the surrounding wilderness day after day; the juices of its trees and plants he compounded, night after night, long without avail. Not until after a thousand failures did he conceive that he had secured the ingredients but they were many, they were perishable, they must be distilled within five days, for fermentation and decay would set in if he delayed longer. Gathering the herbs and piling his floor with fuel, he began his work, alone; the furnace glowed, the retorts bubbled, and through their long throats trickled drops—golden, ruddy, brown, and crystal—that would be combined into that precious draught.

And none too soon, for under the strain of anxiety he seemed to be aging fast. He took no sleep, except while sitting upright in his chair, for, should he yield entirely to nature's appeal, his fire would die and his work be spoiled. With heavy eyes and aching head he watched his furnace and listened to the constant drip, drip of the precious liquor. It was the fourth day. He had knelt to stir his fire to more active burning. Its brightness made him blink, its warmth was grateful, and he reclined before it, with elbow on the floor and head resting on his hand. How cheerily the logs hummed and crackled, yet how drowsily—how slow the hours were—how dull the watch! Lower, lower sank the head, and heavier grew the eyes. At last he lay full length on the floor, and the long sleep of exhaustion had begun.

He was awakened by the sound of a bell. "The church bell!" he cried, starting up. "And people going through the streets to meeting. How is this? The sun is in the east! My God! I have been asleep! The furnace is cold. The elixir!" He hastily blended the essences that he had made, though one or two ingredients were still lacking, and drank them off. "Faugh!" he exclaimed. "Still unfinished-perhaps spoiled. I must begin again." Taking his hat and coat he uttered a weary sigh and was about to open the door when his cheek blenched with pain, sight seemed to leave him, the cry for help that rose to his lips was stifled in a groan of anguish, a groping gesture brought a shelf of retorts and bottles to the floor, and he fell writhing among their fragments. The elixir of life, unfinished, was an elixir of death.

ELIZA WHARTON

Under the name of Eliza Wharton for a brief time lived a woman whose name was said to be Elizabeth Whitman. Little is known of her, and it is thought that she had gone among strangers to conceal disgrace. She died without telling her story. In 1788 she arrived at the Bell Tavern, Danvers, in company with a man, who, after seeing her properly bestowed, drove away and never returned. A graceful, beautiful, well-bred woman, with face overcast by a tender melancholy, she kept indoors with her books, her sewing, and a guitar, avoiding the gossip of the idle. She said that her husband was absent on a journey, and a letter addressed to "Mrs. Eliza Wharton" was to be seen on her table when she received callers. Once a stranger paused at her door and read the name thereon. As he passed on the woman groaned, "I am undone!" One good woman, seeing her need of care and defiant of village prattling, took her to her home, and there, after giving birth to a dead child, she passed away. Among her effects were letters full of pathetic appeal, and some verses, closing thus:

> "O thou for whose dear sake I bear
>
> A doom so dreadful, so severe,
>
> May happy fates thy footsteps guide
>
> And o'er thy peaceful home preside.
>
> Nor let Eliza's early tomb
>
> Infect thee with its baleful gloom."

A stone was raised above her grave, by whom it is not known, and this inscription was engraved thereon: "This humble stone, in memory of Elizabeth Whitman, is inscribed by her weeping friends, to whom she endeared herself by uncommon tenderness and affection. Endowed with superior genius and acquirements, she was still more endeared by humility and benevolence. Let candor throw a veil over her frailties, for great was her charity for others. She sustained the last painful scene far from every friend, and exhibited an example of calm resignation. Her departure was on the 25th of July, 1788, in the thirty-seventh year of her age, and the tears of strangers watered her grave."

SALE OF THE SOUTHWICKS

Bitter were the persecutions endured by Quakers at the hands of the Puritans. They were flogged if they were restless in church, and flogged if they did not go to it. Their ears were slit and they were set in the stocks if they preached, and if any tender-hearted person gave them bed, bite, or sup, he, too, was liable to punishment. They were charged with the awful offence of preaching false doctrine, and no matter how pure their lives might be, the stern Salemite would concede no good of them while their faith was different from his. They even suspected Cobbler Keezar of mischief when he declared that his magic lapstone which Agrippa had torn from the tower at Nettesheim—gave him a vision of the time when men would be as glad as nature, when the "snuffler of psalms" would sing for joy, when priests and Quakers would talk together kindly, when pillory and gallows should be gone. Poor Keezar! In ecstasy at that prospect he flung up his arms, and his lapstone rolled into the Merrimack. The tired mill-girls of Lowell still frequent the spot to seek some dim vision of future comfort.

In contrast to the tales of habitual tyranny toward the Quakers is the tradition of the Southwicks. Lawrence and Cassandra, of that name, were banished from Salem, in spite of their blameless lives, for they had embraced Quakerism. They died within three days of each other on Shelter Island, but their son and daughter, Daniel and Provided, returned to their birthplace, and were incessantly fined for not going to church. At last, having lost their property through seizures made to satisfy their fines, the General Court of Boston issued an order for their sale, as slaves, to any Englishman of Virginia or Barbadoes. Edward Butter was assigned to sell and take them to their master. The day arrived and Salem market-place was crowded with a throng of the curious. Provided Southwick mounted the block and Butter began to call for bids. While expatiating on the aptness of the girl for field or house-service, the master of the Barbadoes ship on which Butter had engaged passage for himself and his two charges looked into her innocent face, and roared, in noble dudgeon, "If my ship were filled with silver, by God, I'd sink her in harbor rather than take away this child!" The multitude experienced a quick change of feeling and applauded the sentiment. As the judges and officers trudged away with gloomy faces, Provided Southwick descended from the auction-block, and brother and sister went forth into the town free and unharmed.

THE COURTSHIP OF MYLES STANDISH

Myles Standish, compact, hard-headed little captain of the Puritan guard at Plymouth, never knew the meaning of fear until he went a-courting Priscilla Mullins—or was she a Molines, as some say? He had fought white men and red men and never reeked of danger in the doing it, but his courage sank to his boots whenever this demure maiden glanced at him, as he thought, with approval. Odd, too, for he had been married once, and Rose was not so long dead that he had forgotten the ways and likings of women; but he made no progress in his suit, and finally chose John Alden to urge it for him. John—who divides with Mary Chilton the honor of being first to land on Plymouth Rock—was a well-favored lad of twenty-two. Until he could build a house for himself he shared Standish's cottage and looked up to that worthy as a guardian, but it was a hard task that was set for him now. He went to goodman Mullins with a slow step and sober countenance and asked leave to plead his protector's cause. The father gave it, called his daughter in, and left them together; then, with noble faith to his mission, the young man begged the maiden's hand for the captain, dwelling on his valor, strength, wisdom, his military greatness, his certainty of promotion, his noble lineage, and all good attributes he could endow him with.

Priscilla kept at her spinning while this harangue went on, but the drone of the wheel did not prevent her noting a sigh and a catch of the breath that interrupted the discourse now and then. She flushed as she replied, "Why does not Captain Standish come to me himself? If I am worth the winning I ought to be worth the wooing."

But John Alden seemed not to notice the girl's confusion until, in a pause in his eloquence, Priscilla bent her head a little, as if to mend a break in the flax, and said, "Prithee, John, why don't you speak for yourself?"

Then a great light broke on the understanding of John Alden, and a great warmth welled up in his heart, and—they were married. Myles Standish—well, some say that he walked in the wedding procession, while one narrator holds that the sturdy Roundhead tramped away to the woods, where he sat for a day, hating himself, and that he never forgave his protege nor the maiden who took advantage of leap year. However that may be, the wedding was a happy one, and the Aldens of all America claim John and Priscilla for their ancestors.

MOTHER CREWE

Mother Crewe was of evil repute in Plymouth in the last century. It was said that she had taken pay for luring a girl into her old farm-house, where a man lay dead of small-pox, with intent to harm her beauty; she was accused of blighting land and driving ships ashore with spells; in brief, she was called a witch, and people, even those who affected to ignore the craft of wizardry, were content to keep away from her. When the Revolution ended, Southward Howland demanded Dame Crewe's house and acre, claiming under law of entail, though primogeniture had been little enforced in America, where there was room and to spare for all. But Howland was stubborn and the woman's house had good situation, so one day he rode to her door and summoned her with a tap of his whip.

"What do you here on my land?" said he.

"I live on land that is my own. I cleared it, built my house here, and no other has claim to it."

"Then I lay claim. The place is mine. I shall tear your cabin down on Friday."

"On Friday they'll dig your grave on Burying Hill. I see the shadow closing round you. You draw it in with every breath. Quick! Home and make your peace!" The hag's withered face was touched with spots of red and her eyes glared in their sunken sockets.

"Bandy no witch words with me, woman. On Friday I will return." And he swung himself into his saddle. As he did so a black cat leaped on Mother Crewe's shoulder and stood there, squalling. The woman listened to its cries as if they were words. Her look of hate deepened. Raising her hand, she cried, "Your day is near its end. Repent!"

"Bah! You have heard what I have said. If on Friday you are not elsewhere, I'll tear the timbers down and bury you in the ruins."

"Enough!" cried the woman, her form straightening, her voice grown shrill. "My curse is on you here and hereafter. Die! Then go down to hell!"

As she said this the cat leaped from her shoulder to the flank of the horse, spitting and clawing, and the frightened steed set off at a furious pace. As he disappeared in the scrub oaks his master was seen vainly trying to stop him. The evening closed in with fog and chill, and before the light waned a man faring homeward came upon the corpse of Southward Howland stretched along the ground.

AUNT RACHEL'S CURSE

On a headland near Plymouth lived "Aunt Rachel," a reputed seer, who made a scant livelihood by forecasting the future for such seagoing people as had crossed her palm. The crew of a certain brig came to see her on the day before sailing, and she reproached one of the lads for keeping bad company. "Avast, there, granny," interrupted another, who took the chiding to himself. "None of your slack, or I'll put a stopper on your gab." The old woman sprang erect. Levelling her skinny finger at the man, she screamed, "Moon cursers! You have set false beacons and wrecked ships for plunder. It was your fathers and mothers who decoyed a brig to these sands and left me childless and a widow. He who rides the pale horse be your guide, and you be of the number who follow him!"

That night old Rachel's house was burned, and she barely escaped with her life, but when it was time for the brig to sail she took her place among the townfolk who were to see it off. The owner of the brig tried to console her for the loss of the house. "I need it no longer," she answered, "for the narrow house will soon be mine, and you wretches cannot burn that. But you! Who will console you for the loss of your brig?"

"My brig is stanch. She has already passed the worst shoal in the bay."

"But she carries a curse. She cannot swim long."

As each successive rock and bar was passed the old woman leaned forward, her hand shaking, her gray locks flying, her eyes starting, her lips mumbling maledictions, "like an evil spirit, chiding forth the storms as ministers of vengeance." The last shoal was passed, the merchant sighed with relief at seeing the vessel now safely on her course, when the woman uttered a harsh cry, and raised her hand as if to command silence until something happened that she evidently expected. For this the onlookers had not long to wait: the brig halted and trembled—her sails shook in the wind, her crew were seen trying to free the cutter—then she careened and sank until only her mast-heads stood out of the water. Most of the company ran for boats and lines, and few saw Rachel pitch forward on the earth-dead, with a fierce smile of exultation on her face. The rescuers came back with all the crew, save one—the man who had challenged the old woman and revengefully burned her cabin. Rachel's body was buried where her house had stood, and the rock—before unknown—where the brig had broken long bore the name of Rachel's Curse.

NIX'S MATE

The black, pyramidal beacon, called Nix's Mate, is well known to yachtsmen, sailors, and excursionists in Boston harbor. It rises above a shoal,—all that is left of a fair, green island which long ago disappeared in the sea. In 1636 it had an extent of twelve acres, and on its highest point was a gallows where pirates were hanged in chains. One night cries were heard on board of a ship that lay at anchor a little way off shore, and when the watch put off, to see what might be amiss, the captain, named Nix, was found murdered in his bed. There was no direct evidence in the case, and no motive could be assigned for the deed, unless it was the expectancy of promotion on the part of the mate, in case of his commander's death.

It was found, however, that this possibility gave significance to certain acts and sayings of that officer during the voyage, and on circumstantial evidence so slight as this he was convicted and sentenced to death. As he was led to execution he swore that he was not guilty, as he had done before, and from the scaffold he cried aloud, "God, show that I am innocent. Let this island sink and prove to these people that I have never stained my hands with human blood." Soon after the execution of his sentence it was noticed that the surf was going higher on the shore, that certain rocks were no longer uncovered at low tide, and in time the island wasted away. The colonists looked with awe on this manifestation and confessed that God had shown their wrong.

THE WILD MAN OF CAPE COD

For years after Bellamy's pirate ship was wrecked at Wellfleet, by false pilotage on the part of one of his captives, a strange-looking man used to travel up and down the cape, who was believed to be one of the few survivors of that night of storm, and of the hanging that others underwent after getting ashore. The pirates had money when the ship struck; it was found in the pockets of a hundred drowned who were cast on the beach, as well as among the sands of the cape, for coin was gathered there long after. They supposed the stranger had his share, or more, and that he secreted a quantity of specie near his cabin. After his death gold was found under his clothing in a girdle. He was often received at the houses of the fishermen, both because the people were hospitable and because they feared harm if they refused to feed or shelter him; but if his company grew wearisome he was exorcised by reading aloud a portion of the Bible. When he heard the holy words he invariably departed.

And it was said that fiends came to him at night, for in his room, whether he appeared to sleep or wake, there were groans and blasphemy, uncanny words and sounds that stirred the hair of listeners on their scalps. The unhappy creature cried to be delivered from his tormenters and begged to be spared from seeing a rehearsal of the murders he had committed. For some time he was missed from his haunts, and it was thought that he had secured a ship and set to sea again; but a traveller on the sands, while passing his cabin in the small hours, had heard a more than usual commotion, and could distinguish the voice of the wild man raised in frantic appeal to somebody, or something; still, knowing that it was his habit to cry out so, and having misgivings about approaching the house, the traveller only hurried past. A few neighbors went to the lonely cabin and looked through the windows, which, as well as the doors, were locked on the inside. The wild man lay still and white on the floor, with the furniture upset and pieces of gold clutched in his fingers and scattered about him. There were marks of claws about his neck.

NEWBURY'S OLD ELM

Among the venerable relics of Newbury few are better known and more prized than the old elm. It is a stout tree, with a girth of twenty-four and a half feet, and is said to have been standing since 1713. In that year it was planted by Richard Jacques, then a youthful rustic, who had a sweetheart, as all rustics have, and adored her as rustics and other men should do. On one of his visits he stayed uncommonly late. It was nearly ten o'clock when he set off for home. The town had been abed an hour or more; the night was murky and oppressively still, and corpse-candles were dancing in the graveyard. Witch times had not been so far agone that he felt comfortable, and, lest some sprite, bogie, troll, or goblin should waylay him, he tore an elm branch from a tree that grew before his sweetheart's house, and flourished it as he walked. He reached home without experiencing any of the troubles that a superstitious fancy had conjured. As he was about to cast the branch away a comforting vision of his loved one came into his mind, and he determined to plant the branch at his own door, that in the hours of their separation he might be reminded of her who dwelt beneath the parent tree. He did so. It rooted and grew, and when the youth and maid had long been married, their children and grandchildren sported beneath its branches.

SAMUEL SEWALL'S PROPHECY

The peace of Newbury is deemed to be permanently secured by the prophecy of Samuel Sewall, the young man who married the buxom daughter of Mint-Master John Hull, and received, as wedding portion, her weight in fresh-coined pine-tree shillings. He afterward became notorious as one of the witchcraft judges. The prophecy has not been countervailed, nor is it likely to be, whether the conditions are kept or not. It runs in this wise:

"As long as Plum island shall faithfully keep the commanded Post, Notwithstanding the hectoring words and hard blows of the proud and boisterous ocean; As long as any Salmon or Sturgeon shall swim in the streams of Merrimack, or any Perch or Pickeril in Crane Pond; As long as the Sea Fowl shall know the time of their coming, and not neglect seasonably to visit the places of their acquaintance; As long as any Cattel shall be fed with Grass growing in the meadows which doe humbly bow themselves before Turkie Hill; As long as any Sheep shall walk upon Old town Hills, and shall from thence look pleasantly down upon the River Parker and the fruitful Marishes lying beneath; As long as any free and harmless Doves shall find a White Oak or other Tree within the township to perch or feed, or build a careless Nest upon, and shall voluntarily present themselves to perform the office of Gleaners after Barley Harvest; As long as Nature shall not grow old and dote, but shall constantly remember to give the rows of Indian Corn their education by Pairs; So long shall Christians be born there and being first made meet, shall from thence be translated to be made partakers of the Saints of Light."

THE SHRIEKING WOMAN

During the latter part of the seventeenth century a Spanish ship, richly laden, was beset off Marblehead by English pirates, who killed every person on board, at the time of the capture, except a beautiful English lady, a passenger on the ship, who was brought ashore at night and brutally murdered at a ledge of rocks near Oakum Bay. As the fishermen who lived near were absent in their boats, the women and children, who were startled from their sleep by her piercing shrieks, dared not attempt a rescue. Taking her a little way from shore in their boat, the pirates flung her into the sea, and as she came to the surface and clutched the gunwale they hewed at her hands with cutlasses. She was heard to cry, "Lord, save me! Mercy! O, Lord Jesus, save me!" Next day the people found her mangled body on the rocks, and, with bitter imprecations at the worse than beasts that had done this wrong, they prepared it for burial. It was interred where it was found, but, although it was committed to the earth with Christian forms, for one hundred and fifty years the victim's cries and appeals were repeated, on each anniversary of the crime, with such distinctness as to affright all who heard them—and most of the citizens of Marblehead claimed to be of that number.

AGNES SURRIAGE

When, in 1742, Sir Henry Frankland, collector of the port of Boston, went to Marblehead to inquire into the smuggling that was pretty boldly carried on, he put up at the Fountain Inn. As he entered that hostelry a barefooted girl, of sixteen, who was scrubbing the floor, looked at him. The young man was handsome, well dressed, gallant in bearing, while Agnes Surriage, maid of all work, was of good figure, beautiful face, and modest demeanor. Sir Henry tossed out a coin, bidding her to buy shoes with it, and passed to his room. But the image of Agnes rose constantly before him. He sought her company, found her of ready intelligence for one unschooled, and shortly after this visit he obtained the consent of her parents—humble folk—to take this wild flower to the city and cultivate it.

He gave her such an education as the time and place afforded, dressed her well, and behaved with kindness toward her, while she repaid this care with the frank bestowal of her heart. The result was not foreseen—not intended—but they became as man and wife without having wedded. Colonial society was scandalized, yet the baronet loved the girl sincerely and could not be persuaded to part from her. Having occasion to visit England he took Agnes with him and introduced her as Lady Frankland, but the nature of their alliance had been made known to his relatives and they refused to receive her. The thought of a permanent union with the girl had not yet presented itself to the young man. An aristocrat could not marry a commoner. A nobleman might destroy the honor of a girl for amusement, but it was beneath his dignity to make reparation for the act.

Sir Henry was called to Portugal in 1755, and Agnes went with him. They arrived inopportunely in one respect, though the sequel showed a blessing in the accident; for while they were sojourning in Lisbon the earthquake occurred that laid the city in ruins and killed sixty thousand people. Sir Henry was in his carriage at the time and was buried beneath a falling wall, but Agnes, who had hurried from her lodging at the first alarm, sped through the rocking streets in search of her lover. She found him at last, and, instead of crying or fainting, she set to work to drag away the stones and timbers that were piled upon him. Had she been a delicate creature, her lover's equal in birth, such as Frankland was used to dance with at the state balls, she could not have done this, but her days of service at the inn had given her a strength that received fresh accessions from hope and love. In an hour she had liberated him, and, carrying him to a place of safety, she cherished the spark of life until health returned. The nobleman had received sufficient proof of Agnes's love and courage. He realized, at last, the superiority of worth to birth. He gave his name, as he had already given his heart, to her, and their married life was happy.

SKIPPER IRESON'S RIDE

Flood, Fluid, or Floyd Ireson (in some chronicles his name is Benjamin) was making for Marblehead in a furious gale, in the autumn of 1808, in the schooner Betsy. Off Cape Cod he fell in with the schooner Active, of Beverly, in distress, for she had been disabled in the heavy sea and was on her beam ends, at the mercy of the tempest. The master of the Active hailed Ireson and asked to be taken off, for his vessel could not last much longer, but the Betsy, after a parley, laid her course again homeward, leaving the exhausted and despairing crew of the sinking vessel to shift as best they might. The Betsy had not been many hours in port before it was known that men were in peril in the bay, and two crews of volunteers set off instantly to the rescue. But it was too late. The Active was at the bottom of the sea. The captain and three of his men were saved, however, and their grave accusation against the Betsy's skipper was common talk in Marblehead ere many days.

On a moonlight night Flood Ireson was roused by knocking at his door. On opening it he was seized by a band of his townsmen, silently hustled to a deserted spot, stripped, bound, and coated with tar and feathers. At break of day he was pitched into an old dory and dragged along the roads until the bottom of the boat dropped out, when he was mounted in a cart and the procession continued until Salem was reached. The selectmen of that town turned back the company, and for a part of the way home the cart was drawn by a jeering crowd of fishwives. Ireson was released only when nature had been taxed to the limit of endurance. As his bonds were cut he said, quietly, "I thank you for my ride, gentlemen, but you will live to regret it."

Some of the cooler heads among his fellows have believed the skipper innocent and throw the blame for the abandonment of the sinking vessel on Ireson's mutinous crew. There are others, the universal deniers, who believe that the whole thing is fiction. Those people refuse to believe in their own grandfathers. Ireson became moody and reckless after this adventure. He did not seem to think it worth the attempt to clear himself. At times he seemed trying, by his aggressive acts and bitter speeches, to tempt some hot-tempered townsman to kill him. He died after a severe freezing, having been blown to sea—as some think by his own will—in a smack.

HEARTBREAK HILL

The name of Heartbreak Hill pertains, in the earliest records of Ipswich, to an eminence in the middle of that town on which there was a large Indian settlement, called Agawam, before the white men settled there and drove the inhabitants out. Ere the English colony had been firmly planted a sailor straying ashore came among the simple natives of Agawam, and finding their ways full of novelty he lived with them for a time. When he found means to return to England he took with him the love of a maiden of the tribe, but the girl herself he left behind, comforting her on his departure with an assurance that before many moons he would return. Months went by and extended into years, and every day the girl climbed Heartbreak Hill to look seaward for some token of her lover. At last a ship was seen trying to make harbor, with a furious gale running her close to shore, where breakers were lashing the rocks and sand. The girl kept her station until the vessel, becoming unmanageable, was hurled against the shore and smashed into a thousand pieces. As its timbers went tossing away on the frothing billows a white, despairing face was lifted to hers for an instant; then it sank and was seen nevermore—her lover's face. The "dusky Ariadne" wasted fast from that day, and she lies buried beside the ledge that was her watch-tower.

HARRY MAIN: THE TREASURE AND THE CATS

Ipswich had a very Old Harry in the person of Harry Main, a dark-souled being, who, after a career of piracy, smuggling, blasphemy, and dissipation, became a wrecker, and lured vessels to destruction with false lights. For his crimes he was sent, after death, to do penance on Ipswich bar, where he had sent many a ship ashore, his doom being to twine ropes of sand, though some believe it was to shovel back the sea. Whenever his rope broke he would roar with rage and anguish, so that he was heard for miles, whereon the children would run to their trembling mothers and men would look troubled and shake their heads. After a good bit of cable had been coiled, Harry had a short respite that he enjoyed on Plum Island, to the terror of the populace. When the tide and a gale are rising together people say, as they catch the sound of moaning from the bar, "Old Harry's grumbling again."

Now, Harry Main—to say nothing of Captain Kidd—was believed to have buried his ill-gotten wealth in Ipswich, and one man dreamed for three successive nights that it had been interred in a mill. Believing that a revelation had been made to him he set off with spade, lantern, and Bible, on the first murky night—for he wanted no partner in the discovery—and found a spot which he recognized as the one that had been pictured to his sleeping senses. He set to work with alacrity and a shovel, and soon he unearthed a flat stone and an iron bar. He was about to pry up the stone when an army of black cats encircled the pit and glared into it with eyes of fire.

The poor man, in an access both of alarm and courage, whirled the bar about his head and shouted "Scat!" The uncanny guards of the treasure disappeared instanter, and at the same moment the digger found himself up to his middle in icy water that had poured into the hole as he spoke.

The moral is that you should never talk when you are hunting for treasure. Wet, scared, and disheartened, the man crawled out and made homeward, carrying with him, as proof of his adventure, a case of influenza and the iron bar. The latter trophy he fashioned into a latch, in which shape it still does service on one of the doors of Ipswich.

THE WESSAGUSCUS HANGING

Among the Puritans who settled in Wessaguscus, now Weymouth, Massachusetts, was a brash young fellow, of remarkable size and strength, who, roaming the woods one day, came on a store of corn concealed in the ground, in the fashion of the Indians. As anybody might have done, he filled his hat from the granary and went his way. When the red man who had dug the pit came back to it he saw that his cache had been levied on, and as the footprints showed the marauder to be an Englishman he went to the colonists and demanded justice. The matter could have been settled by giving a pennyworth of trinkets to the Indian, but, as the moral law had been broken, the Puritans deemed it right that the pilferer should suffer.

They held a court and a proposition was made and seriously considered that, as the culprit was young, hardy, and useful to the colony, his clothes should be stripped off and put on the body of a bedridden weaver, who would be hanged in his stead in sight of the offended savages. Still, it was feared that if they learned the truth about that execution the Indians would learn a harmful lesson in deceit, and it was, therefore, resolved to punish the true offender. He, thinking they were in jest, submitted to be bound, though before doing so he could have "cleaned out" the court-room, and ere he was really aware of the purpose of his judges he was kicking at vacancy.

Butler, in "Hudibras," quotes the story, but makes the offence more serious—

> "This precious brother, having slain,
>
> In time of peace, an Indian,
>
> Not out of malice, but mere zeal,
>
> Because he was an infidel,
>
> The mighty Tottipotimoy
>
> Sent to our elders an envoy
>
> Complaining sorely of the breach Of league."

But the Puritans, having considered that the offender was a teacher and a cobbler,

> "Resolved to spare him; yet, to do
>
> The Indian Hoghan Moghan, too,
>
> Impartial justice, in his stead did
>
> Hang an old weaver that was bed-rid."

The whole circumstance is cloudy, and the reader may accept either version that touches his fancy.

THE UNKNOWN CHAMPION

There was that in the very air of the New World that made the Pilgrims revolt against priests and kings. The Revolution was long a-breeding before shots were fired at Lexington. Stout old Endicott, having conceived a dislike to the British flag because to his mind the cross was a relic of popery, paraded his soldiers and with his sword ripped out the offending emblem in their presence. There was a faint cry of "Treason!" but he answered, "I will avouch the deed before God and man. Beat a flourish, drummer. Shout for the ensign of New England. Pope nor tyrant hath part in it now." And a loud huzza of independence went forth.

With this sentiment confirmed among the people, it is not surprising that the judges who had condemned a papist king—Charles I.—to the block should find welcome in this land. For months at a time they lived in cellars and garrets in various parts of New England, their hiding-places kept secret from the royal sheriffs who were seeking them. For a time they had shelter in a cave in West Rock, New Haven, and once in that town they were crouching beneath the bridge that a pursuing party crossed in search of them. In Ipswich the house is pointed out where they were concealed in the cellar, and the superstitious believed that, as a penalty for their regicidal decision, they are doomed to stay there, crying vainly for deliverance.

Philip, the Narragansett chief, had declared war on the people of New England, and was waging it with a persistence and fury that spread terror through the country. It was a struggle against manifest destiny, such as must needs be repeated whenever civilization comes to dispute a place in new lands with savagery, and which has been continued, more and more feebly, to our own day. The war was bloody, and for a long time the issue hung in the balance. At last the Indian king was driven westward. The Nipmucks joined him in the Connecticut Valley, and he laid siege to the lonely settlements of Brookfield, Northfield, Deerfield, and Springfield, killing, scalping, and burning without mercy. On the 1st of September, 1675, he attacked Hadley while its people were at church, the war-yelp interrupting a prayer of the pastor. All the men of the congregation sallied out with pikes and guns and engaged the foe, but so closely were they pressed that a retreat was called, when suddenly there appeared among them a tall man, of venerable and commanding aspect, clad in leather, and armed with sword and gun.

His hair and beard were long and white, but his eye was dark and resolute, and his voice was strong. "Why sink your hearts?" he cried. "Fear ye that God will give you up to yonder heathen dogs? Follow me, and ye shall see that this day there is a champion in Israel."

Posting half the force at his command to sustain the fight, he led the others quickly by a detour to the rear of the Indians, on whom he fell with such energy that the savages, believing themselves overtaken by reinforcements newly come, fled in confusion. When the victors returned to the village the unknown champion signed to the company to fall to their knees while he offered thanks and prayer. Then he was silent for a little, and when they looked up he was gone.

They believed him to be an angel sent for their deliverance, nor, till he had gone to his account, did they know that their captain in that crisis was Colonel William Goffe, one of the regicide judges, who, with his associate Whalley, was hiding from the vengeance of the son of the king they had rebelled against. After leaving their cave in New Haven, being in peril from beasts and human hunters, they went up the Connecticut Valley to Hadley, where the clergyman of the place, Rev. John Russell, gave them shelter for fifteen years. Few were aware of their existence, and when Goffe, pale with seclusion from the light, appeared among the people near whom he had long been living, it is no wonder that they regarded him with awe.

Whalley died in the minister's house and was buried in a crypt outside of the cellar-wall, while Goffe kept much abroad, stopping in many places and under various disguises until his death, which occurred soon after that of his associate. He was buried in New Haven.

GOODY COLE

Goodwife Eunice Cole, of Hampton, Massachusetts, was so "vehemently suspected to be a witch" that in 1680 she was thrown into jail with a chain on her leg. She had a mumbling habit, which was bad, and a wild look, which was worse. The death of two calves had been charged to her sorceries, and she was believed to have raised the cyclone that sent a party of merrymakers to the sea-bottom off the Isles of Shoals, for insulting her that morning. Some said that she took the shapes of eagles, dogs, and cats, and that she had the aspect of an ape when she went through the mummeries that caused Goody Marston's child to die, yet while she was in Ipswich jail a likeness of her was stumping about the graveyard on the day when they buried the child. For such offences as that of making bread ferment and give forth evil odors, that housekeepers could only dispel by prayer, she was several times whipped and ducked by the constable.

At last she lay under sentence of death, for Anna Dalton declared that her child had been changed in its cradle and that she hated and feared the thing that had been left there. Her husband, Ezra, had pleaded with her in vain. "'Tis no child of mine," she cried. "'Tis an imp. Don't you see how old and shrewd it is? How wrinkled and ugly? It does not take my milk: it is sucking my blood and wearing me to skin and bone." Once, as she sat brooding by the fire, she turned to her husband and said, "Rake the coals out and put the child in them. Goody Cole will fly fast enough when she hears it screaming, and will come down chimney in the shape of an owl or a bat, and take the thing away. Then we shall have our little one back."

Goodman Dalton sighed as he looked into the worn, scowling face of his wife; then, laying his hands on her head, he prayed to God that she might be led out of the shadow and made to love her child again. As he prayed a gleam of sunset shone in at the window and made a halo around the face of the smiling babe. Mistress Dalton looked at the little thing in doubt; then a glow of recognition came into her eyes, and with a sob of joy she caught the child to her breast, while Dalton embraced them both, deeply happy, for his wife had recovered her reason. In the midst of tears and kisses the woman started with a faint cry: she remembered that a poor old creature was about to expiate on the gallows a crime that had never been committed. She urged her husband to ride with all speed to justice Sewall and demand that Goody

Cole be freed. This the goodman did, arriving at Newbury at ten o'clock at night, when the town had long been abed and asleep. By dint of alarms at the justice's door he brought forth that worthy in gown and night-cap, and, after the case had been explained to him, he wrote an order for Mistress Cole's release.

With this paper in his hand Dalton rode at once to Ipswich, and when the cock crew in the dawning the victim of that horrible charge walked forth, without her manacles. Yet dark suspicion hung about the beldam to the last, and she died, as she had lived, alone in the little cabin that stood near the site of the academy. Even after her demise the villagers could with difficulty summon courage to enter her cot and give her burial. Her body was tumbled into a pit, hastily dug near her door, and a stake was driven through the heart to exorcise the powers of evil that possessed her in life.

GENERAL MOULTON AND THE DEVIL

Jonathan Moulton, of Hampton, was a general of consequence in the colonial wars, but a man not always trusted in other than military matters. It was even hinted that his first wife died before her time, for he quickly found consolation in his bereavement by marrying her companion. In the middle of the night the bride was awakened with a start, for she felt a cold hand plucking at the wedding-ring that had belonged to the buried Mrs. Moulton, and a voice whispered in her ear, "Give the dead her own." With a scream of terror she leaped out of bed, awaking her husband and causing candles to be brought. The ring was gone.

It was long after this occurrence that the general sat musing at his fireside on the hardness of life in new countries and the difficulty of getting wealth, for old Jonathan was fond of money, and the lack of it distressed him worse than a conscience. "If only I could have gold enough," he muttered, "I'd sell my soul for it." Whiz! came something down the chimney. The general was dazzled by a burst of sparks, from which stepped forth a lank personage in black velvet with clean ruffles and brave jewels. "Talk quick, general," said the unknown, "for in fifteen minutes I must be fifteen miles away, in Portsmouth." And picking up a live coal in his fingers he looked at his watch by its light. "Come. You know me. Is it a bargain?"

The general was a little slow to recover his wits, but the word "bargain" put him on his mettle, and he began to think of advantageous terms. "What proof may there be that you can do your part in the compact?" he inquired. The unknown ran his fingers through his hair and a shower of guineas jingled on the floor. They were pretty warm, but Moulton, in his eagerness, fell on hands and knees and gathered them to his breast.

"Give me some liquor," then demanded Satan, for of course he was no other, and filling a tankard with rum he lighted it with the candle, remarked, affably, "To our better acquaintance," and tossed off the blazing dram at a gulp. "I will make you," said he, "the richest man in the province. Sign this paper and on the first day of every month I will fill your boots with gold; but if you try any tricks with me you will repent it. For I know you, Jonathan. Sign."

Moulton hesitated. "Humph!" sneered his majesty. "You have put me to all this trouble for nothing." And he began to gather up the guineas that

Moulton had placed on the table. This was more than the victim of his wiles could stand. He swallowed a mouthful of rum, seized a pen that was held out to him, and trembled violently as a paper was placed before him; but when he found that his name was to appear with some of the most distinguished in the province his nerves grew steadier and he placed his autograph among those of the eminent company, with a few crooked embellishments and all the t's crossed. "Good!" exclaimed the devil, and wrapping his cloak about him he stepped into the fire and was up the chimney in a twinkling.

Shrewd Jonathan went out the next day and bought the biggest pair of jack-boots he could find in Hampton. He hung them on the crane on the last night of that and all the succeeding months so long as he lived, and on the next morning they brimmed with coins. Moulton rolled in wealth. The neighbors regarded his sudden prosperity with amazement, then with envy, but afterward with suspicion. All the same, Jonathan was not getting rich fast enough to suit himself.

When the devil came to make a certain of his periodical payments he poured guineas down the chimney for half an hour without seeming to fill the boots. Bushel after bushel of gold he emptied into those spacious money-bags without causing an overflow, and he finally descended to the fireplace to see why. Moulton had cut the soles from the boots and the floor was knee-deep in money. With a grin at the general's smartness the devil disappeared, but in a few minutes a smell of sulphur pervaded the premises and the house burst into flames. Moulton escaped in his shirt, and tore his hair as he saw the fire crawl, serpent-like, over the beams, and fantastic smoke-forms dance in the windows. Then a thought crossed his mind and he grew calm: his gold, that was hidden in wainscot, cupboard, floor, and chest, would only melt and could be quarried out by the hundred weight, so that he could be well-to-do again. Before the ruins were cool he was delving amid the rubbish, but not an ounce of gold could he discover. Every bit of his wealth had disappeared. It was not long after that the general died, and to quiet some rumors of disturbance in the graveyard his coffin was dug up. It was empty.

THE SKELETON IN ARMOR

The skeleton of a man wearing a breastplate of brass, a belt made of tubes of the same metal, and lying near some copper arrow-heads, was exhumed at Fall River, Massachusetts, in 1834. The body had been artificially embalmed or else preserved by salts in the soil. His arms and armor suggest Phoenician origin, but the skeleton is thought to be that of a Dane or Norwegian who spent the last winter of his life at Newport. He may have helped to carve the rock at West Newbury, or the better-known Dighton rock at Taunton River that is covered with inscriptions which the tides and frosts are fast effacing, and which have been construed into a record of Norse exploration and discovery, though some will have it that the inevitable Captain Kidd cut the figures there to tell of buried treasure. The Indians have a legend of the arrival of white men in a "bird," undoubtedly a ship, from which issued thunder and lightning. A battle ensued when the visitors landed, and the white men wrote the story of it on the rock. Certain scholars of the eighteenth century declared that the rock bore an account of the arrival of Phoenician sailors, blown across the Atlantic and unable or unwilling to return. A representation of the pillars of Hercules was thought to be included among the sculptures, showing that the castaways were familiar with the Mediterranean. Only this is known about Dighton Rock, however: that it stood where it does, and as it does, when the English settled in this neighborhood. The Indians said there were other rocks near it which bore similar markings until effaced by tides and drifting ice.

Longfellow makes the wraith of the long-buried exile of the armor appear and tell his story: He was a viking who loved the daughter of King Hildebrand, and as royal consent to their union was withheld he made off with the girl, hotly followed by the king and seventy horsemen. The viking reached his vessel first, and hoisting sail continued his flight over the sea, but the chase was soon upon him, and, having no alternative but to fight or be taken, he swung around before the wind and rammed the side of Hildebrand's galley, crushing in its timbers. The vessel tipped and sank, and every soul on board went with her, while the viking's boat kept on her course, and after a voyage of three weeks put in at Narragansett Bay. The round tower at Newport this impetuous lover built as a bower for his lady, and there he guarded her from the dangers that beset those who are first in savage countries. When the princess died she was buried in the tower, and the lonely viking, arraying himself in his armor, fell on his spear, like Brutus, and expired.

MARTHA'S VINEYARD AND NANTUCKET

There is no such place as Martha's Vineyard, except in geography and common speech. It is Martin Wyngaard's Island, and so was named by Skipper Block, an Albany Dutchman. But they would English his name, even in his own town, for it lingers there in Vineyard Point. Bartholomew Gosnold was one of the first white visitors here, for he landed in 1602, and lived on the island for a time, collecting a cargo of sassafras and returning thence to England because he feared the savages.

This scarred and windy spot was the home of the Indian giant, Maushope, who could wade across the sound to the mainland without wetting his knees, though he once started to build a causeway from Gay Head to Cuttyhunk and had laid the rocks where you may now see them, when a crab bit his toe and he gave up the work in disgust. He lived on whales, mostly, and broiled his dinners on fires made at Devil's Den from trees that he tore up by the roots like weeds. In his tempers he raised mists to perplex sea-wanderers, and for sport he would show lights on Gay Head, though these may have been only the fires he made to cook his supper with, and of which some beds of lignite are to be found as remains. He clove No-Man's Land from Gay Head, turned his children into fish, and when his wife objected he flung her to Seconnet Point, where she preyed on all who passed before she hardened into a ledge.

It is reported that he found the island by following a bird that had been stealing children from Cape Cod, as they rolled in the warm sand or paddled on the edge of the sea. He waded after this winged robber until he reached Martha's Vineyard, where he found the bones of all the children that had been stolen. Tired with his hunt he sat down to fill his pipe; but as there was no tobacco he plucked some tons of poke that grew thickly and that Indians sometimes used as a substitute for the fragrant weed. His pipe being filled and lighted, its fumes rolled over the ocean like a mist—in fact, the Indians would say, when a fog was rising, "Here comes old Maushope's smoke"—and when he finished he emptied his pipe into the sea. Falling on a shallow, the ashes made the island of Nantucket. The first Indians to reach the latter place were the parents of a babe that had been stolen by an eagle. They followed the bird in their canoe, but arrived too late, for the little bones had been picked clean. The Norsemen rediscovered the island and called it Naukiton. Is Nantucket a corruption of that word, or was that word the result of a struggle to master the Indian name?

LOVE AND TREASON

The tribes that inhabited Nantucket and Martha's Vineyard before the whites settled the country were constantly at war, and the people of the western island once resolved to surprise those of Nantucket and slay as many as possible before they could arm or organize for battle. The attack was to be made before daybreak, at an hour when their intended victims would be asleep in their wigwams, but on rowing softly to the hostile shore, while the stars were still lingering in the west, the warriors were surprised at finding the enemy alert and waiting their arrival with bows and spears in hand. To proceed would have been suicidal, and they returned to their villages, puzzled and disheartened. Not for some years did they learn how the camp had been apprised, but at the end of that time, the two tribes being at peace, one of their young men married a girl of Nantucket, with whom he had long been in love, and confessed that on the night preceding the attack he had stolen to the beach, crossed to Nantucket on a neck of sand that then joined the islands, and was uncovered only at low tide, sought his mistress, warned her of the attack, that she, at least, might not be killed; then, at a mad run, with waves of the rising tide lapping his feet, he returned to his people, who had not missed him. He set off with a grave and innocent face in the morning, and was as much surprised as any one when he found the enemy in arms.

THE HEADLESS SKELETON OF SWAMPTOWN

The boggy portion of North Kingston, Rhode Island, known as Swamptown, is of queer repute in its neighborhood, for Hell Hollow, Pork Hill, Indian Corner, and Kettle Hole have their stories of Indian crimes and witch-meetings. Here the headless figure of a negro boy was seen by a belated traveller on a path that leads over the hills. It was a dark night and the figure was revealed in a blaze of blue light. It swayed to and fro for a time, then rose from the ground with a lurch and shot into space, leaving a trail of illumination behind it. Here, too, is Goose-Nest Spring, where the witches dance at night. It dries up every winter and flows through the summer, gushing forth on the same day of every year, except once, when a goose took possession of the empty bed and hatched her brood there. That time the water did not flow until she got away with her progeny.

But the most grewsome story of the place is that of the Indian whose skull was found by a roadmender. This unsuspecting person took it home, and, as the women would not allow him to carry it into the house, he hung it on a pole outside. Just as the people were starting for bed, there came a rattling at the door, and, looking out of the windows, they saw a skeleton stalking around in quick and angry strides, like those of a person looking for something. But how could that be when the skeleton had neither eyes nor a place to carry them? It thrashed its bony arms impatiently and its ribs rattled like a xylophone. The spectators were transfixed with fear, all except the culprit, who said, through the window, in a matter-of-fact way, "I left your head on the pole at the back door." The skeleton started in that direction, seized the skull, clapped it into the place where a head should have grown on its own shoulders, and, after shaking its fists in a threatening way at the house, disappeared in the darkness. It is said that he acts as a kind of guard in the neighborhood, to see that none of the other Indians buried there shall be disturbed, as he was. His principal lounging place is Indian Corner, where there is a rock from which blood flows when the moon shines—a memento, doubtless, of some tragedy that occurred there in times before the white men knew the place. There is iron in the soil, and visitors say that the red color is due to that, and that the spring would flow just as freely on dark nights as on bright ones, if any were there to see it, but the natives, who have given some thought to these matters, know better.

THE CROW AND CAT OF HOPKINSHILL

In a wood near Hopkins Hill, Rhode Island, is a bowlder, four feet in diameter, scored with a peculiar furrow. Witch Rock, as it is called, gained its name two centuries ago, when an old woman abode in a deserted cabin close by and made the forest dreaded. Figures were seen flitting through its shadows; articles left out o' nights in neighboring settlements were missing in the morning, though tramps were unknown; cattle were afflicted with diseases; stones were flung in at windows by unseen hands; crops were blighted by hail and frost; and in stormy weather the old woman was seen to rise out of the woods and stir and push the clouds before her with a broom. For a hundred yards around Witch Rock the ground is still accursed, and any attempt to break it up is unavailing. Nearly a century ago a scoffer named Reynolds declared that he would run his plough through the enchanted boundary, and the neighbors watched the attempt from a distance.

He started well, but on arriving at the magic circle the plough shied and the wooden landside—or chip, as it was called—came off. It was replaced and the team started again. In a moment the oxen stood unyoked, while the chip jumped off and whirled away out of sight. On this, most of the people edged away in the direction of home, and directly there came from the north a crow that perched on a dead tree and cawed. John Hopkins, owner of the land, cried to the bird, "Squawk, you damned old Pat Jenkins!" and the crow took flight, dropping the chip at Reynolds's feet, at the same moment turning into a beldam with a cocked hat, who descended upon the rock. Before the men could reach her she changed into a black cat and disappeared in the ground. Hunting and digging came to naught, though the pursuers were so earnest and excited that one of them made the furrow in the rock with a welt from his shovel. After that few people cared to go near the place, and it became overgrown with weeds and trees and bushes.

THE OLD STONE MILL

If the round tower at Newport was not Benedict Arnold's wind-mill, and any one or two of several other things, it is probably a relic of the occupancy of this country by Thorwald and his Norsemen. After coasting Wonderstrands (Cape Cod), in the year 1007, they built a town that is known to historians—if not in their histories—as Norumbega, the lost city of New England. It is now fancied that the city stood on the Charles River, near Waltham, Massachusetts, where a monument may be erected, but it is also believed that they reached the neighborhood of Newport, Rhode Island. After this tower—popularly called the old stone mill-was built, a seer among the Narragansetts had a vision in which he foresaw that when the last remnant of the structure had fallen, and not one stone had been left on another, the Indian race would vanish from this continent. The work of its extermination seems, indeed, to have begun with the possession of the coast by white men, and the fate of the aborigines is easily read.

ORIGIN OF A NAME

The origin of many curious geographical names has become an object of mere surmise, and this is the more the pity because they suggest such picturesque possibilities. We would like to know, for instance, how Burnt Coat and Smutty Nose came by such titles. The conglomerate that strews the fields south of Boston is locally known as Roxbury pudding-stone, and, according to Dr. Holmes, the masses are fragments of a pudding, as big as the State-house dome, that the family of a giant flung about, in a fit of temper, and that petrified where it fell. But that would have been called pudding-stone, anyway, from its appearance. The circumstance that named the reef of Norman's Woe has passed out of record, though it is known that goodman Norman and his son settled there in the seventeenth century. It is Longfellow who has endowed the rock with this legend, for he depicts a wreck there in the fury of a winter storm in 1680—the wreck of the Hesperus, Richard Norman, master, from which went ashore next morning the body of an unknown and beautiful girl, clad in ice and lashed to a broken mast.

But one of the oddest preservations of an apposite in name is found in the legend of Point Judith, Rhode Island, an innocent *double entendre*. About two centuries ago a vessel was driving toward the coast in a gale, with rain and mist. The skipper's eyes were old and dim, so he got his daughter Judith to stand beside him at the helm, as he steered the vessel over the foaming surges. Presently she cried, "Land, father! I see land!" "Where away?" he asked. But he could not see what she described, and the roar of the wind drowned her voice, so he shouted, "Point, Judith! Point!" The girl pointed toward the quarter where she saw the breakers, and the old mariner changed his course and saved his ship from wreck. On reaching port he told the story of his daughter's readiness, and other captains, when they passed the cape in later days, gave to it the name of Point Judith.

MICAH ROOD APPLES

In Western Florida they will show roses to you that drop red dew, like blood, and have been doing so these many years, for they sprang out of the graves of women and children who had been cruelly killed by Indians. But there is something queerer still about the Micah Rood—or "Mike"—apples of Franklin, Connecticut, which are sweet, red of skin, snowy of pulp, and have a red spot, like a blood-drop, near the core; hence they are sometimes known as bloody-hearts. Micah Rood was a farmer in Franklin in 1693. Though avaricious he was somewhat lazy, and was more prone to dream of wealth than to work for it. But people whispered that he did some hard and sharp work on the night after the peddler came to town—the slender man with a pack filled with jewelry and knickknacks—because on the morning after that visit the peddler was found, beneath an apple-tree on Rood farm, with his pack rifled and his skull split open.

Suspicion pointed at Rood, and, while nothing was proved against him, he became gloomy, solitary, and morose, keeping his own counsels more faithfully than ever—though he never was disposed to take counsel of other people. If he had expected to profit by the crime he was obviously disappointed, for he became poorer than ever, and his farm yielded less and less. To be sure, he did little work on it. When the apples ripened on the tree that had spread its branches above the peddler's body, the neighbors wagged their heads and whispered the more, for in the centre of each apple was a drop of the peddler's blood: a silent witness and judgment, they said, and the result of a curse that the dying man had invoked against his murderer. Micah Rood died soon after, without saying anything that his fellow-villagers might be waiting to hear, but his tree is still alive and its strange fruit has been grafted on hundreds of orchards.

A DINNER AND ITS CONSEQUENCES

The Nipmucks were populous at Thompson, Connecticut, where they skilfully tilled the fields, and where their earthworks, on Fort Hill, provided them with a refuge in case of invasion. Their chief, Quinatisset, had his lodge on the site of the Congregational church in Thompson. They believed that Chargoggagmanchogagog Pond was paradise—the home of the Great Spirit and departed souls—and that it would always yield fish to them, as the hills did game. They were fond of fish, and would barter deer-meat and corn for it, occasionally, with the Narragansetts.

Now, these last-named Indians were a waterloving people, and to this day their "fishing fire"—a column of pale flame—rises out of Quinebaug Lake once in seven years, as those say who have watched beside its waters through the night. Knowing their fondness for blue-fish and clams, the Narragansetts asked the Nipmucks to dine with them on one occasion, and this courtesy was eagerly accepted, the up-country people distinguishing themselves by valiant trencher deeds; but, alas, that it should be so! they disgraced themselves when, soon after, they invited the Narragansetts to a feast of venison at Killingly, and quarrelled with their guests over the dressing of the food. This rumpus grew into a battle in which all but two of the invites were slain. Their hosts buried them decently, but grass would never grow above their graves.

This treachery the Great Spirit avenged soon after, when the Nipmucks had assembled for a powwow, with accessory enjoyments, in the grassy vale where Mashapaug Lake now reflects the charming landscape, and where, until lately, the remains of a forest could be seen below the surface. In the height of the revel the god struck away the foundations of the hills, and as the earth sank, bearing the offending men and women, waters rushed in and filled the chasm, so that every person was drowned, save one good old woman beneath whose feet the ground held firm. Loon Island, where she stood, remains in sight to-day.

THE NEW HAVEN STORM SHIP

In 1647 the New Haven colonists, who even at that early day exhibited the enterprise that has been a distinguishing feature of the Yankee, sent a ship to Ireland to try to develop a commerce, their trading posts on the Delaware having been broken up by the Swedes. When their agent, Captain Lamberton, sailed—in January—the harbor was so beset with ice that a track had to be cut through the floes to open water, five miles distant. She had, moreover, to be dragged out stern foremost—an ill omen, the sailors thought—and as she swung before the wind a passing drift of fog concealed her, for a moment, from the gaze of those on shore, who, from this, foretold things of evil. Though large and new, the ship was so "walty"—inclined to roll—that the captain set off with misgiving, and as she moved away the crew heard this solemn and disheartening invocation from a clergyman on the wharf:—"Lord, if it be thy pleasure to bury these, our friends, in the bottom of the sea, take them; they are thine: save them."

Winter passed; so did spring; still the ship came not; but one afternoon in June, just as a rain had passed, some children cried, "There's a brave ship!" for, flying up the harbor, with all sail set and flaunting colors, was a vessel "the very mould of our ship," the clergyman said.

Strange to tell, she was going flat against the wind; no sailors were on her deck; she did not toss with the fling of the waves; there was no ripple at her bow. As she came close to land a single figure appeared on the quarter, pointing seaward with a cutlass; then suddenly her main-top fell, her masts toppled from their holdings, the dismantled hulk careened and went down. A cloud dropped from heaven and brooded for a time above the place where it had vanished, and when it lifted the surface of the sea was empty and still. The good folk of New Haven believed that the fate of the absent ship had been revealed, at last, for she never came back and Captain Lamberton was never heard from.

THE WINDAM FROGS

On a cloudy night in July, 1758, the people of Windham, Connecticut, were awakened by screams and shrill voices. Some sprang up and looked to the priming of their muskets, for they were sure that the Indians were coming; others vowed that the voices were those of witches or devils, flying overhead; a few ran into the streets with knives and fire-arms, while others fastened their windows and prayerfully shrank under the bedclothes. A notorious reprobate was heard blubbering for a Bible, and a lawyer offered half of all the money that he had made dishonestly to any charity if his neighbors would guarantee to preserve his life until morning.

All night the greatest alarm prevailed. At early dawn an armed party climbed the hill to the eastward, and seeing no sign of Indians, or other invaders, returned to give comfort to their friends. A contest for office was waging at that period between two lawyers, Colonel Dyer and Mr. Elderkin, and sundry of the people vowed that they had heard a challenging yell of "Colonel Dyer! Colonel Dyer!" answered by a guttural defiance of "Elderkin, too! Elderkin, too!" Next day the reason of it all came out: A pond having been emptied by drought, the frogs that had lived there emigrated by common consent to a ditch nearer the town, and on arriving there had apparently fought for its possession, for many lay dead on the bank. The night was still and the voices of the contestants sounded clearly into the village, the piping of the smaller being construed into "Colonel Dyer," and the grumble of the bull-frogs into "Elderkin, too." The "frog scare" was a subject of pleasantry directed against Windham for years afterward.

THE LAMB OF SACRIFICE

The Revolution was beginning, homes were empty, farms were deserted, industries were checked, and the levies of a foreign army had consumed the stores of the people. A messenger rode into the Connecticut Valley with tidings of the distress that was in the coast towns, and begged the farmer folk to spare some of their cattle and the millers some of their flour for the relief of Boston. On reaching Windham he was received with good will by Parson White, who summoned his flock by peal of bell, and from the steps of his church urged the needs of his brethren with such eloquence that by nightfall the messenger had in his charge a flock of sheep, a herd of cattle, and a load of grain, with which he was to set off in the morning. The parson's daughter, a shy maid of nine or ten, went to her father, with her pet lamb, and said to him, "I must give this, too, for there are little children who are crying for bread and meat."

"No, no," answered the pastor, patting her head and smiling upon her. "They do not ask help from babes. Run to bed and you shall play with your lamb to-morrow."

But in the red of the morning, as he drove his herd through the village street, the messenger turned at the hail of a childish voice, and looking over a stone wall he saw the little one with her snow-white lamb beside her.

"Wait," she cried, "for my lamb must go to the hungry children of Boston. It is so small, please to carry it for some of the way, and let it have fresh grass and water. It is all I have."

So saying, she kissed the innocent face of her pet, gave it into the arms of the young man, and ran away, her cheeks shining with tears. Folding the little creature to his breast, the messenger looked admiringly after the girl: he felt a glow of pride and hope for the country whose very children responded to the call of patriotism. "Now, God help me, I will carry this lamb to the city as a sacrifice." So saying, he set his face to the east and vigorously strode forward.

MOODUS NOISES

The village of Moodus, Connecticut, was troubled with noises. There is no question as to that. In fact, Machimoodus, the Indian name of the spot, means Place of Noises. As early as 1700, and for thirty years after, there were crackings and rumblings that were variously compared to fusillades, to thunder, to roaring in the air, to the breaking of rocks, to reports of cannon. A man who was on Mount Tom while the noises were violent describes the sound as that of rocks falling into immense caverns beneath his feet and striking against cliffs as they fell. Houses shook and people feared.

Rev. Mr. Hosmer, in a letter written to a friend in Boston in 1729, says that before white settlers appeared there was a large Indian population, that powwows were frequent, and that the natives "drove a prodigious trade at worshipping the devil." He adds:—"An old Indian was asked what was the reason of the noises in this place, to which he replied that the Indian's god was angry because Englishman's god was come here. Now, whether there be anything diabolical in these things I know not, but this I know, that God Almighty is to be seen and trembled at in what has been often heard among us. Whether it be fire or air distressed in the subterranean caverns of the earth cannot be known for there is no eruption, no explosion perceptible but by sounds and tremors which are sometimes very fearful and dreadful."

It was finally understood that Haddam witches, who practised black magic, met the Moodus witches, who used white magic, in a cave beneath Mount Tom, and fought them in the light of a great carbuncle that was fastened to the roof. The noises recurred in 1888, when houses rattled in witch-haunted Salem, eight miles away, and the bell on the village church "sung like a tuning-fork." The noises have occurred simultaneously with earthquakes in other parts of the country, and afterward rocks have been found moved from their bases and cracks have been discovered in the earth. One sapient editor said that the pearls in the mussels in Salmon and Connecticut Rivers caused the disturbance.

If the witch-fights were continued too long the king of Machimoddi, who sat on a throne of solid sapphire in the cave whence the noises came, raised his wand: then the light of the carbuncle went out, peals of thunder rolled through the rocky chambers, and the witches rushed into the air. Dr. Steele, a learned and aged man from England, built a crazy-looking house in a lonely spot on Mount Tom, and was soon as much a mystery as the noises, for it was known that he had come to this country to stop them by magic and to seize the great carbuncle in the cave—if he could find it. Every window, crack, and keyhole was closed, and nobody was admitted while he stayed there, but the clang of hammers was heard in his house all night, sparks shot from his chimney, and strange odors were diffused. When all was ready for his adventure he set forth, his path marked by a faint light that moved before him and stopped at the closed entrance to the cavern.

Loud were the Moodus noises that night. The mountain shook and groans and hisses were heard in the air as he pried up the stone that lay across the pit-mouth. When he had lifted it off a light poured from it and streamed into the heaven like a crimson comet or a spear of the northern aurora. It was the flash of the great carbuncle, and the stars seen through it were as if dyed in blood. In the morning Steele was gone. He had taken ship for England. The gem carried with it an evil fate, for the galley sank in mid-ocean; but, though buried beneath a thousand fathoms of water, the red ray of the carbuncle sometimes shoots up from the sea, and the glow of it strikes fear into the hearts of passing sailors. Long after, when the booming was heard, the Indians said that the hill was giving birth to another beautiful stone.

Such cases are not singular. A phenomenon similar to the Moodus noises, and locally known as "the shooting of Nashoba Hill," occurs at times in the eminence of that name near East Littleton, Massachusetts. The strange, deep rumbling was attributed by the Indians to whirlwinds trying to escape from caves.

Bald Mountain, North Carolina, was known as Shaking Mountain, for strange sounds and tremors were heard there, and every moonshiner who had his cabin on that hill joined the church and was diligent in worship until he learned that the trembling was due to the slow cracking and separation of a great ledge.

At the end of a hot day on Seneca Lake, New York, are sometimes heard the "lake guns," like exploding gas. Two hundred years ago Agayentah, a wise and honored member of the Seneca tribe, was killed here by a lightning-stroke. The same bolt that slew him wrenched a tree from the bank and hurled it into the water, where it was often seen afterward, going about the lake as if driven by unseen currents, and among the whites it got the name of the Wandering Jew. It is often missing for weeks together, and its reappearances are heralded by the low booming of—what? The Indians said that the sound was but the echo of Agayentah's voice, warning them of dangers and summoning them to battle, while the Wandering Jew became his messenger.

HADDAM ENCHANTMENTS

When witchcraft went rampant through New England the Connecticut town of Haddam owned its share of ugly old women, whom it tried to reform by lectures and ducking, instead of killing. It was averred that Goody So-and-So had a black cat for a familiar, that Dame Thus-and-Thus rode on a broomstick on stormy nights and screeched and gibbered down the farm-house chimneys, and there were dances of old crones at Devils' Hop Yard, Witch Woods, Witch Meadows, Giant's Chair, Devil's Footprint, and Dragon's Rock. Farmers were especially fearful of a bent old hag in a red hood, who seldom appeared before dusk, but who was apt to be found crouched on their door-steps if they reached home late, her mole-covered cheeks wrinkled with a grin, two yellow fangs projecting between her lips, and a light shining from her eyes that numbed all on whom she looked. On stormy nights she would drum and rattle at windows, and by firelight and candle-light her face was seen peering through the panes.

At Chapman Falls, where the attrition of a stream had worn pot-holes in the rocks, there were meetings of Haddam witches, to the number of a dozen. They brewed poisons in those holes, cast spells, and talked in harsh tongues with the arch fiend, who sat on the brink of the ravine with his tail laid against his shoulder, like a sceptre, and a red glow emanating from his body.

In Devils' Hop Yard was a massive oak that never bears leaves or acorns, for it has been enchanted since the time that one of the witches, in the form of a crow, perched on the topmost branch, looked to the four points of the compass, and flew away. That night the leaves fell off, the twigs shrivelled, sap ceased to run, and moss began to beard its skeleton limbs.

The appearance of witches in the guise of birds was no unusual thing, indeed, and a farmer named Blakesley shot one of them in that form. He was hunting in a meadow when a rush of wings was heard and he saw pass overhead a bird with long neck, blue feathers, and feet like scrawny hands. It uttered a cry so weird, so shrill, so like mocking laughter that it made him shudder. This bird alighted on a dead tree and he shot at it. With another laughing yell it circled around his head. Three times he fired with the same result. Then he resolved to see if it were uncanny, for nothing evil can withstand silver—except Congress. Having no bullets of that metal he cut two silver buttons from his shirt and rammed them home with a piece of cloth and a prayer. This time the bird screamed in terror, and tried, but vainly, to rise from the limb. He fired. The creature dropped, with a button in its body, and fell on its right side. At that moment an old woman living in a cabin five miles distant arose from her spinning-wheel, gasped, and fell on her right side-dead.

BLOCK ISLAND AND THE PALATINE

Block Island, or Manisees, is an uplift of clayey moorland between Montauk and Gay Head. It was for sailors an evil place and "bad medicine" for Indians, for men who had been wrecked there had been likewise robbed and ill treated—though the honest islanders of to-day deny it—while the Indians had been driven from their birthright after hundreds of their number had fallen in its defence. In the winter of 1750-51 the ship Palatine set forth over the seas with thrifty Dutch merchants and emigrants, bound for Philadelphia, with all their goods. A gale delayed them and kept them beating to and fro on the icy seas, unable to reach land. The captain died—it was thought that he was murdered—and the sailors, a brutal set even for those days, threw off all discipline, seized the stores and arms, and starved the passengers into giving up their money.

When those died of hunger whose money had given out—for twenty guilders were demanded for a cup of water and fifty rix dollars for a biscuit—their bodies were flung into the sea, and when the crew had secured all that excited their avarice they took to their boats, leaving ship and passengers to their fate. It is consoling to know that the sailors never reached a harbor. The unguided ship, in sight of land, yet tossed at the mercy of every wind and tenanted by walking skeletons, struck off Block Island one calm Sunday morning and the wreckers who lived along the shore set out for her. Their first work was to rescue the passengers; then they returned to strip everything from the hulk that the crew had left; but after getting her in tow a gale sprang up, and seeing that she was doomed to be blown off shore, where she might become a dangerous obstruction or a derelict, they set her on fire. From the rocks they watched her drift into misty darkness, but as the flames mounted to the trucks a scream rang across the whitening sea: a maniac woman had been left on board. The scream was often repeated, each time more faintly, and the ship passed into the fog and vanished.

A twelvemonth later, on the same evening of the year, the islanders were startled at the sight of a ship in the offing with flames lapping up her sides and rigging, and smoke clouds rolling off before the wind. It burned to the water's edge in sight of hundreds. In the winter following it came again, and was seen, in fact, for years thereafter at regular intervals, by those who would gladly have forgotten the sight of it (one of the community, an Indian, fell into madness whenever he saw the light), while those who listened caught the sound of a woman's voice raised in agony above the roar of fire and water.

Substantially the same story is told of a point on the North Carolina coast, save that in the latter case the passengers, who were from the Bavarian Palatinate, were put to the knife before their goods were taken. The captain and his crew filled their boats with treasure and pulled away for land, first firing the ship and committing its ghastly freight to the flames. The ship followed them almost to the beach, ere it fell to pieces, as if it were an animate form, bent on vengeance. The pirates landed, but none profited by the crime, all of them dying poor and forsaken.

THE BUCCANEER

Among the natives of Block Island was a man named Lee. Born in the last century among fishermen and wreckers, he has naturally taken to the sea for a livelihood, and, never having known the influences of education and refinement, he is rude and imperious in manner. His ship lies in a Spanish port fitting for sea, but not with freight, for, tired of peaceful trading, Lee is equipping his vessel as a privateer. A Spanish lady who has just been bereaved of her husband comes to him to ask a passage to America, for she has no suspicion of his intent. Her jewels and well-filled purse arouse Lee's cupidity, and with pretended sympathy he accedes to her request, even going so far as to allow Senora's favorite horse to be brought aboard.

Hardly is the ship in deep water before the lady's servants are stabbed in their sleep and Lee smashes in the door of her cabin. Realizing his purpose, and preferring to sacrifice life to honor, she eludes him, climbs the rail, and leaps into the sea, while the ship ploughs on. As a poor revenge for being thus balked of his prey the pirate has the beautiful white horse flung overboard, the animal shrilling a neigh that seems to reach to the horizon, and is like nothing ever heard before. But these things he affects to forget in dice and drinking. In a dispute over a division of plunder Lee stabs one of his men and tosses him overboard. Soon the rovers come to Block Island, where, under cover of night, they carry ashore their stealings to hide them in pits and caves, reserving enough gold to buy a welcome from the wreckers, and here they live for a year, gaming and carousing. Their ship has been reported as a pirate and to baffle search it is set adrift.

One night a ruddy star is seen on the sea-verge and the ruffians leave their revelling to look at it, for it is growing into sight fast. It speeds toward them and they can now see that it is a ship—their shipwrapped in flames. It stops off shore, and out of the ocean at its prow emerges something white that they say at first is a wave-crest rolling upon the sands; but it does not dissolve as breakers do: it rushes on; it scales the bluff it is a milk-white horse, that gallops to the men, who inly wonder if this is an alcoholic vision, and glares at Lee. A spell seems to be laid on him, and, unable to resist it, the buccaneer mounts the animal. It rushes away, snorting and plunging, to the highest bluff, whence Lee beholds, in the light of the burning ship, the bodies of all who have been done to death by him, staring into his eyes through the reddening waves.

At dawn the horse sinks under him and he stands there alone. From that hour even his companions desert him. They fear to share his curse. He wanders about the island, a broken, miserable man, unwilling to live, afraid to die, refused shelter and friendship, and unable to reach the mainland, for no boat will give him passage. After a year of this existence the ship returns, the spectre horse rises from the deep and claims Lee again for a rider. He mounts; the animal speeds away to the cliff, but does not pause at the brink this time: with a sickening jump and fall he goes into the sea. Spurning the wave-tops in his flight he makes a circuit of the burning ship, and in the hellish light, that fills the air and penetrates to the ocean bottom, the pirate sees again his victims looking up with smiles and arms spread to embrace him.

There is a cry of terror as the steed stops short; then a gurgle, and horse and rider have disappeared. The fire ship vanishes and the night is dark.

ROBERT LOCKWOOD'S FATE

In the winter of 1779, General Putnam was stationed at Reading, Connecticut, with a band of ill-fed, unpaid troops. He was quartered at the Marvin house, and Mary, daughter of farmer Marvin, won her way to the heart of this rough soldier through the excellence of her dumplings and the invigorating quality of her flip. He even took her into his confidence, and, being in want of a spy in an emergency, he playfully asked her if she knew any brave fellow who could be trusted to take a false message into the British lines that would avert an impending attack. Yes, she knew such an one, and would guarantee that he would take the message if the fortunes of the colonial army would be helped thereby. Putnam assured her that it would aid the patriot cause, and, farther, that he would reward her; whereat, with a smile and a twinkling eye, the girl received the missive and left the room.

When daylight had left the sky, Mary slipped out of the house, crossed a pasture, entered a ravine, and in a field beyond reached a cattle shelter. On the instant a tall form stepped from the shadows and she sank into its embrace. There was a kiss, a moment of whispered talk, and the girl hurriedly asked her lover if he would carry a letter to the British headquarters, near Ridgefield. Of course he would. But he must not read it, and he must on no account say from whom he had it. The young man consented without a question—that she required it was sufficient; so, thrusting the tiny paper into his hand and bidding him God-speed, she gave him another kiss and they parted—he to go on his errand, she to pass the night with the clergyman's daughter at the parsonage. At about ten o'clock Putnam was disturbed by the tramping of feet and a tall, goodlooking fellow was thrust into his room by a couple of soldiers. The captive had been found inside the lines, they said, in consultation with some unknown person who had escaped the eye of the sentry in the darkness. When captured he had put a piece of paper into his mouth and swallowed it. He gave the name of Robert Lockwood, and when Putnam demanded to know what he had been doing near the camp without a permit he said that he was bound by a promise not to tell.

"Are you a patriot?" asked the general.

"I am a royalist. I do not sympathize with rebellion. I have been a man of peace in this war."

Putnam strode about the room, giving vent to his passion in language neither choice nor gentle, for he had been much troubled by spies and informers since he had been there. Then, stopping, he said:

"Some one was with you to-night-some of my men. Tell me that traitor's name and I'll spare your life and hang him before the whole army."

The prisoner turned pale and dropped his head. He would not violate his promise.

"You are a British spy, and I'll hang you at sunrise!" roared Putnam.

In vain the young man pleaded for time to appeal to Washington. He was not a spy, he insisted, and it would be found, perhaps too late, that a terrible mistake had been committed. His words were unheeded: he was led away and bound, and as the sun was rising on the next morning the sentence of courtmartial was executed upon him.

At noon Mary returned from the parsonage, her eyes dancing and her mouth dimpling with smiles. Going to Putnam, she said, with a dash of sauciness, "I have succeeded, general. I found a lad last night to take your message. I had to meet him alone, for he is a Tory; so he cannot enter this camp. The poor fellow had no idea that he was doing a service for the rebels, for he did not know what was in the letter, and I bound him not to tell who gave it to him. You see, I punished him for abiding by the king."

The general laughed and gazed at her admiringly.

"You're a brave girl," he said, "and I suppose you've come for your reward. Well, what is it to be?"

"I want a pass for Robert Lockwood. He is the royalist I spoke of, but he will not betray you, for he is not a soldier; and—his visits make me very happy."

"The spy you hanged this morning," whispered an aide in Putnam's ear. "Give her the pass and say nothing of what has happened."

The general started, changed color, and paused; then he signed the order with a dash, placed it in the girl's hand, gravely kissed her, watched her as she ran lightly from the house, and going to his bedroom closed the door and remained alone for an hour. From that time he never spoke of the affair, but when his troops were ordered away, soon after, he almost blenched as he gave good-by to Mary Marvin, and met her sad, reproachful look, though to his last day he never learned whether or no she had discovered Robert Lockwood's fate.

LOVE AND RUM

Back in the seventeenth century a number of Yankee traders arrived in Naugatuck to barter blankets, beads, buttons, Bibles, and brandy for skins, and there they met chief Toby and his daughter. Toby was not a pleasing person, but his daughter was well favored, and one of the traders told the chief that if he would allow the girl to go to Boston with him he would give to him—Toby—a quart of rum. Toby was willing enough. He would give a good deal for rum. But the daughter declined to be sold off in such a fashion unless—she coyly admitted—she could have half of the rum herself. Loth as he was to do so, Toby was brought to agree to this proposition, for he knew that rum was rare and good and girls were common and perverse, so the gentle forest lily took her mug of liquor and tossed it off. Now, it is not clear whether she wished to nerve herself for the deed that followed or whether the deed was a result of the tonic, but she made off from the paternal wigwam and was presently seen on the ledge of Squaw Rock, locally known also as High Rock, from which in another moment she had fallen. Toby had pursued her, and on finding her dead he vented a howl of grief and anger and flung the now empty rum-jug after her. A huge bowlder arose from the earth where it struck, and there it remains—a monument to the girl and a warning to Tobies.

Another version of the story is that the girl sprang from the rock to escape the pursuit of a lover who was hateful to her, and who had her almost in his grasp when she made the fatal leap. In the crevice half-way up the cliff her spirit has often been seen looking regretfully into the rich valley that was her home, and on the 20th of March and 20th of September, in every year, it is imposed on her to take the form of a seven-headed snake, the large centre head adorned with a splendid carbuncle. Many have tried to capture the snake and secure this precious stone, for an old prophecy promises wealth to whoever shall wrest it from the serpent. But thus far the people of Connecticut have found more wealth in clocks and tobacco than in snakes and carbuncles.

LIGHTS AND SHADOWS OF THE SOUTH

THE SWIM AT INDIAN HEAD

At Indian Head, Maryland, are the government proving-grounds, where the racket of great guns and splintering of targets are a deterrent to the miscellaneous visitations of picnics. Trouble has been frequently associated with this neighborhood, as it is now suggested in the noisy symbolry of war. In prehistoric days it was the site of an aboriginal town, whose denizens were like other Indians in their love for fight and their willingness to shed blood. Great was the joy of all these citizens when a scouting party came in, one day, bringing with them the daughter of one of their toughest old hunters and a young buck, from another faction, who had come a-courting; her in the neighboring shades.

Capture meant death, usually, and he knew it, but he held himself proudly and refused to ask for mercy. It was resolved that he should die. The father's scorn for his daughter, that she should thus consort with an enemy, was so great that he was on the point of offering her as a joint sacrifice with her lover, when she fell on her knees before him and began a fervent appeal, not for herself, but for the prisoner. She would do anything to prove her strength, her duty, her obedience, if they would set him free. He had done injury to none. What justice lay in putting him to the torture?

Half in earnest, half in humor, the chief answered, "Suppose we were to set him on the farther shore of the Potomac, do you love him well enough to swim to him?"

"I do."

"The river is wide and deep."

"I would drown in it rather than that harm should come to him."

The old chief ordered the captive, still bound, to be taken to a point on the Virginia shore, full two miles away, in one of their canoes, and when the boat was on the water he gave the word to the girl, who instantly plunged in and followed it. The chief and the father embarked in another birch—ostensibly to see that the task was honestly fulfilled; really, perhaps, to see that the damsel did not drown. It was a long course, but the maid was not as many of our city misses are, and she reached the bank, tired, but happy, for she had saved her lover and gained him for a husband.

THE MOANING SISTERS

Above Georgetown, on the Potomac River, are three rocks, known as the Three Sisters, not merely because of their resemblance to each other—for they are parts of a submerged reef—but because of a tradition that, more than a hundred years ago, a boat in which three sisters had gone out for a row was swung against one of these rocks. The day was gusty and the boat was upset. All three of the girls were drowned. Either the sisters remain about this perilous spot or the rocks have prescience; at least, those who live near them on the shore hold one view or the other, for they declare that before every death on the river the sisters moan, the sound being heard above the lapping of the waves. It is different from any other sound in nature. Besides, it is an unquestioned fact that more accidents happen here than at any other point on the river.

Many are the upsets that have occurred and many are the swimmers who have gone down, the dark forms of the sisters being the last shapes that their water-blurred eyes have seen. It is only before a human life is to be yielded that this low wailing comes from the rocks, and when, on a night in May, 1889, the sound floated shoreward, just as the clock in Georgetown struck twelve, good people who were awake sighed and uttered a prayer for the one whose doom was so near at hand. Twelve hours later, at noon, a shell came speeding down the Potomac, with a young athlete jauntily pulling at the oars. As he neared the Three Sisters his boat appeared to be caught in an eddy; it swerved suddenly, as if struck; then it upset and the rower sank to his death.

A RIDE FOR A BRIDE

When the story of bloodshed at Bunker Hill reached Bohemia Hall, in Cecil County, Maryland, Albert De Courcy left his brother Ernest to support the dignity of the house and make patriotic speeches, while he went to the front, conscious that Helen Carmichael, his affianced wife, was watching, in pride and sadness, the departure of his company. Letters came and went, as they always do, until rumor came of a sore defeat to the colonials at Long Island; then the letters ceased.

It was a year later when a ragged soldier, who had stopped at the hall for supper, told of Albert's heroism in covering the retreat of Washington. The gallant young officer had been shot, he said, as he attempted to swim the morasses of Gowanus. But this soldier was in error. Albert had been vexatiously bogged on the edge of the creek. While floundering in the mud a half dozen sturdy red-coats had lugged him out and he was packed off to the prison-ships anchored in the Wallabout. In these dread hulks, amid darkness and miasma, living on scant, unwholesome food, compelled to see his comrades die by dozens every day and their bodies flung ashore where the tide lapped away the sand thrown over them, De Courcy wished that death instead of capture had been his lot, for next to his love he prized his liberty.

One day he was told off, with a handful of others, for transfer to a stockade on the Delaware, and how his heart beat when he learned that the new prison was within twenty miles of home! His flow of spirits returned, and his new jailers liked him for his frankness and laughed at his honest expletives against the king. He had the liberty of the enclosure, and was not long in finding where the wall was low, the ditch narrow, and the abatis decayed—knowledge that came useful to him sooner than he expected, for one day a captured horse was led in that made straight for him with a whinny and rubbed his nose against his breast.

"Why!" he cried,—"it's Cecil! My horse, gentlemen—or, was. Not a better hunter in Maryland!"

"Yes," answered one of the officers. "We've just taken him from your brother. He's been stirring trouble with his speeches and has got to be quieted. But we'll have him to-day, for he's to be married, and a scouting party is on the road to nab him at the altar."

"Married! My brother! What! Ernest, the lawyer, the orator? Ho, ho! Ah, but it's rather hard to break off a match in that style!"

"Hard for him, maybe; but they say the lady feels no great love for him. He made it seem like a duty to her, after her lover died."

"How's that? Her own—what's her name?"

"Helen—Helen Carmichael, or something like that."

Field and sky swam before De Courcy's eyes for a moment; then he resumed, in a calm voice, and with a pale, set face, "Well, you're making an unhappy wedding-day for him. If he had Cecil here he would outride you all. Ah, when I was in practice I could ride this horse and snatch a pebble from the ground without losing pace!"

"Could you do it now?"

"I'm afraid long lodging in your prison-ships has stiffened my joints, but I'd venture at a handkerchief."

"Then try," said the commandant.

De Courcy mounted into the saddle heavily, crossed the grounds at a canter, and dropped a handkerchief on the grass. Then, taking a few turns for practice, he started at a gallop and swept around like the wind. His seat was so firm, his air so noble, his mastery of the steed so complete, that a cheer of admiration went up. He seemed to fall headlong from the saddle, but was up again in a moment, waving the handkerchief gayly in farewell—for he kept straight on toward the weak place in the wall. A couple of musket-balls hummed by his ears: it was neck or nothing now! A tremendous leap! Then a ringing cry told the astonished soldiers that he had reached the road in safety. Through wood and thicket and field he dashed as if the fiend were after him, and never once did he cease to urge his steed till he reached the turnpike, and saw ahead the scouting party on its way to arrest his brother.

Turning into a path that led to the rear of the little church they were so dangerously near, he plied hands and heels afresh, and in a few moments a wedding party was startled by the apparition of a black horse, all in a foam, ridden by a gaunt man, in torn garments, that burst in at the open chancel-door. The bridegroom cowered, for he knew his brother. The bride gazed in amazement. "'Tis the dead come to life!" cried one. De Courcy had little time for words. He rode forward to the altar, swung Helen up behind him, and exclaimed, "Save yourselves! The British are coming! To horse, every one, and make for the manor!" There were shrieks and fainting—and perhaps a little cursing, even if it was in church,—and when the squadron rode up most of the company were in full flight. Ernest was taken, and next morning held his brother's place on the prison-list, while, as arrangements had been made for a wedding, there was one, and a happy one, but Albert was the bridegroom.

SPOOKS OF THE HIAWASSEE

The hills about the head of the Hiawassee are filled with "harnts," among them many animal ghosts, that ravage about the country from sheer viciousness. The people of the region, illiterate and superstitious, have unquestioning faith in them. They tell you about the headless bull and black dog of the valley of the Chatata, the white stag of the Sequahatchie, and the bleeding horse of the Great Smoky Mountains—the last three being portents of illness, death, or misfortune to those who see them.

Other ghosts are those of men. Near the upper Hiawassee is a cave where a pile of human skulls was found by a man who had put up his cabin near the entrance. For some reason, which he says he never understood, this farmer gathered up the old, bleached bones and dumped them into his shed. Quite possibly he did not dare to confess that he wanted them for fertilizers or to burn them for his poultry.

Night fell dark and still, with a waning moon rising over the mountains—as calm a night as ever one slept through. Along toward the middle of it a sound like the coming of a cyclone brought the farmer out of his bed. He ran to the window to see if the house were to be uprooted, but the forest was still, with a strange, oppressive stillness—not a twig moving, not a cloud veiling the stars, not an insect chirping. Filled with a vague fear, he tried to waken his wife, but she was like one in a state of catalepsy.

Again the sound was heard, and now he saw, without, a shadowy band circling about his house like leaves whirled on the wind. It seemed to be made of human shapes, with tossing arms—this circling band—and the sound was that of many voices, each faint and hollow, by itself, but loud in aggregate. He who was watching realized then that the wraiths of the dead whose skulls he had purloined from their place of sepulture were out in lament and protest. He went on his knees at once and prayed with vigor until morning. As soon as it was light enough to see his way he replaced the skulls, and was not troubled by the "haunts" again. All the gold in America, said he, would not tempt him to remove any more bones from the cave-tombs of the unknown dead.

LAKE OF THE DISMAL SWAMP

Drummond's Pond, or the Lake of the Dismal Swamp, is a dark and lonely tarn that lies in the centre of this noted Virginia morass. It is, in a century-old tradition, the Styx of two unhappy ghosts that await the end of time to pass its confines and enjoy the sunshine of serener worlds. A young woman of a family that had settled near this marsh died of a fever caused by its malarial exhalations, and was buried near the swamp. The young man to whom she was betrothed felt her loss so keenly that for days he neither ate nor slept, and at last broke down in mind and body. He recovered a measure of physical health, after a time, but his reason was hopelessly lost.

It was his hallucination that the girl was not dead, but had been exiled to the lonely reaches of this watery wilderness. He was heard to mutter, "I'll find her, and when Death comes I'll hide her in the hollow of a cypress until he passes on." Evading restraint, he plunged into the fen, and for some days he wandered there, eating berries, sleeping on tussocks of grass, with water-snakes crawling over him and poisonous plants shedding their baneful dew on his flesh. He came to the lake at last. A will-o'the-wisp played along the surface. "'Tis she!" he cried. "I see her, standing in the light." Hastily fashioning a raft of cypress boughs he floated it and pushed toward the centre of the pond, but the eagerness of his efforts and the rising of a wind dismembered the frail platform, and he fell into the black water to rise no more. But often, in the night, is seen the wraith of a canoe, with a fire-fly lamp burning on its prow, restlessly urged to and fro by two figures that seem to be vainly searching for an exit from the place, and that are believed to be those of the maiden and her lover.

THE BARGE OF DEFEAT

Rappannock River, in Virginia, used to be vexed with shadowy craft that some of the populace affirmed to be no boats, but spirits in disguise. One of these apparitions was held in fear by the Democracy of Essex County, as it was believed to be a forerunner of Republican victory. The first recorded appearance of the vessel was shortly after the Civil War, on the night of a Democratic mass-meeting at Tappahannock. There were music, refreshments, and jollity, and it was in the middle of a rousing speech that a man in the crowd cried, "Look, fellows! What is that queer concern going down the river?"

The people moved to the shore, and by the light of their torches a hulk was seen drifting with the stream—a hulk of fantastic form unlike anything that sails there in the daytime. As it came opposite the throng, the torchlight showed gigantic negroes who danced on deck, showing horrible faces to the multitude. Not a sound came from the barge, the halloos of the spectators bringing no response, and some boatmen ventured into the stream, only to pull back in a hurry, for the craft had become so strangely enveloped in shadow that it seemed to melt into air.

Next day the Democracy was defeated at the polls, chiefly by the negro vote. In 1880 it reappeared, and, as before, the Republicans gained the day. Just before the election of 1886, Mr. Croxton, Democratic nominee for Congress, was haranguing the people, when the cry of "The Black Barge!" arose. Argument and derision were alike ineffectual with the populace. The meeting broke up in silence and gloom, and Mr. Croxton was defeated by a majority of two thousand.

NATURAL BRIDGE

Though several natural bridges are known in this country, there is but one that is famous the world over, and that is the one which spans Clear Creek, Virginia—the remnant of a cave-roof, all the rest of the cavern having collapsed. It is two hundred and fifteen feet above the water, and is a solid mass of rock forty feet thick, one hundred feet wide, and ninety feet in span. Thomas Jefferson owned it; George Washington scaled its side and carved his name on the rock a foot higher than any one else. Here, too, came the youth who wanted to cut his name above Washington's, and who found, to his horror, when half-way up, that he must keep on, for he had left no resting-places for his feet at safe and reachable distances—who, therefore, climbed on and on, cutting handhold and foothold in the limestone until he reached the top, in a fainting state, his knife-blade worn to a stump. Here, too, in another tunnel of the cavern, flows Lost River, that all must return to, at some time, if they drink of it. Here, beneath the arch, is the dark stain, so like a flying eagle that the French officer who saw it during the Revolution augured from it a success for the united arms of the nations that used the eagle as their symbol.

The Mohegans knew this wonder of natural masonry, for to this point they were pursued by a hostile tribe, and on reaching the gulf found themselves on the edge of a precipice that was too steep at that point to descend. Behind them was the foe; before them, the chasm. At the suggestion of one of their medicine-men they joined in a prayer to the Great Spirit for deliverance, and when again they looked about them, there stood the bridge. Their women were hurried over; then, like so many Horatii, they formed across this dizzy highway and gave battle. Encouraged by the knowledge that they had a safe retreat in case of being overmastered, they fought with such heart that the enemy was defeated, and the grateful Mohegans named the place the Bridge of God.

THE SILENCE BROKEN

It was in 1734 that Joist Hite moved from Pennsylvania to Virginia, with his wife and boys, and helped to make a settlement on the Shenandoah twelve miles south of Woodstock. When picking berries at a distance from the village, one morning, the boys were surprised by Indians, who hurried with them into the wilderness before their friends could be apprised. Aaron, the elder, was strong, and big of frame, with coarse, black hair, and face tanned brown; but his brother was small and fair, with blue eyes and yellow locks, and it was doubtless because he was a type of the hated white race that the Indians spent their blows and kicks on him and spared the sturdy one. Aaron was wild with rage at the injuries put upon his gentle brother, but he was bound and helpless, and all that he could do was to encourage him to bear a stout heart and not to fall behind.

But Peter was too delicate to keep up, and there came a day when he could go no farther. The red men consulted for a few moments, then all of them stood apart but one, who fitted an arrow to his bow. The child's eyes grew big with fear, and Aaron tore at his bonds, but uselessly, and shouted that he would take the victim's place, but no one understood his speech, and in another moment Peter lay dead on the earth, with an arrow in his heart. Aaron gave one cry of hate and despair, and he, too, sank unconscious. On coming to himself he found that he was in a hut of boughs, attended by an old Indian, who told him in rude English that he was recovering from an illness of several weeks' duration, and that it was the purpose of his tribe to adopt him. When the lad tried to protest he found to his amazement that he could not utter a sound, and he learned from the Indian that the fever had taken away his tongue. In the dulness and weakness of his state he submitted to be clothed in Indian dress, smeared with a juice that browned his skin, and greeted by his brother's slayers as one of themselves. When he looked into a pool he found that he had, to all intents, become an Indian. In time he became partly reconciled to this change, for he did not know and could not ask where the white settlements lay; his appearance and his inability to speak would prevent his recognition by his friends, the red men were not unkind to him, and every boy likes a free and out-door life. They taught him to shoot with bow and arrow, but they kept him back if a white settlement was to be plundered.

Three years had elapsed, and Aaron, grown tall and strong, was a good hunter who stood in favor with the tribe. They had roamed back to the neighborhood of Woodstock, when, at a council, Aaron overheard a plot to fall on the village where his parents lived. He begged, by signs, to be allowed to go with them, and, believing that he could now be trusted, they offered no objection. Stoic as he had grown to be, he could not repress a tear as he saw his old home and thought of the peril that it stood in. If only he could give an alarm! The Indians retired into the forest to cook their food where the smoke could not be seen, while Aaron lingered at the edge of the wood and prayed for opportunity. He was not disappointed. Two girls came up through the perfumed dusk, driving cows from the pasture, and as they drew near, Aaron, pretending not to see them, crawled out of the bush with his weapons, and made a show of stealthily examining the town. The girls came almost upon him and screamed, while he dashed into the wood in affected surprise and regained the camp. The Indians had heard and seen nothing. The girls would surely give the alarm in town.

One by one the lights of the village went out, and when it seemed locked in sleep the red marauders crept toward the nearest house—that of Joist Hite. They arose together and rushed upon it, but at that moment a gun was fired, an Indian fell, and in a few seconds more the settlers, whom the girls had not failed to put on their guard, were hurrying from their hiding-places, firing into the astonished crowd of savages, who dashed for the woods again, leaving a dozen of their number on the ground. Aaron remained quietly standing near his father's house, and he was captured, as he hoped to be. When he saw how his parents had aged with time and grief he could not repress a tear, but to his grief was added terror when his father, after looking him steadily in the eye without recognition, began to load a pistol. "They killed my boys," said he, "and I am going to kill him. Bind him to that tree."

In vain the mother pleaded for mercy; in vain the dumb boy's eyes appealed to his father's. He was not afraid to die, and would do so gladly to have saved the settlement; but to die by his father's band! He could not endure it. He was bound to a tree, with the light of a fire shining into his face.

The old man, with hard determination, raised the weapon and aimed it slowly at the boy's heart. A surge of feeling shook the frame of the captive—he threw his whole life into the effort—then the silence of three years was broken, and he cried, "Father!" A moment later his parents were sobbing joyfully, and he could speak to them once more.

SIREN OF THE FRENCH BROAD

Among the rocks east of Asheville, North Carolina, lives the Lorelei of the French Broad River. This stream—the Tselica of the Indians—contains in its upper reaches many pools where the rapid water whirls and deepens, and where the traveller likes to pause in the heats of afternoon and drink and bathe. Here, from the time when the Cherokees occupied the country, has lived the siren, and if one who is weary and downcast sits beside the stream or utters a wish to rest in it, he becomes conscious of a soft and exquisite music blending with the plash of the wave.

Looking down in surprise he sees—at first faintly, then with distinctness—the form of a beautiful woman, with hair streaming like moss and dark eyes looking into his, luring him with a power he cannot resist. His breath grows short, his gaze is fixed, mechanically he rises, steps to the brink, and lurches forward into the river. The arms that catch him are slimy and cold as serpents; the face that stares into his is a grinning skull. A loud, chattering laugh rings through the wilderness, and all is still again.

THE HUNTER OF CALAWASSEE

Through brisk November days young Kedar and his trusty slave, Lauto, hunted along the Calawassee, with hope to get a shot at a buck—a buck that wore a single horn and that eluded them with easy, baffling gait whenever they met it in the fens. Kedar was piqued at this. He drained a deep draught and buttoned his coat with an air of resolution. "Now, by my soul," quoth he, "I'll have that buck to-day or die myself!" Then he laughed at the old slave, who begged him to unsay the oath, for there was something unusual about that animal—as it ran it left no tracks, and it passed through the densest wood without halting at trees or undergrowth. "Bah!" retorted the huntsman. "Have up the dogs. If that buck is the fiend himself, I'll have him before the day is out!" The twain were quickly in their saddles, and they had not been long in the wood before the one-horned buck was seen ahead, trotting with easy pace, yet with marvellous swiftness.

Kedar, who was in advance, whipped up his horse and followed the deer into a cypress grove near the Chechesee. As the game halted at a pool he fired. The report sounded dead in the dense wood, and the deer turned calmly, watched his pursuer until he was close at hand, then trotted away again. All day long he held the chase. The dogs were nowhere within sound, and he galloped through the forest, shouting and swearing like a very devil, beating and spurring the horse until the poor creature's head and flanks were reddened with blood. It was just at sunset that Kedar found himself again on the bank of the Calawassee, near the point he had left in the morning, and heard once more the baying of his hounds. At last his prey seemed exhausted, and, swimming the river, it ran into a thicket on the opposite side and stood still. "Now I have him!" cried the hunter. "Hillio, Lauto! He's mine!" The old negro heard the call and hastened forward. He heard his master's horse floundering in the swamp that edged the river—then came a plash, a curse, and as the slave arrived at the margin a few bubbles floated on the sluggish current. The deer stood in the thicket, staring with eyes that blazed through the falling darkness, and, with a wail of fear and sorrow, old Lauto fled the spot.

REVENGE OF THE ACCABEE

The settlement made by Lord Cardross, near Beaufort, South Carolina, was beset by Spaniards and Indians, who laid it in ashes and slew every person in it but one. She, a child of thirteen, had supposed the young chief of the Accabees to be her father, as he passed in the smoke, and had thrown herself into his arms. The savage raised his axe to strike, but, catching her blue eye raised to his, more in grief and wonder than alarm, the menacing hand fell to his side, and, tossing the girl lightly to a seat on his shoulder, he strode off into the forest. Mile after mile he bore her, and if she slept he held her to his breast as a father holds a babe. When she awoke it was in his lodge on the Ashley, and he was smiling in her face. The chief became her protector; but those who marked, with the flight of time, how his fierceness had softened, knew that she was more to him than a daughter. Years passed, the girl had grown to womanhood, and her captor declared himself her lover. She seemed not ill pleased at this, for she consented to be his wife. After the betrothal the chief joined a hunting party and was absent for a time. On his return the girl was gone. A trader who had been bartering merchandise for furs had seen her, had been inspired by passion, and, favored by suave manners and a white skin, he had won in a day a stronger affection than the Indian could claim after years of loving watchfulness.

When this discovery was made the chief, without a word, set off on the trail, and by broken twig, by bended grass and footprints at the brook-edge, he followed their course until he found them resting beneath a tree. The girl sprang from her new lover's arms with a cry of fear as the savage, with knife and tomahawk girt upon him, stepped into view, and she would have clasped his knees, but he motioned her away; then, ordering them to continue their march, he went behind them until they had reached a fertile spot on the Ashley, near the present site of Charleston, where he halted. "Though guilty, you shall not die," said he to the woman; then, to his rival, "You shall marry her, and a white priest shall join your hands. Here is your future home. I give you many acres of my land, but look that you care for her. As I have been merciful to you, do good to her. If you treat her ill, I shall not be far away."

The twain were married and went to live on the acres that had been so generously ceded to them, and for a time all went well; but the true disposition of the husband, which was sullen and selfish, soon began to disclose itself; disagreements arose, then quarrels; at last the man struck his wife, and, seizing the deed of the Accabee land and a paper that he had forced her to sign without knowing its contents, he started for the settlements, intending to sell the property and sail for England. On the edge of the village his flight was stayed by a tall form that arose in his path—that of the Indian. "I gave you all," said the chief, "the woman who should have been my wife, and then my land. This is your thanks. You shall go no farther."

With a quick stroke of the axe he cleft the skull of the shrinking wretch, and then, cutting off his scalp, the Indian ran to the cottage where sat the abandoned wife, weeping before the embers of her fire. He roused her by tossing on fresh fuel, but she shrank back in grief and shame when she saw who had come to her. "Do not fear," he said. "The man who struck you meant to sell your home to strangers"—and he laid the deed of sale before her, "but he will never play you false or lay hands on you again. Look!" He tossed the dripping scalp upon the paper. "Now I leave you forever. I cannot take you back among my people, who do not know deceit like yours, nor could I ever love you as I did at first." Turning, without other farewell he went out at the door. When this gift of Accabee land was sold—for the woman could no longer bear to live on it, but went to a northern city—a handsome house was built by the new owner, who added game preserves and pleasure grounds to the estate, but it was "haunted by a grief." Illness and ill luck followed the purchase, and the house fell into ruin.

TOCCOA FALLS

Early in the days of the white occupation of Georgia a cabin stood not far from the Falls of Toccoa (the Beautiful). Its only occupant was a feeble woman, who found it ill work to get food enough from the wild fruits and scanty clearing near the house, and she had nigh forgotten the taste of meat; for her two sons, who were her pride no less than her support, had been killed by savages. She often said that she would gladly die if she could harm the red men back, in return for her suffering—which was not Christian doctrine, but was natural. She was brooding at her fire, one winter evening, in wonder as to how one so weak and old as she could be revenged, when her door was flung open and a number of red men filled her cabin. She hardly changed countenance. She did not rise. "You may take my life," she said, "for it is useless, now that you have robbed it of all that made it worth living."

"Hush!" said the chief. "What does the warrior want with the scalps of women? We war on your men because they kill our game and steal our land."

"Is it possible that you come to our homes except to kill?"

"We are strangers and have lost our way. You must guide us to the foot of Toccoa and lead us to our friends."

"I lead you? Never!"

The chief raised his axe, but the woman did not flinch. There was a pause, in which the iron still hung menacing. Suddenly the dame looked up and said, "If you promise to protect me, I will lead you."

The promise was given and the band set forth, the aged guide in advance, bending against the storm and clasping her poor rags about her. In the darkest part of the wood, where the roaring of wind and groaning of branches seemed the louder for the booming of waters, she cautioned the band to keep in single file, but to make haste, for the way was far and the gloom was thickening. Bending their heads against the wind they pressed forward, she in advance. Suddenly, yet stealthily, she sprang aside and crouched beneath a tree that grew at the very brink of the fall. The Indians came on, following blindly, and in an instant she descried the leader as he went whirling over the edge, and one after another the party followed. When the last had gone to his death she arose to her feet with a laugh of triumph. "Now I, too, can die!" she cried. So saying, she fell forward into the grayness of space.

TWO LIVES FOR ONE

The place of Macon, Georgia, in the early part of this century was marked only by an inn. One of its guests was a man who had stopped there on the way to Alabama, where he had bought land. The girl who was, to be his wife was to follow in a few days. In the morning when he paid his reckoning he produced a well-filled pocket-book, and he did not see the significant look that passed between two rough black-bearded fellows who had also spent the night there, and who, when he set forth, mounted their horses and offered to keep him company. As they rode through the deserted village of Chilicte one of the twain engaged the traveller in talk while the other, falling a little behind, dealt him a blow with a loaded whip that unseated him. Divining their purpose, and lacking weapons for his own defence, he begged for mercy, and asked to be allowed to return to his bride to be, but the robbers had already made themselves liable to penalty, and two knife-thrusts in the breast silenced his appeals. The money was secured, the body was dropped into a hollow where the wolves would be likely to find and mangle it, and the outlaws went on their way.

Men of their class do not keep money long, and when the proceeds of the robbery had been wasted at cards and in drink they separated. As in fulfilment of the axiom that a murderer is sure to revisit the scene of his crime, one of the men found himself at the Ocmulgee, a long time afterward, in sight of the new town—Macon. In response to his halloo a skiff shot forth from the opposite shore, and as it approached the bank he felt a stir in his hair and a touch of ice at his heart, for the ferryman was his victim of years ago. Neither spoke a word, but the criminal felt himself forced to enter the boat when the dead man waved his hand, and he was rowed across, his horse swimming beside the skiff. As the jar of the keel was felt on the gravel he leaped out, urged his horse to the road, sprang to the saddle, and rushed away in an agony of fear, that was heightened when a hollow voice called, "Stay!"

After a little he slackened pace, and a farmer, who was standing at the roadside, asked, in astonishment, "How did you get across? There is a freshet, and the ferryman was drowned last night." With a new thrill he spurred his horse forward, and made no other halt until he reached the tavern, where he fell in a faint on the steps, for the strain was no longer to be endured. A crowd gathered, but he did not see it when he awoke—he saw only one pair of eyes, that seemed to be looking into his inmost soul—the eyes of the man he had slain. With a yell of terror and of insane fury he rushed upon the ghost and thrust a knife into its breast. The frenzy passed. It was no ghost that lay on the earth before him, staring up with sightless eyes. It was his fellow-murderer—his own brother. That night the assassin's body hung from a tree at the cross-roads.

A GHOSTLY AVENGER

In Cuthbert, Georgia, is a gravestone thus inscribed: "Sacred to the memory of Jim Brown." No date, no epitaph—for Jim Brown was hanged. And this is the story: At the close of the Civil War a company of Federal soldiers was stationed in Cuthbert, to enforce order pending the return of its people to peaceful occupations. Charles Murphy was a lieutenant in this company. His brother, an officer quartered in a neighboring town, was sent to Cuthbert one day to receive funds for the payment of some men, and left camp toward evening to return to his troop. That night Charles Murphy was awakened by a violent flapping of his tent. It sounded as though a gale was coming, but when he arose to make sure that the pegs and poles of his canvas house were secure, the noise ceased, and he was surprised to find that the air was clear and still. On returning to bed the flapping began again, and this time he dressed himself and went out to make a more careful examination. In the shadow of a tree a man stood beckoning. It was his brother, who, in a low, grave voice, told him that he was in trouble, and asked him to follow where he should lead him. The lieutenant walked swiftly through fields and woods for some miles with his relative—he had at once applied for and received a leave of absence for a few hours—and they descended together a slope to the edge of a swamp, where he stumbled against something. Looking down at the object on which he had tripped, he saw that it was his brother's corpse—not newly dead, but cold and rigid— the pockets rifled, the clothing soaked with mire and blood.

Dazed and terrified, he returned to camp, roused some of his men, and at daybreak secured the body. An effort to gain a clue to the murderer was at once set on foot. It was not long before evidence was secured that led to the arrest of Jim Brown, and there was a hint that his responsibility for the crime was revealed through the same supernatural agency that had apprised Lieutenant Murphy of his bereavement. Brown was an ignorant farm laborer, who had conceived that it was right to kill Yankees, and whose cupidity had been excited by learning that the officer had money concealed about him. He had offered, for a trifling sum, to take his victim by a short cut to his camp, but led him to the swamp instead, where he had shot him through the heart. On the culprit's arrival in Cuthbert he was lynched by the soldiers, but was cut down by their commander before life was extinct, and was formally and conclusively hanged in the next week, after trial and conviction.

THE WRAITH RINGER OF ATLANTA

A man was killed in Elliott Street, Atlanta, Georgia, by a cowardly stroke from a stiletto. The assassin escaped. Strange what a humming there was in the belfry of St. Michael's Church that night! Had the murderer taken refuge there? Was it a knell for his lost soul, chasing him through the empty streets and beginning already an eternal punishment of terror? Perhaps the guilty one did not dare to leave Atlanta, for the chimes sang in minor chords on several nights after. The old policeman who kept ward in an antiquated guardhouse that stood opposite the church—it was afterward shaken down by earthquake—said that he saw a human form, which he would avouch to be that of the murdered man, though it was wrapped in a cloak, stalk to the doors, enter without opening them, glide up the winding stair, albeit he bent neither arm nor knee, pass the ropes by which the chimes were rung, and mount to the belfry. He could see the shrouded figure standing beneath the gloomy mouths of metal. It extended its bony hands to the tongues of the bells and swung them from side to side, but while they appeared to strike vigorously they seemed as if muffled, and sent out only a low, musical roar, as if they were rung by the wind. Was the murderer abroad on those nights? Did he, too, see that black shadow of his victim in the belfry sounding an alarm to the sleeping town and appealing to be avenged? It may be. At all events, the apparition boded ill to others, for, whenever the chimes were rung by spectral hands, mourners gathered at some bedside within hearing of them and lamented that the friend they had loved would never know them more on earth.

THE SWALLOWING EARTHQUAKE

The Indian village that in 1765 stood just below the site of Oxford, Alabama, was upset when the news was given out that two of the squaws had given simultaneous birth to a number of children that were spotted like leopards. Such an incident betokened the existence of some baneful spirit among them that had no doubt leagued itself with the women, who were at once tried on the charge of witchcraft, convicted, and sentenced to death at the stake, while a watch was to be set on the infants, so early orphaned, lest they, too, should show signs of malevolent possession. The whole tribe, seventeen hundred in number, assembled to see the execution, but hardly were the fires alight when a sound like thunder rolled beneath their feet, and with a hideous crack and groan the earth opened and nearly every soul was engulfed in a fathomless and smoking pit-all, indeed, save two, for a couple of young braves who were on the edge of the crowd flung themselves flat on the heaving ground and remained there until the earthquake wave had passed. The hollow afterward filled with water and was called Blue Pond. It is popularly supposed to be fathomless, but it was shown that a forest once spread across the bottom, when, but a few years ago, a great tree arose from the water, lifting first its branches, then turning so as to show its roots above the surface, and afterward disappeared.

LAST STAND OF THE BILOXI

The southern part of this country was once occupied by a people called the Biloxi, who had kept pace with the Aztecs in civilization and who cultivated especially the art of music. In lives of gentleness and peace they so soon forgot the use of arms that when the Choctaws descended on their fields they were powerless to prevent the onset. Town after town they evacuated before the savages, and at last the Biloxi, reduced to a few thousands, were driven to the mouth of the Pascagoula River, Mississippi, where they intrenched themselves, and for a few months withstood the invaders. But the time came when their supplies were exhausted, and every form was pinched with hunger. Flight was impossible. Surrender commonly meant slaughter and outrage. They resolved to die together.

On a fair spring morning the river-ward gates of their fort were opened and the survivors of that hapless tribe marched forth, their chief in advance, with resolution on his wasted face, then the soldiers and counsellors, the young men, the women and children, and the babes asleep on the empty breasts of their mothers. As they emerged from the walls with slow but steady step they broke into song, and their assailants, who had retired to their tents for their meal, listened with surprise to the chorus of defiance and rejoicing set up by the starving people. Without pause or swerving they entered the bay and kept their march. Now the waters closed over the chief, then the soldiers—at last only a few voices of women were heard in the chant, and in a few moments all was still. Not one shrank from the sacrifice. And for years after the echo of that death-song floated over he waves.

Another version of the legend sets forth that the Biloxi believed themselves the children of the sea, and that they worshipped the image of a lovely mermaid with wondrous music. After the Spaniards had come among this gay and gentle people, they compelled them, by tyranny and murder, to accept the religion of the white man, but of course it was only lip-service that they rendered at the altar. The Biloxi were awakened one night by the sound of wings and the rising of the river. Going forth they saw the waters of Pascagoula heaped in a quivering mound, and bright on its moonlit crest stood a mermaid that sang to them, "Come to me, children of the sea. Neither bell, book, nor cross shall win you from your queen." Entranced by her song and the potency of her glances, they moved forward until they encircled the hill of waters. Then, with hiss and roar, the river fell back to its level, submerging the whole tribe. The music that haunts the bay, rising through the water when the moon is out, is the sound of their revels in the caves below—dusky Tannhausers of a southern Venusberg. An old priest, who was among them at the time of this prodigy, feared that the want of result to his teachings was due to his not being in a perfect state of grace. On his death-bed he declared that if a priest would row to the spot where the music sounded, at midnight on Christmas, and drop a crucifix into the water, he would instantly be swallowed by the waves, but that every soul at the bottom would be redeemed. The souls have never been ransomed.

THE SACRED FIRE OF NACHEZ

The Indians of the South, being in contact with the civilized races of Central America, were among the most progressive and honorable of the red men. They were ruled by intelligence rather than force, and something of the respect that Europeans feel for their kingly families made them submit to woman's rule. The valley of Nacooche, Georgia, indeed, perpetuates in its name one of these princesses of a royal house, for though she ruled a large tribe with wisdom she was not impervious to the passions of common mortals. The "Evening Star" died by her own hand, being disappointed in love affair. Her story is that of Juliet, and she and her lover—united in death, as they could not be in life—are buried beneath a mound in the centre of he valley.

The Indians of that region had towns built for permanency, and possessed some knowledge of the arts, while in religion their belief and rites were curiously like those of the Persian fire-worshippers. It was on the site of the present city in Mississippi which bears their name that the Natchez Indians built their Temple of the Sun. When it was finished a meteor fell from heaven and kindled the fire on their altar, and from that hour the priests guarded he flame continually, until one night when it was extinguished by mischance. This event was believed to be an omen, and the people so took it to heart that when the white men came, directly after, they had little courage to prosecute a war, and fell back before the conqueror, never to hold their ancient home again.

PASS CHRISTIAN

Senhor Vineiro, a Portuguese, having wedded Julia Regalea, a Spaniard, in South America, found it needful to his fortunes to leave Montevideo, for a revolution was breeding, and no less needful to his happiness to take his wife with him from that city, for he was old and she was young. But he chose the wrong ship to sail on, for Captain Dane, of the Nightingale, was also young, presentable, and well schooled, but heartless. On the voyage to New Orleans he not only won the affection of the wife, but slew the husband and flung his body overboard. Vainly the wife tried to repress the risings of remorse, and vainly, too, she urged Dane to seek absolution from her church. She had never loved her husband, and she had loved Dane from the first, but she was not at heart a bad woman and her peace was gone. The captain was disturbed and suspicious. His sailors glanced at him out of the corners of their eyes in a way that he did not like. Had the woman in some unintentional remark betrayed him? Could he conceal his crime, save with a larger one?

Pass Christian was a village then. On a winter night its people saw a glare in the sky, and hurrying to their doors found a ship burning in the gulf. Smacks and row-boats put off to the rescue, but hardly were they under way ere the ship disappeared as suddenly as if the sea had swallowed it. As the night was thick the boats returned, but next morning five men were encountered on the shore-all that were left of the crew of the Nightingale. Captain Dane was so hospitably received by the people of the district, and seemed to take so great a liking for the place, that he resolved to live there. He bought a plantation with a roomy old house upon it and took his fellow-survivors there to live, as he hoped, an easy life. That was not to be. Yellow fever struck down all the men but Dane, and one of them, in dying, raved to his negro nurse that Dane had taken all the treasure from the ship and put it into a boat, after serving grog enough to intoxicate all save the trusted ones of the crew; that he and his four associates fired the ship and rowed away, leaving an unhappy woman to a horrible fate. Senhora Vineiro was pale but composed when she saw the manner of death she was to die. She brought from her cabin a harp which had been a solace of her husband and herself and began to play and sing an air that some of the listeners remembered. It was an "Ave Maria," and the sound of it was so plaintive that even Dane stopped rowing; but he set his teeth when his shoe touched the box of gold at his feet and ordered the men to row on. There was an explosion and the vessel disappeared. On reaching shore the treasure was buried at the foot of a large oak.

This story was repeated by the nurse, but she was ignorant, she had no proofs, so it was not generally believed; yet there was a perceptible difference in the treatment of Dane by his neighbors, and among the superstitious negroes it was declared that he had sold himself to the devil. If he had, was it an air from hell that sounded in his ears when he was alone?—the "Ave Maria" of a sinning but repentant woman. The coldness and suspicion were more than he could stand. Besides, who could tell? Evidence might be found against him. He would dig up his treasure and fly the country. It was a year from the night when he had fired his ship. Going out after dark, that none might see him, he stole to the tree and began to dig. Presently a red light grew through the air, and looking up he saw a flaming vessel advancing over the sea. It stopped, and he could see men clambering into a boat at its side. They rowed toward him with such miraculous speed that the ocean seemed to steam with a blue light as they advanced. He stood like a stone, for now he could see the faces of the rowers, and every one was the face of a corpse—a corpse that had been left on board of that vessel and had been in the bottom of the sea for the last twelvemonth. They sprang on shore and rushed upon him. Next morning Dane's body was found beneath the oak with his hands filled with gems and gold.

THE UNDER LAND

When the Chatas looked into the still depths of Bayou Lacombe, Louisiana, they said that the reflection of the sky was the empyrean of the Under Land, whither all good souls were sure to go after death. Their chief, Opaleeta, having fallen into this bayou, was so long beneath the water that he was dead when his fellows found him, but by working over him for hours, and through resort to prayers and incantations of medicine men, his life returned and he stood on his feet once more. Then he grieved that his friends had brought him back, for he had been at the gates of the Under Land, where the air is blithe and balmy, and so nourishing that people live on it; where it is never winter; where the sun shines brightly, but never withers and parches; and where stars dance to the swing of the breezes. There no white man comes to rob the Indian and teach him to do wrong. Gorgeous birds fly through changing skies that borrow the tints of flowers, the fields are spangled with blossoms of red and blue and gold that load each wind with perfume, the grass is as fine as the hair of deer, and the streams are thick with honey.

At sunset those who loved each other in life are gathered to their lodges, and raise songs of joy and thankfulness. Their voices are soft and musical, their faces are young again and beam with smiles, and there is no death. It was only the chiefs who heard his story, for, had all the tribe known it, many who were old and ill and weary would have gone to the bayou, and leaped in, to find that restful, happy Under Land. Those who had gone before they sometimes tried to see, when the lake was still and dappled with pictures of sunset clouds, but the dead never came back—they kept away from the margin of the water lest they should be called again to a life of toil and sorrow. And Opaleeta lived for many years and ruled his tribe with wisdom, yet he shared in few of the merry-makings of his people, and when, at last, his lodge was ready in the Under Land, he gave up his life without a sigh.

THE CENRAL STATES AND THE GREAT LAKES

AN AVERTED PERIL

In 1786 a little building stood at North Bend, Ohio, near the junction of the Miami and Ohio Rivers, from which building the stars and stripes were flying. It was one of a series of blockhouses built for the protecting of cleared land while the settlers were coming in, yet it was a trading station rather than a fort, for the attitude of government toward the red men was pacific. The French of the Mississippi Valley were not reconciled, however, to the extension of power by a Saxon people, and the English in Canada were equally jealous of the prosperity of those provinces they had so lately lost. Both French and English had emissaries among the Shawnees when it had become known that the United States intended to negotiate a treaty with them.

It was the mild weather that comes for a time in October, when Cantantowit blesses the land from his home in the southwest with rich colors, plaintive perfumes of decay, soft airs, and tender lights a time for peace; but the garrison at the fort realized that the situation was precarious. The Shawnees had camped about them, and the air was filled with the neighing of their ponies and the barking of their dogs. To let them into the fort was to invite massacre; to keep them out after they had been summoned was to declare war.

Colonel George Rogers Clarke, of Virginia, who was in command, scoffed at the fears of his men, and would not give ear to their appeals for an adjournment of the meeting or a change of the place of it. At the appointed hour the doors were opened and the Indians came in. The pipe of peace was smoked in the usual form, but the red men were sullen and insolent, and seemed to be seeking a cause of quarrel. Clarke explained that the whites desired only peace, and he asked the wise men to speak for their tribe. A stalwart chief arose, glanced contemptuously at the officer and his little guard, and, striding to the table where Clarke was seated, threw upon it two girdles of wampum—the peace-belt and the war-belt. "We offer you these belts," he said. "You know what they mean. Take which you like."

It was a deliberate insult and defiance. Both sides knew it, and many of the men held their breath. Clarke carelessly picked up the war-belt on the point of his cane and flung it among the assembled chiefs. Every man in the room sprang to his feet and clutched his weapon. Then, with a sternness that was almost ferocious, Clarke pointed to the door with an imperative action, and cried, "Dogs, you may go!"

The Indians were foiled in their ill intent by his self-possession and seeming confidence, which made them believe that he had forces in the vicinity that they were not prepared to meet. They had already had a bitter experience of his strength and craft, and in the fear that a trap had been set for them they fled tumultuously. The treaty was ratified soon after.

THE OBSTINACY OF SAINT CLAIR

When the new First Regiment of United States Infantry paused at Marietta, Ohio, on its way to garrison Vincennes, its officers made a gay little court there for a time. The young Major Hamtramck—contemptuously called by the Indians "the frog on horseback," because of his round shoulders—found especial pleasure in the society of Marianne Navarre, who was a guest at the house of General Arthur St. Clair; but the old general viewed this predilection with disfavor, because he had hoped that his own daughter would make a match with the major. But Louisa longed for the freedom of the woods. She was a horsewoman and a hunter, and she had a sentimental fondness for Indians.

When Joseph Brandt (Thayendanegea) camped with his dreaded band near the town, it was she who—without her father's knowledge, and in the disguise of an Indian girl—took the message that had been entrusted to a soldier asking the tribe to send delegates to a peace council at the fort. Louisa and Brandt had met in Philadelphia some years before, when both were students in that city, and he was rejoiced to meet her again, for he had made no secret of his liking for her, and in view of the bravery she had shown in thus riding into a hostile camp his fondness increased to admiration. After she had delivered the message she said, "Noble warrior, I have risked my life to obtain this interview. You must send some one back with me." Brandt replied, "It is fitting that I alone should guard so courageous a maiden," and he rode with her through the lines, under the eyes of a wondering and frowning people, straight to the general's door. Soon after, Brandt made a formal demand for the hand of this dashing maid, but the stubborn general refused to consider it. He was determined that she ought to love Major Hamtramck, and he told her so in tones so loud that they reached the ears of Marianne, as she sat reading in her room. Stung by this disclosure of the general's wishes, and doubting whether the major had been true to her—fearful, too, that she might be regarded as an interloper—she made a pretext to return as quickly as possible to her home in Detroit, and left no adieus for her lover.

It was not long after that war broke out between the settlers and the Indians, for Brandt now had a personal as well as a race grudge to gratify, though when he defeated St. Clair he spared his life in the hope that the general would reward his generosity by resigning to him his daughter. At all events, he resolved that the "frog on horseback," whom he conceived to be his rival, should not win her. The poor major, who cared nothing for Louisa, and who was unable to account for the flight of Marianne, mourned her absence until it was rumored that she had been married, when, as much in spite as in love, he took to himself a mate. After he had been for some time a widower he met Marianne again, and learned that she was still a maiden. He renewed his court with ardor, but the woman's love for him had died when she learned of his marriage. Affecting to make light of this second disappointment, he said, "Since I cannot be united to you in life, I shall be near you in death."

"A soldier cannot choose where he shall die," she answered.

"No matter. I shall sleep in the shadow of your tomb."

As it fell out they were indeed buried near each other in Detroit. Thus, the stupidity and obstinacy of General St. Clair, in supposing that he could make young folks love to order, thwarted the happiness of four people and precipitated a war.

THE HUNDREDTH SKULL

In the early part of this century Bill Quick, trapper and frontiersman, lived in a cabin on the upper Scioto, not far from the present town of Kenton, Ohio. One evening when he returned from the hunt he found his home rifled of its contents and his aged father weltering in his blood on the floor. He then and there took oath that he would be revenged a hundredfold. His mission was undertaken at once, and for many a year thereafter the Indians of the region had cause to dread the doom that came to them from brake and wood and fen,—now death by knife that flashed at them from behind a tree, and the next instant whirled through the air and was buried to the hilt in a red man's heart; now, by bullet as they rowed across the rivers; now, by axe that clove their skulls as they lay asleep.

Bill Quick worked secretly, and, unlike other men of the place and time, he did not take his trophies Indian-fashion. The scalp was not enough. He took the head. And presently a row of grinning skulls was ranged upon his shelves. Ninety-nine of these ghastly prizes occupied his cabin, and the man was confident that he should accomplish his intent. But the Indians, in terror, were falling away toward the lakes; they were keeping better guard; and ere the hundredth man had fallen before his rifle he was seized with fatal illness. Calling to him his son, Tom, he pointed to the skulls, and charged him to fulfil the oath he had taken by adding to the list a hundredth skull. Should he fail in this the murdered ancestor and he himself would come back to haunt the laggard. Tom accepted the trust, but everything seemed to work against him. He never was much of a hunter nor a very true shot, and he had no liking for war; besides, the Indians had left the country, as he fancied. So he grumbled at the uncongenial task appointed for him and kept deferring it from week to week and from year to year. When his conscience pricked him he allayed the smart with drink, and his conscience seemed to grow more active as he grew older.

On returning to the cabin after a carouse he declared that he had heard voices, that the skulls gibbered and cracked their teeth together as if mocking his weakness, and that a phosphorescent glare shone through the sockets of their eyes. In his cups he prattled his secret, and soon the whole country knew that he was under oath to kill a red-skin-and the country laughed at him. On a certain day it was reported that a band of Indians had been seen in the neighborhood, and what with drink and the taunts of his friends, he was impelled to take his rifle and set out once more on the war-path. A settler heard a shot fired not long after. Next day a neighbor passing Tom Quick's cabin tapped at the door, and, receiving no answer, pushed it open and entered. The hundredth skull was there, on the shelves, a bullet-hole in the forehead, and the scalp gone. The head was Quick's.

THE CRIME OF BLACK SWAMP

Two miles south of Munger, Ohio, in the heart of what used to be called the Black Swamp, stood the Woodbury House, a roomy mansion long gone to decay. John Cleves, the last to live in it, was a man whose evil practices got him into the penitentiary, but people had never associated him with the queer sights and sounds in the lower chambers, nor with the fact that a man named Syms, who had gone to that house in 1842, had never been known to leave it. Ten years after Syms's disappearance it happened that Major Ward and his friend John Stow had occasion to take shelter there for the night—it being then deserted,—and, starting a blaze in the parlor fireplace, they lit their pipes and talked till late. Stow would have preferred a happier topic, but the major, who feared neither man nor devil, constantly turned the talk on the evil reputation of the house.

While they chatted a door opened with a creak and a human skeleton appeared before them.

"What do you want? Speak!" cried Ward. But waiting for no answer he drew his pistols and fired two shots at the grisly object. There was a rattling sound, but the skeleton was neither dislocated nor disconcerted. Advancing deliberately, with upraised arm, it said, in a husky voice, "I, that am dead, yet live in a sense that mortals do not know. In my earthly life I was James Syms, who was robbed and killed here in my sleep by John Cleves." With bony finger it pointed to a rugged gap in its left temple. "Cleves cut off my head and buried it under the hearth. My body he cast into his well." At these words the head disappeared and the voice was heard beneath the floor, "Take up my skull." The watchers obeyed the call, and after digging a minute beneath the hearth a fleshless head with a wound on the left temple came to view. Ward took it into his hands, but in a twinkling it left them and reappeared on the shoulders of the skeleton.

"I have long wanted to tell my fate," it resumed, "but could not until one should be found brave enough to speak to me. I have appeared to many, but you are the first who has commanded me to break my long silence. Give my bones a decent burial. Write to my relative, Gilmore Syms, of Columbus, Georgia, and tell him what I have revealed. I have found peace." With a grateful gesture it extended its hand to Ward, who, as he took it, shook like one with an ague, his wrist locked in its bony clasp. As it released him it raised its hand impressively. A bluish light burned at the doorway for an instant. The two men found themselves alone.

THE HOUSE ACCURSED

Near Gallipolis, Ohio, there stood within a few years an old house of four rooms that had been occupied by Herman Deluse. He lived there alone, and, though his farming was of the crudest sort, he never appeared to lack for anything. The people had an idea that the place was under ban, and it was more than suspected that its occupant had been a pirate. In fact, he called his place the Isle of Pines, after a buccaneers' rendezvous in the West Indies, and made no attempt to conceal the strange plunder and curious weapons that he had brought home with him, but of money he never appeared to have much at once. When it came his time to die he ended his life alone, so far as any knew—at least, his body was found in his bed, without trace of violence or disorder. It was buried and the public administrator took charge of the estate, locking up the house until possible relatives should come to claim it, and the rustic jury found that Deluse "came to his death by visitation of God."

It was but a few nights after this that the Rev. Henry Galbraith returned from a visit of a month to Cincinnati and reached his home after a night of boisterous storm. The snow was so deep and the roads so blocked with windfalls that he put up his horse in Gallipolis and started for his house on foot.

"But where did you pass the night?" inquired his wife, after the greetings were over. "With old Deluse in the Isle of Pines," he answered. "I saw a light moving about the house, and rapped. No one came; so, as I was freezing, I forced open the door, built a fire, and lay down in my coat before it. Old Deluse came in presently and I apologized, but he paid no attention to me. He seemed to be walking in his sleep and to be searching for something. All night long I could hear his footsteps about the house, in pauses of the storm."

The clergyman's wife and son looked at each other, and a friend who was present—a lawyer, named Maren—remarked, "You did not know that Deluse was dead and buried?" The clergyman was speechless with amazement. "You have been dreaming," said the lawyer. "Still, if you like, we will go there to-night and investigate."

The clergyman, his son, and the lawyer went to the house about nine o'clock, and as they approached it a noise of fighting came from within—blows, the clink of steel, groans, and curses. Lights appeared, first at one window, then at another. The men rushed forward, burst in the door, and were inside—in darkness and silence. They had brought candles and lighted them, but the light revealed nothing. Dust lay thick on the floor except in the room where the clergyman had passed the previous night, and the door that he had then opened stood ajar, but the snow outside was drifted and unbroken by footsteps. Then came the sound of a fall that shook the building. At the same moment it was noticed by the other two men that young Galbraith was absent. They hurried into the room whence the noise had come. A board was wrenched from the wall there, disclosing a hollow that had been used for a hiding-place, and on the floor lay young Galbraith with a sack of Spanish coins in his hand. His father stooped to pick him up, but staggered back in horror, for the young man's life had gone. A post-mortem examination revealed no cause of death, and a rustic jury again laid it to a "visitation of God." MARQUETTE'S MAN-EATER

Until it was worn away by the elements a curious relief was visible on the bluffs of the Mississippi near Alton, Illinois. It was to be seen as late as 1860, and represented a monster once famous as the "piasa bird." Father Marquette not only believed it but described it as a man-eater in the account of his explorations, where he mentions other zoological curiosities, such as unicorns with shaggy mane and land-turtles three feet long with two heads, "very mischievous and addicted to biting." He even showed a picture of the maneater that accorded rudely with the picture on the rocks. It was said to prey on human flesh, and to be held in fear by the Indians, who encountered it on and near the Mississippi. It had the body of a panther, wings like a bat, and head and horns of a deer. Father Marquette gave it a human face. The sculpture was undoubtedly made by Indians, but its resemblance to the winged bulls of Assyria and the sphinxes of Egypt has been quoted as confirmation of a prehistoric alliance of Old and New World races or the descent of one from the other. It has also been thought to stand for the totem of some great chief-symbolizing, by its body, strength; by its wings, speed; by its head, gentleness and beauty. But may not the tradition of it have descended from the discovery of comparatively late remains, by primitive man, of the winged saurians that crawled, swam, dived, or flew, lingering on till the later geologic period? The legend of the man-eater may even have been told by those who killed the last of the pterodactyls.

MICHEL DE COUCY'S TROUBLES

Michel De Coucy, of Prairie de Rocher, Illinois, sat before his door humming thoughtfully, and trying to pull comfort out of a black pipe.. He was in debt, and he did not like the sensation. As hunter, boatman, fiddler he had done well enough, but having rashly ventured into trade he had lost money, and being unable to meet a note had applied to Pedro Garcia for a loan at usurious interest. Garcia was a black-whiskered Spaniard who was known to have been a gambler in New Orleans, and as Michel was in arrears in his payments he was now threatening suit. Presently the hunter jumped up with a glad laugh, for two horsemen were approaching his place—the superior of the Jesuit convent at Notre Dame de Kaskaskia and the governor of the French settlements in Illinois, of whom he had asked advice, and who had come from Fort Chartres, on the Mississippi, to give it in person. It was good advice, too, for the effect of it was that there was no law of that time—1750—by which a Spaniard could sue a Frenchman on French territory. Moreover, the bond was invalid because it was drawn up in Spanish, and Garcia could produce no witness to verify the cross at the bottom of the document as of Michel's making.

Great was the wrath of the Spaniard when Michel told him this, nor was it lessened when the hunter bade him have no fear—that he might be obliged to repudiate part of the interest, but that every livre of the principal would be forthcoming, if only a little time were allowed. The money lender walked away with clenched fists, muttering to himself, and Michel lit his pipe again.

At supper-time little Genevieve, the twelve-year-old daughter of Michel, did not appear. The table was kept waiting for an hour. Michel sat down but could not eat, and, after scolding awhile in a half-hearted fashion, he went to the clearing down the road, where the child had been playing. A placard was seen upon a tree beside the way, and he called a passing neighbor to read to him these words: "Meshell Coosy. French rascal. Pay me my money and you have your daughter. Pedro Garcia."

Accustomed as he was to perils, and quick as he generally was in expedient, Michel was overwhelmed by this stroke. The villagers offered to arm themselves and rescue the child, but he would not consent to this, for he was afraid that Garcia might kill her, if he knew that force was to be set against him. In a day or two Michel was told to go to Fort Chartres, as favorable news awaited him. He rode with all speed to that post, went to the official quarters, where the governor was sitting, and as he entered he became almost insane with rage, for Garcia stood before him. Nothing but the presence of others saved the Spaniard's life, and it was some time before Michel could be made to understand that Garcia was there under promise of safe conduct, and that the representatives of King Louis were in honor bound to see that he was not injured. The points at issue between the two men were reviewed, and the governor gave it as his decision that Michel must pay his debt without interest, that being forfeit by the Spaniard's abduction of Genevieve, and that the Spaniard was to restore the girl, both parties in the case being remanded to prison until they had obeyed this judgment.

"But I have your promise of safe conduct!" cried the Spaniard, blazing with wrath.

"And you shall have it when the girl returns," replied the governor. "You shall be protected in going and coming, but there is no reference in the paper that you hold as to how long we may wish to keep you with us."

Both men were marched away forthwith, but Michel was released in an hour, for in that time the people had subscribed enough to pay his debt. The Spaniard sent a messenger to a renegade who had little Genevieve in keeping, and next day he too went free, swearing horribly, but glad to accept the service of an armed escort until he was well out of town. Michel embraced his child with ardor when once she was in his arms again; then he lighted his pipe and set out with her for home, convinced that French law was the best in the world, that Spaniards were not to be trusted, and that it is safer to keep one's earnings under the floor than to venture them in trade.

WALLEN'S RIDGE

A century ago this rough eminence, a dozen miles from Chattanooga, Tennessee, was an abiding place of Cherokee Indians, among whom was Arinook, their medicine-man, and his daughter. The girl was pure and fair, and when a white hunter saw her one day at the door of her father's wigwam he was so struck with her charm of person and her engaging manner that he resolved not to return to his people until he had won her for his wife. She had many lovers, though she favored none of them, and while the Cherokees were at first loth to admit a stranger to their homes they forgot their jealousy when they found that this one excelled as a hunter and fisherman, that he could throw the knife and tomahawk better than themselves, and that he was apt in their work and their sports.

They even submitted to the inevitable with half a grace when they found that the stranger and the girl of whom they were so fond were in love. With an obduracy that seems to be characteristic of fathers, the medicine-man refused his consent to the union, and the hearts of the twain were heavy. Though the white man pleaded with her to desert her tribe, she refused to do so, on the score of duty to her father, and the couple forlornly roamed about the hill, watching the sunset from its top and passing the bright summer evenings alone, sitting hand in hand, loving, sorrowing, and speaking not. In one of their long rambles they found themselves beside the Tennessee River at a point where the current swirls among rocks and sucks down things that float, discharging them at the surface in still water, down the stream. Here for a time they stood, when the girl, with a gush of tears, began to sing—it was her death-song. The white man grasped her hand and joined his voice to hers. Then they took a last embrace and flung themselves into the water, still hand in hand.

When the river is low you may hear their death-song sounding there. The manitous of the river and the wood were offended with the medicine-man because of his stubbornness and cruelty, although he suffered greatly because of the death his daughter died, and he the cause of it. For now strange Indians appeared among the Cherokees and drove the deer and bear away. Tall, strong, and large were these intruders, and they hung about the village by day and night—never speaking, yet casting a fear about them, for they would throw great rocks farther than a warrior could shoot an arrow with the wind behind him; they had horns springing from their heads; their eyes were the eyes of wild-cats, and shone in the dark; they growled like animals, shaking the earth when they did so, and breathing flame; they were at the bedside, at the council-fire, at the banquet, seeming only to wait for a show of enmity to annihilate the tribe.

At length the people could endure their company no longer, and taking down their lodges they left Wallen's Ridge and wandered far away until they came to a valley where no foot had left its impress, and there they besought the Great Spirit to forgive the wrong their medicine-man had done, and to free them from the terrible spirits that had been living among them. The prayer was granted, and the lodges stood for many years in a safe and happy valley.

THE SKY WALKER OF HURON

Here is the myth of Endymion and Diana, as told on the shores of Saginaw Bay, in Michigan, by Indians who never heard of Greeks. Cloud Catcher, a handsome youth of the Ojibways, offended his family by refusing to fast during the ceremony of his coming of age, and was put out of the paternal wigwam. It was so fine a night that the sky served him as well as a roof, and he had a boy's confidence in his ability to make a living, and something of fame and fortune, maybe. He dropped upon a tuft of moss to plan for his future, and drowsily noted the rising of the moon, in which he seemed to see a face. On awaking he found that it was not day, yet the darkness was half dispelled by light that rayed from a figure near him—the form of a lovely woman.

"Cloud Catcher, I have come for you," she said. And as she turned away he felt impelled to rise and follow. But, instead of walking, she began to move into the air with the flight of an eagle, and, endowed with a new power, he too ascended beside her. The earth was dim and vast below, stars blazed as they drew near them, yet the radiance of the woman seemed to dull their glory. Presently they passed through a gate of clouds and stood on a beautiful plain, with crystal ponds and brooks watering noble trees and leagues of flowery meadow; birds of brightest colors darted here and there, singing like flutes; the very stones were agate, jasper, and chalcedony. An immense lodge stood on the plain, and within were embroideries and ornaments, couches of rich furs, pipes and arms cut from jasper and tipped with silver. While the young man was gazing around him with delight, the brother of his guide appeared and reproved her, advising her to send the young man back to earth at once, but, as she flatly refused to do so, he gave a pipe and bow and arrows to Cloud Catcher, as a token of his consent to their marriage, and wished them happiness, which, in fact, they had.

This brother, who was commanding, tall, and so dazzling in his gold and silver ornaments that one could hardly look upon him, was abroad all day, while his sister was absent for a part of the night. He permitted Cloud Catcher to go with him on one of his daily walks, and as they crossed the lovely Sky Land they glanced down through open valley bottoms on the green earth below. The rapid pace they struck gave to Cloud Catcher an appetite and he asked if there were no game. "Patience," counselled his companion. On arriving at a spot where a large hole had been broken through the sky they reclined on mats, and the tall man loosing one of his silver ornaments flung it into a group of children playing before a lodge. One of the little ones fell and was carried within, amid lamentations. Then the villagers left their sports and labors and looked up at the sky. The tall man cried, in a voice of thunder, "Offer a sacrifice and the child shall be well again." A white dog was killed, roasted, and in a twinkling it shot up to the feet of Cloud Catcher, who, being empty, attacked it voraciously.

Many such walks and feasts came after, and the sights of earth and taste of meat filled the mortal with a longing to see his people again. He told his wife that he wanted to go back. She consented, after a time, saying, "Since you are better pleased with the cares, the ills, the labor, and the poverty of the world than with the comfort and abundance of Sky Land, you may return; but remember you are still my husband, and beware how you venture to take an earthly maiden for a wife."

She arose lightly, clasped Cloud Catcher by the wrist, and began to move with him through the air. The motion lulled him and he fell asleep, waking at the door of his father's lodge. His relatives gathered and gave him welcome, and he learned that he had been in the sky for a year. He took the privations of a hunter's and warrior's life less kindly than he thought to, and after a time he enlivened its monotony by taking to wife a bright-eyed girl of his tribe. In four days she was dead. The lesson was unheeded and he married again. Shortly after, he stepped from his lodge one evening and never came back. The woods were filled with a strange radiance on that night, and it is asserted that Cloud Catcher was taken back to the lodge of the Sun and Moon, and is now content to live in heaven.

THE COFFIN OF SNAKES

No one knew how it was that Lizon gained the love of Julienne, at L'Anse Creuse (near Detroit), for she was a girl of sweet and pious disposition, the daughter of a God-fearing farmer, while Lizon was a dark, ill-favored wretch, who had come among the people nobody knew whence, and lived on the profits of a tap-room where the vilest liquor was sold, and where gaming, fighting, and carousing were of nightly occurrence. Perhaps they were right in saying that it was witchcraft. He impudently laid siege to her heart, and when she showed signs of yielding he told her and her friends that he had no intention of marrying her, because he did not believe in religion.

Yet Julienne deserted her comfortable home and went to live with this disreputable scamp in his disreputable tavern, to the scandal of the community, and especially of the priest, who found Lizon's power for evil greater than his own for good, for as the tavern gained in hangers-on the church lost worshippers. One Sunday morning Julienne surprised the people by appearing in church and publicly asking pardon for her wrong-doing. It was the first time she had appeared there since her flight, and she was as one who had roused from a trance or fever-sleep. Her father gladly took her home again, and all went well until New-Year's eve, when the young men called d'Ignolee made the rounds of the settlement to sing and beg meat for the poor—a custom descended from the Druids. They came to the house of Julienne's father and received his welcome and his goods, but their song was interrupted by a cry of distress—Lizon was among the maskers, and Julienne was gone. A crowd of villagers ran to the cabaret and rescued the girl from the room into which the fellow had thrust her, but it was too late—she had lost her reason. Cursing and striking and blaspheming, Lizon was at last confronted by the priest, who told him he had gone too far; that he had been a plague to the people and an enemy to the church. He then pronounced against him the edict of excommunication, and told him that even in his grave he should not rest; that the church, abandoned by so many victims of his wiles and tyrannies, should be swept away.

The priest left the place forthwith, and the morals of the village fell lower and lower. Everything was against it, too. Blight and storm and insect pest ravaged the fields and orchards, as if nature had engaged to make an expression of the iniquity of the place. Suddenly death came upon Lizon. A pit was dug near his tavern and he was placed in a coffin, but as the box was lowered it was felt to grow lighter, while there poured from it a swarm of fat and filthy snakes. The fog that overspread the earth that morning seemed to blow by in human forms, the grave rolled like a wave after it had been covered, and after darkness fell a blue will-o'-the-wisp danced over it. A storm set in, heaping the billows on shore until the church was undermined, and with a crash it fell into the seething flood. But the curse had passed, and when a new chapel was built the old evils had deserted L'Anse Crease.

MACKINACK

Not only was Mackinack the birthplace of Hiawatha: it was the home of God himself—Gitchi Manitou, or Mitchi Manitou—who placed there an Indian Adam and Eve to watch and cultivate his gardens. He also made the beaver, that his children might eat, and they acknowledged his goodness in oblations. Bounteous sacrifices insured entrance after death to the happy hunting-grounds beyond the Rocky Mountains. Those who had failed in these offerings were compelled to wander about the Great Lakes, shelterless, and watched by unsleeping giants who were ten times the stature of mortals.

These giants still exist, but in the form of conical rocks, one of which-called Sugar-Loaf, or Manitou's Wigwam—is ninety feet high. A cave in this obelisk is pointed out as Manitou's abiding-place, and it was believed that every other spire in the group had its wraith, whence has come the name of the island—Michillimackinack (place of great dancing spirits). Arch Rock is the place that Manitou built to reach his home from Sunrise Land the better. There were many such monuments of divinities in the north. They are met with all about the lakes and in the wooded wilderness, the most striking one being the magnificent spire of basalt in the Black Hills region of Wyoming. It is known as Devil's Tower, or Mateo's Tepee, and by the red men is held to be the wigwam of a were-animal that can become man at pleasure. This singular rock towers above the Belle Fourche River to a height of eight hundred feet.

Deep beneath Mackinack was a stately and beautiful cavern hall where spirits had their revels. An Indian who got leave to quit his body saw it in company with one of the spirits, and spread glowing reports of its beauties when he had clothed himself in flesh again. When Adam and Eve died they, too, became spirits and continued to watch the home of Manitou.

Now, there is another version of this tradition which gives the, original name of the island as Moschenemacenung, meaning "great turtle." The French missionaries and traders, finding the word something too large a mouthful, softened it to Michillimackinack, and, when the English came, three syllables served them as well as a hundred, so Mackinack it is to this day. Manitou, having made a turtle from a drop of his own sweat, sent it to the bottom of Lake Huron, whence it brought a mouthful of mud, and from this Mackinack was created. As a reward for his service the turtle was allowed to sleep there in the sun forever.

Yet another version has it that the Great Spirit plucked a sand-grain from the primeval ocean, set it floating on those waters, and tended it until it grew so large that a young wolf, running constantly, died of old age before reaching its limits. The sand became the earth. Prophecy has warned the Winnebagoes that Manibozho (Michabo or Hiawatha) shall smite by pestilence at the end of their thirteenth generation. Ten are gone. All shall perish but one pure pair, who will people the recreated world. Manibozho, or Minnebojou, is called a "culture myth," but the Indians have faith in him. They say that he lies asleep on the north shore of Lake Superior, beneath the "hill of four knobs," known as the Sleeping Giant. There offerings are made to him, and it was a hope of his speedy rising that started the Messiah craze in the West in 1890.

LAKE SUPERIOR WATER GODS

There were many water gods about Lake Superior to whom the Indians paid homage, casting implements, ornaments, and tobacco into the water whenever they passed a spot where one of these manitous sat enthroned. At Thunder Cape, on the north shore, lies Manibozho, and in the pillared recess of La Chapelle, among the Pictured Rocks, dwelt powerful rulers of the storm to whose mercy the red men commended themselves with quaint rites whenever they were to set forth on a voyage over the great unsalted sea. At Le Grand Portal were hidden a horde of mischievous imps, among whose pranks was the repetition of every word spoken by the traveller as he rested on his oars beneath this mighty arch. The Chippewas worked the copper mines at Keweenaw Point before the white race had learned of a Western land, but they did so timidly, for they believed that a demon would visit with injury or death the rash mortal who should presume to pillage his treasure, unless he had first bestowed gifts upon him. Even then they went ashore with fear, lighted fires around a surface of native copper, hacked off a few pounds of the softened metal, and ran to their canoes without looking behind them.

There was another bad manitou at the mouth of Superior Bay, where conflicting currents make a pother of waters. This spirit sat on the bottom of the lake, gazing upward, and if any boatman ventured to cross his domain without dropping a pipe or beads or hatchet into it, woe betide him, for his boat would be caught in a current and smashed against a rocky shore. Perhaps the most vexatious god was he who ruled the Floating Islands. These islands were beautiful with trees and flowers, metal shone and crystals sparkled on their ledges, sweet fruits grew in plenty, and song-birds flitted over them. In wonder and delight the hunter would speed toward them in his canoe, but as he neared their turfy banks the jealous manitou, who kept these fairy lands for his own pleasure, would throw down a fog and shut them out of sight. Never could the hunter set foot on them, no matter how long he kept up his search.

THE WITCH OF PICTURED ROCKS

On the Pictured Rocks of Lake Superior dwelt an Ojibway woman, a widow, who was cared for by a relative. This relative was a hunter, the husband of an agreeable wife, the father of two bright children. Being of a mean and jealous nature, the widow begrudged every kindness that the hunter showed to his wife—the skins he brought for her clothing, the moose's lip or other dainty that he saved for her; and one day, in a pretence of fine good-nature, the old woman offered to give the younger a swing in a vine pendent from a tree that overhung the lake.

The wife accepted, and, seating herself on the vine, was swayed to and fro, catching her breath, yet laughing as she swept out over the water. When the momentum was greatest the old woman cut the stem. A splash was heard—then all was silent. Returning to the lodge, the hag disguised herself in a dress of the missing woman, and sitting in a shadow, pretended to nurse the infant of the household. The hunter, returning, was a little surprised that his wife should keep her face from him, and more surprised that the old woman did not appear for her share of the food that he had brought; but after their meal he took his little ones to the lake, to enjoy the evening breeze, when the elder burst into tears, declaring that the woman in the lodge was not his mother, and that he feared his own mother was dead or lost.

The hunter hurled his spear into the earth and prayed that, if his wife were dead, her body might be found, so he could mourn over it and give it burial. Instantly a bolt of lightning came from a passing cloud and shot into the lake, while the thunder-peal that followed shook the stones he stood on. It also disturbed the water and presently something was seen rising through it. The man stepped into a thicket and watched. In a few moments a gull arose from the lake and flew to the spot where the children were seated.

Around its body was a leather belt, embroidered with beads and quills, which the hunter recognized, and, advancing softly, he caught the bird—that changed at once into the missing woman. The family set forth toward home, and as they entered the lodge the witch—for such she was—looked up, with a start, then uttered a cry of despair. Bending low, she moved her arms in both imprecation and appeal. A moment later a black, ungainly bird flew from the wigwam and passed from sight among the trees. The witch never came back to plague them.

THE ORIGIN OF WHITE-FISH

An Indian who lived far in the north was so devoted to the chase that he was never at home for the whole of a day, to the sorrow of his two boys, who liked nothing so much as to sport with him and to be allowed to practise with his weapons. Their mother told them that on no account were they to speak to him of the young man who visited the lodge while their father was away, and it was not until they were well grown and knew what the duty of wives should be that they resolved to disobey her. The hunter struck the woman dead when he learned of her perfidy. So greatly did her spirit trouble them, however, that they could no longer abide in their old home in peace and comfort, and they left the country and journeyed southward until they came to the Sault Sainte Marie.

As they stood beside the falls a head came rolling toward them on the earth—the head of the dead woman. At that moment, too, a crane was seen riding on the surface of the water, whirling about in its strongest eddies, and when one of the boys called to it, "O Grandfather, we are persecuted by a spirit; take us across the falls," the crane flew to them. "Cling to my back and do not touch my head," it said to them, and landed them safely on the farther shore.

But now the head screamed, "Come, grandfather, and carry me over, for I have lost my children and am sorely distressed," and the bird flew to her likewise. "Be careful not to touch my head," it said. The head promised obedience, but succumbed to curiosity when half-way over and touched the bird's head to see what was the matter with him. With a lurch the crane flung off his burden and it fell into the rapids. As it swept down, bumping against the rocks, the brains were pounded out and strewn over the water. "You were useless in life," cried the crane. "You shall not be so in death. Become fish!" And the bits of brain changed to roe that presently hatched to a delicate white fish, the flesh whereof is esteemed by Indians of the lakes, and white men, likewise. The family pitched a lodge near the spot and took the crane as their totem or name-mark. Many of their descendants bear it to this day.

THE SPIRIT OF CLOUDY

Among the lumbermen of Alger, Michigan, was William Cloud, an Indian, usually called Cloudy, who was much employed on a chute a mile and a half out of the village. The rains were heavy one spring, and a large raft of logs had been floated down to the chute, where they were held back by a gate until it was time to send them through in a mass. When the creek had reached its maximum height the foreman gave word to the log-drivers to lower the gate and let the timber down. This order came on a chilly April night, and, as it was pitchy dark and rain was falling in sheets, the lumbermen agreed to draw cuts to decide which of them should venture out and start the logs. Cloudy drew the fatal slip. He was a quiet fellow, and without a word he opened the door, bent against the storm, and passed into the darkness. An hour went by, and the men in the cabin laughed as they described the probable appearance of their comrade when he should return, soaked through and through, and they wondered if he was waiting in some shelter beside the path for the middle of the night to pass, for the Indians believed that an evil spirit left the stream every night and was abroad until that hour.

As time lengthened the jest and talk subsided and a moody silence supervened. At length one of the number resolved to sally out and see if any mishap had fallen to the Indian. He was joined by three others, and the party repaired to the creek. Above the chute it was seen that the gate—which was released by the withdrawal of iron pins and sank of its own weight-had not quite settled into place, and by the light of a lantern held near the surface of the rushing current an obstruction could be dimly seen. The gate was slightly raised and the object drawn up with pike-poles. It was the mangled body of Cloudy. He was buried beside the creek; but the camp was soon abandoned and the chute is in decay, for between the hours of ten and twelve each night the wraith of the Indian, accompanied by the bad spirit of the stream, ranges through the wood, his form shining blue in the gloom, his groans sounding above the swish and lap of the waters.

THE SUN FIRE AT SAULT SAINTE MARIE

Father Marquette reached Sault Sainte Marie, in company with Greysolon Du Lhut, in August, 1670, and was received in a manner friendly enough, but the Chippewas warned him to turn back from that point, for the Ojibways beyond were notoriously hostile to Europeans, their chief—White Otter—having taken it on himself to revenge, by war, his father's desertion of his mother. His father was a Frenchman. Inspired by his mission, and full of the enthusiasm of youth and of the faith that had led him safely through a host of dangers and troubles, Marquette refused to change his plans, and even ventured the assertion that he could tame the haughty Otter and bring him to the cross. At dawn he and his doughty henchman set off in a war-canoe, but, on arriving in White Otter's camp and speaking their errand, they were seized and bound, to await death on the morrow. The wife of the chief spoke, out of the kindness of her heart, and asked mercy for the white men. To no avail. The brute struck her to the ground. That night his daughter, Wanena, who had seen Du Lhut at the trading post and had felt the stir of a generous sentiment toward him, appeared before the prisoners when sleep was heaviest in the camp, cut their bonds, led them by an obscure path to the river, where she enjoined them to enter a canoe, and guided the boat to the Holy Isle. This was where the Ojibways came to lay offerings before the image of Manitou, whose home was there believed to be. There the friendly red men would be sure to find and rescue them, she thought, and after a few hours of sleep she led them into a secluded glen where stood the figure rudely carved from a pine trunk, six feet high, and tricked with gewgaws. As they stood there, stealthy steps were heard, and before they could conceal themselves White Otter and eight of his men were upon them. Du Lhut grasped a club from among the weapons that—with other offerings—strewed the earth at the statue's feet and prepared to sell his life dearly. The priest drew forth his crucifix and prayed. The girl dropped to the ground, drew her blanket over her head, and began to sing her death-song.

"So the black-coat and the woman-stealer have come to die before the Indian's god?" sneered the chief.

"If it be God's will, we will die defying your god and you," replied Marquette. "Yet we fear not death, and if God willed he could deliver us as easily as he could destroy that worthless image." He spoke in an undertone to Du Lhut, and continued, confidently, "challenge your god to withstand mine. I shall pray my God to send his fire from the sky and burn this thing. If he does so will you set us free and become a Christian?"

"I will; but if you fail, you die."

"And if I win you must pardon your daughter."

White Otter grunted his assent.

The sun was high and brought spicy odors from the wood; an insect hummed drowsily, and a bird-song echoed from the distance. Unconscious of what was being enacted about her, Wanena kept rocking to and fro, singing her death-song, and waiting the blow that would stretch her at her father's feet. The savages gathered around the image and watched it with eager interest. Raising his crucifix with a commanding gesture, the priest strode close to the effigy, and in a loud voice cried, in Chippewa, "In the name of God, I command fire to destroy this idol!"

A spot of light danced upon the breast of the image. It grew dazzling bright and steady. Then a smoke began to curl from the dry grass and feathers it was decked with. The Indians fell back in amazement, and when a faint breeze passed, fanning the sparks into flame, they fell on their faces, trembling with apprehension, for Marquette declared, "As my God treats this idol, so can he treat you!"

Then, looking up to see the manitou in flames, White Otter exclaimed, "The white man's God has won. Spare us, O mighty medicine!"

"I will do so, if you promise to become as white men in the faith and be baptized." Tamed by fear, the red men laid aside their weapons and knelt at a brook where Marquette, gathering water in his hands, gave the rite of baptism to each, and laid down the moral law they were to live by. Wanena, who had fainted from sheer fright when she saw the idol burning, was restored, and it may be added that the priest who Christianized her also married her to Du Lhut, who prospered and left his name to the city of the lake. News of the triumph of the white men's God went far and wide, and Marquette found his missions easier after that. Du Lhut alone, of all those present, was in the father's secret. He had perpetrated a pious fraud, justified by the results as well as by his peril. A burning-glass had been fastened to the crucifix, and with that he had destroyed the idol.

Trading thus on native ignorance a Frenchman named Lyons at another time impressed the Indians at Dubuque and gained his will by setting a creek on fire. They did not know that he had first poured turpentine over it.

THE SNAKE GOD OF BELLE ISLE

The Indian demi-god, Sleeping Bear, had a daughter so beautiful that he kept her out of the sight of men in a covered boat that swung on Detroit River, tied to a tree on shore; but the Winds, having seen her when her father had visited her with food, contended so fiercely to possess her that the little cable was snapped and the boat danced on to the keeper of the water-gates, who lived at the outlet of Lake Huron. The keeper, filled with admiration for the girl's beauty, claimed the boat and its charming freight, but he had barely received her into his lodge when the angry Winds fell upon him, buffeting him so sorely that he died, and was buried on Peach Island (properly Isle au Peche), where his spirit remained for generations—an oracle sought by Indians before emprise in war. His voice had the sound of wind among the reeds, and its meanings could not be told except by those who had prepared themselves by fasting and meditation to receive them. Before planning his campaign against the English, Pontiac fasted here for seven days to "clear his ear" and hear the wisdom of the sighing voice.

But the Winds were not satisfied with the slaying of the keeper. They tore away his meadows and swept them out as islands. They smashed the damsel's boat and the little bark became Belle Isle. Here Manitou placed the girl, and set a girdle of vicious snakes around the shore to guard her and to put a stop to further contests. These islands in the straits seem to have been favorite places of exile and theatres of transformation. The Three Sisters are so called because of three Indian women who so scolded and wrangled that their father was obliged to separate them and put one on each of the islands for the sake of peace.

It was at Belle Isle that the red men had put up and worshipped a natural stone image. Hearing of this idol, on reaching Detroit, Dollier and De Galinee crossed over to it, tore it down, smashed it, flung the bigger piece of it into the river, and erected a cross in its place. The sunken portion of the idol called aloud to the faithful, who had assembled to wonder at the audacity of the white men and witness their expected punishment by Manitou, and told them to cast in the other portions. They did so, and all the fragments united and became a monster serpent that kept the place from further intrusion. Later, when La Salle ascended the straits in his ship, the Griffin, the Indians on shore invoked the help of this, their manitou, and strange forms arose from the water that pushed the ship into the north, her crew vainly singing hymns with a hope of staying the demoniac power.

WERE-WOLVES OF DETROIT

Long were the shores of Detroit vexed by the Snake God of Belle Isle and his children, the witches, for the latter sold enchantments and were the terror of good people. Jacques Morand, the *coureur de bois*, was in love with Genevieve Parent, but she disliked him and wished only to serve the church. Courting having proved of no avail, he resolved on force when she had decided to enter a convent, and he went to one of the witches, who served as devil's agent, to sell his soul. The witch accepted the slight commodity and paid for it with a grant of power to change from a man's form to that of a were-wolf, or *loup garou*, that he might the easier bear away his victim. Incautiously, he followed her to Grosse Pointe, where an image of the Virgin had been set up, and as Genevieve dropped at the feet of the statue to implore aid, the wolf, as he leaped to her side, was suddenly turned to stone.

Harder was the fate of another maiden, Archange Simonet, for she was seized by a were-wolf at this place and hurried away while dancing at her own wedding. The bridegroom devoted his life to the search for her, and finally lost his reason, but he prosecuted the hunt so vengefully and shrewdly that he always found assistance. One of the neighbors cut off the wolf's tail with a silver bullet, the appendage being for many years preserved by the Indians. The lover finally came upon the creature and chased it to the shore, where its footprint is still seen in one of the bowlders, but it leaped into the water and disappeared. In his crazy fancy the lover declared that it had jumped down the throat of a catfish, and that is why the French Canadians have a prejudice against catfish as an article of diet.

The man-wolf dared as much for gain as for love. On the night that Jean Chiquot got the Indians drunk and bore off their beaver-skins, the wood witches, known as "the white women," fell upon him and tore a part of his treasure from him, while a were-wolf pounced so hard on his back that he lost more. He drove the creatures to a little distance, but was glad to be safe inside of the fort again, though the officers laughed at him and called him a coward. When they went back over the route with him they were astonished to find the grass scorched where the women had fled before him, and little springs in the turf showed where they had been swallowed up. Sulphur-water was bubbling from the spot where the wolf dived into the earth when the trader's rosary fell out of his jacket. Belle Fontaine, the spot was called, long afterward.

THE ESCAPE OF FRANCOIS NAVARRE

When the Hurons came to Sandwich, opposite the Michigan shore, in 1806, and camped near the church for the annual "festival of savages," which was religious primarily, but incidentally gastronomic, athletic, and alcoholic, an old woman of the tribe foretold to Angelique Couture that, ere long, blood would be shed freely and white men and Indians would take each other's lives. That was a reasonably safe prophecy in those days, and, though Angelique repeated it to her friends, she did not worry over it. But when the comet of 1812 appeared the people grew afraid—and with cause, for the war soon began with England. The girl's brothers fought under the red flag; her lover, Francois Navarre, under the stars and stripes.

The cruel General Proctor one day passed through Sandwich with prisoners on his way to the Hurons, who were to put them to death in the usual manner. As they passed by, groaning in anticipation of their fate, footsore and covered with dust, Angelique nearly swooned, for among them she recognized her lover. He, too, had seen her, and the recognition had been noticed by Proctor. Whether his savage heart was for the moment softened by their anguish, or whether he wished to heighten their pain by a momentary taste of joy, it is certain that on reaching camp he paroled Francrois until sunset. The young man hastened to the girl's house, and for one hour they were sadly happy. She tried to make him break his parole and escape, but he refused, and as the sun sank he tore himself from her arms and hastened to rejoin his companions in misery.

His captors admired him for this act of honor, and had he so willed he could have been then and there received into their tribe. As it was, they allowed him to remain unbound. Hardly had the sun gone down when a number of boats drew up at the beach with another lot of prisoners, and with yells of rejoicing the Indians ran to the river to drive them into camp. Francois's opportunity was brief, but he seized it. In the excitement he had been unobserved. He was not under oath now, and with all speed he dashed into the wood. Less than a minute had elapsed before his absence was discovered, but he was a cunning woodman, and by alternately running and hiding, with gathering darkness in his favor, he had soon put the savages at a distance.

A band of English went to Angelique's home, thinking that he would be sure to rejoin her; but he was too shrewd for that, and it was in vain that they fired guns up the chimneys and thrust bayonets into beds. Angelique was terrified at this intrusion, but the men had been ordered not to injure the woman, and she was glad, after all, to think that Francois had escaped. Some days later one of the Hurons came to her door and pointed significantly to a fresh scalp that hung at his belt. In the belief that it was her lover's she grew ill and began to fade, but one evening there came a faint tap at the door. She opened it to find a cap on the door-step.

There was no writing, yet her heart rose in her bosom and the color came back to her cheeks, for she recognized it as her lover's. Later, she learned that Francois had kept to the forest until he reached the site of Walkerville, where he had found a canoe and reached the American side in safety. She afterward rejoined him in Detroit, and they were married at the end of the war, through which he served with honor and satisfaction to himself, being enabled to pay many old scores against the red-coats and the Indians.

THE OLD LODGER

In 1868 there died in Detroit a woman named Marie Louise Thebault, more usually called Kennette. She was advanced in years, and old residents remembered when she was one of the quaintest figures and most assertive spirits in the town, for until a few years before her death she was rude of speech, untidy in appearance, loved nothing or respected nothing unless it might be her violin and her money, and lived alone in a little old house on the river-road to Springwells. Though she made shoes for a living, she was of so miserly a nature that she accepted food from her neighbors, and in order to save the expense of light and fuel she spent her evenings out. Yet she read more or less, and was sufficiently acquainted with Volney, Voltaire, and other skeptics to shock her church acquaintances. Love of gain, not of company, induced her to lease one of her rooms to a pious old woman, from whom she got not only a little rent, but the incidental use of her fuel and light.

When the pious one tried to win her to the church it angered her, and then, too, she had a way of telling ghost stories that Kennette laughed at. One of these narratives that she would dwell on with especial self-conviction was that of Lieutenant Muir, who had left his mistress, when she said No to his pleadings, supposing that she spoke the truth, whereas she was merely trying to be coquettish.

He fell in an attack on the Americans that night, and came back, bleeding, to the girl who had made him throw his life away; he pressed her hand, leaving the mark of skeleton fingers there, so that she always kept it gloved afterward. Then there was the tale of the two men of Detroit who were crushed by a falling tree: the married one, who was not fatally hurt, begged his mate to call his wife, as soon as his soul was free, and the woman, hearing the mournful voice at her door, as the spirit passed on its way to space, ran out and rescued her husband from his plight. She told, too, of the *feu follet*, or will-o'-the-wisp, that led a girl on Grosse Isle to the swamp where her lover was engulfed in mire and enabled her to rescue him. There was Grand'mere Duchene, likewise, who worked at her spinning-wheel for many a night after death, striking fear to her son's heart, by its droning, because he had not bought the fifty masses for the repose of her soul, but when he had fulfilled the promise she came no more. Another yarn was about the ghost-boat of hunter Sebastian that ascends the straits once in seven years, celebrating his return, after death, in accordance with the promise made to Zoe, his betrothed, that—dead or alive—he would return to her from the hunt at a certain time.

To all this Kennette turned the ear of scorning. "Bah!" she cried. "I don't believe your stories. I don't believe in your hell and your purgatory. If you die first, come back. If I should, and I can, I will come. Then we may know whether there is another world."

The bargain was made to this effect, but the women did not get on well together, and soon Kennette had an open quarrel with her lodger that ended by her declaring that she never could forgive her, but that she would hold her to her after-death compact. The lodger died, and while talking of her death at the house of a neighbor a boy, who had arrived from town, casually asked Kennette—knowing her saving ways—why she had left the light burning in her house. Grasping a poker, she set off at once to punish the intruder who had dared to enter in her absence, but when she arrived there was no light. On several evenings the light was reported by others, but as she was gadding in the neighborhood she never saw it until, one night, resolved to see for herself, she returned early, softly entered at the back door, and went to bed. Hardly had she done so when she saw a light coming up-stairs. Sitting bolt upright in bed she waited. The light came up noiselessly and presently stood in the room—not a lantern or candle, but a white phosphorescence. It advanced toward her, changing its form until she saw a cloudy likeness to a human being. For the first time in her life she feared. "Come no nearer!" she cried. "I know you. I believe you, and I forgive."

The light vanished. From that night it was remarked that Kennette began to age fast—she began to change and become more like other women. She went to church and her face grew softer and kinder. It was the only time that she saw the spirit, but the effect of the visit was permanent.

THE NAIN ROUGE

Among all the impish offspring of the Stone God, wizards and witches, that made Detroit feared by the early settlers, none were more dreaded than the Nain Rouge (Red Dwarf), or Demon of the Strait, for it appeared only when there was to be trouble. In that it delighted. It was a shambling, red-faced creature, with a cold, glittering eye and teeth protruding from a grinning mouth. Cadillac, founder of Detroit, having struck at it, presently lost his seigniory and his fortunes. It was seen scampering along the shore on the night before the attack on Bloody Run, when the brook that afterward bore this name turned red with the blood of soldiers. People saw it in the smoky streets when the city was burned in 1805, and on the morning of Hull's surrender it was found grinning in the fog. It rubbed its bony knuckles expectantly when David Fisher paddled across the strait to see his love, Soulange Gaudet, in the only boat he could find—a wheel-barrow, namely—but was sobered when David made a safe landing.

It chuckled when the youthful bloods set off on Christmas day to race the frozen strait for the hand of buffer Beauvais's daughter Claire, but when her lover's horse, a wiry Indian nag, came pacing in it fled before their happiness. It was twice seen on the roof of the stable where that sour-faced, evil-eyed old mumbler, Jean Beaugrand, kept his horse, Sans Souci—a beast that, spite of its hundred years or more, could and did leap every wall in Detroit, even the twelve-foot stockade of the fort, to steal corn and watermelons, and that had been seen in the same barn, sitting at a table, playing seven-up with his master, and drinking a liquor that looked like melted brass. The dwarf whispered at the sleeping ear of the old chief who slew Friar Constantine, chaplain of the fort, in anger at the teachings that had parted a white lover from his daughter and led her to drown herself—a killing that the red man afterward confessed, because he could no longer endure the tolling of a mass bell in his ears and the friar's voice in the wind.

The Nain Rouge it was who claimed half of the old mill, on Presque Isle, that the sick and irritable Josette swore that she would leave to the devil when her brother Jean pestered her to make her will in his favor, giving him complete ownership. On the night of her death the mill was wrecked by a thunder-bolt, and a red-faced imp was often seen among the ruins, trying to patch the machinery so as to grind the devil's grist. It directed the dance of black cats in the mill at Pont Rouge, after the widow's curse had fallen on Louis Robert, her brother-in-law. This man, succeeding her husband as director of the property, had developed such miserly traits that she and her children were literally starved to death, but her dying curse threw such ill luck on the place and set afloat such evil report about it that he took himself away. The Nain Rouge may have been the Lutin that took Jacques L'Esperance's ponies from the stable at Grosse Pointe, and, leaving no tracks in sand or snow, rode them through the air all night, restoring them at dawn quivering with fatigue, covered with foam, bloody with the lash of a thornbush. It stopped that exercise on the night that Jacques hurled a font of holy water at it, but to keep it away the people of Grosse Pointe still mark their houses with the sign of a cross.

It was lurking in the wood on the day that Captain Dalzell went against Pontiac, only to perish in an ambush, to the secret relief of his superior, Major Gladwyn, for the major hoped to win the betrothed of Dalzell; but when the girl heard that her lover had been killed at Bloody Run, and his head had been carried on a pike, she sank to the ground never to rise again in health, and in a few days she had followed the victims of the massacre. There was a suspicion that the Nain Rouge had power to change his shape for one not less offensive. The brothers Tremblay had no luck in fishing through the straits and lakes until one of them agreed to share his catch with St. Patrick, the saint's half to be sold at the church-door for the benefit of the poor and for buying masses to relieve souls in purgatory. His brother doubted if this benefit would last, and feared that they might be lured into the water and turned into fish, for had not St. Patrick eaten pork chops on a Friday, after dipping them into holy water and turning them into trout? But his good brother kept on and prospered and the bad one kept on grumbling. Now, at Grosse Isle was a strange thing called the rolling muff, that all were afraid of, since to meet it was a warning of trouble; but, like the *feu follet*, it could be driven off by holding a cross toward it or by asking it on what day of the month came Christmas. The worse of the Tremblays encountered this creature and it filled him with dismay. When he returned his neighbors observed an odor—not of sanctity—on his garments, and their view of the matter was that he had met a skunk. The graceless man felt convinced, however, that he had received a devil's baptism from the Nain Rouge, and St. Patrick had no stancher allies than both the Tremblays, after that.

TWO REVENGES

It is no more possible to predicate the conduct of an Indian than that of a woman. In Detroit lived Wasson, one of the warriors of the dreaded Pontiac, who had felt some tender movings of the spirit toward a girl of his tribe. The keeper of the old red mill that stood at the foot of Twenty-fourth Street adopted her, with the consent of her people, and did his best to civilize her. But Wasson kept watch. He presently discovered that whenever the miller was away a candle shone in the window until a figure wrapped in a military cloak emerged from the shadows, knocked, and was admitted. On the night that Wasson identified his rival as Colonel Campbell, an English officer, he stole into the girl's room through the window and cut her down with his hatchet. Colonel Campbell, likewise, he slew after Pontiac had made prisoners of the garrison. The mill was shunned, after that, for the figure of a girl, with a candle in her hand, frightened so many people by moving about the place that it was torn down in 1795.

But the red man was not always hostile. Kenen, a Huron, loved a half-breed girl, whom he could never persuade into a betrothal. One day he accidentally wounded a white man in the wood, and lifting him on his shoulder he hurried with him to camp. It was not long before he found that the soft glances of the half-breed girl were doing more to cure his victim than the incantations of the medicine-man, and in a fit of anger, one day, he plucked forth his knife and fell upon the couple. Her look of innocent surprise shamed him. He rushed away, with an expression of self-contempt, and flung his weapon far into the river. Soon after, the white man was captured by the Iroquois. They were preparing to put him to the torture when a tall Indian leaped in among them, with the cry, "I am Kenen. Let the pale face go, for a Huron chief will take his place." And, as the bonds fell from the prisoner's wrists and ankles, he added, "Go and comfort the White Fawn." The white man was allowed to enter a canoe and row away, but as he did so his heart misgave him: the words of a deathsong and the crackling of flames had reached his ears.

HIAWATHA

The story of Hiawatha—known about the lakes as Manabozho and in the East as Glooskapis the most widely disseminated of the Indian legends. He came to earth on a Messianic mission, teaching justice, fortitude, and forbearance to the red men, showing them how to improve their handicraft, ridding the woods and hills of monsters, and finally going up to heaven amid cries of wonder from those on whose behalf he had worked and counselled. He was brought up as a child among them, took to wife the Dakota girl, Minnehaha ("Laughing Water"), hunted, fought, and lived as a warrior; yet, when need came, he could change his form to any shape of bird, fish, or plant that he wished. He spoke to friends in the voice of a woman and to enemies in tones like thunder. A giant in form, few dared to resist him in battle, yet he suffered the common pains and adversities of his kind, and while fishing in one of the great lakes in his white stone canoe, that moved whither he willed it, he and his boat were swallowed by the king of fishes. He killed the creature by beating at its heart with a stone club, and when the gulls had preyed on its flesh, as it lay floating on the surface, until he could see daylight, he clambered through the opening they had made and returned to his lodge.

Believing that his father had killed his mother, he fought against him for several days, driving him to the edge of the world before peace was made between them. The evil Pearl Feather had slain one of his relatives, and to avenge that crime Hiawatha pressed through a guard of fire-breathing serpents which surrounded that fell personage, shot them with arrows as they struck at him, and having thus reached the lodge of his enemy he engaged him in combat. All day long they battled to no purpose, but toward evening a woodpecker flew overhead and cried, "Your enemy has but one vulnerable point. Shoot at his scalp-lock." Hiawatha did so and his foe fell dead. Anointing his finger with the blood of his foe, he touched the bird, and the red mark is found on the head of every woodpecker to this day. A duck having led him a long chase when he was trying to capture it for food, he angrily kicked it, thus flattening its back, bowing its legs, despoiling it of half of its tail-feathers, and that is why, to this day, ducks are awkward.

In return for its service in leading him to where the prince of serpents lived, he invested the kingfisher with a medal and rumpled the feathers of its head in putting it on; hence all kingfishers have rumpled knots and white spots on their breasts. After slaying the prince of serpents he travelled all over America, doing good work, and on reaching Onondaga he organized a friendly league of thirteen tribes that endured for many years. This closed his mission. As he stood in the assemblage of chiefs a white bird, appearing at an immense height, descended like a meteor, struck Hiawatha's daughter with such force as to drive her remains into the earth and shattered itself against the ground. Its silvery feathers were scattered, and these were preserved by the beholders as ornaments for their hair—so the custom of wearing feather head-dresses endures to our time. Though filled with consternation, Hiawatha recognized the summons. He addressed his companions in tones of such sweetness and terms of such eloquence as had never been heard before, urging them to live uprightly and to enforce good laws, and unhappy circumstance!—promising to come back when the time was ripe. The expectancy of his return has led to ghost-dances and similar demonstrations of enmity against the whites. When he had ended he entered his stone canoe and began to rise in air to strains of melting music. Higher and higher he arose, the white vessel shining in the sunlight, until he disappeared in the spaces of the sky.

Incidents of the Hiawatha legend are not all placed, but he is thought to have been born near the great lakes, perhaps at Mackinack. Some legends, indeed, credit him with making his home at Mackinack, and from that point, as a centre, making a new earth around him. The fight with his father began on the upper Mississippi, and the bowlders found along its banks were their missiles. The south shore of Lake Superior was the scene of his conflict with the serpents. He hunted the great beaver around Lake Superior and brought down his dam at the Sault Sainte Marie. A depression in a rock on the southern edge of Michipicotea Bay is where he alighted after a jump across the lake. In a larger depression, near Thunder Bay, he sat when smoking his last pipe. The big rocks on the east side of Grand Traverse Bay, near Antrim City, Michigan, are the bones of a stone monster that he slew.

So trifling an incident as the kicking of the duck has been localized at Lake Itasca. [It is worth passing mention that this name, which sounds as if it were of Indian origin, is held by some to be composed of the last syllables of *veritas* and the first letters of *caput*, these words-signifying "the true head"—being applied by early explorers as showing that they were confident of having found the actual source of the Mississippi.] Minnehaha lived near the fall in Minneapolis that bears her name. The final apotheosis took place on the shores of Lake Onondaga, New York, though Hiawatha lies buried under a mountain, three miles long, on the east side of Thunder Bay, Lake Superior, which, from the water, resembles a man lying on his back. The red man makes oblation, as he rows past, by dropping a pinch of tobacco into the water. Some say that Hiawatha now lives at the top of the earth, amid the ice, and directs the sun. He has to live in a cold country because, if he were to return, he would set the earth on fire with his footsteps.

THE INDIAN MESSIAH

The promise of the return to earth of various benign spirits has caused much trouble among the red men, and incidentally to the white men who are the objects of their fanatic dislike. The New Mexicans believed that when the Emperor Montezuma was about to leave the earth he planted a tree and bade them watch it, for when it fell he would come back in glory and lead them to victory, wealth, and power. The watch was kept in secret on account of the determination of the Spaniards to breakup all fealty to tribal heroes and traditions. As late as 1781 they executed a sentence of death on a descendant of the Peruvian Incas for declaring his royal origin. When Montezuma's tree fell the people gathered on the house-tops to watch the east-in vain, for the white man was there. In 1883 the Sanpoels, a small tribe in Washington, were stirred by the teaching of an old chief, who told them that the wicked would soon be destroyed, and that the Great Spirit had ordered him to build an ark for his people. The remains of this vessel, two hundred and eighty-eight feet long, are still to be seen near one of the tributaries of the Columbia.

A frenzy swept over the West in 1890, inspiring the Indians by promise of the coming of one of superhuman power, who was generally believed to be Hiawatha, to threaten the destruction of the white population, since it had been foretold that the Messiah would drive the white men from their land. Early in the summer of that year it was reported that the Messiah had appeared in the north, and the chiefs of many tribes went to Dakota, as the magi did to Bethlehem, to learn if this were true. Sitting Bull, the Sioux chief, told them, in assembly, that it was so, and declared that he had seen the new Christ while hunting in the Shoshone Mountains. One evening he lost his way and was impelled by a strange feeling to follow a star that moved before him. At daybreak it paused over a beautiful valley, and, weary with his walk, he sank on a bed of moss. As he sat there throngs of Indian warriors appeared and began a spirit dance, led by chiefs who had long been dead. Presently a voice spoke in his ear, and turning he saw a strange man dressed in white. The man said he was the same Christ who had come into the world nineteen hundred years before to save white men, and that now he would save the red men by driving out the whites. The Indians were to dance the ghost-dance, or spirit dance, until the new moon, when the globe would shiver, the wind would glow, and the white soldiers and their horses would sink into the earth. The Messiah showed to Sitting Bull the nail-wounds in his hands and feet and the spear-stab in his side. When night came on the form in white had disappeared—and, returning, the old chief taught the ghost-dance to his people.

THE VISION OF RESCUE

Surmounting Red Banks, twelve miles north of Green Bay, Wisconsin, on the eastern shore, and one hundred feet above the water, stands an earthwork that the first settlers found there when they went into that country. It was built by the Sauks and Outagamies, a family that ruled the land for many years, rousing the jealousy of neighboring tribes by their wealth and power. The time came, as it did in the concerns of nearly every band of Indians, when war was declared against this family, and the enemy came upon them in the darkness, their canoes patroling the shore while the main body formed a line about the fort. So silently was this done that but one person discovered it—a squaw, who cried, "We are all dead!"

There was nothing to see or hear, and she was rated for alarming the camp with foolish dreams; but dawn revealed the beleaguering line, and at the lifting of the sun a battle began that lasted for days, those within the earthworks sometimes fighting while ankle-deep in the blood of their fellows. The greatest lack of the besieged was that of water, and they let down earthen jars to the lake to get it, but the cords were cut ere they could be drawn up, the enemy shouting, derisively, "Come down and drink!" Several times they tried to do so, but were beaten back at every sally, and it seemed at last as if extermination was to be their fate.

When matters were at their darkest one of the young men who had been fasting for ten days—the Indian custom when divine direction was sought—addressed his companions to this effect: "Last night there stood by me the form of a young man, clothed in white, who said, 'I was once alive, but I died, and now I live forever. Trust me and I will deliver you. Be fearless. At midnight I will cast a sleep on your enemies. Go forth boldly and you shall escape.'" The condition was too desperate to question any means of freedom, and that night all but a handful of disbelievers left the fort, while the enemy was in a slumber of exhaustion, and got away in safety. When the besiegers, in the morning, found that the fort had been almost deserted, they fell on the few that remained to repent their folly, and put them to the knife and axe, for their fury was excessive at the failure of the siege.

DEVIL'S LAKE

Any of the noble rivers and secluded lakes of Wisconsin were held in esteem or fear by the northern tribes, and it was the now-forgotten events and superstitions connected with them, not less than the frontier tendency for strong names, that gave a lurid and diabolical nomenclature to parts of this region. Devils, witches, magicians, and manitous were perpetuated, and Indians whose prowess was thought to be supernatural left dim records of themselves here and there—as near the dells of the Wisconsin, where a chasm fifty feet wide is shown as the ravine leaped by chief Black Hawk when flying from the whites. Devil's Lake was the home of a manitou who does not seem to have been a particularly evil genius, though he had unusual power. The lake fills what is locally regarded as the crater of an extinct volcano, and the coldness and purity kept by the water, in spite of its lacking visible inlets or outlets, was one cause for thinking it uncanny.

This manitou piled the heavy blocks of Devil's Door-Way and set up Black Monument and the Pedestalled Bowlder as thrones where he might sit and view the landscape by day—for the Indians appreciated the beautiful in nature and supposed their gods did, too—while at night he could watch the dance of the frost spirits, the aurora borealis. Cleft Rock was sundered by one of his darts aimed at an offending Indian, who owed his life to the manitou's bad aim. The Sacrifice Stone is shown where, at another time, a girl was immolated to appease his anger. Cleopatra's Needle, as it is now called, is the body of an ancient chief, who was turned into stone as a punishment for prying into the mysteries of the lake, a stone on East Mountain being the remains of a squaw who had similarly offended. On the St. Croix the Devil's Chair is pointed out where he sat in state. He had his play spells, too, as you may guess when you see his toboggan slide in Weber Canon, Utah, while Cinnabar Mountain, in the Yellowstone country, he scorched red as he coasted down.

The hunter wandering through this Wisconsin wilderness paused when he came within sight of the lake, for all game within its precincts was in the manitou's protection; not a fish might be taken, and not even a drop of water could be dipped to cool the lips of the traveller. So strong was this fear of giving offence to the manitou that Indians who were dying of wounds or illness, and were longing for a swallow of water, would refuse to profane the lake by touching their lips to it.

THE KEUSCA ELOPEMENT

Keusca was a village of the Dakota Indians on the Wisconsin bluffs of the Mississippi eighteen hundred miles from its mouth. The name means, to overthrow, or set aside, for it was here that a tribal law was broken. Sacred Wind was a coquette of that village, for whose hand came many young fellows wooing with painted faces. For her they played the bone flute in the twilight, and in the games they danced and leaped their hardest and shot their farthest and truest when she was looking on. Though they amused her she cared not a jot for these suitors, keeping her love for the young brave named the Shield—and keeping it secret, for he was her cousin, and cousins might not wed. If a relative urged her to marry some young fellow for whom she had no liking, she would answer that if forced to do so she would fling herself into the river, and spoke of Winonah and Lovers' Leap.

She was afraid to wed the Shield, for the medicine-men had threatened all who dared to break the marriage laws with unearthly terrors; yet when the Shield had been absent for several weeks on the war-path she realized that life without his companionship was too hollow to be endured—and she admired him all the more when he returned with two scalps hanging at his belt. He renewed his wooing. He allayed her fears by assurances that he, too, was a medicine-man and could counteract the spells that wizards might cast on them. Then she no longer repressed the promptings of her heart, but yielded to his suit. They agreed to elope that night.

As they left the little clearing in the wood where their interview had taken place, a thicket stirred and a girl stole from it, looking intently at their retreating forms. The Swan, they had named her; but, with a flush in her dusky cheeks, her brows dark, her eyes glittering, she more recalled the vulture—for she, too, loved the Shield; and she had now seen and heard that her love was hopeless. That evening she alarmed the camp; she told the parents of Sacred Wind of the threatened violation of custom, and the father rose in anger to seek her. It was too late, for the flight had taken place. The Swan went to the river and rowed out in a canoe. From the middle of the stream she saw a speck on the water to the southward, and knew it to be Sacred Wind and her lover, henceforth husband. She watched until the speck faded in the twilight—then leaning over the side of the boat she capsized it, and passed from the view of men.

PIPESTONE

Pipestone, a smooth, hard, even-textured clay, of lively color, from which thousands of red men cut their pipe-bowls, forms a wall on the Coteau des Prairies, in Minnesota, that is two miles long and thirty feet high. In front of it lie five bowlders, the droppings from an iceberg to the floor of the primeval sea, and beneath these masses of granite live the spirits of two squaws that must be consulted before the stone can be dug. This quarry was neutral ground, and here, as they approached it, the men of all tribes sheathed their knives and belted up their axes, for to this place the Great Spirit came to kill and eat the buffalo, and it is the blood of this animal that has turned the stone to red. Here, too, the Thunder Bird had her nest, and her brood rent the skies above it with the clashing of their iron wings.

A snake having crawled into this nest to steal the unhatched thunders, Manitou caught up a piece of pipestone, hastily pressed it between his hands, giving it the shape of a man, and flung it at the reptile. The stone man's feet stuck fast in the ground, and there he stood for a thousand years, growing like a tree and drawing strength and knowledge out of the earth. Another shape grew up beside him—woman. In time the snake gnawed them free from their foundations and the red-earth pair wandered off together. From them sprang all people.

Ages after, the Manitou called the red men to the quarry, fashioned a pipe for them, told them it was a part of their flesh, and smoked it over them, blowing the smoke to north, south, east, and west, in token that wherever the influence of the pipe extended there was to be brotherhood and peace. The place was to be sacred from war and they were to make their pipes from this rock. As the smoke rolled about him he gradually disappeared from view. At the last whiff the ashes fell out and the surface of the rock for miles burst into flame, so that it melted and glazed. Two ovens opened at its foot, and through the fire entered the two spirits Tsomecostee and Tsomecostewondee—that are still its guardians, answering the invocations of the medicine-men and accepting the oblations of those who go to make pipes or carve their totems on the rock.

THE VIRGINS' FEAST

A game of lacrosse was played by Indian girls on the ice near the present Fort Snelling, one winter day, and the victorious trophies were awarded to Wenonah, sister of the chief, to the discomfiture of Harpstenah, her opponent, an ill-favored woman, neglected by her tribe, and jealous of Wenonah's beauty and popularity. This defeat, added to some fancied slights, was almost more than she could bear, and during the contest she had been cut in the head by one of the rackets—an accident that she falsely attributed to her adversary in the game. She had an opportunity of proving her hatred, for directly that it was known how Wenonah had refused to marry Red Cloud, a stalwart boaster, openly preferring a younger warrior of the tribe, the ill-thinking Harpstenah sought out the disappointed suitor, who sat moodily apart, and thus advised him, "To-morrow is the Feast of Virgins, when all who are pure will sit at meat together. Wenonah will be there. Has she the right to be? Have you not seen how shamelessly she favors your rival's suit? Among the Dakotas to accuse is to condemn, and the girl who is accused at the Virgins' Feast is disgraced forever. She has shown for Red Cloud nothing but contempt. If he shows no anger at it the girls will laugh at him."

With this she turned away and left Red Cloud to his meditations. Wenonah, at the door of her brother's wigwam, looked into the north and saw the stars grow pale through streams of electric fire. "The Woman of the North warns us of coming evil," muttered the chief. "Some danger is near. Fire on the lights!" And a volley of musketry sent a shock through the still air.

"They shine for me," said Wenonah, sadly. "For I shall soon join our father, mother, and sister in the land of spirits. Before the leaves fell I sat beside the Father of Waters and saw a manitou rise among the waves. It said that my sisters in the sunset world were calling to me and I must soon go to them." The chief tried to laugh away her fancies and comforted her as well as he might, then leading her to the wigwam he urged her to sleep.

Next day is the Virgins' Feast and Wenonah is among those who sit in the ring, dressed in their gayest. None who are conscious of a fault may share in the feast; nor, if one were exposed and expelled, might any interpose to ask for mercy; yet a groan of surprise and horror goes through the company when Red Cloud, stalking up to the circle, seizes the girl roughly by the shoulder and orders her away. No use to deny or appeal. An Indian warrior would not be so treacherous or unjust as to act in this way unless he had proofs. Without a word she enters the adjacent wood, draws her knife, and strikes it to her heart. With summer came the fever, and it ravaged through the band, laying low the infant and the counsellor. Red Cloud was the first to die, and as he was borne away Harpstenah lifted her wasted form and followed him with dimming eyes, then cried, "He is dead. He hated Wenonah because she slighted him. I hated her because she was happy. I told him to denounce her. But she was innocent."

FALLS OF ST. ANTHONY

Several of the Dakotas, who had been in camp near the site of St. Paul, left their families and friends, when the hunting season opened, and went into the north. On their arrival at another village of their tribe, they stayed to rest for a little, and one of the men used the time to ill-advantage, as it fell out, for he conceived an attachment for a girl of this northern family, and on his way southward he wedded her and took her home with him. Proper enough to do, if he had not been married already. The first wife knew that any warrior might take a second, if he could support both; but the woman was stronger than the savage in her nature, and when her husband came back, with a red-cheeked woman walking beside him, she felt that she should never know his love again. The man was all attention to the young wife, whether the tribe tarried or travelled. When they shifted camp the elder walked or rowed behind with her boy, a likely lad of ten or twelve.

It was when they were returning down the river after a successful hunt that the whole company was obliged to make a carry around the quick water near the head of St. Anthony's Falls. While the others were packing the boats and goods for transportation by hand to the foot of the cataract, the forsaken wife chose a moment when none were watching to embark with her boy in one of the canoes. Rowing out to an island, she put on all her ornaments, and dressed the lad in beads and feathers as if he were a warrior. Her husband, finding her absent from the party, looked anxiously about for some time, and was horrified to see her put out from the island into the rapid current. She had placed the child high in the boat, and was rowing with a steady stroke down the stream. He called and beckoned frantically. She did not seem to hear him, nor did she turn her head when the others joined their cries to his. For a moment those who listened heard her death-song, then the yeasty flood hid them from sight, and the husband on the shore fell to the earth with a wail of anguish.

FLYING SHADOW AND TRACK MAKER

The Chippewas and Sioux had come together at Fort Snelling to make merry and cement friendships. Flying Shadow was sad when the time came for the tribes to part, for Track Maker had won her heart, and no less strong than her love was the love he felt for her. But a Chippewa girl might not marry among the Sioux, and, if she did, the hand of every one would be against her should ever the tribes wage war upon each other, and war was nearer than either of them had expected. The Chippewas left with feelings of good will, Flying Shadow concealing in her bosom the trinkets that testified to the love of Track Maker and sighing as she thought of the years that might elapse ere they met again.

Two renegade Chippewas, that had lingered behind the band, played the villain after this pleasant parting, for they killed a Sioux. Hardly was the news of this outrage received at the fort ere three hundred warriors were on the trail of their whilom guests and friends, all clamoring for revenge. Among them was Track Maker, for he could not, as a warrior, remain behind after his brother had been shot, and, while his heart sank within him as he thought of the gentle Flying Shadow, he marched in advance, and early in the morning the Chippewas were surprised between St. Anthony's Falls and Rum River, where they had camped without fear, being alike ignorant and innocent of the murder for which so many were to be punished.

The Sioux fell upon them and cut down all alike—men, women, and children. In the midst of the carnage Track Maker comes face to face with Flying Shadow, and with a cry of gladness she throws herself into his arms. But there is no refuge there. Gladly as he would save her, he knows too well that the thirst for blood will not be sated until every member of that band is dead. He folds her to his bosom for an instant, looks into her eyes with tenderness—then bowing his head he passes on and never glances back. It is enough. She falls insensible, and a savage, rushing upon her, tears the scalp from her head.

The Sioux win a hundred scalps and celebrate their victory with dance and song. Track Maker has returned with more scalps than any, and the maidens welcome him as a hero, but he keeps gravely apart from all, and has no share in the feasting and merry-making. Ever the trusting, pleading, wondering face of Flying Shadow comes before him. It looks out at him in the face of the deer he is about to kill. He sees it in the river, the leaves, the clouds. It rises before him in dreams. The elder people say he is bewitched, but he will have none of their curatives. When war breaks out he is the first to go, the first to open battle. Rushing among his enemies he lays about him with his axe until he falls, pierced with a hundred spears and arrows. It is the fate he has courted, and as he falls his face is lighted with a smile.

SAVED BY A LIGHTNING-STROKE

There was rough justice in the West in the old days. It had to be dealt severely and quickly, for it was administered to a kind of men that became dangerous if they saw any advantage or any superiority in their strength or numbers over the decent people with whom they were cast. They were uncivilized foreigners and native renegades, for the most part, who had drifted to the frontier in the hope of making a living without work more easily than in the cities. As there were no lawyers or courts and few recognized laws, the whole people constituted themselves a jury, and if a man were known to be guilty it was foolishness for any one to waste logic on his case. And there is almost no record of an innocent man being hanged by lynchers in the West. For minor offences the penalty was to be marched out of camp, with a warning to be very cautious about coming that way again, but for graver ones it was death.

In 1840 a number of desperate fellows had settled along Cedar River, near its confluence with the Iowa, who subsisted by means of theft from the frugal and industrious. Some of these men applied themselves especially to horse-stealing, and in thinly settled countries, where a man has often to go twenty or thirty miles for supplies, or his mail, or medical attendance, it is thought to be a calamity to be without a horse.

At last the people organized themselves into a vigilance committee and ran down the thieves. As the latter were a conscienceless gang of rascals, it was resolved that the only effectual way of reforming them would be by hanging. One man of the nine, it is true, was supposed before his arrest to be a respectable citizen, but his evil communications closed the ears of his neighbors to his appeals, and it was resolved that he, too, should hang.

Not far away stood an oak with nine stout branches, and to this natural gallows the rogues were taken. As a squall was coming up the ceremonies were short, and presently every limb was weighted with the form of a captive. The formerly respectable citizen was the last one to be drawn up, and hardly had his halter been secured before the storm burst and a bolt of lightning ripped off the limb on which he hung. During the delay caused by this accident the unhappy man pleaded so earnestly for a rehearing that it was decided to give it to him, and when he had secured it he conclusively proved his innocence and was set free. The tree is still standing. To the ruffians it was a warning and they went away. Even the providential saving of one man did not detract from the value of the lesson to avoid bad company.

THE KILLING OF CLOUDY SKY

In the Dakota camp on the bank of Spirit Lake, or Lake Calhoun, Iowa, lived Cloudy Sky, a medicine-man, who had been made repellent by age and accident, but who was feared because of his magic power. At eighty years of age he looked for a third wife, and chose the daughter of a warrior, his presents of blankets and calicoes to the parents winning their consent. The girl, Harpstenah (a common name for a third daughter among the Sioux), dreaded and hated this man, for it was rumored that he had killed his first wife and basely sold his second. When she learned what had been decided for her she rushed from the camp in tears and sat in a lonely spot near the lake to curse and lament unseen. As she sat there the waters were troubled. There was no wind, yet great waves were thrown up, and tumbled hissing on the shore. Presently came a wave higher than the rest, and a graceful form leaped from it, half shrouded in its own long hair.

"Do not tremble," said the visitant, for Harpstenah had hidden her face. "I am the daughter of Unktahe, the water god. In four days your parents will give you to Cloudy Sky, as his wife, though you love Red Deer. It is with you to wed the man you hate or the man you love. Cloudy Sky has offended the water spirits and we have resolved upon his death. If you will be our agent in destroying him, you shall marry Red Deer and live long and happily. The medicine-man wandered for years through the air with the thunder birds, flinging his deadly fire-spears at us, and it was for killing the son of Unktahe that he was last sent to earth, where he has already lived twice before. Kill him while he sleeps and we will reward you."

As Harpstenah went back to the village her prospective bridegroom ogled her as he sat smoking before his lodge, his face blackened and blanket torn in mourning for an enemy he had killed. She resolved to heed the appeal of the manitou. When Red Deer heard how she had been promised to the old conjurer, he was filled with rage. Still, he became thoughtful and advised caution when she told him of the water spirit's counsel, for the dwellers in the lakes were, of all immortals, most deceitful, and had ever been enemies of the Dakotas. "I will do as I am bidden," she said, sternly. "Go away and visit the Tetons for a time. It is now the moon of strawberries" (June), "but in the moon when we gather wild rice" (September) "return and I will be your wife."

Red Deer obeyed, after finding that she would not elope with him, and with the announcement that he was going on a long hunt he took his leave of the village. Harpstenah made ready for the bridal and greeted her future husband with apparent pleasure and submissiveness. He gave a medicine feast in token of the removal of his mourning, and appeared in new clothing, greased and braided hair, and a white blanket decorated with a black hand—the record of a slain enemy.

On the night before the wedding the girl creeps to his lodge, but hesitates when she sees his medicine-bag hanging beside the door—the medicine that has kept its owner from evil and is sacred from the touch of woman. As she lingers the night-breeze seems to bring a voice from the water: "Can a Dakota woman want courage when she is forced to marry the man she hates?"

She delays no longer. A knife-blade glitters for an instant in the moonlight—and Cloudy Sky is dead. Strange, is it not, that the thunder birds flap so heavily along the west at that moment and a peal of laughter sounds from the lake? She washes the blood from the blade, steals to her father's lodge, and pretends to sleep. In the morning she is loud in her grief when it is made known to her that the medicine-man was no more, and the doer of the deed is never discovered. In time her wan face gets its color and when the leaves begin to fall Red Deer returns and weds her.

They seem to be happy for a time, and have two sons who promise to be famous hunters, but consumption fastens on Red Deer and he dies far from the village. The sons are shot by enemies, and while their bodies are on their way to Harpstenah's lodge she, too, is stricken dead by lightning. The spirit of Cloudy Sky had rejoined the thunder birds, and the water manitou had promised falsely.

PROVIDENCE HOLE

The going of white men into the prairies aroused the same sort of animosity among the Indians that they have shown in other parts of the country when retiring before the advance of civilization, and many who tried to plant corn on the rolling lands of Iowa, though they did no harm to the red men, paid for the attempt with their lives. Such was the fate of a settler who had built his cabin on the Wyoming hills, near Davenport. While working in his fields an arrow, shot from a covert, laid him low, and his scalp was cut away to adorn the belt of a savage. His little daughter, left alone, began to suffer from fears and loneliness as the sun went lower and lower, and when it had come to its time of setting she put on her little bonnet and went in search of him. As she gained the slope where he had last been seen, an Indian lifted his head from the grass and looked at her.

Starting back to run, she saw another behind her. Escape seemed hopeless, and killing or captivity would have been her lot had not a crevice opened in the earth close to where she stood. Dropping on hands and knees she hastily crawled in, and found herself in what seemed to be an extensive cavern. Hardly had she time to note the character of the place when the gap closed as strangely as it had opened and she was left in darkness. Not daring to cry aloud, lest Indians should hear her, she sat upright until her young eyes could keep open no longer; then, lying on a mossy rock, she fell asleep. In the morning the sun was shining in upon her and the way to escape was open. She ran home, hungry, but thankful, and was found and cared for by neighbors. "Providence Hole" then passed into the legends of the country. It has closed anew, however.

THE SCARE CURE

Early in this century a restless Yankee, who wore the uninspiring name of Tompkinson, found his way into Carondelet—or Vuide Poche, the French settlement on the Mississippi since absorbed by St. Louis—and cast about for something to do. He had been in hard luck on his trip from New England to the great river. His schemes for self-aggrandizement and the incidental enlightenment and prosperity of mankind had not thriven, and it was largely in pity that M. Dunois gave shelter to the ragged, half-starved, but still jaunty and resourceful adventurer. Dunois was the one man in the place who could pretend to some education, and the two got on together famously.

As soon as Tompkinson was in clothes and funds—the result of certain speculations—he took a house, and hung a shingle out announcing that there he practised medicine. Now, the fellow knew less about doctoring than any village granny, but a few sick people that he attended had the rare luck to get well in spite of him, and his reputation expanded to more than local limits in consequence. In the excess of spirits that prosperity created he flirted rather openly with a number of virgins in Carondelet, to the scandal of Dunois, who forbade him his house, and of the priest, who put him under ban.

For the priest he cared nothing, but Dunois's anger was more serious—for the only maid of all that he really loved was Marie Dunois, his daughter. He formally proposed for her, but the old man would not listen to him. Then his "practice" fell away. The future looked as dark for him as his recent past had been, until a woman came to him with a bone in her throat and begged to be relieved. His method in such cases was to turn a wheel-of-fortune and obey it. The arrow this time pointed to the word, "Bleeding."

He grasped a scalpel and advanced upon his victim, who, supposing that he intended to cut her throat open to extract the obstacle, fell a-screaming with such violence that the bone flew out. What was supposed to be his ready wit in this emergency restored him to confidence, and he was able to resume the practice that he needed so much. In a couple of years he displayed to the wondering eyes of Dunois so considerable an accumulation of cash that he gave Marie to him almost without the asking, and, as Tompkinson afterward turned Indian trader and quadrupled his wealth by cheating the red men, he became one of the most esteemed citizens of the West.

TWELFTH NIGHT AT CAHOKIA

It was Twelfth Night, and the French village of Cahokia, near St. Louis, was pleasantly agitated at the prospect of a dance in the old court saloon, which was assembly-room and everything else for the little place. The thirteen holy fires were alight—a large one, to represent Christ; a lesser one, to be trampled out by the crowd, typing Judas. The twelfth cake, one slice with the ring in it, was cut, and there were drink and laughter, but, as yet, no music. Gwen Malhon, a drift-wood collector, was the most anxious to get over the delay, for he had begged a dance from Louison. Louison Florian was pretty, not badly off in possessions and prospects, and her lover, Beaurain, had gone away. She was beginning to look a little scornful and impatient, so Gwen set off for a fiddler.

He had inquired at nearly every cabin without success, and was on his way toward the ferry when he heard music. Before him, on the moonlit river, was a large boat, and near it, on the bank, he saw a company of men squatted about a fire and bousing together from a bottle. At a little distance, on a stump, sat a thin, bent man, enveloped in a cloak, and it was he who played. Gwen complimented him and pleaded the disappointment of the dancers in excuse of an urgent appeal that he should hurry with him to the court saloon. The stranger was courteous. He sprang into the road with a limping bound, shook down his cloak so as to disclose a curled moustache, shaggy brows, a goat's beard, and a pair of glittering eyes. "I'll give them a dance!" he exclaimed. "I know one tune. They call it 'Returned from the Grave.' Pay? We'll see how you like my playing."

On entering the room where the caperish youth were already shuffling in corners, the musician met Mamzel Florian, who offered him a slice of the cake. He bent somewhat near to take it, and she gave a little cry. He had found the ring, and that made him king of the festival, with the right to choose the prettiest girl as queen. A long drink of red wine seemed to put him in the best of trim, and he began to fiddle with a verve that was irresistible. In one minute the whole company—including the priest, some said—was jigging it lustily. "Whew!" gasped one old fellow. "It is the devil who plays. Get some holy water and sprinkle the floor."

Gwen watched the musician as closely as his labors would allow, for he did not like the way the fiddler had of looking at Louison, and he thought to himself that Louison never blushed so prettily for him. Forgetting himself when he saw the fiddler smile at the girl, he made a rush for the barrel where that artist was perched. He bumped against a dancer and fell. At that moment the light was put out and the hall rang with screams and laughter. The tones of one voice sounded above the rest: "By right of the ring the girl is mine."

"He has me," Louison was heard to say, yet seemingly not in fear. Lights were brought. Louison and the fiddler were gone, the stranger's cloak and half of a false moustache were on the floor, while Gwen was jammed into the barrel and was kicking desperately to get out. When released he rushed for the river-side where he had seen the boat. Two figures flitted before him, but he lost sight of them, and in the silence and loneliness his choler began to cool. Could it really have been the devil? An owl hooted in the bush. He went away in haste. There was a rumor in after years that Beaurain was an actor in a company that went up and down the great river on a barge, and that a woman who resembled Louison was also in the troupe. But Gwen never told the story of his disappointment without crossing himself.

THE SPELL OF CREVE CIUR LAKE

Not far west of St. Louis the Lake of Creve Coeur dimples in the breezes that bend into its basin of hills, and there, in summer, swains and maidens go to confirm their vows, for the lake has an influence to strengthen love and reunite contentious pairs. One reason ascribed for the presence of this spell concerns a turbulent Peoria, ambitious of leadership and hungry for conquest, who fell upon the Chawanons at this place, albeit he was affianced to the daughter of their chief. The girl herself, enraged at the treachery of the youngster, put herself at the head of her band—a dusky Joan of Arc,—and the fight waged so furiously that the combatants, what were left of them, were glad when night fell that they might crawl away to rest their exhausted bodies and nurse their wounds. Neither tribe daring to invite a battle after that, hostilities were stopped, but some time later the young captain met the girl of his heart on the shore, and before the amazon could prepare for either fight or flight he had caught her in his arms. They renewed their oaths of fidelity, and at the wedding the chief proclaimed eternal peace and blessed the waters they had met beside, the blessing being potent to this day.

Another reason for the enchantments that are worked here may be that the lake is occupied by a demon-fish or serpent that crawls, slimy and dripping, through the underbrush, whenever it sees two lovers together, and listens to their words. If the man prove faithless he would best beware of returning to this place, for the demon is lurking there to destroy him. This monster imprisons the soul of an Ozark princess who flung herself into the lake when she learned that the son of the Spanish governor, who had vowed his love to her, had married a woman of his own rank and race in New Orleans. So they call the lake Creve Coeur, or Broken Heart. On the day after the suicide the Ozark chief gathered his men about him and paddled to the middle of the water, where he solemnly cursed his daughter in her death, and asked the Great Spirit to confine her there as a punishment for giving her heart to the treacherous white man, the enemy of his people. The Great Spirit gave her the form in which she is occasionally seen, to warn and punish faithless lovers.

HOW THE CRIME WAS REVEALED

In 1853 a Hebrew peddler, whose pack was light and his purse was full, asked leave to pass the night at the house of Daniel Baker, near Lebanon, Missouri. The favor was granted, and that was the last seen of Samuel Moritz; although, when some neighbors shook their heads and wondered how it was that Baker was so well in funds, there were others who replied that it was impossible to keep track of peddlers, and that if Moritz wanted to start on his travels early in the morning, or to return to St. Louis for goods, it mattered to nobody. On an evening in 1860 when there was a mist in the gullies and a new moon hung in the west, Rev. Mr. Cummings, a clergyman of that region, was driving home, and as he came to a bridge near "old man" Baker's farm he saw a man standing on it, with a pack on his back and a stick in his hand, who was staring intently at something beneath the bridge. The clergyman greeted him cheerily and asked him if he would like to ride, whereat the man looked him in the face and pointed to the edge of the bridge. Mr. Cummings glanced down, saw nothing, and when he looked up again the man with the pack had disappeared. His horse at the same moment gave a snort and plunged forward at a run, so that the clergyman's attention was fully occupied until he had brought the animal under control again; when he glanced back and saw that the man was still standing in the bridge and looking over the edge of it. The minister told his neighbors of this adventure, and on returning with two of them to the spot next morning they found the body of old man Baker swinging by the neck from a beam of the bridge exactly beneath where the apparition had stood—for it must have been an apparition, inasmuch as the dust, damped though it had been with dew, showed no trace of footprint. In taking down the body the men loosened the earth on a shelving bank, and the gravel rolling away disclosed a skeleton with some bits of clothing on it that were identified as belongings of Samuel Moritz. Was it conscience, craziness, or fate that led old man Baker to hang himself above the grave of his victim?

BANSHEE OF THE BAD LANDS

"Hell, with the fires out," is what the Bad Lands of Dakota have been called. The fearless Western nomenclature fits the place. It is an ancient sea-bottom, with its clay strata worn by frost and flood into forms like pagodas, pyramids, and terraced cities. Labyrinthine canons wind among these fantastic peaks, which are brilliant in color, but bleak, savage, and oppressive. Game courses over the castellated hills, rattlesnakes bask at the edge of the crater above burning coal seams, and wild men have made despairing stand here against advancing civilization. It may have been the white victim of a red man's jealousy that haunts the region of the butte called "Watch Dog," or it may have been an Indian woman who was killed there, but there is a banshee in the desert whose cries have chilled the blood that would not have cooled at the sight of a bear or panther. By moonlight, when the scenery is most suggestive and unearthly, and the noises of wolves and owls inspire uneasy feelings, the ghost is seen on a hill a mile south of the Watch Dog, her hair blowing, her arms tossing in strange gestures.

If war parties, emigrants, cowboys, hunters, any who for good or ill are going through this country, pass the haunted butte at night, the rocks are lighted with phosphor flashes and the banshee sweeps upon them. As if wishing to speak, or as if waiting a question that it has occurred to none to ask, she stands beside them in an attitude of appeal, but if asked what she wants she flings her arms aloft and with a shriek that echoes through the blasted gulches for a mile she disappears and an instant later is seen wringing her hands on her hill-top. Cattle will not graze near the haunted butte and the cowboys keep aloof from it, for the word has never been spoken that will solve the mystery of the region or quiet the unhappy banshee.

The creature has a companion, sometimes, in an unfleshed skeleton that trudges about the ash and clay and haunts the camps in a search for music. If he hears it he will sit outside the door and nod in time to it, while a violin left within his reach is eagerly seized and will be played on through half the night. The music is wondrous: now as soft as the stir of wind in the sage, anon as harsh as the cry of a wolf or startling as the stir of a rattler. As the east begins to brighten the music grows fainter, and when it is fairly light it has ceased altogether. But he who listens to it must on no account follow the player if the skeleton moves away, for not only will it lead him into rocky pitfalls, whence escape is hopeless, but when there the music will intoxicate, madden, and will finally charm his soul from his body.

STANDING ROCK

The stone that juts from one of the high banks of the Missouri, in South Dakota, gives its name to the Standing Rock Agency, which, by reason of many councils, treaties, fights, feasts, and dances held there, is the best known of the frontier posts. It was a favorite gathering place of the Sioux before the advent of the white man. The rock itself is only twenty-eight inches high and fifteen inches wide, and could be plucked up and carried away without difficulty, but no red man is brave enough to do that, for this is the transformed body of a squaw who was struck into stone by Manitou for falsely suspecting her husband of unfaithfulness.

After her transformation she not only remained sentient but acquired supernatural powers that the Sioux propitiated by offerings of beads, tobacco, and ribbons, paint, fur, and game—a practice that was not abandoned until the teachings of missionaries began to have effect among them. Soldiers and trappers think the story an ingenious device to prevent too close inquiry into the lives of some of the nobility of the tribe. The Arickarees, however, regard this stone as the wife of one of their braves, who was so pained and mortified when her husband took a second wife that she went out into the prairie and neither ate nor drank until she died, when the Great Spirit turned her into the Standing Stone. The squaws still resort to it in times of domestic trouble.

THE SALT WITCH

A pillar of snowy salt once stood on the Nebraska plain, about forty miles above the point where the Saline flows into the Platte, and white men used to hear of it as the Salt Witch. An Indian tribe was for a long time quartered at the junction of the rivers, its chief a man of blood and muscle in whom his people gloried, but so fierce, withal, that nobody made a companion of him except his wife, who alone could check his tigerish rages.

In sooth, he loved her so well that on her death he became a recluse and shut himself within his lodge, refusing to see anybody. This mood endured with him so long that mutterings were heard in the tribe and there was talk of choosing another chief. Some of this talk he must have heard, for one morning he emerged in war-dress, and without a word to any one strode across the plain to westward. On returning a full month later he was more communicative and had something unusual to relate. He also proved his prowess by brandishing a belt of fresh scalps before the eyes of his warriors, and he had also brought a lump of salt.

He told them that after travelling far over the prairie he had thrown himself on the earth to sleep, when he was aroused by a wailing sound close by. In the light of a new moon he saw a hideous old woman brandishing a tomahawk over the head of a younger one, who was kneeling, begging for mercy, and trying to shake off the grip from her throat. The sight of the women, forty miles from the village, so surprised the chief that he ran toward them. The younger woman made a desperate effort to free herself, but in vain, as it seemed, for the hag wound her left hand in her hair while with the other she raised the axe and was about to strike.

At that moment the chief gained a view of the face of the younger woman-it was that of his dead wife. With a snarl of wrath he leaped upon the hag and buried his own hatchet in her brain, but before he could catch his wife in his arms the earth had opened and both women disappeared, but a pillar of salt stood where he had seen this thing. For years the Indians maintained that the column was under the custody of the Salt Witch, and when they went there to gather salt they would beat the ground with clubs, believing that each blow fell upon her person and kept her from working other evil.

ALONG THE ROCKY RANGE

OVER THE DIVIDE

The hope of finding El Dorado, that animated the adventurous Spaniards who made the earlier recorded voyages to America, lived in the souls of Western mountaineers as late as the first half of this century. Ample discoveries of gold in California and Colorado gave color to the belief in this land of riches, and hunger, illness, privation, the persecutions of savages, and death itself were braved in the effort to reach and unlock the treasure caves of earth. Until mining became a systematic business, prospectors were dissatisfied with the smaller deposits of precious metal and dreamed of golden hills farther away. The unknown regions beyond the Rocky Mountains were filled by imagination with magnificent possibilities, and it was the hope of the miner to penetrate the wilderness, "strike it rich," and "make his pile."

Thus, the region indicated as "over the divide" meaning the continental water-shed-or "over the range" came to signify not a delectable land alone, but a sum of delectable conditions, and, ultimately, the goal of posthumous delights. Hence the phrase in use to-day: "Poor Bill! He's gone over the divide."

The Indian's name of heaven—"the happy hunting ground"—is of similar significance, and among many of the tribes it had a definite place in the far Southwest, to which their souls were carried on cobweb floats. Just before reaching it they came to a dark river that had to be crossed on a log. If they had been good in the world of the living they suffered no harm from the rocks and surges, but if their lives had been evil they never reached the farther shore, for they were swept into a place of whirlpools, where, for ever and ever, they were tossed on the torrent amid thousands of clinging, stinging snakes and shoals of putrid fish. From the far North and East the Milky Way was the star-path across the divide.

THE PHANTOM TRAIN OF MARSHALL PASS

Soon after the rails were laid across Marshall Pass, Colorado, where they go over a height of twelve thousand feet above the sea, an old engineer named Nelson Edwards was assigned to a train. He had travelled the road with passengers behind him for a couple of months and met with no accident, but one night as he set off for the divide he fancied that the silence was deeper, the canon darker, and the air frostier than usual. A defective rail and an unsafe bridge had been reported that morning, and he began the long ascent with some misgivings. As he left the first line of snow-sheds he heard a whistle echoing somewhere among the ice and rocks, and at the same time the gong in his cab sounded and he applied the brakes.

The conductor ran up and asked, "What did you stop for?"

"Why did you signal to stop?"

"I gave no signal. Pull her open and light out, for we've got to pass No. 19 at the switches, and there's a wild train climbing behind us."

Edwards drew the lever, sanded the track, and the heavy train got under way again; but the whistles behind grew nearer, sounding danger-signals, and in turning a curve he looked out and saw a train speeding after him at a rate that must bring it against the rear of his own train if something were not done. He broke into a sweat as he pulled the throttle wide open and lunged into a snow-bank. The cars lurched, but the snow was flung off and the train went roaring through another shed. Here was where the defective rail had been reported. No matter. A greater danger was pressing behind. The fireman piled on coal until his clothes were wet with perspiration, and fire belched from the smoke-stack. The passengers, too, having been warned of their peril, had dressed themselves and were anxiously watching at the windows, for talk went among them that a mad engineer was driving the train behind.

As Edwards crossed the summit he shut off steam and surrendered his train to the force of gravity. Looking back, he could see by the faint light from new snow that the driving-wheels on the rear engine were bigger than his own, and that a tall figure stood atop of the cars and gestured frantically. At a sharp turn in the track he found the other train but two hundred yards behind, and as he swept around the curve the engineer who was chasing him leaned from his window and laughed. His face was like dough. Snow was falling and had begun to drift in the hollows, but the trains flew on; bridges shook as they thundered across them; wind screamed in the ears of the passengers; the suspected bridge was reached; Edwards's heart was in his throat, but he seemed to clear the chasm by a bound. Now the switch was in sight, but No. 19 was not there, and as the brakes were freed the train shot by like a flash. Suddenly a red light appeared ahead, swinging to and fro on the track. As well be run into behind as to crash into an obstacle ahead. He heard the whistle of the pursuing locomotive yelp behind him, yet he reversed the lever and put on brakes, and for a few seconds lived in a hell of dread.

Hearing no sound, now, he glanced back and saw the wild train almost leap upon his own—yet just before it touched it the track seemed to spread, the engine toppled from the bank, the whole train rolled into the canon and vanished. Edwards shuddered and listened. No cry of hurt men or hiss of steam came up—nothing but the groan of the wind as it rolled through the black depth. The lantern ahead, too, had disappeared. Now another danger impended, and there was no time to linger, for No. 19 might be on its way ahead if he did not reach the second switch before it moved out. The mad run was resumed and the second switch was reached in time. As Edwards was finishing the run to Green River, which he reached in the morning ahead of schedule, he found written in the frost of his cab-window these words: "A frate train was recked as yu saw. Now that yu saw it yu will never make another run. The enjine was not ounder control and four sexshun men wor killed. If yu ever run on this road again yu will be recked." Edwards quit the road that morning, and returning to Denver found employment on the Union Pacific. No wreck was discovered next day in the canon where he had seen it, nor has the phantom train been in chase of any engineer who has crossed the divide since that night.

THE RIVER OF LOST SOULS

In the days when Spain ruled the Western country an infantry regiment was ordered out from Santa Fe to open communication with Florida and to carry a chest of gold for the payment of the soldiers in St. Augustine. The men wintered on the site of Trinidad, comforted by the society of their wives and families, and in the spring the women and camp-followers were directed to remain, while the troops set forward along the canon of the Purgatoire—neither to reach their destination nor to return. Did they attempt to descend the stream in boats and go to wreck among the rapids? Were they swept into eternity by a freshet? Did they lose their provisions and starve in the desert? Did the Indians revenge themselves for brutality and selfishness by slaying them at night or from an ambush? Were they killed by banditti? Did they sink in the quicksands that led the river into subterranean canals? None will ever know, perhaps; but many years afterward a savage told a priest in Santa Fe that the regiment had been surrounded by Indians, as Custer's command was in Montana, and slain, to a man. Seeing that escape was hopeless, the colonel—so said the narrator—had buried the gold that he was transporting. Thousands of doubloons are believed to be hidden in the canon, and thousands of dollars have been spent in searching for them.

After weeks had lapsed into months and months into years, and no word came of the missing regiment, the priests named the river El Rio de las Animas Perdidas—the River of Lost Souls. The echoing of the flood as it tumbled through the canon was said to be the lamentation of the troopers. French trappers softened the suggestion of the Spanish title when they renamed it Purgatoire, and—"bullwhackers" teaming across the plains twisted the French title into the unmeaning "Picketwire." But Americo-Spaniards keep alive the tradition, and the prayers of many have ascended and do ascend for the succor of those who vanished so strangely in the valley of Las Animas.

RIDERS OF THE DESERT

Among the sandstone columns of the Colorado foot-hills stood the lodge of Ta-in-ga-ro (First Falling Thunder). Though swift in the chase and brave in battle, he seldom went abroad with neighboring tribes, for he was happy in the society of his wife, Zecana (The Bird). To sell beaver and wild sheep-skins he often went with her to a post on the New Mexico frontier, and it was while at this fort that a Spanish trader saw the pretty Zecana, and, determining to win her, sent the Indian on a mission into the heart of the mountains, with a promise that she should rest securely at the settlement until his return.

On his way Ta-in-ga-ro stopped at the spring in Manitou, and after drinking he cast beads and wampum into the well in oblation to its deity. The offering was flung out by the bubbling water, and as he stared, distressed at this unwelcome omen, a picture formed on the surface—the anguished features of Zecana. He ran to his horse, galloped away, and paused neither for rest nor food till he had reached the post. The Spaniard was gone. Turning, then, to the foot-hills, he urged his jaded horse toward his cabin, and arrived, one bright morning, flushed with joy to see his wife before his door and to hear her singing. When he spoke she looked up carelessly and resumed her song. She did not know him. Reason was gone.

It was his cry of rage and grief, when, from her babbling, Ta-in-ga-ro learned of the Spaniard's treachery, that brought the wandering mind back for an instant. Looking at her husband with a strange surprise and pain, she plucked the knife from his belt. Before he could realize her purpose she had thrust it into her heart and had fallen dead at his feet. For hours he stood there in stupefaction, but the stolid Indian nature soon resumed its sway. Setting his lodge in order and feeding his horse, he wrapped Zecana's body in a buffalo-skin, then slept through the night in sheer exhaustion. Two nights afterward the Indian stood in the shadow of a room in the trading fort and watched the Spaniard as he lay asleep. Nobody knew how he passed the guard.

In the small hours the traitor was roused by the strain of a belt across his mouth, and leaping up to fling it off, he felt the tug of a lariat at his throat. His struggles were useless. In a few moments he was bound hand and foot. Lifting some strips of bark from the low roof, Ta-in-ga-ro pushed the Spaniard through the aperture and lowered him to the ground, outside the enclosure of which the house formed part. Then, at the embers of a fire he kindled an arrow wrapped in the down of cottonwood and shot it into a haystack in the court. In the smoke and confusion thus made, his own escape was unseen, save by a guardsman drowsily pacing his beat outside the square of buildings. The sentinel would have given the alarm, had not the Indian pounced on him like a panther and laid him dead with a knife-stroke.

Catching up the Spaniard, the Indian tied him to the back of a horse and set off beside him. Thus they journeyed until they came to his lodge, where he released the trader from his horse and fed him, but kept his hands and legs hard bound, and paid no attention to his questions and his appeals for liberty. Tying a strong and half-trained horse at his door, Ta-in-ga-ro placed a wooden saddle on him, cut off the Spaniard's clothes, and put him astride of the beast. After he had fastened him into his seat with deer-skin thongs, he took Zecana's corpse from its wrapping and tied it to his prisoner, face to face.

Then, loosing the horse, which was plunging and snorting to be rid of his burden, he saw him rush off on the limitless desert, and followed on his own strong steed. At first the Spaniard fainted; on recovering he struggled to get free, but his struggles only brought him closer to the ghastly thing before him. Noon-day heat covered him with sweat and blood dripped from the wales that the cords cut in his flesh. At night he froze uncovered in the chill air, and, if for an instant his eyes closed in sleep, a curse, yelled into his ear, awoke him. Ta-inga-ro gave him drink from time to time, but never food, and so they rode for days. At last hunger overbore his loathing, and sinking his teeth into the dead flesh before him he feasted like a ghoul.

Still they rode, Ta-in-ga-ro never far from his victim, on whose sufferings he gloated, until a gibbering cry told him that the Spaniard had gone mad. Then, and not till then, he drew rein and watched the horse with its dead and maniac riders until they disappeared in the yellow void. He turned away, but nevermore sought his home. To and fro, through the brush, the sand, the alkali of the plains, go the ghost riders, forever.

THE DIVISION OF TWO TRIBES

When white men first penetrated the Western wilderness of America they found the tribes of Shoshone and Comanche at odds, and it is a legend of the springs of Manitou that their differences began there. This "Saratoga of the West," nestling in a hollow of the foot-hills in the shadow of the noble peak of Pike, was in old days common meeting-ground for several families of red men. Councils were held in safety there, for no Indian dared provoke the wrath of the manitou whose breath sparkled in the "medicine waters." None? Yes, one. For, centuries ago a Shoshone and a Comanche stopped here on their return from a hunt to drink. The Shoshone had been successful; the Comanche was empty handed and ill tempered, jealous of the other's skill and fortune. Flinging down the fat deer that he was bearing homeward on his shoulders, the Shoshone bent over the spring of sweet water, and, after pouring a handful of it on the ground, as a libation to the spirit of the place, he put his lips to the surface. It needed but faint pretext for his companion to begin a quarrel, and he did so in this fashion: "Why does a stranger drink at the spring-head when one of the owners of the fountain contents himself with its overflow? How does a Shoshone dare to drink above me?"

The other replied, "The Great Spirit places the water at the spring that his children may drink it undefiled. I am Ausaqua, chief of Shoshones, and I drink at the head-water. Shoshone and Comanche are brothers. Let them drink together."

"No. The Shoshone pays tribute to the Comanche, and Wacomish leads that nation to war. He is chief of the Shoshone as he is of his own people."

"Wacomish lies. His tongue is forked, like the snake's. His heart is black. When the Great Spirit made his children he said not to one, 'Drink here,' and to another, 'Drink there,' but gave water that all might drink."

The other made no answer, but as Ausaqua stooped toward the bubbling surface Wacomish crept behind him, flung himself against the hunter, forced his head beneath the water, and held him there until he was drowned. As he pulled the dead body from the spring the water became agitated, and from the bubbles arose a vapor that gradually assumed the form of a venerable Indian, with long white locks, in whom the murderer recognized Waukauga, father of the Shoshone and Comanche nation, and a man whose heroism and goodness made his name revered in both these tribes. The face of the patriarch was dark with wrath, and he cried, in terrible tones, "Accursed of my race! This day thou hast severed the mightiest nation in the world. The blood of the brave Shoshone appeals for vengeance. May the water of thy tribe be rank and bitter in their throats."

Then, whirling up an elk-horn club, he brought it full on the head of the wretched man, who cringed before him. The murderer's head was burst open and he tumbled lifeless into the spring, that to this day is nauseous, while, to perpetuate the memory of Ausaqua, the manitou smote a neighboring rock, and from it gushed a fountain of delicious water. The bodies were found, and the partisans of both the hunters began on that day a long and destructive warfare, in which other tribes became involved until mountaineers were arrayed against plainsmen through all that region.

BESIEGED BY STARVATION

A hundred years before the white men set up their trading-posts on the Arkansas and Platte, a band of mountain hunters made a descent on what they took to be a small company of plainsmen, but who proved to be the enemy in force, and who, in turn, drove the Utes—for the aggressors were of that tribe—into the hills. Most of them took refuge on a castellated rock on the south side of Bowlder Canon, where they held their own for several days, rolling down huge rocks whenever an attempt was made to storm the height; wherefore, seeing that the mountain was too secure a stronghold to be taken in that way, the besiegers camped about it, and, by cutting off the access of the beleaguered party to game and to water, starved every one of them to death.

This, too, is the story of Starved Rock, on Illinois River, near Ottawa, Illinois. It is a sandstone bluff, one hundred and fifty feet high, with a slope on one side only. Its summit is an acre in extent, and at the order of La Salle his Indian lieutenant, Tonti, fortified the place and mounted a small cannon on it. He died there afterward. After the killing of Pontiac at Cahokia, some of his people—the Ottawas—charged the crime against their enemies, the Illinois. The latter, being few in number, entrenched themselves on Starved Rock, where they kept their enemies at bay, but were unable to break their line to reach supplies. For a time they secured water by letting down bark vessels into the river at the end of thongs, but the Ottawas came under the bluff in canoes and cut the cords. Unwilling to surrender, the Illinois remained there until all had died of starvation. Bones and relics are found occasionally at the top.

There is yet another place of which a similar narrative is extant—namely, Crow Butte, Nebraska, which is two hundred feet high and vertical on all sides save one, but on that a horseman may ascend in safety. A company of Crows, flying from the Sioux, gained this citadel and defended the path so vigorously that their pursuers gave over all attempts to follow them, but squatted calmly on the plain and proceeded to starve them out. On a dark night the besieged killed some of their ponies and made lariats of their hides, by which they reached the ground on the unguarded side of the rock. They slid down, one at a time, and made off all but one aged Indian, who stayed to keep the camp-fire burning as a blind. He went down and surrendered on the next day, but the Sioux, respecting his age and loyalty, gave him freedom.

A YELLOWSTONE TRAGEDY

Although the Indians feared the geyser basins of the upper Yellowstone country, believing the hissing and thundering to be voices of evil spirits, they regarded the mountains at the head of the river as the crest of the world, and whoso gained their summits could see the happy hunting-grounds below, brightened with the homes of the blessed. They loved this land in which their fathers had hunted, and when they were driven back from the settlements the Crows took refuge in what is now Yellowstone Park. Even here the soldiers pursued them, intent on avenging acts that the red men had committed while suffering under the sting of tyranny and wrong. A mere remnant of the fugitive band gathered at the head of that mighty rift in the earth known as the Grand Canon of the Yellowstone—a remnant that had succeeded in escaping the bullets of the soldiery,—and with Spartan courage they resolved to die rather than be taken and carried away to pine in a distant prison. They built a raft and placed it on the river at the foot of the upper fall, and for a few days they enjoyed the plenty and peace that were their privilege in former times. A short-lived peace, however, for one morning they are aroused by the crack of rifles—the troops are upon them.

Boarding their raft they thrust it toward the middle of the stream, perhaps with the idea of gaining the opposite shore, but, if such is their intent, it is thwarted by the rapidity of the current. A few among them have guns, that they discharge with slight effect at the troops, who stand wondering on the shore. The soldiers forbear to fire, and watch, with something like dread, the descent of the raft as it passes into the current, and, with many a turn and pitch, whirls on faster and faster. The death-song rises triumphant above the lash of the waves and that distant but awful booming that is to be heard in the canon. Every red man has his face turned toward the foe with a look of defiance, and the tones of the death-chant have in them something of mockery no less than hate and vaunting.

The raft is now between the jaws of rock that yawn so hungrily. Beyond and below are vast walls, shelving toward the floor of the gulf a thousand feet beneath—their brilliant colors shining in the sun of morning that sheds as peaceful a light on wood and hill as if there were no such thing as brother hunting brother in this free land of ours. The raft is galloping through the foam like a racehorse, and, hardened as the soldiers are, they cannot repress a shudder as they see the fate that the savages have chosen for themselves. Now the brink is reached. The raft tips toward the gulf, and with a cry of triumph the red men are launched over the cataract, into the bellowing chasm, where the mists weep forever on the rocks and mosses.

THE BROAD HOUSE

Down in the canon of Chaco, New Mexico, stands a building evidently coeval with those of the cliff dwellers, that is still in good preservation and is called the Broad House. When Noqoilpi, the gambling god, came on earth he strayed into this canon, and, finding the Moquis a prosperous people, he envied them and resolved to win their property. To do that he laid off a race-track at the bottom of the ravine and challenged them to meet him there in games of chance and strength and skill. They accepted his challenge, and, as he could turn luck to his own side, he soon won not their property alone, but their women and children, and, finally, some of the men themselves.

In his greed he had acquired more than he wanted, and as the captives were a burden to him he offered to make a partial restoration if the people would build this house for him. They did so and he gave up some of the men and women. The other gods looked with disapproval on this performance, however, and they agreed to give the wind god power to defeat him, for, now that he had secured his house, he had gone to gambling again. The wind god, in disguise as a Moqui, issued a challenge, and the animals agreed to help him.

When the contest in tree-pulling took place the wind god pulled up a large tree while Noqoilpi was unable to stir a smaller one. That was because the beavers had cut the roots of the larger. In the ball contest Noqoilpi drove the ball nearly to the bounds, but the wind god sent his far beyond, for wrapped loosely in it was a bird that freed itself before touching the ground and flew away. In brief, Noqoilpi was beaten at every point and the remaining captives left him, with jeers, and returned to their people.

The gambler cursed and raged until the wind god seized him, fitted him to a bow, like an arrow, and shot him into the sky. He flew far out of sight, and presently came to the long row of stone houses where the man lives who carries the moon. He pitied the gambler and made new animals and people for him and let him down to the earth in old Mexico, the moon people becoming Mexicans. He returned to his old haunts and came northward, building towns along the Rio Grande until he had passed the site of Santa Fe, when his people urged him to go back, and after his return they made him their god—Nakai Cigini.

THE DEATH WALTZ

Years ago, when all beyond the Missouri was a waste, the military post at Fort Union, New Mexico, was the only spot for miles around where any of the graces of social life could be discovered. Among the ladies at the post was a certain gay young woman, the sister-in-law of a captain, who enjoyed the variety and spice of adventure to be found there, and enjoyed, too, the homage that the young officers paid to her, for women who could be loved or liked were not many in that wild country. A young lieutenant proved especially susceptible to her charms, and devoted himself to her in the hope that he should ultimately win her hand. His experience with the world was not large enough to enable him to distinguish between the womanly woman and the coquette.

One day messengers came dashing into the fort with news of an Apache outbreak, and a detachment was ordered out to chase and punish the marauding Indians. The lieutenant was put in command of the expedition, but before starting he confided his love to the young woman, who not only acknowledged that she returned his affection, but promised that if the fortune of war deprived him of life she would never marry another. As he bade her good-by he was heard to say, "That is well. Nobody else shall have you. I will come back and make my claim."

In a few days the detachment came back, but the lieutenant was missing. It was noticed that the bride-elect grieved but little for him, and nobody was surprised when she announced her intention of marrying a young man from the East. The wedding-day arrived. All was gayety at the post, and in the evening the mess-room was decorated for a ball. As the dance was in full swing a door flew open with a bang, letting in a draught of air that made the candles burn dim, and a strange cry, unlike that of any human creature, sounded through the house. All eyes turned to the door. In it stood the swollen body of a dead man dressed in the stained uniform of an officer. The temple was marked by a hatchet-gash, the scalp was gone, the eyes were wide open and, burned with a terrible light.

Walking to the bride the body drew her from the arms of her husband, who, like the rest of the company, stood as in a trance, without the power of motion, and clasping her to its bosom began a waltz. The musicians, who afterward declared that they did not know what they were doing, struck up a demoniac dance, and the couple spun around and around, the woman growing paler and paler, until at last the fallen jaw and staring eyes showed that life was also extinct in her. The dead man allowed her to sink to the floor, stood over her for a moment, wrung his hands as he sounded his fearful cry again, then vanished through the door. A few days after, a troop of soldiers who had been to the scene of the Apache encounter returned with the body of the lieutenant.

THE FLOOD AT SANTA FE

Many are the scenes of religious miracles in this country, although French Canada and old Mexico boast of more. So late as the prosaic year of 1889 the Virgin was seen to descend into the streets of Johnstown, Pennsylvania, to save her image on the Catholic church in that place, when it was swept by a deluge in which hundreds of persons perished. It was the wrath of the Madonna that caused just such a flood in New Mexico long years ago. There is in the old Church of Our Lady of Guadalupe, in Santa Fe, a picture that commemorates the appearance of the Virgin to Juan Diego, an Indian in Guadalupe, old Mexico, in the sixteenth century. She commanded that a chapel should be built for her, but the bishop of the diocese declared that the man had been dreaming and told him to go away. The Virgin came to the Indian again, and still the bishop declared that he had no evidence of the truth of what he said. A third time the supernatural visitor appeared, and told Juan to climb a certain difficult mountain, pick the flowers he would find there, and take them to the bishop.

After a long and dangerous climb they were found, to the Indian's amazement, growing in the snow. He filled his blanket with them and returned to the episcopal residence, but when he opened the folds before the dignitary, he was more amazed to find not flowers, but a glowing picture painted on his blanket. It hangs now in Guadalupe, but is duplicated in Santa Fe, where a statue of the Virgin is also kept. These treasures are greatly prized and are resorted to in time of illness and threatened disaster, the statue being taken through the streets in procession when the rainy season is due. Collections of money are then made and prayers are put up for rain, to which appeals the Virgin makes prompt response, the priests pointing triumphantly to the results of their intercession. One year, however, the rain did not begin on time, though services were almost constantly continued before the sacred picture and the sacred statue, and the angry people stripped the image of its silks and gold lace and kicked it over the ground for hours. That night a violent rain set in and the town was nearly washed away, so the populace hastened the work of reparation in order to save their lives. They cleansed the statue, dressed it still more brilliantly, and addressed their prayers to the Virgin with more energy and earnestness than ever before.

GODDESS OF SALT

Between Zuni and Pescado is a steep mesa, or table-land, with fantastic rocks weathered into tower and roof-like prominences on its sides, while near it is a high natural monument of stone. Say the Zunis: The goddess of salt was so troubled by the people who lived near her domain on the seashore, and who took away her snowy treasures without offering any sacrifice in return, that she forsook the ocean and went to live in the mountains far away. Whenever she stopped beside a pool to rest she made it salt, and she wandered so long about the great basins of the West that much of the water in them is bitter, and the yield of salt from the larger lake near Zuni brings into the Zuni treasury large tolls from other tribes that draw from it.

Here she met the turquoise god, who fell in love with her at sight, and wooed so warmly that she accepted and married him. For a time they lived happily, but when the people learned that the goddess had concealed herself among the mountains of New Mexico they followed her to that land and troubled her again until she declared that she would leave their view forever. She entered this mesa, breaking her way through a high wall of sandstone as she did so. The arched portal through which she passed is plainly visible. As she went through, one of her plumes was broken off, and falling into the valley it tipped upon its stem and became the monument that is seen there. The god of turquoise followed his wife, and his footsteps may be traced in outcrops of pale-blue stone.

THE COMING OF THE NAVAJOS

Many fantastic accounts of the origin of man are found among the red tribes. The Onondagas say that the Indians are made from red earth and the white men from sea-foam. Flesh-making clay is seen in the precipitous bank in the ravine west of Onondaga Valley, where at night the fairies "little fellows" sport and slide. Among others, the Noah legend finds a parallel. Several tribes claim to have emerged from the interior of the earth. The Oneidas point to a hill near the falls of Oswego River, New York, as their birthplace; the Wichitas rose from the rocks about Red River; the Creeks from a knoll in the valley of Big Black River in the Natchez country, where dwelt the Master of Breath; the Aztecs were one of seven tribes that came out from the seven caverns of Aztlan, or Place of the Heron; and the Navajos believe that they emerged at a place known to them in the Navajo Mountains.

In the under world the Navajos were happy, for they had everything that they could wish: there was no excess of heat or cold, trees and flowers grew everywhere, and the day was marked by a bright cloud that arose in the east, while a black cloud that came out of the west made the night. Here they lived for centuries, and might have been there to this day had not one of the tribe found an opening in the earth that led to some place unknown. He told of it to the whole tribe. They set off up the passage to see where it led, and after long and weary climbing the surface was reached. Pleased with the novelty of their surroundings, they settled here, but on the fourth day after their arrival their queen disappeared.

Their search for her was unavailing until some of the men came to the mouth of the tunnel by which they had reached the upper land, when, looking down, they saw their queen combing her long, black locks. She told them that she was dead and that her people could go to her only after death, but that they would be happy in their old home. With that the earth shut together and the place has never since been open to the eye of mortals. Soon came the cannibal giants who ravaged the desert lands and destroyed all of the tribe but four families, these having found a refuge in a deep canon of the Navajo Mountains. From their retreat they could see a beam of light shining from one of the hills above them, and on ascending to the place they found a beautiful girl babe.

This child grew to womanhood under their care, and her charms attracted the great manitou that rides on a white horse and carries the sun for a shield. He wooed and married her, and their children slew the giants that had destroyed the Navajos. After a time the manitou carried his wife to his floating palace in the western water, which has since been her home. To her the prayers of the people are addressed, and twelve immortals bear their petitions to her throne.

THE ARK ON SUPERSTITION MOUNTAINS

The Pima Indians of Arizona say that the father of all men and animals was the butterfly, Cherwit Make (earth-maker), who fluttered down from the clouds to the Blue Cliffs at the junction of the Verde and Salt Rivers, and from his own sweat made men. As the people multiplied they grew selfish and quarrelsome, so that Cherwit Make was disgusted with his handiwork and resolved to drown them all. But first he told them, in the voice of the north wind, to be honest and to live at peace. The prophet Suha, who interpreted this voice, was called a fool for listening to the wind, but next night came the east wind and repeated the command, with an added threat that the ruler of heaven would destroy them all if they did not reform.

Again they scoffed, and on the next night the west wind cautioned them. But this third warning was equally futile. On the fourth night came the south wind. It breathed into Suha's ear that he alone had been good and should be saved, and bade him make a hollow ball of spruce gum in which he might float while the deluge lasted. Suha and his wife immediately set out to gather the gum, that they melted and shaped until they had made a large, rounded ark, which they ballasted with jars of nuts, acorn-meal and water, and meat of bear and venison.

On the day assigned Suha and his wife were looking regretfully down into the green valleys from the ledge where the ark rested, listening to the song of the harvesters, and sighing to think that so much beauty would presently be laid waste, when a hand of fire was thrust from a cloud and it smote the Blue Cliffs with a thunder-clang. It was the signal. Swift came the clouds from all directions, and down poured the rain. Withdrawing into their waxen ball, Suha and his wife closed the portal. Then for some days they were rolled and tossed on an ever-deepening sea. Their stores had almost given out when the ark stopped, and breaking a hole in its side its occupants stepped forth.

There was a tuna cactus growing at their feet, and they ate of its red fruit greedily, but all around them was naught but water. When night came on they retired to the ark and slept—a night, a month, a year, perhaps a century, for when they awoke the water was gone, the vales were filled with verdure, and bird-songs rang through the woods. The delighted couple descended the Superstition Mountains, on which the ark had rested, and went into its valleys, where they lived for a thousand years, and became the parents of a great tribe.

But the evil was not all gone. There was one Hauk, a devil of the mountains, who stole their daughters and slew their sons. One day, while the women were spinning flax and cactus fibre and the men were gathering maize, Hauk descended into the settlement and stole another of Suha's daughters. The patriarch, whose patience had been taxed to its limit, then made a vow to slay the devil. He watched to see by what way he entered the valley. He silently followed him into the Superstition Mountains; he drugged the cactus wine that his daughter was to serve to him; then, when he had drunk it, Suha emerged from his place of hiding and beat out the brains of the stupefied fiend.

Some of the devil's brains were scattered and became seed for other evil, but there was less wickedness in the world after Hauk had been disposed of than there had been before. Suha taught his people to build adobe houses, to dig with shovels, to irrigate their land, to weave cloth, and avoid wars. But on his death-bed he foretold to them that they would grow arrogant with wealth, covetous of the lands of others, and would wage wars for gain. When that time came there would be another flood and not one should be saved—the bad should vanish and the good would leave the earth and live in the sun. So firmly do the Pimas rely on this prophecy that they will not cross Superstition Mountains, for there sits Cherwit Make—awaiting the culmination of their wickedness to let loose on the earth a mighty sea that lies dammed behind the range.

THE PALE FACED LIGHTNING

Twenty miles from the capital of Arizona stands Mount Superstition—the scene of many traditions, the object of many fears. Two centuries ago a tribe of Pueblo dwarfs arrived near it and tilled the soil and tended their flocks about the settlements that grew along their line of march. They were little people, four feet high, but they were a thousand strong and clever. They were peaceful, like all intelligent people, and the mystery surrounding their incantations and sun-worship was more potent than a show of arms to frighten away those natural assassins, the Apaches.

After they had lived near the mountain for five years the "little people" learned that the Zunis were advancing from the south and made preparations for defence. Their sheep were concealed in obscure valleys; provisions, tools, and arms were carried up the mountain; piles of stone were placed along the edges of cliffs commanding the passes. This work was superintended by a woman with a white face, fair hair, and commanding form, who was held in reverence by the dwarfs; and she it was—the Helen of a New-World Troy—who was causing this trouble, for the Zunis claimed her on the ground that they had brought her from the waters of the rising sun, and that it was only to escape an honorable marriage with their chief that she had fled to the dwarfs.

Be that as it might, the Zunis marched on, meeting with faint resistance until, on a bright afternoon, they massed on a slope of the mountain, seven hundred in number. The Apaches, expecting instant defeat of the "little men," watched, from neighboring hills, the advance of the invaders as they climbed nimbly toward the stone fort on the top of the slope, brandishing clubs and stone spears, and bragging, as the fashion of a red man is—and sometimes of a white one.

At a pool outside of the walls stood the pale woman, queenly and calm, and as her white robe and brown hair fluttered in the wind both her people and the foe looked upon her with admiration. When but a hundred yards away the Zunis rushed toward her with outstretched arms, whereupon she stooped, picked up an earthen jar, emptied its contents into the pool, and ran back. In a moment sparks and balls of fire leaped from crevices in the rocks, and as they touched the Indians many fell dead. Others plunged blindly over the cliffs and were dashed to pieces.

In a few minutes the remainder of the force was in full retreat and not an arrow had been shot. The Apaches, though stricken with terror at these pyrotechnics, overcame the memory of them sufficiently in a couple of years to attempt the sack of the fort on their own account, but the queen repelled them as she had forced back the Zunis, and with even greater slaughter. From that time the dwarfs were never harmed again, but they went away, as suddenly as they had come, to a secret recess in the mountains, where the Pale Faced Lightning still rules them.

Some of the Apaches maintain that her spirit haunts a cave on Superstition Mountain, where her body vanished in a blaze of fire, and this cave of the Spirit Mother is also pointed out on the south side of Salt River. A skeleton and cotton robes, ornamented and of silky texture, were once found there. It is said that electrical phenomena are frequent on the mountain, and that iron, copper, salt, and copperas lying near together may account for them.

THE WEIRD SENTINEL AT SQUAW PEAK

There is a cave under the highest butte of the Squaw Peak range, Arizona, where a party of Tonto Indians was found by white men in 1868. The white men were on the war-path, and when the Tontos fell into their hands they shot them unhesitatingly, firing into the dark recesses of the cavern, the fitful but fast-recurring flashes of their rifles illuminating the interior and exposing to view the objects of their hatred.

The massacre over, the cries and groans were hushed, the hunters strode away, and over the mountains fell the calm that for thousands of years had not been so rudely broken. That night, when the moon shone into this pit of death, a corpse arose, walked to a rock just within the entrance, and took there its everlasting seat.

Long afterward a man who did not know its story entered this place, when he was confronted by a thing, as he called it, that glared so fearfully upon him that he fled in an ecstasy of terror. Two prospectors subsequently attempted to explore the cave, but the entrance was barred by "the thing." They gave one glance at the torn face, the bulging eyes turned sidewise at them, the yellow fangs, the long hair, the spreading claws, the livid, mouldy flesh, and rushed away. A Western paper, recounting their adventure, said that one of the men declared that there was not money enough in Maricopa County to pay him to go there again, while the other had never stopped running—at least, he had not returned to his usual haunts since "the thing" looked at him. Still, it is haunted country all about here. The souls of the Mojaves roam upon Ghost Mountain, and the "bad men's hunting-grounds" of the Yumas and Navajos are over in the volcanic country of Sonora. It is, therefore, no unusual thing to find signs and wonders in broad daylight.

SACRIFICE OF THE TOLTECS

Centuries ago, when Toltec civilization had extended over Arizona, and perhaps over the whole West, the valleys were occupied by large towns—the towns whose ruins are now known as the City of Ovens, City of Stones, and City of the Dead. The people worked at trades and arts that had been practised by their ancestors before the pyramids were built in Egypt. Montezuma had come to the throne of Mexico, and the Aztecs were a subject people; Europe had discovered America and forgotten it, and in America the arrival of Europeans was recalled only in traditions. But, like other nations, the Toltecs became a prey to self-confidence, to luxury, to wastefulness, and to deadening superstitions. Already the fierce tribes of the North were lurking on the confines of their country in a faith of speedy conquest, and at times it seemed as if the elements were against them.

The villagers were returning from the fields, one day, when the entire region was smitten by an earthquake. Houses trembled, rumblings were heard, people fell in trying to reach the streets, and reservoirs burst, wasting their contents on the fevered soil. A sacrifice was offered. Then came a second shock, and another mortal was offered in oblation. As the earth still heaved and the earthquake demon muttered underground, the king gave his daughter to the priests, that his people might be spared, though he wrung his hands and beat his brow as he saw her led away and knew that in an hour her blood would stream from the altar.

The girl walked firmly to the cave where the altar was erected—a cave in Superstition Mountains. She knelt and closed her eyes as the officiating-priest uttered a prayer, and, gripping his knife of jade stone, plunged it into her heart. She fell without a struggle. And now, the end.

Hardly had the innocent blood drained out and the fires been lighted to consume the body, when a pall of cloud came sweeping across the heavens; a hot wind surged over the ground, laden with dust and smoke; the storm-struck earth writhed anew beneath pelting thunder-bolts; no tremor this time, but an upheaval that rent the rocks and flung the cities down. It was an hour of darkness and terror. Roars of thunder mingled with the more awful bellowing beneath; crash on crash told that houses and temples were falling in vast ruin; the mountainsides were loosened and the rush of avalanches added to the din; the air was thick, and through the clouds the people groped their way toward the fields; rivers broke from their confines and laid waste farms and gardens! The gods had indeed abandoned them, and the spirit of the king's daughter took its flight in company with thousands of souls in whose behalf she had suffered uselessly.

The king was crushed beneath his palace-roof and the sacerdotal executioner perished in a fall of rock. The survivors fled in panic and the Ishmaelite tribes on their frontier entered their kingdom and pillaged it of all abandoned wealth. The cities never were rebuilt and were rediscovered but a few years ago, when the maiden's skeleton was also found. Nor does any Indian cross Superstition Mountains without a sense of apprehension.

TA-VWOTS CONQUERS THE SUN

The Indian is a great story-teller. Every tribe has its traditions, and the elderly men and women like to recount them, for they always find listeners. And odd stories they tell, too. Just listen to this, for example. It is a legend among the tribes of Arizona.

While Ta-Vwots, the hare god, was asleep in the valley of Maopa, the Sun mischievously burned his back, causing him to leap up with a howl. "Aha! It's you, is it, who played this trick on me?" he cried, looking at the Sun. "I'll make it warm for you. See if I don't."

And without more ado he set off to fight the Sun. On the way he stopped to pick and roast some corn, and when the people who had planted it ran out and tried to punish him for the theft he scratched a hole in the ground and ran in out of sight. His pursuers shot arrows into the hole, but Ta-Vwots had his breath with him, and it was an awfully strong breath, for with it he turned all the arrows aside. "The scamp is in here," said one of the party. "Let's get at him another way." So, getting their flints and shovels, they began to dig.

"That's your game, is it?" mumbled Ta-Vwots. "I know a way out of this that you don't know." With a few puffs of his breath and a few kicks of his legs he reached a great fissure that led into the rock behind him, and along this passage he scrambled until he came to the edge of it in a niche, from which he could watch his enemies digging. When they had made the hole quite large he shouted, "Be buried in the grave you have dug for yourselves!" And, hurling down a magic ball that he carried, he caved the earth in on their heads. Then he paced off, remarking, "To fight is as good fun as to eat. Vengeance is my work. Every one I meet will be an enemy. No one shall escape my wrath." And he sounded his war-whoop.

Next day he saw two men heating rocks and chipping arrow-heads from them. "Let me help you, for hot rocks will not hurt me," he said.

"You would have us to believe you are a spirit, eh?" they questioned, with a jeer.

"No ghost," he answered, "but a better man than you. Hold me on those rocks, and, if I do not burn, you must let me do the same to you."

The men complied, and heating the stones to redness in the fire they placed him against them, but failed to see that by his magic breath he kept a current of air flowing between him and the hot surface. Rising unhurt, he demanded that they also should submit to the torture, and, like true Indians, they did so. When their flesh had been burned half through and they were dead, he sounded his warwhoop and went on.

On the day following he met two women picking berries, and told them to blow the leaves and thorns into his eyes. They did so, as they supposed, but with his magic breath he kept the stuff away from his face.

"You are a ghost!" the women exclaimed.

"No ghost," said he. "Just a common person. Leaves and thorns can do no harm. See, now." And he puffed thorns into their faces and made them blind. "Aha! You are caught with your own chaff I am on my way to kill the Sun. This is good practice." And he slew them, sounded his war-whoop, and went on.

The morning after this affair some women appeared on Hurricane Cliff and the wind brought their words to his ears. They were planning to kill him by rolling rocks upon him as he passed. As he drew near he pretended to eat something with such enjoyment that they asked him what it was. He called out, "It is sweet. Come to the edge and I will throw it up to you." With that he tossed something so nearly within their reach that in bending forward to catch it they crowded too near the brink, lost their balance, fell over, and were killed. "You are victims of your own greed. One should never be so anxious as to kill one's self." This was his only comment, and, sounding the warwhoop, he went on.

A day later he came upon two women making water jugs of willow baskets lined with pitch, and he heard one whisper to the other, "Here comes that bad Ta-Vwots. How shall we destroy him?"

"What were you saying?" asked the hare god.

"We just said, 'Here comes our grandson.'" (A common form of endearment.)

"Is that all? Then let me get into one of these water jugs while you braid the neck."

He jumped in and lay quite still as they wove the neck, and they laughed to think that it was braided so small that he could never escape, when—puff! the jug was shattered and there was Ta-Vwots. They did not know anything about his magic breath. They wondered how he got out.

"Easily enough," replied the hare god. "These things may hold water, but they can't hold men and women. Try it, and see if they can." With their consent, Ta-Vwots began weaving the osiers about them, and in a little while he had them caged. "Now, come out," he said. But, try as they might, not a withe could they break. "Ha, ha! You are wise women, aren't you? Bottled in your own jugs! I am on my way to kill the Sun. In time I shall learn how." Then, sounding his war-whoop, he struck them dead with his magic ball and went on.

He met the Bear next day, and found him digging a hole to hide in, for he had heard of the hare god and was afraid. "Don't be frightened, friend Bear," said the rogue. "I'm not the sort of fellow to hide from. How could a little chap like me hurt so many people?" And he helped the Bear to dig his den, but when it was finished he hid behind a rock, and as the Bear thrust his head near him he launched his magic ball at his face and made an end of him. "I was afraid of this warrior," said Ta-Vwots, "but he is dead, now, in his den." And sounding his war-whoop he went on.

It was on the day following that he met the Tarantula, a clever rascal, who had a club that would deal a fatal blow to others, but would not hurt himself. He began to groan as Ta-Vwots drew near, and cried that he had a pain caused by an evil spirit in his head. Wouldn't Ta-Vwots thump it out? Indeed, he would. He grasped the club and gave him the soundest kind of a thwacking, but when the Tarantula shouted "Harder," he guessed that it was an enchanted weapon, and changing it for his magic ball he finished the Tarantula at a blow. "That is a stroke of your own seeking," he remarked. "I am on my way to kill the Sun. Now I know that I can do it." And sounding his war-whoop he went on.

Next day he came to the edge of the world and looked off into space, where thousands of careless people had fallen, and there he passed the night under a tree. At dawn he stood on the brink of the earth and the instant that the Sun appeared he flung the magic ball full in his face. The surface of the Sun was broken into a thousand pieces that spattered over the earth and kindled a mighty conflagration. Ta-Vwots crept under the tree that had sheltered him, but that was of no avail against the increasing heat. He tried to run away, but the fire burned off his toes, then his feet, then his legs, then his body, so that he ran on his hands, and when his hands were burned off he walked on the stumps of his arms. At last his head alone remained, and that rolled over hill and valley until it struck a rock, when the eyes burst and the tears that gushed forth spread over the land, putting out the flames. The Sun was conquered, and at his trial before the other gods was reprimanded for his mischievous pranks and condemned thereafter to travel across the sky every day by the same trail.

THE COMANCHE RIDER

The ways of disposing of the Indian dead are many. In some places ground sepulture is common; in others, the corpses are placed in trees. South Americans mummified their dead, and cremation was not unknown. Enemies gave no thought to those that they had slain, after plucking off their scalps as trophies, though they sometimes added the indignity of mutilation in killing.

Sachem's Head, near Guilford, Connecticut, is so named because Uncas cut a Pequot's head off and placed it in the crotch of an oak that grew there. It remained withering for years. It was to save the body of Polan from such a fate, after the fight on Sebago Lake in 1756, that his brothers placed it under the root of a sturdy young beech that they had pried out of the ground. He was laid in the hollow in his war-dress, with silver cross on his breast and bow and arrows in his hand; then, the weight on the trunk being released, the sapling sprang back to its place and afterward rose to a commanding height, fitly marking the Indian's tomb. Chief Blackbird, of the Omahas, was buried, in accordance with his wish, on the summit of a bluff near the upper Missouri, on the back of his favorite horse, fully equipped for travel, with the scalps that he had taken hung to the bridle.

When a Comanche dies he is buried on the western side of the camp, that his soul may follow the setting sun into the spirit world the speedier. His bow, arrows, and valuables are interred with him, and his best pony is killed at the grave that he may appear among his fellows in the happy hunting grounds mounted and equipped. An old Comanche who died near Fort Sill was without relatives and poor, so his tribe thought that any kind of a horse would do for him to range upon the fields of paradise. They killed a spavined old plug and left him. Two weeks from that time the late unlamented galloped into a camp of the Wichitas on the back of a lop-eared, bob-tailed, sheep-necked, ring-boned horse, with ribs like a grate, and said he wanted his dinner. Having secured a piece of meat, formally presented to him on the end of a lodge-pole, he offered himself to the view of his own people, alarming them by his glaring eyes and sunken cheeks, and told them that he had come back to haunt them for a stingy, inconsiderate lot, because the gate-keeper of heaven had refused to admit him on so ill-conditioned a mount. The camp broke up in dismay. Wichitas and Comanches journeyed, en masse, to Fort Sill for protection, and since then they have sacrificed the best horses in their possession when an unfriended one journeyed to the spirit world.

Myths and Legends

HORNED TOAD AND GIANTS

The Moquis have a legend that, long ago, when the principal mesa that they occupy was higher than it is now, and when they owned all the country from the mountains to the great river, giants came out of the west and troubled them, going so far as to dine on Moquis. It was hard to get away, for the monsters could see all over the country from the tops of the mesas. The king of the tribe offered the handsomest woman in his country and a thousand horses to any man who would deliver his people from these giants. This king was eaten like the rest, and the citizens declined to elect another, because they were beginning to lose faith in kings. Still, there was one young brave whose single thought was how to defeat the giants and save his people.

As he was walking down the mesa he saw a lizard, of the kind commonly known as a horned toad, lying under a rock in pain. He rolled the stone away and was passing on, when a voice, that seemed to come out of the earth, but that really came from the toad, asked him if he wished to destroy the giants. He desired nothing so much. "Then take my horned crest for a helmet."

Lolomi—that was the name of him—did as he was bid, and found that in a moment the crest had swelled and covered his head so thickly that no club could break through it.

"Now take my breastplate," continued the toad. And though it would not have covered the Indian's thumb-nail, when he put it on it so increased in bulk that it corseleted his body and no arrow could pierce it.

"Now take the scales from my eyes," commanded the toad, and when he had done so Lolomi felt as light as a feather.

"Go up and wait. When you see a giant, go toward him, looking in his eyes, and he will walk backward. Walk around him until he has his back to a precipice, then advance. He will back away until he reaches the edge of the mesa, when he will fall off and be killed."

Lolomi obeyed these instructions, for presently a giant loomed in the distance and came striding across the plains half a mile at a step. As he drew near he flung a spear, but it glanced from the Indian's armor like hail from a rock. Then an arrow followed, and was turned. At this the giant lost courage, for he fancied that Lolomi was a spirit. Fearing a blow if he turned, he kept his face toward Lolomi, who manoeuvred so skilfully that when he had the giant's back to the edge of a cliff he sprang at him, and the giant, with a yell of alarm, fell and broke his bones on the rocks below. So Lolomi killed many giants, because they all walked back before him, and after they had fallen the people heaped rocks on their bodies. To this day the place is known as "the giants' fall." Then the tribe made Lolomi king and gave him the most beautiful damsel for a wife. As he was the best king they ever had, they treasured his memory after he was dead, and used his name as a term of greeting, so that "Lolomi" is a word of welcome, and will be until the giants come again.

THE SPIDER TOWER

In Dead Man's Canon—a deep gorge that is lateral to the once populated valley of the Rio de Chelly, Arizona—stands a stark spire of weathered sandstone, its top rising eight hundred feet above its base in a sheer uplift. Centuries ago an inhabitant of one of the cave villages was surprised by hostiles while hunting in this region, and was chased by them into this canon. As he ran he looked vainly from side to side in the hope of securing a hiding-place, but succor came from a source that was least expected, for on approaching this enormous obelisk, with strength well-nigh exhausted, he saw a silken cord hanging from a notch at its top. Hastily knotting the end about his waist, that it might not fall within reach of his pursuers, he climbed up, setting his feet into roughnesses of the stone, and advancing, hand over hand, until he had reached the summit, where he stayed, drinking dew and feeding on eagles' eggs, until his enemies went away, for they could not reach him with their arrows, defended as he was by points of rock. The foemen having gone, he safely descended by the cord and reached his home. This help had come from a friendly spider who saw his plight from her perch at the top of the spire, and, weaving a web of extra thickness, she made one end fast to a jag of rock while the other fell within his grasp—for she, like all other of the brute tribe, liked the gentle cave-dwellers better than the remorseless hunters. Hence the name of the Spider Tower.

THE LOST TRAIL

The canon of Oak Creek is choked by a mass of rock, shaped like a keystone, and wedged into the jaws of the defile. An elderly Ute tells this story of it. Acantow, one of the chiefs of his tribe, usually placed his lodge beside the spring that bubbled from a thicket of wild roses in the place where Rosita, Colorado, stands to-day. He left his wife—Manetabee (Rosebud)—in the lodge while he went across the mountains to attend a council, and was gone four sleeps. On his return he found neither wife nor lodge, but footprints and hoofprints in the ground showed to his keen eye that it was the Arapahoes who had been there.

Getting on their trail he rode over it furiously, and at night had reached Oak Canon, along which he travelled until he saw the gleam of a small fire ahead. A squall was coming up, and the noise of it might have enabled him to gallop fairly into the group that he saw huddled about the glow; but it is not in the nature of an Indian to do that, and, tying his horse, he crawled forward.

There were fifteen of the Arapahoes, and they were gambling to decide the ownership of Manetabee, who sat bound beneath a willow near them. So engrossed were the savages in the contest that the snake-like approach of Acantow was unnoticed until he had cut the thongs that bound Manetabee's wrists and ankles—she did not cry out, for she had expected rescue—and both had imperceptibly slid away from them. Then, with a yell, one of the gamblers pointed to the receding forms, and straightway the fifteen made an onset.

Swinging his wife lightly to his shoulders Acantow set off at a run and he had almost reached his horse when his foot caught in a root and he fell headlong. The pursuers were almost upon him when the storm burst in fury. A flood of fire rushed from the clouds and struck the earth with an appalling roar. Trees were snapped, rocks were splintered, and a whirlwind passed. Acantow was nearly insensible for a time—then he felt the touch of the Rosebud's hand on his cheek, and together they arose and looked about them. A huge block of riven granite lay in the canon, dripping blood. Their enemies were not to be seen.

"The trail is gone," said Acantow. "Manitou has broken it, that the Arapahoes may never cross it more. He would not allow them to take you. Let us thank the Manitou." So they went back to where the spring burst amid the rose-bushes.

A BATTLE IN THE AIR

In the country about Tishomingo, Indian Territory, troubles are foretold by a battle of unseen men in the air. Whenever the sound of conflict is heard it is an indication that many dead will lie in the fields, for it heralds battle, starvation, or pestilence. The powerful nation that lived here once was completely annihilated by an opposing tribe, and in the valley in the western part of the Territory there are mounds where hundreds of men lie buried. Spirits occupy the valley, and to the eyes of the red men they are still seen, at times, continuing the fight.

In May, 1892, the last demonstration was made in the hearing of John Willis, a United States marshal, who was hunting horse-thieves. He was belated one night and entered the vale of mounds, for he had no scruples against sleeping there. He had not, in fact, ever heard that the region was haunted. The snorting of his horse in the middle of the night awoke him and he sprang to his feet, thinking that savages, outlaws, or, at least, coyotes had disturbed the animal. Although there was a good moon, he could see nothing moving on the plain. Yet the sounds that filled the air were like the noise of an army, only a trifle subdued, as if they were borne on the passing of a wind. The rush of hoofs and of feet, the striking of blows, the fall of bodies could be heard, and for nearly an hour these fell rumors went across the earth. At last the horse became so frantic that Willis saddled him and rode away, and as he reached the edge of the valley the sounds were heard going into the distance. Not until he reached a settlement did he learn of the spell that rested on the place.

ON THE PACIFIC COAST

THE VOYAGER OF WHULGE

Like the ancient Greeks, the Siwash of the Northwest invest the unseen world with spiritual intelligence. Every tree has a soul; the forests were peopled with good and evil genii, the latter receiving oblation at the devil-dances, for it was not worth while to appease those already good; and the mountains are the home of tamanouses, or guardian spirits, that sometimes fight together—as, when the spirits of Mount Tacoma engaged with those of Mount Hood, fire and melted stone burst from their peaks, their bellowing was heard afar, and some of the rocks flung by Tacoma fell short, blocking the Columbia about the Dalles.

Across these fantastic reports of older time there come echoes of a later instruction, adapted and blended into native legend so that the point of division cannot be indicated. Such is that of the mysterious voyager of the Whulge—the Siwash name for the sound that takes the name of Puget from one of Vancouver's officers. Across this body of water the stranger came in a copper canoe that borrowed the glories of the morning. When he had landed and sent for all the red men, far and near, he addressed to them a doctrine that provoked expressions of contempt—a doctrine of love.

To fight and steal no more, to give of their goods to men in need, to forgive their enemies,—they could not understand such things. He promised—this radiant stranger—to those who lived right, eternal life on seas and hills more fair than these of earth, but they did not heed him. At last, wearying of his talk, they dragged him to a tree and nailed him fast to it, with pegs through his hands and feet, and jeered and danced about him, as they did about their victims in the devil-dance, until his head fell on his breast and his life went out.

A great storm, with thunderings and earthquakes! They took the body down and would have buried it, but, lo! it arose to its feet, as the sun burst forth, and resumed its preaching. Then they took the voyager's word for truth and never harmed him more, while they grew less warlike as each year went by until, of all Indians, they were most peaceable.

TAMANOUS OF TACOMA

Mount Tacoma has always been a place of superstitious regard among the Siwash (Sauvage) of the Northwest. In their myths it was the place of refuge for the last man when the Whulge was so swollen after long rain that its waters covered the earth. All other men were drowned. The waves pursued the one man as he climbed, rising higher and higher until they came to his knees, his waist, his breast. Hope was almost gone, and he felt that the next wave would launch him into the black ocean that raged about him, when one of the tamanouses of the peak, taking pity on him, turned his feet to stone. The storm ceased, and the waters fell away. The man still stood there, his feet a part of the peak, and he mourned that he could not descend to where the air was balmy and the flowers were opening. The Spirit of all Things came and bade him sleep, and, after his eyes were closed, tore out one of his ribs and changed it to a woman. When lifted out of the rock the man awoke, and, turning with delight to the woman, he led her to the seashore, and there in a forest bower they made their home. There the human race was recreated.

On the shore of the Whulge in after years lived an Indian miser—rare personage—who dried salmon and jerked the meat that he did not use, and sold it to his fellow-men for hiaqua—the wampum of the Pacific tribes. The more of this treasure he got, the more he wanted—even as if it were dollars. One day, while hunting on the slopes of Mount Tacoma, he looked along its snow-fields, climbing to the sky, and, instead of doing homage to the tamanous, or divinity of the mountain, he only sighed, "If I could only get more hiaqua!"

Sounded a voice in his ear: "Dare you go to my treasure caves?"

"I dare!" cried the miser.

The rocks and snows and woods roared back the words so quick in echoes that the noise was like that of a mountain laughing. The wind came up again to whisper the secret in the man's ear, and with an elk-horn for pick and spade he began the ascent of the peak. Next morning he had reached the crater's rim, and, hurrying down the declivity, he passed a rock shaped like a salmon, next, one in the form of a kamas-root, and presently a third in likeness of an elk's head. "'Tis a tamanous has spoken!" he exclaimed, as he looked at them.

At the foot of the elk's head he began to dig. Under the snow he came to crusts of rock that gave a hollow sound, and presently he lifted a scale of stone that covered a cavity brimful of shells more beautiful, more precious, more abundant than his wildest hopes had pictured. He plunged his arms among them to the shoulder—he laughed and fondled them, winding the strings of them about his arms and waist and neck and filling his hands. Then, heavily burdened, he started homeward.

In his eagerness to take away his treasure he made no offerings of hiaqua strings to the stone tamanouses in the crater, and hardly had he begun the descent of the mountain's western face before he began to be buffeted with winds. The angry god wrapped himself in a whirling tower of cloud and fell upon him, drawing darkness after. Hands seemed to clutch at him out of the storm: they tore at his treasure, and, in despair, he cast away a cord of it in sacrifice. The storm paused for a moment, and when it returned upon him with scream and flash and roar he parted with another. So, going down in the lulls, he reached timber just as the last handful of his wealth was wrenched from his grasp and flung upon the winds. Sick in heart and body, he fell upon a moss-heap, senseless. He awoke and arose stiffly, after a time, and resumed his journey.

In his sleep a change had come to the man. His hair was matted and reached to his knees; his joints creaked; his food supply was gone; but he picked kamas bulbs and broke his fast, and the world seemed fresh and good to him. He looked back at Tacoma and admired the splendor of its snows and the beauty of its form, and had never a care for the riches in its crater. The wood was strange to him as he descended, but at sunset he reached his wigwam, where an aged woman was cooking salmon. Wife and husband recognized each other, though he had been asleep and she a-sorrowing for years. In his joy to be at home the miser dug up all his treasure that he had secreted and gave of his wealth and wisdom to whoso needed them. Life, love, and nature were enough, he found, and he never braved the tamanous again.

THE DEVIL AND THE DALLES

In days when volcanoes were playing in the Northwest and the sternly beautiful valley of the Columbia was a hell of ash and lava, the fiend men of the land met at intervals on the heated rocks to guzzle and riot together. It was at one of these meetings in the third summer after Tacoma had stopped spouting that the devil urged a lesson from the growing peace and joy of nature, and prayed the fiend men to desist from killing and eating each other and live in love.

With a howl of rage at such a proposal they set upon him, tossing their tails in such a threatening manner that he deemed it best to be off, and as his hoofs clattered over the country his brain was busy in devising an escape. Nearing the mountain bulwarks of an inland sea, whose breakers' rhythmic roar he heard above the yells of his pursuers, a hope came into his head, and new vigor into his tail, though you might have thought the latter accession was not needed, for his tail was of prodigious length and strength. He whirled this limb aloft and beat it on the earth. A chasm opened at the stroke, and the devil skipped across to the safe side of it.

Safe? No; for the fiend men in advance took the leap and came beside him. The tormented one could thrash any two of them at once, but he was not equal to a thousand. He brandished his weapon once more and it fell with a crash. Earth shook, dust arose in clouds, and a deeper cleft than before yawned through the valley. Again the fiend men tried to reach him, and, though the gap was bigger and many fell into it, hundreds made the jump and overtook him. He must make one more attempt. The tail revolved for a third time, and with the energy of despair he flailed the ground with it.

A third ravine was split through the rock, and this time the earth's crust cracked away to the eastward, giving outlet to the sea, which came pouring through the canon, breaking rocks from mountains and grinding them to powder in its terrific progress. Gasping with fatigue, the unhappy one toiled up a hill and surveyed his work with satisfaction, for the flood engulfed the fiend men and they left no member of their race behind them.

When they had all been happily smashed or drowned, the devil skipped lightly over the channels he had cut and sought his family, though with a subdued expression of countenance, for his tail—his strength and pride—was bruised and broken beyond repair, and all the little imps that he fathered to the world afterward had little dangling tails like monkeys' instead of megatheriums', and in time these appendages disappeared. But what was the use of them? The fiend men they had fought against were dead and the rising race they could circumvent by subtler means. The inland sea drained off. Its bed is now the prairie, and the three strokes of the devil's tail are indelibly recorded in the bed of the Columbia at the Dalles. And the devil never tried to be good again.

CASCADES OF THE COLUMBIA

When the Siwash, as the Northwestern Indians called themselves, were few, Mount Hood was kept by the Spirit of Storms, who when he shook his robe caused rain or snow to fall over the land, while the Fire Spirit flashed his lightnings from Mount Adams. Across the vale between them stretched a mighty bridge of stone, joining peak to peak, and on this the Siwash laid his offering of salmon and dressed skins. Here, too, the tribal festivals were kept. The priestess of the arch-Mentonee, who fed the fire on the tribal altar "unimpassioned by a mortal throb"—had won the love of the wild tamanouses of the mountains, but she was careless alike of coaxing and threats, and her heart was as marble to them.

Jealous of each other, these two spirits fell to fighting, and, appalled by the whirl of fire and cloud, of splintering trees and crumbling rocks, the Indians fled in terror toward the lowlands, but she, unhurt and undaunted, kept in her place, and still offered praise to the one god. Yet she was not alone, for watchful in the shadow of a rock stood a warrior who had loved her so long, without the hope of lovers, that he, too, had outgrown fear. Though she had given him but passing words and never a smile, his own heart was the warmer and the heavier with its freight, and it was his way to be ever watching her in some place where she might not be troubled by the sight of him.

The war waxed fiercer, and at last the spirits met at the centre of the arch, and in roar and quake and deluge the great bridge swayed and cracked. The young man sprang forward. He seized Mentonee in his arms. There was time for one embrace that cheated death of sorrow. Then, with a thunder like a bursting world, the miles of masonry crashed down and buried the two forever. The Columbia leaps the ruins of the bridge in the rapids that they call the Cascades, and the waters still brawl on, while the sulky tamanouses watch the whitened floods from their mountain-tops, knowing that never again will they see so fair a creature as Mentonee.

THE DEATH OF UMATILLA

Umatilla, chief of the Indians at the Cascades of the Columbia, was one of the few red men of his time who favored peace with the white settlers and lent no countenance to the fierce revels of the "potlatch." In these "feasts of gifts" the savages, believing themselves to be "possessed by the spirit," lashed themselves into a frenzy that on several occasions was only quieted by the shedding of blood. Black Eagle's Feather—or Benjamin, as he was called by the settlers—was the only one of the children of the old chief who survived a summer of plague, and on this boy Umatilla had put all his hopes and affections.

The lad had formed a great trust in his white teacher, a college-bred man from the East, who had built a little school-house beside the Columbia and was teaching the Indian idea how to shoot something beside white people. This boy and his teacher had hunted together; they had journeyed in the same canoe; had tramped over the same trail to the great falls of the Missouri; and at the Giant Spring had seen the Piegans cast in their gifts, in the belief that the manitou of the place would deliver them in the hereafter to the sun-god, whom they worshipped. One day Benjamin fell ill, and the schoolmaster saw that he, too, was to die of the plague. Old Umatilla received the news with Indian stoicism, but he went into the forest to be alone for a time.

When he returned day was breaking and a flock of wild-geese trumpeted overhead. The boy heard them, and said, "Boston tilicum" (white man), "does the Great Father tell the geese where to go?"

"Yes."

"Then he will tell me, too?"

"Yes."

"We shall never go back to the Missouri together. My father—"

"We will watch over him."

"That is well." And, in a few hours, he had intrusted the guidance of his soul through the world of shadows to the white man's unseen father.

Umatilla sat beside the body through the night, and in the morning he called his people together. He told them that he was prepared to follow his boy out of the world, but that first he wanted to have their promise that they would no longer war on the whites, but look to them for friendship and guidance. There was some murmuring at this, for the ruder fellows were already plotting a descent on the settlers, but Umatilla had given them great store of goods at the last potlatch, and they reluctantly consented. The venerable chief ordered them to make a grave for Benjamin like the white man's, and, when it had been dug, four warriors laid the body of his son within it. Then, standing at the brink, the chief said, "My heart is growing cold, for it is in the grave there with my son. When I take three steps to the side of him, I, too, shall die. Be good to the white men, as you have said, and bury us both together. Great Spirit, I come." And, sinking to the ground, the old man's life ebbed in a breath. They buried him and his son in a single grave, and next day they went to the teacher and asked him to lead and instruct them. And with that year ended all trouble between red and white men along the Columbia.

HUNGER VALLEY

East of San Francisco is a narrow valley opening to the bay of San Pablo. In spite of its pleasant situation and fruitful possibilities, it had no inhabitants until 1820, when Miguel Zamacona and his wife Emilia strayed into it, while on a journey, and, being delighted with its scenery, determined to make it their home. In playful mockery of its abundance they gave to it the name El Hambre [Hunger] valley.

After some weeks of such hardship as comes to a Mexican from work, Miguel had built an adobe cabin and got a garden started, while he caught a fish or shot a deer now and then, and they got on pretty well. At last it became necessary that he should go to Yerba Buena, as San Francisco was then called, for goods. His burros were fat and strong, and there should be no danger. Emilia cried at being left behind, but the garden had to be tended, and he was to be back in exactly three weeks. She waited for twenty-two days; then, her anxiety becoming unendurable, she packed an outfit on a burro and started on the trail. From time to time she called his name, and "Miguel!" echoed sweetly from hills and groves, but there was no other answer, save when an owl would hoot. Rolled in a blanket she slept on lupin boughs, but was off at peep of day again, calling—calling—high and clear among the solitudes.

During the second day her burro gave a rasping bray, and a hee-haw answered from the bush. It was Miguel's burro. He had come at last! Leaping to her feet, in her impatience, she ran to meet him, and found him lying on the earth, staring silently at the sky. All that day she sat beside him, caressing his hand, talking, crying, bathing his face with water from the marsh—the poison marsh—and it was not until sunset that she could bring herself to admit that he was dead—had been dead for at least two days.

She put the blanket over him, weighted it with stones, and heaped reeds upon it; then she started for home. A wandering trader heard her story, but years elapsed before any other settler entered Hunger valley. They found her skeleton then in the weedy garden. The adobe stands tenantless in the new village of Martinez, and the people have so often heard that the ghosts of the Zamaconas haunt the place that they have begun to disbelieve it.

THE WRATH OF MANITOU

The county called Kern, in California, lies mostly in a circular valley, and long, long before the evil one had created the pale face it was the home of a nation advanced in arts, who worshipped the Great Spirit in a building with a lofty dome. But the bravery and wisdom of one of their own people made them forget the Manitou and idolize the man who seemed the most like him. They brought him to the temple and prayed and sang to him, and held their sacred dances there, so angering God that he rent the earth and swallowed them. Nothing was seen of this people for years after, but their stone tools were left on neighboring hill-sides. Manitou even poured water into the valley, and great creatures sported in the inland sea.

But, ere long, he repented his anger, and, in a fit of impatience at what he had done, he threw up quantities of earth that smoked with heat, and thus created the Sierra Nevada, while he broke away the hills at the foot of the lake, and the waters drained into the sea at the Golden Gate. This again made dry land of the valley, and, opening the earth once more, he released the captive tribe. The imprisoned people had not forgotten their arts nor their boldness; they made the place blossom again; they conquered other tribes, and Manitou declared them his chosen ones, from whom alone he would accept sacrifice. But their chief became so ambitious that he wanted to supplant the Manitou in the worship of the people, and finally, in a lunacy of self-conceit, he challenged the god to single combat.

Under pretence of accepting the challenge, the Great Spirit set the offenders to wander through the desert until they reached a valley in the Sierras, opposite Tehachapi, where he caused them to be exterminated by a horde of savages from the Mojave desert. Then, in a fit of disgust at refractory humanity, he evoked a whirlwind and stripped away every living thing from the country of the savages, declaring that it should be empty of human beings from that time forward. And it was so.

THE SPOOK OF MISERY HILL

Tom Bowers, who mined on Misery Hill, near Pike City, California, never had a partner, and he never took kindly to the rough crowd about the place. One day he was missing. They traced his steps through the snow from his cabin to the brink of a great slope where he had been prospecting, but there they vanished, for a landslide had blotted them out. His body was exhumed far below and decently buried, yet it was said that it was so often seen walking about the mouth of his old shaft that other men avoided the spot.

Thriftless Jim Brandon, in a spasm of industry, began work on the abandoned mine, and for a while he made it pay, for he got money and squared accounts with his creditors; but after a time it appeared that somebody else was working on the claim, for every morning he found that the sluice had been tampered with and the water turned on. He searched for the trespasser in vain, and told "the boys" that if they called that joking it had grown tiresome.

One night he loaded his rifle, and, from a convenient nook, he watched for the intruder. The tamaracks crooned in the wind, the Yuba mumbled in the canon, the Sierras lay in a line of white against the stars. As he crept along to a point of better vantage he came to a tree with something tacked on it—something that shone in the dark like a match. In its own light he read, "Notice! I, Thomas Bowers, claim this ground for placer mining." Raising his hand to tear off the paper, he was amazed to feel a thrill pass through it, and his arm fell palsied at his side. But the notice was gone.

Now came the sound of water flowing, and, as he angrily caught his gun and turned toward the sluice, the letters shone again in phosphorescence on the tree. There was the sound of a pick in the gravel now, and, crawling stealthily towards the sluice, he saw, at work there, Tom Bowers—dead, lank, his head and face covered with white hair, his eyes glowing from black sockets. Half unconsciously Jim brought his rifle to his shoulder and fired. A yell followed the report, then the dead man came running at him like the wind, with pick and shovel in either hand.

Away went Brandon, and the spectre followed, up hill, in and out of woods, over ditches, through scrub, on toward Pike City. The miners were celebrating a new find with liberal potations and a dance in the saloon when, high above the crash of boots, the shouted jokes, the laughter, and the clink of glasses, came a sound of falling, a scream-then silence. They hurried into the road. There lay Brandon's rifle, and a pick and shovel with "T. B." cut in the handles. Jim returned no more, and the sluice is running every night on Misery Hill.

THE QUEEN OF DEATH VALLEY

In the southern part of California, near the Arizona line, is the famous Death Valley—a tract of arid, alkaline plain hemmed in by steep mountains and lying below the level of the sea. For years it was believed that no human being could cross that desert and live, for horses sink to their knees in drifts of soda dust; there is no water, though the traveller requires much drink; and the heat is terrific. Animals that die in the neighborhood mummify, but do not decay, and it is surmised that the remains of many a thoughtless or ignorant prospector lie bleached in the plain. On the east side of Dead Mountain are points of whitened rock that at a distance look like sheeted figures, and these, the Indians say, are the ghosts of their brethren.

In the heart of this desert is said to be the ruin of a pueblo, or village, though the shape and size of it suggest that it was made for a few persons rather than for a tribe or family. Long ago, the tale runs, this place of horrors was a fair and fertile kingdom, ruled by a beautiful but capricious queen. She ordered her subjects to build her a mansion that should surpass those of her neighbors, the Aztecs, and they worked for years to make one worthy of her, dragging the stones and timbers for miles. Fearing lest age, accident, or illness should forbid her to see the ending of her dream, she ordered so many of her subjects to assist that her tribe was reduced to practical slavery.

In her haste and heartlessness she commanded her own daughter to join the bearers of burdens, and when the toilers flagged in step in the noonday heat she strode among them and lashed their naked backs. As royalty was sacred, they did not complain, but when she struck her daughter the girl turned, threw down her load of stone, and solemnly cursed her mother and her kingdom; then, overcome by heat and weariness, she sank to the earth and died. Vain the regrets and lamentations of the queen. The sun came out with blinding heat and light, vegetation withered, animals disappeared, streams and wells dried up, and at last the wretched woman gave up her life on a bed of fever, with no hand to soothe her dying moments, for her people, too, were dead. The palace, half-completed, stands in the midst of this desolation, and sometimes it seems to lift into view of those at a distance in the shifting mirage that plays along the horizon.

BRIDAL VEIL FALL

The vast ravine of Yo Semite (Grizzly Bear), formed by tearing apart the solid Sierras, is graced by many water-falls raining down the mile-high cliffs. The one called Bridal Veil has this tale attached to it. Centuries ago, in the shelter of this valley, lived Tutokanula and his tribe—a good hunter, he, a thoughtful saver of crops and game for winter, a wise chief, trusted and loved by his people. While hunting, one day, the tutelary spirit of the valley—the lovely Tisayac—revealed herself to him, and from that moment he knew no peace, nor did he care for the well-being of his people; for she was not as they were: her skin was white, her hair was golden, and her eyes like heaven; her speech was as a thrush-song and led him to her, but when he opened his arms she rose lighter than any bird and vanished in the sky.

Lacking his direction Yo Semite became a desert, and when Tisayac returned she wept to see the corn lands grown with bushes and bears rooting where the huts had been. On a mighty dome of rock she knelt and begged the Great Spirit to restore its virtue to the land. He did so, for, stooping from the sky, he spread new life of green on all the valley floor, and smiting the mountains he broke a channel for the pent-up meltings of the snows, and the water ran and leaped far down, pooling in a lake below and flowing off to gladden other land. The birds returned, the flowers sprang up, corn swayed in the breeze, and the people, coming back, gave the name of Tisayac to South Dome, where she had knelt.

Then came the chief home again, and, hearing that the spirit had appeared, was smitten with love more strong than ever. Climbing to the crest of a rock that spires three thousand feet above the valley, he carved his likeness there with his hunting-knife, so that his memory might live among his tribe. As he sat, tired with his work, at the foot of the Bridal Veil, he saw, with a rainbow arching around her, the form of Tisayac shining from the water. She smiled on him and beckoned. His quest was at an end. With a cry of joy he sprang into the fall and disappeared with Tisayac. Two rainbows quivered on the falling water, and the sun went down.

THE GOVERNOR'S RIGHT EYE

Old Governor Hermenegildo Salvatierra, of Presidio, California, sported only one eye—the left—because the other had been shot out by an Indian arrow. With his sound one he was gazing into the fire, on a windy afternoon in the rainy season, when a chunky man in a sou'wester was ushered into his presence, and after announcing that he was no other than Captain Peleg Scudder, of the schooner General Court, from Salem, he was made welcome in a manner quite out of proportion in its warmth to the importance that such a disclosure would have for the every-day citizen.

He was hailed with wassail and even with wine. The joy of the commandant was so great that at the third bowl he sang a love ballad, in a voice somewhat cracked, and got on the table to teach the Yankee how to dance the cachuca. The law forbade any extended stay of Americans in Spanish waters, and the General Court took herself off that very night—for this, mind you, was in 1797, when the Spaniard ruled the farther coast.

Next day Salvatierra appeared before his astonished people with a right eye. The priests attached to the fort gave a special service of praise, and told the miracle to the red men of their neighborhood as an illustration of the effect of goodness, prayer, and faith. People came from far and near that they might go to church and see this marvel for themselves. But, alas, for the governor's repute for piety! It soon began to be whispered around that the new eye was an evil one; that it read the deepest thoughts of men with its inflexible, cold stare; that under its influence some of the fathers had been betrayed into confessing things that the commandant had never supposed a clergyman to be guilty of. The people feared that eye, and ascribed such rogueries to the old man as had been entirely foreign to his nature hitherto.

This common fear and suspicion reacted, inevitably, and Salvatierra began, unconsciously, to exhibit some of the traits that his subjects said he possessed. He changed slowly from the indulgent parent to the stern and exacting law-giver. He did not know, however, what the people had been saying about him, and never suspected that his eye was likely to get him into trouble.

It was a warm night and he had gone to bed with his windows open—windows that opened from his garden, and were level, at the bottom, with the floor. A shadowy form stole along the gravel path and entered one of these windows. It was that of a mission Indian. He had gathered from the talk of the faithful that it would be a service to the deity as well as to men to destroy the power of that evil eye. He came beside the bed and looked attentively at the governor, sleeping there in the light of a candle. Then he howled with fright—howled so loudly that the old man sprang to his feet—for while the left eye had been fast asleep the evil one was broad awake and looking at him with a ghostly glare.

In another second the commandant was at the window whirling his trusty Toledo about his head, lopping ears and noses from the red renegades who had followed in the track of the first. In the scrimmage he received another jab in the right eye with a fist. When day dawned it was discovered, with joy, that the evil eye was darkened—and forever. The people trusted him once more. Finding that he was no longer an object of dread, his voice became kinder, his manner more gentle. A heavy and unusual rain, that had been falling, passed off that very day, so that the destruction from flood, which had been prophesied at the missions, was stayed, and the clergy sang "Te Deum" in the church. The old commandant never, to his dying day, had the heart to confess that the evil eye was only a glass one.

THE PRISONER IN AMERICAN SHAFT

An Indian seldom forgets an injury or omits to revenge it, be it a real or a fancied one. A young native of the New Almaden district, in California, fell in love with a girl of the same race, and supposed that he was prospering in his suit, for he was ardent and the girl was, seemingly, not averse to him; but suddenly she became cold, avoided him, and answered his greetings, if they met, in single words. He affected to care not greatly for this change, but he took no rest until he had discovered the cause of it. Her parents had conceived a dislike to him that later events proved to be well founded, and had ordered or persuaded her to deny his suit.

His retaliation was prompt and Indian-like. He killed the father and mother at the first opportunity, seized the girl when she was at a distance from the village, and carried her to the deserted quicksilver mine near Spanish Camp. In a tunnel that branched from American Shaft he had fashioned a rude cell of stone and wood, and into that he forced and fastened her. He had stocked it with water and provisions, and for some weeks he held the wretched girl a captive in total darkness, visiting her whenever he felt moved to do so until, his passion sated, he resolved to leave the country.

As an act of partial atonement for the wrong he had done, he hung a leather coat at the mouth of the tunnel, on which, in picture writing, he indicated the whereabouts of the girl. Search parties had been out from the time of her disappearance, and one of them chanced on this clue and rescued her as she was on the point of death. The savage who had exacted so brutal and excessive a revenge fled afar, and his whereabouts were never known.

AS TO BURIED RICHES

KIDD'S TREASURE

Captain Kidd is the most ubiquitous gentleman in history. If his earnings in the gentle craft of piracy were frugally husbanded, he has possibly left some pots of money in holes in the ground between Key West and Halifax. The belief that large deposits of gold were made at Gardiner's Island, Dunderberg, Cro' Nest, New York City, Coney Island, Ipswich, the marshes back of Boston, Cape Cod, Nantucket, Isles of Shoals, Money Island, Ocean Beach, the Bahamas, the Florida Keys, and elsewhere has caused reckless expenditure of actual wealth in recovering doubloons and guineas that disappointed backers of these enterprises are beginning to look upon—no, not to look upon, but to think about—as visionary. A hope of getting something for nothing has been the impetus to these industries, and interest in the subject is now and then revived by reports of the discovery—usually by a farmer ploughing near the shore—of an iron kettle with a handful of gold and silver coins in it, the same having doubtless been buried for purposes of concealment during the wars of 1776 and 1812.

Gardiner's Island, a famous rendezvous for pirates, is the only place known to have been used as a bank of deposit, for in 1699 the Earl of Bellomont recovered from it seven hundred and eighty-three ounces of gold, six hundred and thirty-three ounces of silver, cloth of gold, silks, satins, and jewels. In the old Gardiner mansion, on this island, was formerly preserved a costly shawl given to Mrs. Gardiner by Captain Kidd himself. This illustrious Kidd—or Kydd—was born in New York, began his naval career as a chaser of pirates, became a robber himself, was captured in Boston, where he was ruffling boldly about the streets, and was hanged in London in 1701. In sea superstitions the apparition of his ship is sometimes confused with that of the Flying Dutchman.

At Lion's Rock, near Lyme, Connecticut, a part of his treasure is under guard of a demon that springs upon intruders unless they recite Scripture while digging for the money.

Charles Island, near Milford, Connecticut, was dug into, one night, by a company from that town that had learned of Kidd's visit to it—and what could Kidd be doing ashore unless he was burying money? The lid of an iron chest had been uncovered when the figure of a headless man came bounding out of the air, and the work was discontinued right then. The figure leaped into the pit that had been dug, and blue flames poured out of it. When the diggers returned, their spades and picks were gone and the ground was smooth.

Monhegan Island, off the Maine coast, contains a cave, opening to the sea, where it was whispered that treasure had been stored in care of spirits. Searchers found within it a heavy chest, which they were about to lift when one of the party—contrary to orders—spoke. The spell was broken, for the watchful spirits heard and snatched away the treasure. Some years ago the cave was enlarged by blasting, in a hope of finding that chest, for an old saying has been handed down among the people of the island—from whom it came they have forgotten—that was to this effect: "Dig six feet and you will find iron; dig six more and you will find money."

On Damariscotta Island, near Kennebec, Maine, is a lake of salt water, which, like dozens of shallow ones in this country, is locally reputed to be bottomless. Yet Kidd was believed to have sunk some of his valuables there, and to have guarded against the entrance of boats by means of a chain hung from rock to rock at the narrow entrance, bolts on either side showing the points of attachment, while ring bolts were thought to have been driven for the purpose of tying buoys, thus marking the spots where the chests went down. This island, too, has been held in fear as haunted ground.

Appledore, in the Isles of Shoals, was another such a hiding-place, and Kidd put one of his crew to death that he might haunt the place and frighten searchers from their quest. For years no fisherman could be induced to land there after nightfall, for did not an islander once encounter "Old Bab" on his rounds, with a red ring around his neck, a frock hanging about him, phosphorescence gleaming from his body, who peered at the intruder with a white and dreadful face, and nearly scared him to death?

A spot near the Piscataqua River was another hiding-place, and early in this century the ground was dug over, two of the seekers plying pick and spade, while another stood within the circle they had drawn about the spot and loudly read the Bible. Presently their implements clicked on an iron chest, but it slid sideway into the ground as they tried to uncover it, and at last an interruption occurred that caused them to stop work so long that when they went to look for it again it had entirely disappeared. This diversion was the appearance of a monster horse that flew toward them from a distance without a sound, but stopped short at the circle where the process of banning fiends was still going on, and, after grazing and walking around them for a time, it dissolved into air.

Kidd's plug is a part of the craggy steep known as Cro' Nest, on the Hudson. It is a projecting knob, like a bung closing an orifice, which is believed to conceal a cavern where the redoubtable captain placed a few barrels of his wealth. Though it is two hundred feet up the cliff, inaccessible either from above or below, and weighs many tons, still, as pirates and devils have always been friendly, it may be that the corking of the cave was accomplished with supernatural help, and that if blasts or prayers ever shake the stone from its place a shower of doubloons and diamonds may come rattling after it.

The shore for several hundred feet around Dighton Rock, Massachusetts, has been examined, for it was once believed that the inscriptions on it were cut by Kidd to mark the place of burial for part of his hoard.

The Rock Hill estate, Medford, Massachusetts, was plagued by a spectre that some thought to be that of a New Hampshire farmer who was robbed and murdered there, but others say it is the shade of Kidd, for iron treasure chests were found in the cellar that behaved like that on the Piscataqua River, sinking out of sight whenever they were touched by shovels.

Misery Islands, near Salem, Massachusetts, were dug over, and under spiritual guidance, too, for other instalments of Mr. Kidd's acquisitions, but without avail.

It takes no less than half a dozen ghosts to guard what is hidden in Money Hill, on Shark River, New Jersey, so there must be a good deal of it. Some of these guardians are in sailor togs, some in their mouldy bones, some peaceable, some noisy with threats and screams and groans—a "rum lot," as an ancient mariner remarked, who lives near their graves and daytime hiding-places. Many heirlooms are owned by Jerseymen hereabout that were received from Kidd's sailors in exchange for apple-jack and provisions, and two sailor-looking men are alleged to have taken a strong-box out of Money Hill some years ago, from which they abstracted two bags of gold. After that event the hill was dug over with great earnestness, but without other result to the prospectors than the cultivation of their patience.

Sandy Hook, New Jersey, near "Kidd's tree," and the clay banks of the Atlantic highlands back of that point, are suspected hiding-places; but the cairn or knoll called Old Woman's Hill, at the highlands, is not haunted by Kidd's men, as used to be said, but by the spirit of a discontented squaw. This spirit the Indians themselves drove away with stones.

At Oyster Point, Maryland, lived Paddy Dabney, who recognized Kidd from an old portrait on meeting him one evening in 1836. He was going home late from the tavern when a light in a pine thicket caused him to turn from the road. In a clearing among the trees, pervaded by a pale shine which seemed to emanate from its occupants, a strange company was playing at bowls. A fierce-looking reprobate who was superintending the game glanced up, and, seeing Paddy's pale face, gave such a leap in his direction that the Irishman fled with a howl of terror and never stopped till he reached his door, when, on turning about, he found that the phantom of the pirate chief had vanished. The others, he conceived, were devils, for many a sea rover had sold himself to Satan. Captain Teach, or Blackbeard, proved as much to his crew by shutting himself in the hold of his ship, where he was burning sulphur to destroy rats, and withstanding suffocation for several hours; while one day a dark man appeared on board who was not one of the crew at the sailing, and who had gone as mysteriously as he came on the day before the ship was wrecked. It was known that Kidd had buried his Bible in order to ingratiate the evil one.

A flat rock on the north shore of Liberty Island, in New York harbor, was also thought to mark the place of this pervasive wealth of the pirates. As late as 1830, Sergeant Gibbs, one of the garrison at the island, tried to unearth it, with the aid of a fortune-teller and a recruit, but they had no sooner reached a box about four feet in length than a being with wings, horns, tail, and a breath, the latter palpable in blue flames, burst from the coffer. Gibbs fell unconscious into the water and narrowly escaped drowning, while his companions ran away, and the treasure may still be there for aught we know.

Back in the days before the Revolution, a negro called Mud Sam, who lived in a cabin at the Battery, New York City, was benighted at about the place where One Hundredth Street now touches East River while waiting there for the tide to take him up the Sound. He beguiled the time by a nap, and, on waking, he started to leave his sleeping place under the trees to regain his boat, when the gleam of a lantern and the sound of voices coming up the bank caused him to shrink back into the shadow. At first he thought that he might be dreaming, for Hell Gate was a place of such repute that one might readily have bad dreams there, and the legends of the spot passed quickly through his mind: the skeletons that lived in the wreck on Hen and Chickens and looked out at passing ships with blue lights in the eye-sockets of their skulls; the brown fellow, known as "the pirate's spuke," that used to cruise up and down the wrathful torrent, and was snuffed out of sight for some hours by old Peter Stuyvesant with a silver bullet; a black-looking scoundrel with a split lip, who used to brattle about the tavern at

Corlaer's Hook, and who tumbled into East River while trying to lug an iron chest aboard of a suspicious craft that had stolen in to shore in a fog. This latter bogy was often seen riding up Hell Gate a-straddle of that very chest, snapping his fingers at the stars and roaring Bacchanalian odes, just as skipper Onderdonk's boatswain, who had been buried at sea without prayers, chased the ship for days, sitting on the waves, with his shroud for a sail, and shoving hills of water after the vessel with the plash of his hands.

These grewsome memories sent a quake through Mud Sam's heart, but when the bushes cracked under the strangers' tread, he knew that they were of flesh and bone, and, following them for a quarter-mile into the wood, he saw them dig a hole, plant a strong-box there, and cover it. A threatening remark from one of the company forced an exclamation from the negro that drew a pistol-shot upon him, and he took to his heels. Such a fright did he receive that he could not for several years be persuaded to return, but when that persuasion came in the form of a promise of wealth from Wolfert Webber, a cabbage-grower of the town, and promises of protection from Dr. Knipperhausen, who was skilled in incantations, he was not proof against it, and guided the seekers to the spot.

After the doctor had performed the proper ceremonies they fell to work, but no sooner had their spades touched the lid of an iron-bound chest than a sturdy rogue with a red flannel cap leaped out of the bushes. They said afterward that he had the face of the brawler who was drowned at Corlaer's Hook, but, in truth, they hardly looked at him in their flight; nor, when the place was revisited, could any mark of digging be found, nor any trace of treasure, so that part of Kidd's wealth may be at this moment snugly stowed in the cellar of a tenement. Webber had engaged in so many crazy enterprises of this nature that he had neglected cabbage culture, and had grown so poor that the last disappointment nearly broke his heart. He retired to his chamber and made his will, but on learning that a new street had been run across his farm and that it would presently be worth ten times as much for building-lots as it ever had been for cabbages, he leaped out of bed, dressed himself, and prospered for many a day after.

OTHER BURIED WEALTH

The wealth of the Astors hardly exceeds the treasure that is supposed to be secreted here and there about the country, and thousands of dollars have been expended in dredging rivers and shallow seas, and in blasting caves and cellars. Certain promoters of these schemes have enjoyed salaries as officers in the stock companies organized for their furtherance, and they have seen the only tangible results from such enterprises.

One summer evening, in the middle of the seventeenth century, a bark dropped anchor at the mouth of Saugus River, Massachusetts, and four of the crew rowed to the woods that skirt its banks and made a landing. The vessel had disappeared on the following morning, but in the forge at the settlement was found a paper stating that if a certain number of shackles and handcuffs were made and secretly deposited at a specified place in the forest, a sum of money equal to their value would be found in their stead on the next day. The order was filled and the silver was found, as promised, but, though a watch was set, nothing further was seen of men or ship for several months.

The four men did return, however, and lived by themselves amid the woods of Saugus, the gossips reporting that a beautiful woman had been seen in their company—the mistress of the pirate chief, for, of course, the mysterious quartette had followed the trade of robbery on the high seas. Three of these men were captured, taken to England, and hanged, but the fourth-Thomas Veale—escaped to a cavern in the wood, where, it was reputed, great treasures were concealed, and there he lived until the earthquake of 1658, when a rock fell from the roof of the cave, closing the entrance and burying the guilty man in a tomb where, it is presumed, he perished of thirst and hunger. Dungeon Rock, of Lynn, is the name that the place has borne ever since.

In 1852 Hiram Marble announced that he had been visited by spirits, who not only told him that the pirates' spoils were still in their olden hiding-place, but pointed out the spot where the work of excavation should begin. Aided by his son he tunnelled the solid granite for a distance of one hundred and thirty-five feet, the passage being seven feet high and seven wide. Whenever he was wearied the "mediums" that he consulted would tell him to make cuttings to the right or left, and for every fresh discouragement they found fresh work. For thirty years this task was carried on, both father and son dying without gaining any practical result, other than the discovery of an ancient scabbard in a rift. The heiress of the house of Marble alone reaped benefit from their labors, for-resuming on a petty scale the levies of the first dwellers in the rock—she boldly placarded the entrance to the workings "Ye who enter here leave twenty-five cents behind."

In several cases the chasms that have been caused by wear of water or convulsions of nature (their opposite sides being matched) were believed to have been hiding-places, but, in the old days in New England, it was believed that all such fractures were caused by the earthquake at the time of the crucifixion—a testimony of the power of God to shake sinners.

The Heart of Greylock is the name given to the crater-like recess, a thousand feet deep, in the tallest of the Berkshire peaks, but it was formerly best known as Money Hole, and the stream that courses through it as Money Brook, for a gang of counterfeiters worked in that recess, and there some spurious coinage may still be concealed. The stream is also known as Spectre Brook, for late wandering hunters and scouting soldiers, seeing the forgers moving to and fro about their furnaces, took them for ghosts.

Province Island, in Lake Memphremagog, Vermont, is believed to contain some of the profits of an extensive smuggling enterprise that was carried on near the lake for several years.

A little company of Spanish adventurers passed along the base of the Green Mountains early in the last century, expecting to return after having some dealings with the trading stations on the St. Lawrence; so they deposited a part of their gold on Ludlow Mountain, Vermont, and another pot of it on Camel's Hump. They agreed that none should return without his companions, but they were detained in the north and separated, some of them going home to Spain. Late in life the sole survivor of the company went to Camel's Hump and tried to recall where the treasure had been hidden, but in vain.

While flying from the people whose declaration of independence had already been written in the blood of the king's troops at Concord, the royal governor—Wentworth—was embarrassed by a wife and a treasure-chest. He had left his mansion, at Smith's Pond, New Hampshire, and was making toward Portsmouth, where he was to enjoy the protection of the British fleet, but the country was up in arms, time was important, and as his wearied horses could not go on without a lightening of the burden, he was forced to leave behind either Lady Wentworth or his other riches. As the lady properly objected to any risk of her own safety, the chest was buried at an unknown spot in the forest, and for a century and more the whereabouts of the Wentworth plate and money-bags have been a matter of search and conjecture.

When the Hessian troops marched from Saratoga to Boston, to take ship after Burgoyne's surrender, they were in wretched condition-war-worn, ragged, and ill fed,—and having much with them in the form of plate and jewels that had been spared by their conquerors, together with some of the money sent from England for their hire, they were in constant fear of attack from the farmers, who, though they had been beaten, continued to regard them with an unfavorable eye. On reaching Dalton, Massachusetts, the Hessians agreed among themselves to put their valuables into a howitzer, which they buried in the woods, intending that some of their number should come back at the close of the war and recover it. An Indian had silently followed them for a long distance, to gather up any unconsidered trifles that might be left in their bivouacs, and he marked the route by blazes on the trees; but if he saw the burial of this novel treasury it meant nothing to him, and the knowledge of the hiding-place was lost. For years the populace kept watch of all strangers that came to town, and shadowed them if they went to the woods, but without result. In about the year 1800 the supposed hiding-place was examined closely and excavations were made, but, as before, nothing rewarded the search.

A tree of unknown age—the Old Elm—stood on Boston Common until within a few years. This veteran, torn and broken by many a gale and lightning-stroke, was a gallows in the last century, and Goody Glover had swung from it in witch-times. On tempestuous nights, when the boughs creaked together, it was said that dark shapes might be seen writhing on the branches and capering about the sward below in hellish glee. On a gusty autumn evening in 1776 a muffled form presented itself, unannounced, at the chamber of Mike Wild, and, after that notorious miser had enough recovered from the fear created by the presence to understand what it said to him, he realized that it was telling him of something that in life it had buried at the foot of the Old Elm. After much hesitancy Mike set forth with his ghostly guide, for he would have risked his soul for money, but on arriving at his destination he was startled to find himself alone. Nothing daunted, he set down his lantern and began to dig. Though he turned up many a rood of soil and sounded with his spade for bags and chests of gold, he found nothing. Strange noises overhead—for the wind was high and the twigs seemed to snicker eerily as they crossed each other-sent thrills along his back from time to time, and he was about to return, half in anger, half in fear, when his spirit visitor emerged from behind the tree and stood before him. The mien was threatening, the nose had reddened and extended, the hair was rumpled, and the brow was scowling. The frown of the gold monster grew more awful, the stare of his eye in the starlight more unbearable, and he was crouching and creeping as if for a spring. Mike could endure no more. He fainted, and awakened in the morning in his own chamber, where, to a neighbor who made an early call, he told—with embellishments—the story of the encounter; but before he had come to the end of the narrative the visitor burst into a roar of laughter and confessed that he had personated the supernatural visitant, having wagered a dozen bottles of wine with the landlord of the Boar's Head that he could get the better of Mike Wild. For all this the old tree bore, for many years, an evil reputation.

A Spanish galleon, the Saints Joseph and Helena, making from Havana to Cadiz in 1753 was carried from her course by adverse winds and tossed against a reef, near New London, Connecticut, receiving injuries that compelled her to run into that port for repairs. To reach her broken ribs more easily her freight was put on shore in charge of the collector of the port, but when it was desired to ship the cargo again, behold! the quarter part of it had disappeared, none could say how. New London got a bad name from this robbery, and the governor, though besought by the assembly to make good the shortage, failed to do so, and lost his place at the next election. It was reputed that some of the treasure was buried on the shore by the robbers. In 1827 a woman who was understood to have the power of seership published a vision to a couple of young blades, who had paid for it, to the effect that hidden under one of the grass-grown wharves was a box of dollars. By the aid of a crystal pebble she received this really valuable information, but the pebble was not clear enough to reveal the exact place of the box. She could see, however, that the dollars were packed edgewise. When New London was sound asleep the young men stole out and by lantern-light began their work. They had dug to water-level when they reached an iron chest, and they stooped to lift it-but, to their amazement, the iron was too hot to handle! Now they heard deep growls, and a giant dog peered at them from the pit-mouth; red eyes flashed at them from the darkness; a wild-goose, with eyes of blazing green, hovered and screamed above them. Though the witch had promised them safety, nothing appeared to ward off the fantastic shapes that began to crowd about them. Too terrified to work longer they sprang out and made away, and when-taking courage from the sunshine— they renewed the search, next day, the iron chest had vanished.

On Crown Point, Lake Champlain, is the ruin of a fort erected by Lord Amherst above the site of a French work that had been thrown up in 1731 to guard a now vanished capital of fifteen hundred people. It was declared that when the French evacuated the region they buried money and bullion in a well, in the northwest corner of the bastion, ninety feet deep, in the full expectancy of regaining it, and half a century ago this belief had grown to such proportions that fifty men undertook to clear the well, pushing their investigations into various parts of the enclosure and over surrounding fields. They found quantities of lead and iron and no gold.

Follingsby's Pond, in the Adirondacks, was named for a recluse, who, in the early part of this century, occupied a lonely but strongly guarded cabin there. It was believed afterward that he was an English army officer, of noble birth, who had left his own country in disgust at having discovered an attachment between his wife and one of his fellow-officers. He died in a fever, and while raving in a delirium spoke of a concealed chest. A trapper, who was his only attendant in his last moments, dug over the ground floor of the hut and found a box containing a jewelled sword, costly trinkets, and letters that bore out the presumption of Follingsby's aristocratic origin. What became of these valuables after their exhumation is not known, and the existence of more has been suspected.

Coney Island is declared to have been used by a band of pirates as the first national sand bank, and, as these rascals were caught and swung off with short shrift, they do say that the plunder is still to be had—by the man who finds it. But the hotel-keepers and three-card-monte men are not waiting for that discovery to grow rich.

In Shandaken Valley, in the Catskills, it was affirmed that a party of British officers buried money somewhere, when they were beset by the farmers and hunters of that region, and never got it out of the earth again.

On Tea Island, Lake George, the buried treasures of Lord Abercrombie have remained successfully hidden until this day.

The oldest house at Fort Neck, Long Island, was known for years as the haunted house, and the grave of its owner—Captain Jones—was called the pirate's grave, for, in the last century, Jones was accused of piracy and smuggling, and there have been those who suspected worse. A hope of finding gold and silver about the premises has been yearly growing fainter. Just before the death of Jones, which occurred here in an orderly manner, a crow, so big that everybody believed it to be a demon, flew in at the window and hovered over the bed of the dying man until he had drawn his last breath, when, with a triumphant cry, it flew through the west end of the house. The hole that it broke through the masonry could never be stopped, for, no matter how often it was repaired, the stone and cement fell out again, and the wind came through with such a chill and such shriekings that the house had to be abandoned.

The owner of an estate on Lloyd's Neck, Long Island, had more wealth than he thought it was safe or easy to transport when he found the colonies rising against Britain in 1775, and flight was imperative, for he was known by his neighbors to be a Tory. Massing his plate, coin, and other movables into three barrels, he caused his three slaves to bury them in pits that they had dug beneath his house. Then, as they were shovelling back the earth, he shot them dead, all three, and buried them, one on each barrel. His motive for the crime may have been a fear that the slaves would aid the Americans in the approaching struggle, or that they might return and dig up the wealth or reveal the hiding-place to the enemies of the king. Then he made his escape to Nova Scotia, though he might as well have stayed at home, for the British possessed themselves of Long Island, and his house became a place of resort for red-coats and loyalists. It was after the turn of the century when a boat put in, one evening, at Cold Spring Bay, and next morning the inhabitants found footprints leading to and from a spot where some children had discovered a knotted rope projecting from the soil. Something had been removed, for the mould of a large box was visible at the bottom of a pit. Acres of the neighborhood were then dug over by treasure hunters, who found a box of cob dollars and a number of casks. The contents of the latter, though rich and old, were not solid, and when diffused through the systems of several Long Islanders imparted to them a spirituous and patriotic glow—for in thus destroying the secreted stores of a royalist were they not asserting the triumph of democratic principles?

The clay bluffs at Pottery Beach, Brooklyn, were pierced with artificial caves where lawless men found shelter in the unsettled first years of the republic. A wreck lay rotting here for many years, and it was said to be the skeleton of a ship that these fellows had beached by false beacons. She had costly freight aboard, and on the morning after she went ashore crew and freight had vanished. It was believed that much of the plunder was buried in the clay near the water's edge. In the early colonial days, Grand Island, in Niagara River, was the home of a Frenchman, Clairieux, an exile or refugee who was attended by a negro servant. During one summer a sloop visited the island frequently, laden on each trip with chests that never were taken away in the sight of men, and that are now supposed to be buried near the site of the Frenchman's cabin. Report had it that these boxes were filled with money, but if well or ill procured none could say, unless it were the Frenchman, and he had no remarks to offer on the subject. In the fall, after these visits of the sloop, Clairieux disappeared, and when some hunters landed on the island they found that his cabin had been burned and that a large skeleton, evidently that of the negro, was chained to the earth in the centre of the place where the house had stood. The slave had been killed, it was surmised, that his spirit might watch the hoard and drive away intruders; but the Frenchman met his fate elsewhere, and his secret, like that of many another miser, perished with him. In 1888, when a northeast gale had blown back the water of the river, a farmer living on the island discovered, just under the surface, a stone foundation built in circular form, as if it had once supported a tower. In the mud within this circle he found a number of French gold and silver coins, one of them minted in 1537. Close by, other coins of later date were found, and a systematic examination of the whole channel has been proposed, as it was also said that two French frigates, scuttled to keep them out of the hands of the English, lie bedded in sand below the island, one of them with a naval paymaster's chest on board.

On the shore of Oneida Lake is an Indian's grave, where a ball of light is wont to swing and dance. A farmer named Belknap dreamed several times of a buried treasure at this point, and he was told, in his vision, that if he would dig there at midnight he could make it his own. He made the attempt, and his pick struck a crock that gave a chink, as of gold. He should, at that moment, have turned around three times, as his dream directed, but he was so excited that he forgot to. A flash of lightning rent the air and stretched him senseless on the grass. When he recovered the crock was gone, the hole filled in, and ever since then the light has hovered about the place. Some say that this is but the will-o'-the-wisp: the soul of a bad fellow who is doomed to wander in desolate regions because, after dying, Peter would not allow him to enter heaven, and the devil would not let him go into the other place, lest he should make the little devils unmanageable; but he is allowed to carry a light in his wanderings.

In Indian Gap, near Wernersville, Pennsylvania, the Doane band of Tories and terrorists hid a chest of gold, the proceeds of many robberies. It is guarded by witches, and, although it has been seen, no one has been able to lay hands on it. The seekers are always blinded by blue flame, and frightened away by roaring noises. The Dutch farmers of the vicinity are going to dig for it, all the same, for it is said that the watch of evil spirits will be given over at midnight, but they do not know of what date. They will be on hand at the spot revealed to them through the vision of a "hex layer" (a vision that cost them fifty cents), until the night arrives when there are no blue flames.

In the southern part of Chester County, Pennsylvania, is money, too, but just where nobody knows. A lonely, crabbed man, who died there in a poor hut after the Revolution, owned that he had served the British as a spy, but said that he had spent none of the gold that he had taken from them. He was either too sorry for his deeds, or too mean to do so. He had put it in a crock and buried it, and, on his death-bed, where he made his statement, he asked that it might be exhumed and spent for some good purpose. He was about to tell where it was when the death-rattle choked his words.

The Isle of the Yellow Sands, in Lake Superior, was supposed by Indians to be made of the dust of gold, but it was protected by vultures that beat back those who approached, or tore them to pieces if they insisted on landing. An Indian girl who stole away from her camp to procure a quantity of this treasure was pursued by her lover, who, frightened at the risk she was about to run from the vultures, stopped her flight by staving in the side of her canoe, so that she was compelled to take refuge in his, and he rowed home with her before the birds had come to the attack.

Old Francois Fontenoy, an Indian trader, buried a brass kettle full of gold at Presque Isle, near Detroit, that is still in the earth.

On the banks of the Cumberland, in Tennessee, is a height where a searcher for gold was seized by invisible defenders and hurled to the bottom of the cliff, receiving a mortal hurt.

The Spaniards were said to have entombed three hundred thousand dollars in gold near Natchez. A man to whom the secret had descended offered to reveal it, but, as he was a prisoner, his offer was laughed at. Afterward an empty vault was found where he said it would be. Somebody had accidentally opened it and had removed the treasure.

Caverns have frequently been used as hiding-places for things of more or less value—generally less. Saltpetre Cave, in Georgia, for instance, was a factory and magazine for saltpetre, gunpowder, and other military stores during the Civil War. The Northern soldiers wrecked the potash works and broke away tons of rock, so as to make it dangerous to return. Human bones have been found here, too, but they are thought to be those of soldiers that entered the cave in pursuit of an Indian chief who had defied the State in the '40's. He escaped through a hole in the roof, doubled on his pursuers, fired a pile of dead leaves and wood at the mouth, and suffocated the white men with the smoke.

Spaniards worked the mines in the Ozark Hills of Missouri two hundred years ago. One of the mines containing lead and silver, eighteen miles southwest of Galena, was worked by seven men, who could not agree as to a division of the yield. One by one they were killed in quarrels until but a single man was left, and he, in turn, was set upon by the resurrected victims and choked to death by their cold fingers. In 1873 a Vermonter named

Johnson went there and said he would find what it was the Spaniards had been hiding, in spite of the devil and his imps. He did work there for one day, and was then found dead at the mouth of the old shaft with marks of bony fingers on his throat.

The seven cities of Cibola, that Coronado and other Spanish adventurers sought in the vast deserts of the Southwest, were pueblos. A treacherous guide who had hoped to take Coronado into the waterless plain and lose him, but who first lost his own head, had told him a tale of the Quivira, a tribe that had much gold. So far from having gold these Indians did not know the stuff, but the myth that they had hoarded quantities of it has survived to this day and has caused waste of lives and money. Towns in New Mexico that have lain in ruins since 1670, when the Apaches butchered their people—towns that were well built and were lorded by solid old churches and monasteries erected by the Spanish missionaries—these towns have often been dug over, and the ruinous state of Abo, Curari, and Tabira is due, in part, to their foolish tunnelling and blasting.

A Spanish bark, one day in 1841, put in for water off the spot where Columbia City, Oregon, now stands. She had a rough crew on board, and it had been necessary for her officers to watch the men closely from the time the latter discovered that she was carrying a costly cargo. Hardly had the anchorchains run out before the sailors fell upon the captain, killed him, seized all of value that they could gather, and took it to the shore. What happened after is not clear, but it is probable that in a quarrel, arising over the demands of each man to have most of the plunder, several of the claimants were slain. Indians were troublesome, likewise, so that it was thought best to put most of the goods into the ground, and this was done on the tract known as Hez Copier's farm. Hardly was the task completed before the Indians appeared in large numbers and set up their tepees, showing that they meant to remain. The mutineers rowed back to the ship, and, after vainly waiting for several days for a chance to go on shore again, they sailed away. Two years of wandering, fighting, and carousal ensued before the remnant of the crew returned to Oregon. The Indians were gone, and an earnest search was made for the money—but in vain. It was as if the ground had never been disturbed. The man who had supervised its burial was present until the mutineers went back to their boats, when it was discovered that he was mysteriously missing.

More than forty years after these events a meeting of Spiritualists was held in Columbia City, and a "medium" announced that she had received a revelation of the exact spot where the goods had been concealed. A company went to the place, and, after a search of several days, found, under a foot of soil, a quantity of broken stone. While throwing out these fragments one of the party fell dead. The spirit of the defrauded and murdered captain had claimed him, the medium explained. So great was the fright caused by this accident that the search was again abandoned until March, 1890, when another party resumed the digging, and after taking out the remainder of the stone they came on a number of human skeletons. During the examination of these relics—possibly the bones of mutineers who had been killed in the fight on shore—a man fell into a fit of raving madness, and again the search was abandoned, for it is now said that an immutable curse rests on the treasure.

STORIED WATERS, CLIFFS AND MOUNTAINS

MONSTERS AND SEA-SERPENTS

It is hardly to be wondered at that two prominent scientists should have declared on behalf of the sea-serpent, for that remarkable creature has been reported at so many points, and by so many witnesses not addicted to fish tales nor liquor, that there ought to be some reason for him. He has been especially numerous off the New England coast. He was sighted off Cape Ann in 1817, and several times off Nahant. Though alarming in appearance—for he has a hundred feet of body, a shaggy head, and goggle eyes—he is of lamb-like disposition, and has never justified the attempts that have been made to kill or capture him. Rewards were at one time offered to the seafaring men who might catch him, and revenue cutters cruising about Massachusetts Bay were ordered to keep a lookout for him and have a gun double shotted for action. One fisherman emptied the contents of a ducking gun into the serpent's head, as he supposed, but the creature playfully wriggled a few fathoms of its tail and made off. John Josselyn, gentleman, reports that when he stirred about this neighborhood in 1638 an enormous reptile was seen "quoiled up on a rock at Cape Ann." He would have fired at him but for the earnest dissuasion of his Indian guide, who declared that ill luck would come of the attempt. The sea-serpent sometimes shows amphibious tendencies and occasionally leaves the sea for fresh water. Two of him were seen in Devil's Lake, Wisconsin, in 1892, by four men. They confess, however, that they were fishing at the time. The snakes had fins and were a matter of fifty feet long.

When one of these reptiles found the other in his vicinage he raised his head six feet above water and fell upon him tooth and nail—if he had nails. In their struggles these unpleasant neighbors made such waves that the fishermen's boat was nearly upset.

Even the humble Wabash has its terror, for at Huntington, Indiana, three truthful damsels of the town saw its waters churned by a tail that splashed from side to side, while far ahead was the prow of the animal—a leonine skull, with whiskers, and as large as the head of a boy of a dozen years. As if realizing what kind of a report was going to be made about him, the monster was overcome with bashfulness at the sight of the maidens and sank from view.

In April, 1890, a water-snake was reported in one of the Twin Lakes, in the Berkshire Hills, but the eye-witnesses of his sports let him off with a length of twenty-five feet.

Sysladobosis Lake, in Maine, has a snake with a head like a dog's, but it is hardly worth mentioning because it is only eight feet long-hardly longer than the name of the lake. More enterprise is shown across the border, for Skiff Lake, New Brunswick, has a similar snake thirty feet long.

In Cotton Mather's time a double-headed snake was found at Newbury, Massachusetts,—it had a head at each end,—and before it was killed it showed its evil disposition by chasing and striking at the lad who first met it.

A snake haunts Wolf Pond, Pennsylvania, that is an alleged relic of the Silurian age. It was last seen in September, 1887, when it unrolled thirty feet of itself before the eyes of an alarmed spectator—again a fisherman. The beholder struck him with a pole, and in revenge the serpent capsized his boat; but he forbore to eat his enemy, and, diving to the bottom, disappeared. The creature had a black body, about six inches thick, ringed with dingy-yellow bands, and a mottled-green head, long and pointed, like a pike's.

Silver Lake, near Gainesville, New York, was in 1855 reported to be the lair of a great serpent, and old settlers declare that he still comes to the surface now and then.

A tradition among the poor whites of the South Jruns to the effect that the sea-monster that swallowed Jonah—not a whale, because the throat of that animal is hardly large enough to admit a herring—crossed the Atlantic and brought up at the Carolinas. His passenger was supplied with tobacco and beguiled the tedium of the voyage by smoking a pipe. The monster, being unused to that sort of thing, suffered as all beginners in nicotine poisoning do, and expelled the unhappy man with emphasis. On being safely landed, Jonah attached himself to one of the tribes that peopled the barrens, and left a white progeny which antedated Columbus's arrival by several centuries. God pitied the helplessness of these ignorant and uncourageous whites and led them to Looking-Glass Mountain, North Carolina, where He caused corn and game to be created, and while this race endured it lived in plenty.

Santa Barbara Island, off the California coast, was, for a long time, the supposed head-quarters of swimming and flying monsters and sirens, and no Mexican would pass in hearing of the yells and screams and strange songs without crossing himself and begging the captain to give the rock a wide berth. But the noise is all the noise of cats. A shipwrecked tabby peopled the place many years ago, and her numerous progeny live there on dead fish and on the eggs and chicks of sea-fowl.

Spirit Canon, a rocky gorge that extends for three miles along Big Sioux River, Iowa, was hewn through the stone by a spirit that took the form of a dragon. Such were its size and ferocity that the Indians avoided the place, lest they should fall victims to its ire.

The Hurons believed in a monster serpent—Okniont—who wore a horn on his head that could pierce trees, rocks, and hills. A piece of this horn was an amulet of great value, for it insured good luck.

The Zunis tell of a plumed serpent that lives in the water of sacred springs, and they dare not destroy the venomous creatures that infest the plains of Arizona because, to them, the killing of a snake means a reduction in their slender water-supply. The gods were not so kind to the snakes as men were, for the agatized trees of Chalcedony Park, in Arizona, are held to be arrows shot by the angry deities at the monsters who vexed this region.

Indians living on the shore of Canandaigua Lake, New York, tamed a pretty spotted snake, and fed and petted it until it took a deer at a meal. It grew so large that it eventually encircled the camp and began to prey on its keepers. Vainly they tried to kill the creature, until a small boy took an arrow of red willow, anointed it with the blood of a young woman, and shot it from a basswood bow at the creature's heart. It did not enter at once; it merely stuck to the scales. But presently it began to bore and twist its way into the serpent's body. The serpent rolled into the lake and made it foam in its agony. It swallowed water and vomited it up again, with men dead and alive, before it died.

The monster Amhuluk, whose home is a lake near Forked Mountain, Oregon, had but one passion-to catch and drown all things; and when you look into the lake you see that he has even drowned the sky in it, and has made the trees stand upside down in the water. Wherever he set his feet the ground would soften. As three children were digging roots at the edge of the water he fell on them and impaled two of them on his horns, the eldest only contriving to escape. When this boy reached home his body was full of blotches, and the father suspected how it was, yet he went to the lake at once. The bodies of the children came out of the mud at his feet to meet him, but went down again and emerged later across the water. They led him on in this way until he came to the place where they were drowned. A fog now began to steam up from the water, but through it he could see the little ones lifted on the monster's horns, and hear them cry, "We have changed our bodies." Five times they came up and spoke to him, and five times he raised a dismal cry and begged them to return, but they could not. Next morning he saw them rise through the fog again, and, building a camp, he stayed there and mourned for several days. For five days they showed themselves, but after that they went down and he saw and heard no more of them. Ambuluk had taken the children and they would live with him for ever after.

Crater Lake, Oregon, was a haunt of water-devils who dragged into it and drowned all who ventured near. Only within a few years could Indians be persuaded to go to it as guides. Its discoverers saw in it the work of the Great Spirit, but could not guess its meaning. All but one of these Klamaths stole away after they had looked into its circular basin and sheer walls. He fancied that if it was a home of gods they might have some message for men, so camping on the brink of the lofty cliffs he waited. In his sleep a vision came to him, and he heard voices, but could neither make out appearances nor distinguish a word. Every night this dream was repeated. He finally went down to the lake and bathed, and instantly found his strength increased and saw that the people of his dreams were the genii of the waters—whether good or bad he could not guess. One day he caught a fish for food. A thousand water-devils came to the surface, on the instant, and seized him. They carried him to a rock on the north side of the lake, that stands two thousand feet above the water, and from that they dashed him down, gathering the remains of his shattered body below and devouring them. Since that taste they have been eager for men's blood. The rock on the south side of the lake, called the Phantom Ship, is believed by the Indians to be a destructive monster, innocent as it looks in the daytime.

So with Rock Lake, in Washington. A hideous reptile sports about its waters and gulps down everything that it finds in or on them. Only in 1853 a band of Indians, who had fled hither for security against the soldiers, were overtaken by this creature, lashed to death, and eaten.

The Indians of Louisiana, Mississippi, and Texas believed that the King Snake, or God Snake, lived in the Gulf of Mexico. It slept in a cavern of pure crystal at the bottom, and its head, being shaped from a solid emerald, lighted the ocean for leagues when it arose near the surface.

Similar to this is the belief of the Cherokees in the kings of rattlesnakes, "bright old inhabitants" of the mountains that grew to a mighty size, and drew to themselves every creature that they looked upon. Each wore a crown of carbuncle of dazzling brightness.

The Indians avoided Klamath Lake because it was haunted by a monster that was half dragon, half hippopotamus.

Hutton Lake, Wyoming, is the home of a serpent queen, whose breathing may be seen in the bubbles that well up in the centre. She is constantly watching for her lover, but takes all men who come in her way to her grotto beneath the water, when she finds that they are not the one she has expected, and there they become her slaves. To lure victims into the lake she sets there a decoy of a beautiful red swan, and should the hunter kill this bird he will become possessed of divine power. Should he see "the woman," as the serpent queen is called, he will never live to tell of it, unless he has seen her from a hiding-place near the shore—for so surely as he is noticed by this Diana of the depths, so surely will her spies, the land snakes, sting him to death. In appearance she is a lovely girl in all but her face, and that is shaped like the head of a monster snake. Her name is never spoken by the Indians, for fear that it will cost them their lives.

Michael Pauw, brave fisherman of Paterson, New Jersey, hero of the fight with the biggest snapping-turtle in Dover Slank, wearer of a scar on his seat of honor as memento of the conflict, member of the Kersey Reds—he whose presence of mind was shown in holding out a chip of St. Nicholas's staff when he met the nine witches of the rocks capering in the mists of Passaic Falls—gave battle from a boat to a monster that had ascended to the cataract. One of the Kersey Reds, leaning out too far, fell astride of the horny beast, and was carried at express speed, roaring with fright, until unhorsed by a projecting rock, up which he scrambled to safety. Falling to work with bayonets and staves, the company despatched the creature and dragged it to shore. One Dutchman—who was quite a traveller, having been as far from home as Albany—said that the thing was what the Van Rensselaers cut up for beef, and that he believed they called it a sturgeon.

STONE-THROWING DEVILS

There is an odd recurrence among American legends of tales relating to assaults of people or their houses by imps of darkness. The shadowy leaguers of Gloucester, Massachusetts, kept the garrison of that place in a state of fright until they were expelled from the neighborhood by a silver bullet and a chaplain's prayers. Witchcraft was sometimes manifested in Salem by the hurling of missiles from unseen hands. The "stone-throwing devil" of Portsmouth is the subject of a tradition more than two centuries of age, but, as the stone-thrower appears rather as an avenger than as a gratuitously malignant spirit, he is ill treated in having the name of devil applied to him. In this New Hampshire port lived a widow who had a cabin and a bit of land of her own. George Walton, a neighbor, wanted her land, for its situation pleased him, and as the old woman had neither money nor influential friends he charged her with witchcraft, and, whether by legal chicanery or mere force is not recorded, he got his hands upon her property.

The charge of witchcraft was not pressed, because the man had obtained what he wanted, but the poor, houseless creature laid a ban on the place and told the thief that he would never have pleasure nor profit out of it. Walton laughed at her, bade her go her way, and moved his family into the widow's house. It was Sunday night, and the family had gone to bed, when at ten o'clock there came a fierce shock of stones against the roof and doors. All were awake in a moment. A first thought was that Indians were making an assault, but when the occupants peered cautiously into the moonlight the fields were seen to be deserted. Yet, even as they looked, a gate was lifted from its hinges and thrown through the air.

Walton ventured out, but a volley of stones, seemingly from a hundred hands, was delivered at his head, and he ran back to shelter. Doors and windows were barred and shuttered, but it made no difference. Stones, too hot to hold a hand upon, were hurled through glass and down the chimney, objects in the rooms themselves were picked up and flung at Walton, candles were blown out, a hand without a body tapped at the window, locks and bars and keys were bent as if by hammer-blows, a cheese-press was smashed against the wall and the cheese spoiled, hay-stacks in the field were broken up and the hay tossed into branches of trees. For a long time Walton could not go out at night without being assailed with stones. Bell, book, candle, and witch-broth availed nothing, and it was many a day before peace came to the Walton household.

In 1802 an epidemic of assault went through the Berkshire Hills. The performance began in a tailor's shop in Salisbury, Connecticut, at eleven of the clock on the night of November 2, when a stick and lumps of stone, charcoal, and mortar were flung through a window. The moon was up, but nothing could be seen, and the bombardment was continued until after daylight. After doing some damage here the assailants went to the house of Ezekiel Landon and rapped away there for a week. Persons were struck by the missiles, and quantities of glass were destroyed. Nothing could be seen coming toward the windows until the glass broke, and it was seldom that anything passed far into a room. No matter how hard it was thrown, it dropped softly and surely on the sill, inside, as if a hand had put it there. Windows were broken on both sides of buildings at the same time, and many sticks and stones came through the same holes in the panes, as if aimed carefully by a gunner.

A hamlet that stood in Sage's ravine, on the east side of the Dome of the Taconics, was assailed in the same way after nightfall. One house was considerably injured. No causes for the performance were ever discovered, and nobody in the place was known to have an enemy—at least, a malicious one.

At Whitmire Hill, Georgia, the spot where two murders were committed before the war, is a headless phantom that comes thundering down on the wayfarer on the back of a giant horse and vanishes at the moment when the heart of his prospective victim is bumping against his palate. At times, however, this spook prefers to remain invisible, and then it is a little worse, for it showers stones and sods on the pedestrian until his legs have carried him well beyond the phantom's jurisdiction.

The legends of buried treasure, instanced in another place, frequently include assaults by the ghosts of pirates and misers on the daring ones who try to resurrect their wealth.

Forty-seven years ago, in the township of St. Mary's, Illinois, two lads named Groves and a companion named Kirk were pelted with snowballs while on their way home from a barn where they had been to care for the stock for the night. The evening had shut in dark, and the accuracy of the thrower's aim was the more remarkable because it was hardly possible to see more than a rod away. The snowballs were packed so tightly that they did not break on striking, though they were thrown with force, and Kirk was considerably bruised by them. Mr. Groves went out with a lantern, but its rays lit up a field of untrodden snow, and there was no sound except that made by the wind as it whistled past the barn and fences. Toward dawn another inspection was made, and in the dim light the snowballs were seen rising from the middle of a field that had not a footprint on it, and flying toward the spectators like bullets. They ran into the field and laid about them with pitchforks, but nothing came of that, and not until the sun arose was the pelting stopped. Young Kirk, who was badly hurt, died within a year.

The men of Sharon, Connecticut, having wheedled their town-site from the Indians in 1754, were plagued thereafter by whoops and whistlings and the throwing of stones. Men were seen in the starlight and were fired upon, but without effect, and the disturbances were not ended until the Indians had received a sum of money.

Without presuming to doubt the veracity of tradition in these matters, an incident from the writer's boyhood in New England may be instanced. The house of an unpopular gentleman was assailed—not in the ostentatious manner just described, yet in a way that gave him a good deal of trouble. Dead cats appeared mysteriously in his neighborhood; weird noises arose under his windows; he tried to pick up letters from his doorstep that became mere chalk-marks at his touch, so that he took up only splinters under his nails. One night, as a seance was about beginning in his yard, he emerged from a clump of bushes, flew in the direction of the disturbance, laid violent hands on the writer's collar, and bumped his nose on a paving-stone. Then the manifestations were discontinued, for several nights, for repairs.

STORIED SPRINGS

Like the Greeks, the red men endowed the woods and waters with tutelary sprites, and many of the springs that are now resorted to as fountains of healing were known long before the settlement of Europeans here, the gains from drinking of them being ascribed to the beneficence of spirit guardians. The earliest comers to these shores—or, rather, the earliest of those who entertained such beliefs—fancied that the fabled fountain of eternal youth would be found among the other blessings of the land. To the Spaniards Florida was a land of promise and mystery. Somewhere in its interior was fabled to stand a golden city ruled by a king whose robes sparkled with precious dust, and this city was named for the adventurer—El Dorado, or the Place of the Gilded One. Here, they said, would be found the elixir of life. The beautiful Silver Spring, near the head of the Ocklawaha, with its sandy bottom plainly visible at the depth of eighty feet, was thought to be the source of the life-giving waters, but, though Ponce de Leon heard of this, he never succeeded in fighting his way to it through the jungle.

In Georgia, in the reputed land of Chicora, were a sacred stream that made all young again who bathed there, and a spring so delectable that a band of red men, chancing on it in a journey, could not leave it, and are there forever.

In the island of "Bimini," one of the Lucayos (Bahamas), was another such a fountain.

Between the Flint and Ocmulgee Rivers the Creeks declared was a spring of life, on an island in a marsh, defended from approach by almost impenetrable labyrinths,—a heaven where the women were fairer than any other on earth.

The romantic and superstitious Spaniards believed these legends, and spent years and treasure in searching for these springs. And, surely, if the new and striking scenes of this Western world caused Columbus to "boast that he had found the seat of paradise, it will not appear strange that Ponce de Leon should dream of discovering the fountain of youth."

The Yuma Apaches had been warned by one of their oracles never to enter a certain canon in Castle Dome range, Arizona, but a company of them forgot this caution while in chase of deer, and found themselves between walls of pink and white fluorite with a spring bubbling at the head of the ravine. Tired and heated, they fell on their faces to drink, when they found that the crumbling quartz that formed the basin of the spring was filled with golden nuggets. Eagerly gathering up this precious substance, for they knew what treasure of beads, knives, arrows, and blankets the Mexicans would exchange for it, they attempted to make their way out of the canon; but a cloudburst came, and on the swiftly rising tide all were swept away but one, who survived to tell the story. White men have frequently but vainly tried to find that spring.

In Southwestern Kansas, on a hill a quarter-mile from Solomon River, is the Sacred Water, pooled in a basin thirty feet across. When many stand about the brink it slowly rises. Here two Panis stopped on their return from a buffalo hunt, and one of them unwittingly stepped on a turtle a yard long. Instantly he felt his feet glued to the monster's back, for, try as he might, he could not disengage himself, and the creature lumbered away to the pool, where it sank with him. There the turtle god remains, and beads, arrows, ear-rings, and pipes that are dropped in, it swallows greedily. The Indians use the water to mix their paint with, but never for drinking.

The mail rider, crossing the hot desert of Arizona, through the cacti and over holes where scorpions hide, makes for Devil's Well, under El Diablo—a dark pool surrounded with gaunt rocks. Here, coming when the night is on, he lies down, and the wind swishing in the sage—brush puts him to sleep. At dawn he wakens with the frightened whinny of his horse in his ears and, all awake, looks about him. A stranger, wrapped in a tattered blanket, is huddled in a recess of the stones, arrived there, like himself, at night, perhaps. Poising his rifle on his knee, the rider challenges him, but never a sign the other makes. Then, striding over to him, he pulls away the blanket and sees a shrivelled corpse with a face that he knows—his brother. Hardly is this meeting made when a hail of arrows falls around. His horse is gone. The Apaches, who know no gentleness and have no mercy, have manned every gap and sheltering rock. With his rifle he picks them off, as they rise in sight with arrows at the string, and sends them tumbling into the dust; but, when his last bullet has sped into a red man's heart, they rise in a body and with knives and hatchets hew him to death. And that is why the Devil's Well still tastes of blood.

Among the Balsam Mountains of Western North Carolina is a large spring that promises refreshment, but, directly that the wayfarer bends over the water, a grinning face appears at the bottom and as he stoops it rises to meet his. So hideous is this demon that few of the mountaineers have courage to drink here, and they refuse to believe that the apparition is caused by the shape of the basin, or aberrated reflection of their own faces. They say it is the visage of a "haunt," for a Cherokee girl, who had uncommon beauty, once lived hard by, and took delight in luring lovers from less favored maidens. The braves were jealous of each other, and the women were jealous of her, while she—the flirt!—rejoiced in the trouble that she made. A day fell for a wedding—that of a hunter with a damsel of his tribe, but at the hour appointed the man was missing. Mortified and hurt, the bride stole away from the village and began a search of the wood, and she carried bow and arrows in her hand. Presently she came on the hunter, lying at the feet of the coquette, who was listening to his words with encouraging smiles. Without warning the deserted girl drew an arrow to the head and shot her lover through the heart—then, beside his lifeless body, she begged Manitou to make her rival's face so hideous that all would be frightened who looked at it. At the words the beautiful creature felt her face convulse and shrivel, and, rushing to the mirror of the spring, she looked in, only to start back in loathing. When she realized that the frightful visage that glared up at her was her own, she uttered a cry of despair and flung herself into the water, where she drowned.

It is her face—so altered as to disclose the evil once hid behind it—that peers up at the hardy one who passes there and knows it as the Haunted Spring.

The medicinal properties of the mineral springs at Ballston and Saratoga were familiar to the Indians, and High Rock Spring, to which Sir William Johnson was carried by the Mohawks in 1767 to be cured of a wound, was called "the medicine spring of the Great Spirit," for it was believed that the leaping and bubbling of the water came from its agitation by hands not human, and red men regarded it with reverence.

The springs at Manitou, Colorado (see "Division of Two Tribes"), were always approached with gifts for the manitou that lived in them.

The lithia springs of Londonderry, New Hampshire, used to be visited by Indians from the Merrimack region, who performed incantations and dances to ingratiate themselves with the healing spirit that lived in the water. Their stone implements and arrow-heads are often found in adjacent fields.

The curative properties of Milford Springs, New Hampshire, were revealed in the dream of a dying boy.

A miracle spring flowed in the old days near the statue of the Virgin at White Marsh, Maryland.

Biddeford Pool, Maine, was a miracle pond once a year, for whoso bathed there on the 26th of June would be restored to health if he were ill, because that day was the joint festival of Saints Anthelm and Maxentius.

There was a wise and peaceable chief of the Ute tribe who always counselled his people to refrain from war, but when he grew old the fiery spirits deposed him and went down to the plains to give battle to the Arapahoe. News came that they had been defeated in consequence of their rashness. Then the old man's sorrow was so keen that his heart broke. But even in death he was beneficent, for his spirit entered the earth and forthwith came a gush of water that has never ceased to flow—the Hot Sulphur Springs of Colorado. The Utes often used to go to those springs to bathe—and be cured of rheumatism—before they were driven away.

Spring River, Arkansas, is nearly as large at its source as at its mouth, for Mammoth Spring, in the Ozark Mountains, where it has its rise, has a yield of ninety thousand gallons a minute, so that it is, perhaps, the largest in the world. Here, three hundred years ago, the Indians had gathered for a month's feast, for chief Wampahseesah's daughter—Nitilita—was to wed a brave of many ponies, a hundred of which he had given in earnest of his love. For weeks no rain had fallen, and, while the revel was at its height, news came that all the rivers had gone dry. Several young men set off with jars, to fill them at the Mississippi, and, confident that relief would come, the song and dance went on until the men and women faltered from exhaustion. At last, Nitilita died, and, in the wildness of his grief, the husband smote his head upon a rock and perished too. Next day the hunters came with water, but, incensed by their delay, the chief ordered them to be slain in sacrifice to the manes of the dead. A large grave was dug and the last solemnities were begun when there was a roaring and a shaking in the earth—it parted, and the corpses disappeared in the abyss. Then from the pit arose a flood of water that went foaming down the valley. Crazed with grief, remorse, and fear, Wampahseesah flung himself into the torrent and was borne to his death. The red men built a dam there later, and often used to sit before it in the twilight, watching, as they declared, the faces of the dead peering at them through the foam.

During the rush for the California gold-fields in the '50's a party took the route by Gila River, and set across the desert. The noon temperature was 120, the way was strewn with skeletons of wagons, horses, and men, and on the second night after crossing the Colorado the water had given out. The party had gathered on the sands below Yuma, the men discussing the advisability of returning, the women full of apprehension, the young ones crying, the horses panting; but presently the talk fell low, for in one of the wagons a child's voice was heard in prayer: "Oh, good heavenly Father,

I know I have been a naughty girl, but I am so thirsty, and mamma and papa and baby all want a drink so much! Do, good God, give us water, and I never will be naughty again." One of the men said, earnestly, "May God grant it!" In a few moments the child cried, "Mother, get me water. Get some for baby and me. I can hear it running." The horses and mules nearly broke from the traces, for almost at their feet a spring had burst from the sand-warm, but pure. Their sufferings were over. The water continued to flow, running north for twenty miles, and at one point spreading into a lake two miles wide and twenty feet deep. When emigration was diverted, two years later, to the northern route and to the isthmus, New River Spring dried up. Its mission was over.

LOVERS' LEAPS

So few States in this country—and so few countries, if it comes to that—are without a lover's leap that the very name has come to be a by-word. In most of these places the disappointed ones seem to have gone to elaborate and unusual pains to commit suicide, neglecting many easy and equally appropriate methods. But while in some cases the legend has been made to fit the place, there is no doubt that in many instances the story antedated the arrival of the white men. The best known lovers' leaps are those on the upper Mississippi, on the French Broad, Jump Mountain, in Virginia, Jenny Jump Mountain, New Jersey, Mackinac, Michigan, Monument Mountain, Massachusetts, on the Wissahickon, near Philadelphia, Muscatine, Iowa, and Lefferts Height. There are many other declivities,—also, that are scenes of leaps and adventures, such as the Fawn's Leap, in Kaaterskill Clove; Rogers's Rock, on Lake George; the rocks in Long Narrows, on the Juniata, where the ghost of Captain Jack, "the wild hunter" of colonial days, still ranges; Campbell's Ledge, Pittston, Pennsylvania, where its name-giver jumped off to escape Indians; and Peabody's leap, of thirty feet, on Lake Champlain, where Tim Peabody, a scout, escaped after killing a number of savages.

At Jump Mountain, near Lexington, Virginia, an Indian couple sprang off because there were insuperable bars to their marriage.

At the rock on the Wissahickon a girl sought death because her lover was untrue to her.

At Muscatine the cause of a maid's demise and that of her lover was the severity of her father, who forbade the match because there was no war in which the young man could prove his courage.

At Lefferts Height a girl stopped her recreant lover as he was on his way to see her rival, and urging his horse to the edge of the bluff she leaped with him into the air.

Monument Mountain, a picturesque height in the Berkshires, is faced on its western side by a tall precipice, from which a girl flung herself because the laws of her tribe forbade her marriage with a cousin to whom she had plighted troth. She was buried where her body was found, and each Indian as he passed the spot laid a stone on her grave—thus, in time, forming a monument.

"Purgatory," the chasm at Newport, Rhode Island, through which the sea booms loudly after a storm, was a scene of self-sacrifice to a hopeless love on the part of an Indian pair in a later century, though there is an older tradition of the seizure of a guilty squaw, by no less a person than the devil himself, who flung her from the cliff and dragged her soul away as it left her body. His hoof-marks were formerly visible on the rocks.

At Hot Springs, North Carolina, two conspicuous cliffs are pointed out on the right bank of the French Broad River: Paint Rock—where the aborigines used to get ochre to smear their faces, and which they decorated with hieroglyphics—and Lover's Leap. It is claimed that the latter is the first in this country known to bear this sentimental and tragically suggestive title. There are two traditions concerning it, one being that an Indian girl was discovered at its top by hostiles who drove her into the gulf below, the other relating to the wish of an Indian to marry a girl of a tribe with which his own had been immemorially at war. The match was opposed on both sides, so, instead of doing as most Indians and some white men would do nowadays—marry the girl and let reconciliation come in time,—he scaled the rock in her company and leaped with her into the stream. They awoke as man and wife in the happy hunting-ground.

In 1700 there lived in the village of Keoxa, below Frontenac, Minnesota, on the Mississippi River, a Dakota girl named Winona (the First Born), who was loved by a hunter in her tribe, and loved him in return. Her friends commended to her affections a young chief who had valiantly defended the village against an attack of hostiles, but Juliet would none of this dusky Count de Paris, adhering faithfully to her Romeo. Unable to move her by argument, her family at length drove her lover away, and used other harsh measures to force her into a repugnant union, but she replied, "You are driving me to despair. I do not love this chief, and cannot live with him. You are my father, my brothers, my relatives, yet you drive from me the only man with whom I wish to be united. Alone he ranges through the forest, with no one to build his lodge, none to spread his blanket, none to wait on him. Soon you will have neither daughter, sister, nor relative to torment with false professions." Blazing with anger at this unsubmissive speech, her father declared that she should marry the chief on that very day, but while the festival was in preparation she stole to the top of the crag that has since been known as Maiden's Rock, and there, four hundred feet above the heads of the people, upbraided those who had formerly professed regard for her. Then she began her death-song. Some of the men tried to scale the cliff and avert the tragedy that it was evident would shortly be enacted, and her father, his displeasure forgotten in an agony of apprehension, called to her that he would no longer oppose her choice. She gave no heed to their appeals, but, when the song was finished, walked to the edge of the rock, leaped out, and rolled lifeless at the feet of her people.

When we say that the real name of Lover's Leap in Mackinac is Mechenemockenungoqua, we trust that it will not be repeated. It has its legend, however, as well as its name, for an Ojibway girl stood on this spire of rock, watching for her lover after a battle had been fought and her people were returning. Eagerly she scanned the faces of the braves as their war-canoes swept by, but the face she looked for was not among them. Her lover was at that moment tied to a tree, with an arrow in his heart. As she looked at the boats a vision of his fate revealed itself, and the dead man, floating toward her, beckoned. Her death-song sounded in the ears of the men, but before they could reach her she had gone swiftly to the verge, her hands extended, her eyes on vacancy, and her spirit had met her lover's.

From this very rock, in olden time, leaped the red Eve when the red Adam had been driven away by a devil who had fallen in love with her. Adam, who was paddling by the shore, saw she was about to fall, rushed forward, caught her, and saved her life. The law of gravitation in those days did not act with such distressing promptitude as now. Manitou, hearing of these doings, restored them to the island and banished the devil, who fell to a world of evil spirits underground, where he became the father of the white race, and has ever since persecuted the Indians by proxy.

On the same island of Mackinac the English had a fort, the garrison of which was massacred in 1763. A sole survivor—a young officer named Robinson—owed his life to a pretty half-breed who gave him hiding in a secluded wigwam. As the spot assured him of safety, and the girl was his only companion, they lived together as man and wife, rather happily, for several years. When the fort had been built again, Robinson re-entered the service, and appeared at head-quarters with a wife of his own color. His Indian consort showed no jealousy. On the contrary, she consented to live apart in a little house belonging to the station, on the cliff, called Robinson's Folly. She did ask her lover to go there and sit with her for an hour before they separated forever, and he granted this request. While they stood at the edge of the rock she embraced him; then, stepping back, with her arms still around his neck, she fell from the cliff, dragging him with her, and both were killed. The edge of the rock fell shortly after, carrying the house with it.

Matiwana, daughter of the chief of the Omahas, whose village was near the mouth of Omaha Creek, married a faithless trader from St. Louis, who had one wife already, and who returned to her, after an absence among his own people, with a third, a woman of his own color. He coldly repelled the Indian woman, though he promised to send her boy—and his—to the settlements to be educated. She turned away with only a look, and a few days later was found dead at the foot of a bluff near her home.

White Rocks, one hundred and fifty feet above Cheat River, in Fayette County, Pennsylvania, were the favorite tryst of a handsome girl, the daughter of a well-to-do farmer of that region, and a dashing fellow who had gone into that country to hunt. They had many happy days there on the hill together, but after making arrangements for the wedding they quarrelled, nobody knew for what. One evening they met by accident on the rocks, and appeared to be in formal talk when night came on and they could no longer be seen. The girl did not return, and her father set off with a search party to look for her. They found her, dead and mangled, at the foot of the rocks. Her lover, in a fit of impatience, had pushed her and she had staggered and fallen over. He fled at once, and, under a changed name and changed appearance, eluded pursuit. When the War of the Rebellion broke out, he entered the army and fought recklessly, for by that time he had tired of life and hoped to die. But it was of no use. He was only made captain for a bravery that he was not conscious of showing, and the old remorse still preyed on him. It was after the war that something took him back to Fayette County, and on a pleasant day he climbed the rocks to take a last look at the scenes that had been brightened by love and saddened by regret. He had not been long on its summit when an irresistible impulse came upon him to leap down where the girl had fallen, and atone with his own blood for the shedding of hers. He gave way to this prompting, and the fall was fatal.

Some years before the outbreak of the Civil War a man with his wife and daughter took up their residence in a log cabin at the foot of Sunrise Rock, near Chattanooga, Tennessee. It seemed probable that they had known better days, for the head of the household was notoriously useless in the eyes of his neighbors, and was believed to get his living through "writin' or book-larnin'," but he was so quiet and gentle that they never upbraided him, and would sometimes, after making a call, wander into his garden and casually weed it for him for an hour or so. The girl, Stella, was a well-schooled, quick-witted, rosy-cheeked lass, whom all the shaggy, big-jointed farmer lads of the neighborhood regarded with hopeless admiration. A year or two after the settlement of the family it began to be noticed that she was losing color and had an anxious look, and when a friendly old farmer saw her talking in the lane with a lawyer from Chattanooga, who wore broadcloth and had a gold watch, he was puzzled that the "city chap" did not go home with her, but kissed his hand to her as he turned away.

Afterward the farmer met the pair again, and while the girl smiled and said, "Howdy, Uncle Joe?" the lawyer turned away and looked down the river. It was the last time that a smile was seen on Stella's face. A few evenings later she was seen standing on Sunrise Rock, with her look bent on Chattanooga. The shadow of night crept up the cliff until only her figure stood in sunlight, with her hair like a golden halo about her face. At that moment came on the wind the sound of bells-wedding-bells. Pressing her hands to her ears, the girl walked to the edge of the rock, and a few seconds later her lifeless form rolled through the bushes at its foot into the road. At her funeral the people came from far and near to offer sympathy to the mother, garbed in black, and the father, with his hair turned white, but the lawyer from Chattanooga was not there.

The name of Indian Maiden's Cliff—applied to a precipice that hangs above the wild ravine of Stony Clove, in the Catskills—commemorates the sequel to an elopement from her tribe of an Indian girl and her lover. The parents and relatives had opposed the match with that fatal fatuity that appears to be characteristic of story-book Indians, and as soon as word of her flight came to the village they set off in chase. While hurrying through the tangled wood the young couple were separated and the girl found herself on the edge of the cliff. Farther advance was impossible. Her pursuers were close behind. She must yield or die. She chose not to yield, and, with a despairing cry, flung herself into the shadows.

Similar to this is the tale of Lover's Leap in the dells of the Sioux, among the Black Hills of South Dakota.

At New Milford, Connecticut, they show you Falls Mountain, with the cairn erected by his tribe in 1735 to chief Waramaug, who wished to be buried there, so that, when he was cold and lonely in the other life, he could return to his body and muse on the lovely landscape that he so enjoyed. The will-o'-the-wisp flickered on the mountain's edge at night, and flecks of dew-vapor that floated from the wood by day were sometimes thought to be the spirit of the chief. He had a daughter, Lillinonah, whose story is related to Lover's Leap, on the riverward side of the mountain. She had led to the camp a white man, who had been wandering beside the Housatonic, ill and weak, vainly seeking a way out of the wilderness, and, in spite of the dark looks that were cast at him and her, she succeeded in making him, for that summer, a member of the tribe. As the man grew strong with her care he grew happy and he fell in love. In the autumn he said to her, "I wish to see my people, and when I have done so I will come back to you and we shall be man and wife." They parted regretfully and the winter passed for the girl on leaden feet. With spring came hope. The trails were open, and daily she watched for her white lover. The summer came and went, and the autumn was there again. She had grown pale and sad, and old Waramaug said to young Eagle Feather, who had looked softly on her for many years, "The girl sickens in loneliness. You shall wed her." This is repeated to her, and that evening she slips away to the river, enters a canoe, casts away the paddle, and drifts down the stream. Slowly, at first, but faster and faster, as the rapids begin to draw it, skims the boat, but above the hoarse brawling of the waters she hears a song in a voice that she knows—the merry troll of a light heart. The branches part at Lover's Leap and her lover looks down upon her. The joyous glance of recognition changes to a look of horror, for the boat is caught. The girl rises and holds her arms toward him in agonized appeal. Life, at any cost! He, with a cry, leaps into the flood as the canoe is passing. It lurches against a rock and Lillinonah is thrown out. He reaches her. The falls bellow in their ears. They take a last embrace, and two lives go out in the growing darkness.

GOD ON THE MOUNTAINS

From the oldest time men have associated the mountains with visitations of God. Their height, their vastness, their majesty made them seem worthy to be stairs by which the Deity might descend to earth, and they stand in religious and poetic literature to this day as symbols of the largest mental conceptions. Scriptural history is intimately associated with them, and the giving of the law on Sinai, amid thunder and darkness, is one of the most tremendous pictures that imagination can paint. Ararat, Hermon, Horeb, Pisgah, Calvary, Adam's Peak, Parnassus, Olympus! How full of suggestion are these names! And poetic figures in sacred writings are full of allusion to the beauty, nobility, and endurance of the hills.

It is little known that many of our own mountains are associated with aboriginal legends of the Great Spirit. According to the Indians of California, Mount Shasta was the first part of the earth to be made. The Great Spirit broke a hole through the floor of heaven with a rock, and on the spot where this rock had stopped he flung down more rocks, with earth and snow and ice, until the mass had gained such a height that he could step from the sky to its summit. Running his hands over its sides he caused forests to spring up. The leaves that he plucked he breathed upon, tossed into the air, and, lo! they were birds. Out of his own staff he made beasts and fishes, to live on the hills and in the streams, that began to appear as the work of worldbuilding went on. The earth became so joyous and so fair that he resolved at last to live on it, and he hollowed Shasta into a wigwam, where he dwelt for centuries, the smoke of his lodge-fire (Shasta is a volcano) being often seen pouring from the cone before the white man came.

According to the Oregon Indians the first man was created at the base of the Cascade Range, near Wood River, by Kmukamtchiksh, "the old man of the ancients," who had already made the world. The Klamaths believe Kmukamtchiksh a treacherous spirit, "a typical beast god," yet that he punishes the wicked by turning them into rocks on the mountain-sides or by putting them into volcanic fires.

Sinsinawa Mound, Wisconsin, was the home of strange beings who occupied caverns that few dared to enter. Enchanted rivers flowed through these caves to heaven. The Catskills and Adirondacks were abodes of powerful beings, and the Highlands of the Hudson were a wall within which Manitou confined a host of rebellious spirits. When the river burst through this bulwark and poured into the sea, fifty miles below, these spirits took flight, and many succeeded in escaping. But others still haunt the ravines and bristling woods, and when Manitou careers through the Hudson canon on his car of cloud, crying with thunder voice, and hurling his lightnings to right and left as he passes, the demons scream and howl in rage and fear lest they be recaptured and shut up forever beneath the earth.

The White Mountains were held in awe by Indians, to whom they were homes of great and blessed spirits. Mount Washington was their Olympus and Ararat in one, for there dwelt God, and there, when the earth was covered with a flood, lived the chief and his wife, whom God had saved, sending forth a hare, after the waters had subsided, to learn if it were safe to descend. From them the whole country was peopled with red men. Yet woe betide the intruder on this high and holy ground, for an angered deity condemned him to wander for ages over the desolate peaks and through the shadowy chasms rifted down their sides. The despairing cries of these condemned ones, in winter storms, even frightened the early white settlers in this region, and in 1784 the women of Conway petitioned three clergymen "to lay the spirits."

Other ark and deluge legends relate to the Superstition Mountains, in Arizona, Caddoes village, on Red River, Cerro Naztarny, on the Rio Grande, the peak of Old Zuni, in Mexico, Colhuacan, on the Pacific coast, Mount Apaola, in upper Mixteca, and Mount Neba, in Guaymi. The Northwestern Indians tell of a flood in which all perished save one man, who fled to Mount Tacoma. To prevent him from being swept away a spirit turned him into stone. When the flood had fallen the deity took one of his ribs and made a woman of it. Then he touched the stone man back to life.

There were descendants of Manitou on the mountains, too, of North Carolina, but the Cherokees believe that those heights are bare because the devil strode over them on his way to the Devil's Court House (Transylvania County, North Carolina), where he sat in judgment and claimed his own. Monsters were found in the White Mountains. Devil's Den, on the face of Mount Willard, was the lair of one of them—a strange, winged creature that strewed the floor of its cave with brute and human skeletons, after preying on their flesh.

The ideas of supernatural occurrences in these New Hampshire hills obtained until a recent date, and Sunday Mountain is a monument to the dire effects of Sabbath-breaking that was pointed out to several generations of New Hampshire youth for their moral betterment. The story goes that a man of the adjacent town of Oxford took a walk one Sunday, when he should have taken himself to church; and, straying into the woods here, he was delivered into the claws and maws of an assemblage of bears that made an immediate and exemplary conclusion of him.

The grand portrait in rock in Profile Notch was regarded with reverence by the few red men who ventured into that lonely defile. When white men saw it they said it resembled Washington, and a Yankee orator is quoted as saying, "Men put out signs representing their different trades. Jewellers hang out a monster watch, shoemakers a huge boot, and, up in Franconia, God Almighty has hung out a sign that in New England He makes men."

To Echo Lake, close by, the deity was wont to repair that he might contemplate the beauties of nature, and the clear, repeated echoes were his voice, speaking in gentleness or anger. Moosilauke—meaning a bald place, and wrongly called Moose Hillock—was declared by Waternomee, chief of the Pemigewassets, to be the home of the Great Spirit, and the first time that red men tried to gain the summit they returned in fear, crying that Gitche Manitou was riding home in anger on a storm—which presently, indeed, burst over the whole country. Few Indians dared to climb the mountain after that, and the first fruits of the harvest and first victims of the chase were offered in propitiation to the deity. At Seven Cascades, on its eastern slope, one of Rogers's Rangers, retreating after the Canadian foray, fell to the ground, too tired for further motion, when a distant music of harps mingled with the cascade's plash, and directly the waters were peopled with forms glowing with silver-white, like the moonstone, that rose and circled, hand in hand, singing gayly as they did so. The air then seemed to be flooded with rosy light and thousands of sylvan genii ascended altars of rock, by steps of rainbow, to offer incense and greet the sun with song. A dark cloud passed, daylight faded, and a vision arose of the massacre at St. Francis, a retreat through untried wilderness, a feast on human heads, torture, and death; then his senses left the worn and starving man. But a trapper who had seen his trail soon reached him and led him to a friendly settlement, where he was told that only to those who were about to take their leave of earth was it given to know those spirits of fountain and forest that offered their voices, on behalf of nature, in praise of the Great Spirit. To those of grosser sense, on whom the weight of worldliness still rested, this halcyon was never revealed.

It was to Mount Washington that the Great Spirit summoned Passaconaway, when his work was done, and there was his apotheosis.

The Indians account in this manner for the birth of the White Mountains: A red hunter who had wandered for days through the forest without finding game dropped exhausted on the snow, one night, and awaited death. But he fell asleep and dreamed. In his vision he saw a beautiful mountain country where birds and beasts and fruits were plenty, and, awaking from his sleep, he found that day had come. Looking about the frozen wilderness in despair, he cried, "Great Master of Life, where is this country that I have seen?" And even as he spoke the Master appeared and gave to him a spear and a coal. The hunter dropped the coal on the ground, when a fire spread from it, the rocks burning with dense smoke, out of which came the Master's voice, in thunder tones, bidding the mountains rise. The earth heaved and through the reek the terrified man saw hills and crags lifting—lifting—until their tops reached above the clouds, and from the far summits sounded the promise, "Here shall the Great Spirit live and watch over his children." Water now burst from the rocks and came laughing down the hollows in a thousand brooks and rills, the valleys unfolded in leaf and bloom, birds sang in the branches, butterflies-like winged flowers flitted to and fro, the faint and cheerful noise of insect life came from the herbage, the smoke rolled away, a genial sun blazed out, and, as the hunter looked in rapture on the mighty peaks of the Agiochooks, God stood upon their crest.